Practical Gunsmithing

By The Editors of
American Gunsmith

DBI BOOKS, INC.

PRACTICAL GUNSMITHING STAFF

Senior Staff Editors
Harold A. Murtz
Ray Ordorica

Electronic Publishing Associate
Larry Levine

Production Manager
John L. Duoba

Managing Editor
Pamela Johnson

Publisher
Sheldon L. Factor

About the Editors

The editors of *Practical Gunsmithing* are acknowledged experts in their fields and are represented here in a collection of selected articles from the *American Gunsmith* journal, a monthly technical publication devoted to the repair and maintenance of firearms.

The *American Gunsmith*, since its inception in 1985, has become the standard-bearer for the craft of gunsmithing. The professional gunsmiths who contribute to each issue provide both hobbyist and professional alike with information on the procedures, tips and tricks-of-the-trade for successfully diagnosing and repairing classic firearms as well as the latest production models.

In 1996, the *American Gunsmith* assumed the role of the official publication of the American Gunsmithing Association, an organization for gunsmiths who ply their trade from coast to coast. Dedicated to promoting the craft of gunsmithing, the American Gunsmithing Association encourages quality in workmanship; integrity in business practices; and a greater respect, knowledge and appreciation of firearms. Through a variety of media it provides information and education for the hobbyist and sets standards for the accredited professional while acting as a voice for the community of gunsmiths who share an appreciation for this important craft.

ISBN 0-87349-187-4

Library of Congress Catalog Card #96-83883

Contents

Introduction 5

Section 1: Tools & Techniques

Setting Up a Work Area *by Dennis A. Wood* 8

Precision Measuring Instruments *by Frank Fry* 10

Choosing and Using Files, Part 1 *by Dennis A. Wood* 14

Using Files, Part 2 *by Dennis A. Wood* 17

Working With Pins and Punches *by Chip Todd* 20

Tips for Choosing—and Using—Abrasive Stones *by Chip Todd* 25

The Not-So-Simple Drill Bit *by Chip Todd* 31

Polishing Tools and Techniques *by Frank Fry* 34

Sear and Hammer Fixtures *by Chick Blood* 39

Chamber Identification With Cerrosafe *by Chip Todd* 42

Tapping and Die-Cutting Threads *by Chip Todd* 46

Cold Blueing Tips and Techniques *by Chip Todd* 52

Silversoldering—Useful, But Frustrating *by Chip Todd* 56

Diamonds Are a Gun's Best Friend 59

More About Checkering 64

Checkering Metal Parts *by Dennis A. Wood* 67

Magazine Repair and Lip-Shaping *by Chip Todd* 69

Tricks to the Trade *by Chip Todd* 76

Section 2: Handguns

Basic Work on 1911 Pistols *by Chick Blood* 82

Troubleshooting Smith & Wesson Revolvers *by Chick Blood* 86

Inside the Kahr K9 *by Chick Blood* 93

Smoothing Ruger Single-Action Revolvers *by Thomas Stuntebeck* 97

Fitting 1911 Slides and Frames *by Chick Blood* 101

Mounting Handgun Scopes *by Chip Todd* 103

Handgun Security Devices You Can Make *by Chip Todd* 107

Working Colt Single-Action Revolvers *by Thomas J. Stuntebeck* 110

Repairing Beretta 92 Pistols *by Butch Thomson* 114

Smoothing the T/C Contender's Trigger Assembly *by Chip Todd* 118

Troubleshooting Browning 9mm Hi-Power Pistols *by Chick Blood* 122

Troubleshooting Luger Pistols *by Frank Fry* 125

Contents

Checklist: Charco Revolvers *by Guy Lemieux* 130

Lorcin L9mm Pistols *by Butch Thomson* 131

Easy Revolver Jobs for Beginners *by Chip Todd* 134

Working the Glock Pistols *by Butch Thomson* 142

Correcting a Taurus Revolver's Problems *by Butch Thomson* 145

Installing Melded Rear Sights *by Dennis A. Wood* 149

Working Charco/Charter Arms Revolvers *by Butch Thomson* 152

Fitting M1911 Extractors *by Chick Blood* 156

Smith & Wesson's Third Generation Pistols *by Chick Blood* 158

Troubleshooting Ruger P-Series Pistols *by Butch Thomson* 162

Section 3: Long Guns

Working Chinese SKS Rifles *by Butch Thomson* 168

Troubleshooting the Remington 1100 Shotgun *by Butch Thomson* 172

Working the Winchester 94 *by Butch Thomson* 177

Gunstock Repairs 181

Performing the Ruger 10/22 Team Challenge Conversion *by Dennis Wood* 185

Mounting Rifle Scopes *by Frank Fry* 188

Working the Browning Auto-5 *by Dennis A. Wood* 192

Sporterizing Mauser 98 Rifles *by Dennis A. Wood* 196

Correcting a Bad Muzzle Crown *by Dennis Wood* 201

Installing Recoil Pads *by Chip Todd* 204

Troubleshooting Remington Model 700 Rifles *by Rich Hopkins* 210

Gunsmithing the Winchester 1300 Shotgun *by Butch Thomson* 213

Maintaining Ruger Mini-14 Rifles *by Dennis A. Wood* 217

Repairing and Maintaining the Mossberg 500 *by Butch Thomson* 220

Glass-Bedding for Bolt-Action Rifles *by Thomas J. Stuntebeck* 224

How to Lengthen Chambers and Forcing Cones *by Michael R. Orlen* 228

Reworking Ruger 77/22 Triggers *by Chick Blood* 232

Installing Screw-In Chokes Without a Lathe *by Chick Blood* 234

Installing Steel Butt Plates and Grip Caps *by Dennis A. Wood* 239

Removing Shotgun Barrel Dents *by Chip Todd* 243

Bead Sight Basics 248

Benchworking Winchester Model 70 Rifles *by Dennis A. Wood* 249

Working the Savage Model 110 *by Frank Fry* 253

Introduction

Sooner or later, almost every shooter becomes intrigued by the mechanics of firearms and the methods of repairing, improving, customizing or altering them. A few of these gun buffs eventually become professional gunsmiths, while most simply improve their personal firearms—and their shooting. Whether your goal is to be an enthusiast or professional, PRACTICAL GUNSMITHING will be a valuable addition to your workshop library.

Written by professional gunsmiths for *American Gunsmith* magazine, official publication of the American Gunsmithing Association, PRACTICAL GUNSMITHING covers the broad spectrum of 'smithing challenges in three sections: **Section 1: Tools & Techniques**; **Section 2: Handguns**; and **Section 3: Long Guns**. The writers represented here are some of the best gunsmiths in their field, not only as experienced practitioners of the gunsmithing arts, but also as communicators of gunsmithing trends and technologies. They bring to this book all their years of gunsmithing knowledge and experience in order to teach you, the reader, those skills you will need to perform the projects.

Most firearms manufactured in the United States are designed and built to last a lifetime, but all of them are subject to certain common malfunctions that occur from time-to-time. Worn and broken parts will need to be replaced, trigger assemblies will need adjusting, headspace will need correcting, worn finishes renewed, and a host of other adjustments. In every case, before a gun can be repaired, the problem must first be determined; only then can a definite plan be devised to do the actual repair. Finding out exactly what is wrong with any type of malfunctioning sporting firearm is known as troubleshooting. Troubleshooting covers an enormous range of problems, from replacing a mainspring in a revolver to diagnosing why a repeating shotgun jams or a carbine fails to shoot accurately. And troubleshooting firearms is a big part of what this book is all about, covering the investigation, analysis and corrective action required to eliminate faults in the operation of firearms.

But taking corrective action requires a fundamental knowledge of gunsmithing tools—precision measuring devices, files, abrasive stones, drill bits, pins and punches, polishing tools—and how to use them. It also requires learning technical skills and a systematic, methodical and efficient approach to problem solving in order to perform bench work projects such as installing swivels, mounting

scopes, tapping and die-cutting threads, and adjusting triggers. And, no reference work on gunsmithing is complete without a thorough examination of the advanced techniques required for working with metal and wood, whether the project at hand calls for perfecting wood-to-metal fit, checkering wood and metal surfaces, cold-blueing or silver soldering. All this and more is covered in the kind of depth and detail not found in other gunsmithing manuals. PRACTICAL GUNSMITHING covers these fundamentals in a way that's clear, cogent and timely.

However, all these professional tricks, tips and methodologies aren't any good unless put to use. Springing from these background chapters, you'll find specific projects that help you apply these gunsmithing skills. In **Section 2: Handguns**, projects range from easy revolver jobs for beginners; working slides and frames on the 1911 Colt; mounting handgun rings and scopes; installing sights; smoothing actions and fashioning handgun security devices, to gun-specific projects on Ruger and Colt single-action revolvers, Luger, 1911 Colt, Beretta, Glock, Lorcin, Browning and Ruger P-series semi-automatic pistols, plus double-action revolvers from Smith & Wesson to Colt. You'll even find an in-depth discussion of the trigger work a competent gunsmith may wish to consider for a T/C Contender.

Section 3: Long Guns is replete with a discussion of accessories and enhancements for any rifle or shotgun, from sling swivels to recoil pads, to scope mounting and gunstock repair. Readers are treated to discussions of glass-bedding bolt-action rifles; chamber lengthening; installing screw-in chokes, backboring barrels; and fashioning bead sights on shotguns. In-depth analyses examine the fit, function and repair of such widely used rifles as the Chinese SKS and Ruger 10-22, along with shotguns like the Browning Auto-5 and Remington 1100. Winchester, Savage and Mossberg are among the numerous long gun makers who receive detailed scrutiny in the pages of PRACTICAL GUNSMITHING.

Although intended primarily for home gunsmiths, this book will be an extremely helpful desk reference for professionals as well. Apprentice gunsmiths will also find the material valuable when used with other textbooks. In fact, it will be a useful manual for anyone who is interested in guns and shooting. It is designed to be read through at a sitting, to serve as a reference to solve specific problems, or as a gunsmithing browser—a book that can be opened to virtually any chapter to glean information of substance, value and enjoyment.

Safety

With regard to the mechanical and safety aspects of the guns covered in this book, it is assumed that the guns are in factory original condition with the dimensions of all parts as made by the manufacturer. Since alterations of parts is a simple matter, the reader is advised to have any gun checked by a competent gunsmith.

There are also certain safety rules which apply to everyone who handles firearms. The chief rule is never point a firearm at anyone or anything unless you intend to shoot it. This applies to both loaded and unloaded guns. Get in the habit of always checking the chamber and magazine of every gun you handle before doing anything else. Even after you have assured yourself that the gun is unloaded, always keep the muzzle pointed in a safe direction.

Make certain the firearm you intend to shoot is in good operating condition, with the proper ammunition being used, and that no obstructions—such as a cleaning brush or patch—are in the chamber or bore.

Beyond these, anyone who performs work on firearms should observe the following:

- Never apply heat to any part of a firearm unless you know exactly what you are doing; even then, proceed with caution.
- Never remove excessive amounts of metal from a rifle or shotgun action at points of stress such as receiver rings, locking lugs, and the like.
- When installing replacement parts, make certain that these parts are functioning properly before firing the gun.
- Be careful with trigger pull; and avoid "hair" triggers.
- When inspecting a new gun, make certain it is unloaded; but always treat it as if it were loaded.
- Wear safety goggles when grinding, chipping, sanding or working with caustic solutions.
- Always make certain that you are competent and understand the principles of a gunsmithing job before attempting it.

Whatever your definition of gunsmithing, it is in aggregate a field that requires practical, commonsense solutions to problems intrinsic to firearms repair. If you are interested in workable solutions to common gunsmithing problems, PRACTICAL GUNSMITHING is the reference source for you.

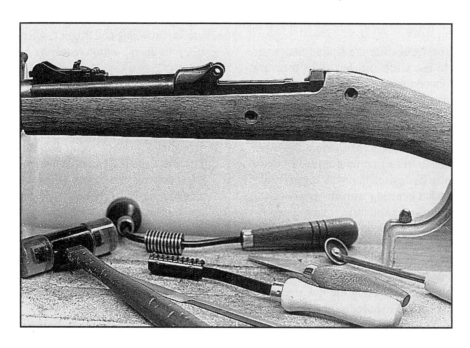

Section 1
Tools & Techniques

Setting Up a Work Area 8

Precision Measuring Instruments . .10

Choosing and Using Files, Part 1 . .14

Using Files, Part 2 17

Working With Pins and Punches . .20

Tips for Choosing—and Using—
    Abrasive Stones 25

The Not-So-Simple Drill Bit 31

Polishing Tools and Techniques . . .34

Sear and Hammer Fixtures 39

Chamber Identification With
    Cerrosafe .42

Tapping and Die-Cutting Threads .46

Cold Blueing Tips and
    Techniques 52

Silversoldering—Useful, But
    Frustrating 56

Diamonds Are a Gun's
    Best Friend 59

More About Checkering 64

Checkering Metal Parts 67

Magazine Repair and
    Lip-Shaping 69

Tricks to the Trade 76

Setting Up A Work Area

You'll find cleaning and basic maintenance easier to manage if you have everything in a designated spot. Here are some ideas.

By Dennis A. Wood

POST-HUNTING SEASON is the time of year that a lot of firearms can get neglected. Cleaning before storage is one of the most important things you can do to prevent damage to your costly firearms. You only have to put an uncleaned gun used during wet, snowy or rainy conditions away for the season one time to learn a costly lesson, especially if it's stored in a carrying case. Next fall, when you pull that firearm out for an anticipated hunt, it will no doubt greet you with a new, furry red skin. A catastrophe like that can be averted with just a little attention to the firearms before they go into storage.

A work bench dedicated just to maintenance of your firearms need not take up a lot of room and, if arranged according to your needs, can remove some of the drudgery of firearms cleaning. The convenience of having an area that contains all your tools makes working on your firearms much more pleasant.

A good start for most beginners is a work bench measuring 4 to 6 feet in length, about 2 feet front to back, and 34 inches high anchored to the wall and floor. Sturdiness and rigidity of construction is an absolute plus. You don't need to be chasing the bench around the room and a wobbly bench is, at best, frustrating to deal with. Consider acquiring some pre-assembled base cabinets that are available at most of the larger lumber yards. These cabinets can be found in pine or birch-faced plywood and are usually priced reasonably. Most of these base cabinets can be purchased with a top drawer and a door that opens to expose a shelved storage area for cleaning supplies. Anchored to the floor and wall, they become quite solid. A $3/4$- to 1-inch top made of plywood and screwed in place makes a nice, flat working surface.

Sealing the top with several coats of varnish will prevent gun crud from permeating the raw plywood top.

Once your bench has been secured, and any movement eliminated, the next item of importance to consider is a sturdy vise. Unfortunately, we were born with only two hands even though a third would be greatly appreciated when disassembling firearms for cleaning or whatever. This is where the vise comes in handy. It doesn't have to be expensive, but it should be sturdy. A cast iron vise, with jaws at least 4 inches wide, that has a swiveling base will not set you back much dollar-wise. Some of the imported vises coming into this country are priced so low that you sometimes wonder if they don't push the people who make them out the tenth floor window on Friday rather than pay them.

When mounted to a sturdy bench with bolts through the vise base and bench you'll have a solid setup. Most vises normally come with serrated jaw faces. As is, such jaw faces are not very kind to the finishes we need to maintain on firearms. A set of false jaws for your vise can be fashioned out of almost any hardwood. With some $1/4$-inch thick leather glued to the inside faces of these false jaws, you'll protect the finish on any gun. If you feel you'd like to get more elaborate, Brownell's sells material for false jaws specifically formulated for dealing with either metal or wood surfaces.

If you are like me, you've had to accompany the wife at least once to shop for carpeting. No doubt you've also had to suffer through the endless viewing of samples that the salesperson is all too willing to show you. These carpet samples, usually sized around 18 x 24 inches, make great bench mats. If you're purchasing carpet, work out a deal with the salesperson to get a half-dozen or so of these sample pads thrown in. Otherwise, they can be found from 50 cents to a dollar anywhere carpet is sold. These pads are great for disassembly of handguns, as parts usually stay on them and, when they get overly dirty, they can be tossed away. I prefer short nap samples, as the deep pile variety has a tendency to allow small pins and screws a place to hide.

The best investment you will ever make as far as firearms maintenance is concerned is a set of good hollow-ground screwdriver bits. The importance of a properly fitting screwdriver blade cannot be overstated. We've all seen screw slots butchered by some gun owner using a tapered blade screwdriver. Battered screw slots can make an otherwise nice firearm look atrocious. Magna-tip hollow-ground screwdriver bits are sold in sets or individually at affordable cost so there is no excuse to not use them.

Every width and thickness ever contrived for screw slots has a representative screwdriver bit available for it. If a bit is broken, a replacement can be found for about $2.

Maintaining firearms so that they remain in reliable condition often means they will need to be taken down in either subassemblies or completely for a thorough cleaning. Another set of tools that will prove invaluable will be a good set of drift pin punches. Starrett and General are two brands that come to mind as they are readily available in sets or individually. Diameters of these punches run from 0.060-inch on up.

A 2-ounce ballpeen hammer will provide enough power for most pin drifting and a pair of safety glasses should always accompany the use of drifting punches. A bench block, either steel or nylon, is also a handy item. These round blocks, which resemble a cup, have several different sizes of holes in them and usually a v-groove. Their job is to support the off side of the firearm over the appropriate hole in the block and catch the drifted out pin. The hollowed out underside of the bench block acts as a catching chamber for the removed pin.

For drifting front or rear sights, the use of a brass drift will often be recommended. I'm not a fan of using brass punches on blued surfaces, because brass drifts almost always leave behind a residual yellow smear that isn't easy to remove.

I purchased a solid copper rod, 6 feet in length and 3/8-inch diameter, well over 10 years ago. I've cut about six 4-inch lengths off it to use for drifting front and rear sights. Copper is softer than brass, but I think it makes a better drift. The smear that's left behind can be wiped off of a blued surface much easier.

All this equipment is not going to do you much good without sufficient lighting to get the cleaning job done properly and thoroughly. Find a good lamp that has a bent arm and swiveling head and can handle a 100-watt bulb. You can point this type of light in almost any direction and peer into the nooks and crannies that hold gunk.

If I had to pick only two of the seemingly infinite variety of gun solvents available, Shooter's Choice and Break-Free CLP would be the ones that would have a spot reserved on my bench. There are a lot of brands out there to choose from, and I try just about every new one in search of the ultimate solution. Most people don't. These brands have served me well, so I don't think you'd go wrong with them.

The aforementioned equipment should set you up with a convenient area to help in the maintenance of your firearms.

A dedicated, organized area, containing all the tools and supplies you need to get the job done somewhat guarantees that the job will get done. If you have to search around gathering up all the things necessary to clean your firearms until the next season arrives the job can all too often get neglected.

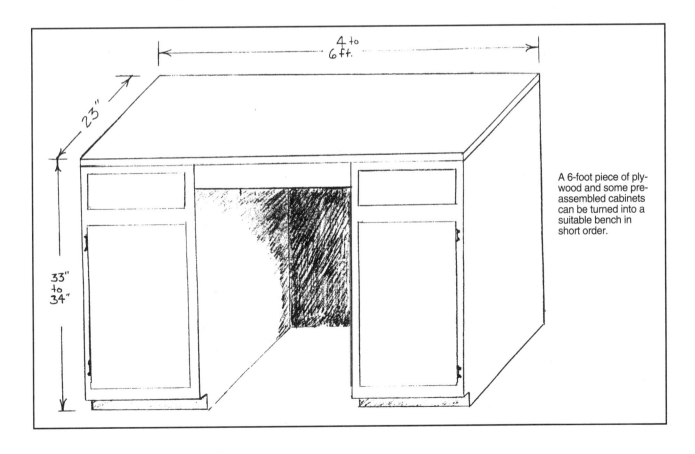

A 6-foot piece of plywood and some pre-assembled cabinets can be turned into a suitable bench in short order.

Precision Measuring Instruments

In gunsmithing, precision is a must—here are some tools to help you.

By Frank Fry

AN IMPORTANT ASPECT of successful gunsmithing—often overlooked by beginners—is measuring tools. Gunsmiths need two types of measuring instruments, direct and indirect (or comparison). The indirect, or comparison, instruments include tools found in the caliper family, such as inside, outside, and hermaphrodite calipers, and dividers. Direct measuring devices include the rule, various micrometers, and dial-faced measuring tools.

Tolerances can be held surprisingly close with calipers, and measurements taken with an outside or inside caliper can be transferred to a rule or to another measuring tool. Unless a measured distance is required, the caliper family is generally useful as a "snap gauge" to transfer an old part's dimensions to a new one during reproduction.

Direct measuring tools such as outside micrometers, depth micrometers, dial, and Vernier calipers are almost an absolute requirement when manufacturing parts to close tolerances. When calculations are needed in machining, these instruments provide the linear measurements needed.

The dial indicator, which does not measure length like a micrometer or dial caliper, is indispensable in "setting up" mills and lathes and monitoring machining processes to close tolerance.

Some of these precision tools are versatile enough to perform several functions and may be easier to read than single-purpose instruments, thus are used more often. The downside to multi-function tools like dial calipers is that some accuracy may be sacrificed to provide this reading ease and multiplicity of use.

Measuring-instrument quality, like any other gunsmithing tool, is directly related to cost, and your purchases should be guided by the item's expected use. For example, a 6-inch plastic dial caliper retailing for $17 to $20 is fine as a snap gauge for measuring cartridge cases or the occasional bench job. But if that piece is used constantly on daily eight-hour shifts, it will soon wear to the point of being useless. On the other hand, a 6-inch Starrett Satin Chrome Master Vernier Caliper at $270 or more is certainly not the tool to purchase if all you measure is the width of slings or recoil pads.

An important rule of tool purchasing is to buy the best quality tool you can afford for the expected use. But be sensible about it. Don't go overboard and buy more quality than you will need just because your budget allows it.

Another rule is to safeguard your investment once it's purchased. Regardless of how much you spend, you need to keep your tools in good shape by wiping them clean before storing. When storing precision measuring tools, leave a small gap between the measuring surfaces. This allows parts of different metals and shapes to expand and contract at different rates as the temperature changes, preventing stresses that could possibly damage the tool's accuracy.

The Dial Caliper

Practicing gunsmiths I consulted with overwhelmingly recommended the 6-inch dial caliper as their first choice in precision tools. Only a few old-timers voted for Vernier calipers, which were once the standard for machinists. Verniers are still available and are useful and accurate instruments, but learning to use Vernier scales can be more difficult than the dial versions, and extra practice may be needed to read the scales accurately. Dials, especially for those of us who are overdue to visit an optician, are far easier to read.

The dial caliper has three standard uses: for outside, inside and depth measurement. Dial calipers usually measure to a thousandth of an inch (0.001) and are generally accurate enough and acceptable for most gun work. In those cases where 0.001-inch is not close enough, and a "tenth," or one ten-thousandth of an inch accuracy, is required, a "tenths" micrometer should be used.

A dial caliper's depth measurement is perhaps not as accurate as it would be from a depth micrometer because holding the caliper exactly parallel or vertical to the measured surface is more difficult. However, adapters are available and can be attached to the caliper to provide a more stable measuring platform.

The major caliper parts are the fixed and movable jaws, slide, dial, scale, and jaw-adjustment knob. The dial has an adjustable bezel or face and a bezel lock. Most, if not all, dial calipers have a lock to keep the jaws from accidentally moving while reading or transferring measurements. The dial indicator is available in two standard types on

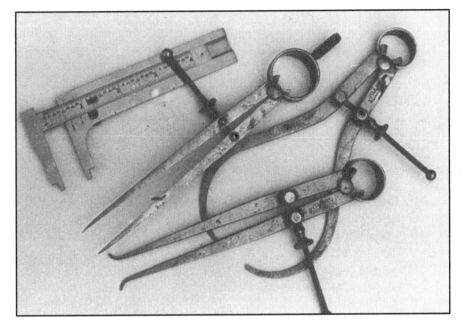

Inside and outside calipers, dividers and a pocket slide caliper are accurate but can't be considered precision measuring instruments.

which a full revolution of the needle can equal either one tenth (0.100) or two tenths (0.200) of an inch. The 0.200 dial will have zeros at its top and midpoint. Of the two, the 0.100 revolution dial provides wider spaces between graduations and is easier to read. Hint: Before you take any measurements, clean and close the jaws of the caliper, then adjust the dial bezel to the zero point.

Apply only enough pressure to the jaws or depth stem to assure that contact with the work has been made. With a little practice, you will develop a feel for this. Consistent pressure will become a habit, contributing toward consistent measurements. Quality calipers have an adjustment knob that "slips" when reading pressures have been reached and automatically provide the consistency needed from one measurement to another.

Many calipers, dial and Vernier alike, have scales that read in millimeters and inches. Since most of our measurements will be in inches, be sure it is the inch scale that is used. Do not mix the scales.

The inch scale is divided into two types of graduations. The largest lines and numbers are inches; the smaller are hundredths of an inch. The dial also divides each tenth into thousandths of an inch.

To read the dial caliper, remember to add the measurement from the scale in increments from left to right, from largest to smallest. Convention says that any numbers smaller than an inch are to be converted to thousandths of an inch to eliminate confusion. One inch plus six-tenths plus fifty-three thousandths equals 1.653 and is read as one and six-hundred fifty-three thousandths of an inch. If these measurements are not precise enough, the micrometer with tenths capabilities will be needed.

Dial Indicators

The next precision measuring tool mentioned by gunsmiths was the .001-inch dial indicator used primarily to prepare milling machines and lathes for specific jobs. It is also used to center items in a four-jawed chuck, to monitor machining progress, and to work to precise dimensions. If quality and precision machining is in order, the dial indicator cannot be overlooked. Costs for the basic indicator will vary from around $20 to more than $250, while an indicator stand will run an additional $20 to $100. The stands come in many styles, but the magnetic base is the most popular. The

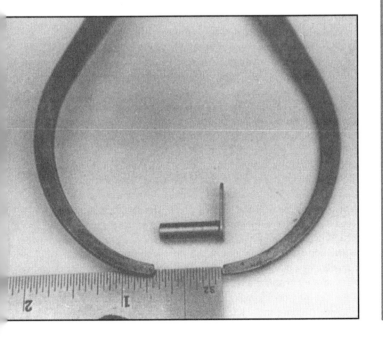

Transfer the measurement you get with the outside calipers to your rule.

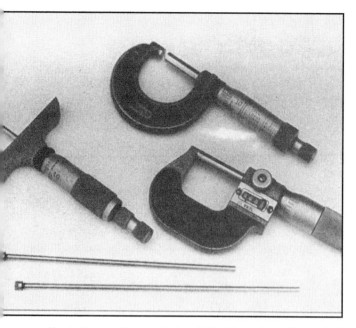

Key tools you will use include outside micrometers with standard and digital scales and a depth micrometer with extension rods.

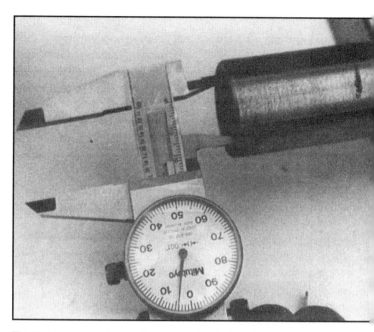

The dial calipers can be used to measure inside diameters of holes or to gauge the diameter of a shaft.

holder arms may be solid or flexible, depending on personal preference and available funds.

The dial indicator differs from the caliper and micrometer in that it produces readings of variance and motion, or continuously monitors the distance of travel from one given point to another. Neither the dial caliper nor micrometer can do this.

From its at-rest position, the dial indicator's needle will indicate in one direction (clockwise) only. The number of needle revolutions around the dial is determined by the length of the stem, which can be 0.050-inch or less to several inches. Some dial indicators have replaceable stems of different lengths, but a stem with 1 inch of travel is probably versatile enough for your needs. These instruments are generally available in 0.001-inch accuracy.

Movable bezels are generally graduated in 0.100-inch per needle revolution. To ease failing memories, pointers are provided and can be set as reference locations or to mark a variation spread.

Some confusion exists between two similar indicator instruments, the dial indicator and the dial *test* indicator. The latter has capabilities to read either left or right from its normal state. The test indicator's range of motion is usually limited to a short amount of travel, and it has dial markings graduated plus and minus right and left of the zero. It is used to measure vertical runout or wobble. The dial indicator reads to the right, its readings limited only by the length of the stem. It can be used for both runout and linear motion.

In lathe work, if we mount the indicator on the lathe bed so it contacts the saddle, we can accurately determine the length of any given longitudinal cut or amount of saddle travel along the bed. Contact with the cross feed can determine very precise cutting depths for finished work. If centering work in a four-jawed chuck, the indicator is mounted with the stem bearing on the work. Any errors in centering are removed by revolving the chuck 180 degrees and removing half the indicated error by loosening and tightening opposing jaws. The chuck is again rotated 180 degrees and checked again. After removing this runout, rotate the work 90 degrees and start the process again. The work is centered when the needle does not move as the work is rotated 360 degrees against the stem.

For milling machine work, the indicator is used to "swing" or "sweep" the table to set the mill head absolutely vertical to the table. This is necessary to produce parallel cuts and prevents "shelving" in successive cuts across wide surfaces. The dial indicator is also required for setups, like scope-mount drilling or slabbing the sides of a barrel, that must have the axis of the work parallel to bed travel. In both of these examples, the bore must be held absolutely parallel to the direction of table travel. This setup is best done with the dial indicator.

To "swing" or "sweep" the table in adjusting the milling head to vertical, hold the indicator on the end of a bar held at 90 degrees in the spindle, the stem pressing 0.025-inch, more or less, against the table. A reading is taken on the long axis of the bed, the indicator rotated 180 degrees and the reading compared. Any change indicates the milling head is not vertical in the Y axis and needs to be adjusted by half of the variation. As this process continues, the indicator is swung back to the starting point. The variation should become smaller on each swing. Additional tests are taken on the X axis (90 degrees from the original setting) and the head adjusted so no variation exists in the Y axis. When the readings are equal in all four quadrants, the head is perpendicular to the table.

If you want to square a vise or work to the table, clamp one end of the vise or work to it. Set the stem of the indicator to get an 0.025-inch reading on the fixed jaw of the vise or on a flat edge of the work. Note the position of the needle on the dial and traverse the table. If the needle shows any motion from its original reading, tap the vise or work in the direction needed to bring the needle back to its original position. A couple of passes should square the vise or work to plus or minus 0.002-inch or less.

If the lathe is used to chamber, the dial indicator can be set up to read motion in 0.001-inch increments as the reamer is fed into the chamber. Reaming distances of less than 0.001-inch can be controlled in this manner and holes drilled to exact depths in the same manner.

Remember that direct-measurement instruments—the dial indicator, outside micrometers and depth micrometers—produce actual linear measurements. The dial indicator measures variation, or motion from one point to another, and is not an instrument that is generally used to measure length directly.

Micrometers

The final family of precision measuring tools needed for those more precise jobs are micrometers. A 1 inch outside micrometer with tenths capability is an excellent choice. A depth micrometer with 1- to 6-inch capabilities is extremely useful for barreling and chambering.

The major components of micrometers are, from top to base, the thimble, barrel, spindle, anvil and yoke. Most micrometers are now equipped with a pressure-regulating thimble or ratcheting top to provide equal force from measurement to measurement. (Don't let customers handle your micrometers. No matter what some people believe, micrometers are not precision "C" clamps.) The cautions of cleaning and verifying the zero apply to micrometers as well as dial calipers. If a zero reading is not obtained when the spindle touches the anvil, follow the manufacturer's instructions for adjusting the micrometer barrel.

Note that the value of the micrometer scale differs from that of the dial indicator. Each large graduation on a micrometer barrel represents 0.100-inch, the same as the scale of the dial caliper. Within each of these major divisions are three smaller graduations producing four spaces from one major line to the next. The distance between these smaller lines represents 0.025-inch.

The thimble is also marked around its circumference with 25 graduations, each representing 0.001-inch. One full turn of the thimble equals 0.025-inch.

To arrive at an outside micrometer reading, use the same principle as we did with the dial caliper, adding from large to small, left to right. As the micrometer is adjusted, the reading is taken from the last graduation that appears under the barrel on the base line.

All graduations on the micrometer, like the dial caliper, are read in thousandths: 0.100 is read as one hundred thousandths, 0.025 as twenty-five thousandths, and 0.003 as three-thousandths. Together they add up to a total reading of 0.128 or one hundred twenty-eight thousandths.

The "tenths" micrometer has a set of markings parallel to the barrel numbered from 0 through 10. These lines break a single thousandth of an inch (0.001) into 10 parts to provide the ability to read in ten-thousandths of an inch.

If a graduation on the thimble does not line up on the base line,

look at the tenths lines on the barrel; one of the graduations on the thimble will line up exactly with one of those lines.

The number of "tenths" is read on the barrel scale, not the thimble, and the number is added to the end of the reading. For example, 0.1287 is read as one hundred twenty-eight thousandths and seven-tenths.

The depth micrometer scale is handled differently than an outside micrometer, but it uses the same additive principle. In both instances, the scale starts at zero, but as the thimble on the depth micrometer is turned, the thimble covers the graduated lines on the barrel instead of revealing them. Remember, the last covered line is the graduation to read. If you use the graduation line that is visible, the measurement will be long by 0.025-inch.

Depth micrometers are especially useful in measuring receiver-ring and barrel-shank lengths, when reaming during chambering to monitor progress, and for seeing how many more thousandths remain before the GO gage is fully seated.

The Tools In Use

You'll find these instruments invaluable if you ever have to reproduce a part for a customer's gun. We need the part's dimensions, overall length, width, depth of retaining slots, and so forth. Many of these measurements can be taken directly from the old part without difficulty, but the new part's dimensions may have to be altered or adjusted to compensate for wear that may have occurred. Special consideration must also be given to those dimensions that concern safety, such as firing pin-tip protrusion, diameter, or loss of length through battering at the rear of the pin by the hammer.

Tip diameter should be matched to the existing hole, not to the old pin. Wear may have taken place on both the pin and in the hole. If this compounded error is not eliminated, the newly manufactured firing pin could indicate a headspace condition by letting the primer flow into the space around the tip and hole. The tip must be long enough to ignite the primer without piercing it. These lengths vary from shotguns to 22 rimfires, so published data should be followed in making them up.

Measurements that you take from old parts need not be drafted professionally into a full-blown blueprint. They are only working guides for reproduction, though it is a good idea to record and save them for future reference just in case another one is needed. Several laws of gunsmithing suggest that if you do not record the data, the next job will be identical and the measurement will have to be taken over again!

A little practice in using dial calipers, micrometers and dial indicators can give the gunsmith an increased ability to make precision measurements. But the quest for accuracy does not end here. The best measuring skills are useless without the ability to transfer and work to those measurements. Without a high level of competence using precision measuring instruments, the mastery of mechanical skills needed to work to close tolerances is a near impossible task.

If precision is important to you—measure with a dial indicator, mark with a finely pointed scriber, machine and file to within 0.001-inch. It will not be long before you are known as a superior quality craftsman!

Choosing and Using Files, Part 1

You can make your stock and metalwork smoother and better by using the proper files. Following is a rundown of the many types from which to choose.

By Dennis A. Wood

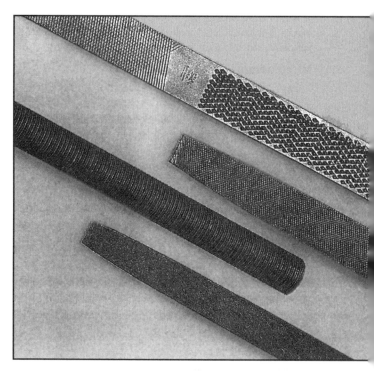

From top: A rasp, which is used to remove large amounts of wood; the bastard cut file, which is used primarily for roughing metal work but which will also serve to work wood; the curved tooth file, used for shaping stocks or other wood work; and the second-cut pattern, which is used for metalwork.

AN OLD TOOLMAKER, who had the responsibility of training young upstarts, once told me, "Give me a trainee who knows how to file and I'll teach him the rest." According to this old gentleman, quite a bit of his early apprenticeship involved the proper use of files, and this old guy used a file like a concert violinist uses a bow.

Gunsmiths, too, have plenty of opportunities to file wood and metal, and using a file properly can speed—or even make possible—your work on internal bolt parts, stocks, and other piecework. For instance, when I'm hand-fitting parts that are purposely made oversize, the proper type and use of a file will make the job go easier. Or when I'm installing so-called drop-in parts for building 1911 auto pistols, more often than not I find myself reaching for a file to give the parts a few swipes so they will actually drop in.

Filing is one of those tasks you develop a feel for, a learn-by-doing process.

Talking the Talk

Files are normally classified according to their shape or cross-cut section and according to the pitch or spacing of their teeth and the nature of the cut. The broad terms used to describe file characteristics are cross-section and outline.

A file's cross section may be triangular, quadrangular, circular, or some special shape. The outline of its contour may be tapered or blunt. In the former the point is reduced in width and/or thickness gradually, usually for one-half to two-thirds of its length. Blunt files' cross sections remain the same from tang to point.

The term *cut* designates the arrangement of teeth such as single, double, rasp, or curved. The single-cut file has a single series of parallel teeth extending across the face of the file at an angle of 45 to 85 degrees to the axis of the file (see sidebar for definitions). This angle depends upon the form of the file and the nature of the work for which the file is intended. The single cut file is normally used with light pressure to produce a smooth finish.

The double-cut file has a large number of small pointed teeth angled toward the point of the file and arranged in two series of diagonal rows that cross each other. For general work, the angle of the first series of rows is from 40 to 45 degrees and the second row from 70 to 80 degrees. For double-cut finishing files, the first series has an angle of about 30 degrees, and the second from 80 to 87 degrees. The second, or upcut, is almost always deeper than the first or overcut. Double-cut files are usually used, along with heavier pressure, for removing material faster and where you can get by with a rougher finish.

The rasp is formed by raising a series of individually rounded teeth from the surface of the file blank and is used with relatively heavy pressure on softer material for faster removal such as roughing out the shape on gun stocks.

The curved-tooth file has teeth that are in the form of parallel arcs extending across the face of the file. The middle portion of each arc is closest to the point or center of the file. Teeth are usually single cut and are relatively coarse.

Coarseness

Files remove material at different rates; the terms coarse, bastard, second, and smooth are normally used to describe those rates. The coarse and bastard-cut files are used to remove a great deal of material from a job, and the second and smooth cut files are used to finish the more exacting gun work.

You'll often find more use for the second and smooth cut files on metal, and the rougher cut files for stock wood shaping. (Degrees of coarseness are only comparable when files of the same length are compared, as the number of teeth per inch decreases as the length of the file increases.) The coarseness range for curved tooth files is given as standard, fine and smooth. In the case of Swiss pattern files a series of numbers is used to designate coarseness instead of a title; numbers 00, 0, 1, 2, 3, 4, and 6 are the most common, with No. 00 the coarsest and No. 6 the finest. The number 5 is not used because it could be mistaken for an "S" on a smooth-cut file.

File Classes

There are five main classes of files: mill or saw files, machinists files, curved tooth files, Swiss-pattern files, and rasps.

The first two classes are more commonly referred to as American pattern files. Mill or saw files are used for sharpening mill or circular saws, large cross-cut saws, lathe work, draw filing brass or bronze and for general smooth filing. Cantsaw files have an obtuse isosceles triangular section, a blunt outline, are single cut and are used for sharpening saws having "M" shaped teeth and teeth of less than a 60-degree angle. Crosscut files have a narrow triangular section with the short side rounded, a blunt outline, a single cut and are used to sharpen cross-cut saws. Machinist files are used throughout industry where metal must be removed rapidly and where the finish is not that important. Except for certain instances in the round or half-round configurations, most of these files are double-cut.

Flat files have a rectangular section, are tapered in width and thickness, cut on both sides and edges and are used for general utility work. Half-round files have a circular segmental section, are tapered in width and thickness, have their flat side double-cut, their rounded side mostly double-cut but sometimes single-cut and are used to file in concave areas. Hand files are similar to flat files but taper in thickness only. One edge is usually uncut or safe. Knife files have a knife blade shaped section, tapered in width only, double-cut and are used by tool and die makers on work having acute angles. General purpose files have a rectangular section, are tapered and have second cut teeth divided by angular sections which produce short cutting edges. These edges help with stock removal but still leave a smooth finish and are suitable for use on various materials including aluminum, bronze, cast iron and mild steels.

Pillar files are similar to hand files but are thicker and narrower and should be included in every gunsmith's arsenal of files. Because these files are thicker, there is less tendency for this type of file to flex. Round files have a circular surface, are tapered, single-cut and are generally used to file round openings or convex radii.

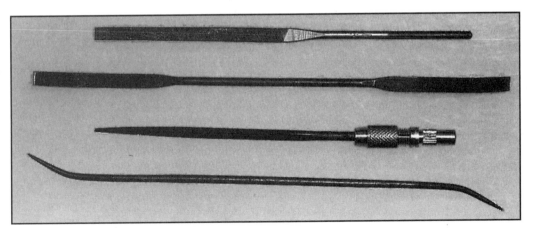

The straight needle files (top and third from top) are used for fine finishing cuts on metal. The bent files (second from top and at bottom), called rifflers, allow you to perform detail work in hard-to-reach places.

Three square files are double-cut and have sharp corners as contrasted with taper triangular files, which are single-cut and have somewhat rounded corners. These files are normally used for filing accurate internal angles such as those used for dovetail sight bases. Warding files have a rectangular section and taper in width to a narrow point. These files are used for getting into narrow areas.

Wood files are made in the same sections as flat and half-round files but with coarser teeth especially suited for rough work on gunstocks. Curved tooth files are made in both rigid and flexible forms. The rigid type has either a tang for a conventional handle or is made with a hole at each end for mounting in a special holder. The flexible type is furnished for use in special holders only. Curved tooth files come in standard, fine and smooth cuts in parallel flat, square, pillar, pillar narrow, half-round and shell types.

Swiss pattern files are used by tool and die makers, model makers and delicate instrument parts finishers. These files are made to closer tolerances than the conventional American pattern files although they have similar cross sections. The points of the Swiss pattern files are smaller, the tapers are longer and they are available in much finer cuts. These files are primarily finishing tools for removing burrs left behind from previous finishing operations, truing up grooves, notches, cleaning out corners and smoothing small parts. For very fine work, round and square handled needle files, available in numerous cross-section shapes in lengths from 4 to 7$\frac{1}{4}$ inches, are used.

Wrapping Up

Regardless of the kinds of files you eventually use for stock and metalwork, you need to know which file to pick and exactly how to employ it.

File Definitions

Axis: The imaginary line extending the entire length of a file equidistant from the faces and edges.

Back: The convex side of a file having the same or similar cross section as in a half-round file.

Bastard Cut: A grade of coarseness that falls between coarse and second cut on American pattern files and rasps.

Blank: A file in any process of manufacture before the teeth are cut.

Blunt: A file whose cross-section dimensions from point to tang remain unchanged.

Coarse Cut: The coarsest of all American pattern files and rasps.

Coarseness: This term describes the relative number of teeth per length of the file. The coarsest have the fewest number of teeth per unit of length; the smoothest files the most. American pattern files and rasps have four degrees of coarseness; coarse, bastard, second and smooth. Swiss pattern files usually have seven stages of coarseness: 00, 0, 1, 2, 3, 4 and 6 (from coarsest to smoothest). Curved-tooth files have three stages of coarseness; standard, fine and smooth.

Curved Cut: File teeth that are made in a curved contour across the file blank.

Cut: This term is used to describe the file teeth with respect to coarseness or character. Single, double, rasp, curved or special are used to describe the cut.

Double-Cut: A file tooth arrangement formed by two series of cuts, namely the overcut followed, at an angle, by the upcut.

Edge: The surface joining faces of a file. Some files have teeth on the edges; some don't.

Face: The widest cutting surface or surfaces that are used for filing. Heel or Shoulder: That portion of a file that abuts the tang.

Hopped: This term is used by file makers to describe the spacing between file teeth.

Length: The measured distance from the heel to the point of the file.

Overcut: The first series of teeth put on a double cut file.

Point: The front end of a file.

Rasp Cut: A file tooth arrangement of round-topped teeth, not usually connected. These teeth are formed individually by means of a narrow punch like tool.

Recut: A worn out file which has had the teeth re-cut into it after annealing and grinding off of the old teeth. The file is then rehardened.

Safe edge: An edge on a file that is smooth and without teeth so that it will not cut into the workpiece.

Second Cut: A grade of file coarseness between bastard and smooth on American pattern files and rasps.

Set: To blunt the sharp edges or corners of file blanks before and after the overcut is made. This is done to prevent weakness or breakage of the teeth along the edges or corners when the file is in use.

Single-Cut: File tooth arrangement where the file teeth are composed of single unbroken rows of parallel teeth formed by a single series of cuts.

Smooth Cut: An American pattern file and rasp cut that is smoother than second cut.

Tang: The narrowed end of the file which enters the handle.

Upcut: The series of teeth superimposed on the overcut and at an angle to it, such as on a double-cut file.

Using Files, Part II

Other than screwdriver bits and punches, files are probably the most useful tools that you can own. Here's how to get more out of them.

By Dennis A. Wood

GIVEN TIME AND patience, any job performed on a milling machine can probably be done by hand with files. Once properly inletted, a decent stock design can be rasped out of a block of walnut, providing a nesting place for a favorite barreled action. A replacement rabbit ear hammer for that antique shotgun can be fashioned out of a piece of steel. The artisans of bygone times did not have all the intricate wood or metal-shaping equipment available today, yet they managed to turn out beautiful work. When filing, patience and the ability to see the finished job in your mind make the difference between success and failure—along with using proper filing techniques.

You already know some of the techniques involved, but there are some basic file-working ideas that are worth reviewing and some advanced techniques that can make your work go faster and look better.

Choosing a File

When working on any surface, the most important step is to choose the right file cut, style, and size.

A milling machine (which removes metal, as does a file) has the incremental capacity for downfeed adjustment. If the mill downfeed scale is accurate, the cutter will remove the desired amount of material from the work piece. Not so with files. The operator deter-

mines how much material is removed with each pass of the file. This is why selecting the right file-cut type is important.

To get a real-world idea of how much material each file removes, place a flat piece of steel stock on your work bench, and with a micrometer or Vernier, measure the thickness of it. Place the steel stock in your vise and take ten or so swipes across the top of it with a smooth-cut file. Measure the piece again, and you will soon see that not much material has been removed by the smooth cut file.

Thus, when a project calls for removing $1/32$-inch of material, start the job with one of the coarser files, such as the bastard cut. Work the surface down with the coarse file until there is about 0.010-inch of remaining material, then finish up with one of the smoother cuts.

Shaping gun stock wood normally calls for coarser files, but this is not to say the finer files do not have a place in working wood. For example, when forming a beaded cheekpiece, it's mighty hard to beat a smooth-cut file to get the definition of a sharp 90-degree shoulder.

Most often, roughing out a stock blank requires using raised tooth rasps in round and half-round shapes. The round or half-round files work around the curves of a cheekpiece or in the grip area with its compound curves. Although sometimes impossible, try to keep the rasps and files going with the direction of the grain in the wood. Excessive cross-grain cutting of the wood fibers results in the need for extra elbow grease when the time comes for

While draw filing, the file teeth are held at 90 degrees to the bore line, and the file is pushed forward and back.

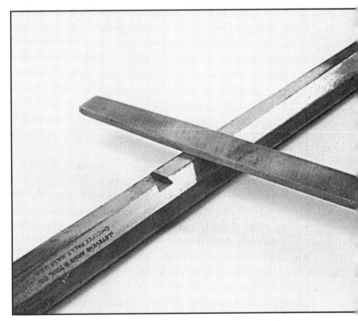

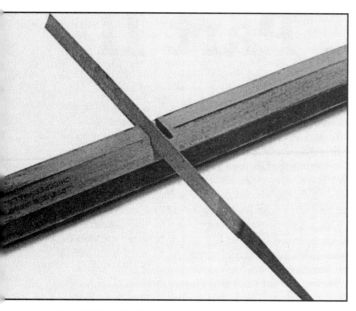

The sight base file has two safe sides; they guide the file when cutting a dovetail wider.

The horseshoe rasp has a curved side and a flat side. It comes in handy when roughing out gunstock shapes.

sanding. The compression and cutting trauma imparted to the wood fibers from rasping can go deeper than what is visible, so whenever possible try to go with the grain.

I employ these types in shaping new stocks for the most common Remington and Winchester bolt-action rifles. I have my own stock patterns made from the lowest grade of walnut I can get. I then reshape these patterns to match the particular needs of the customer. It's a simple matter to build up an area with an auto-body filler, such as Bondo, to get the pattern as close to the customer's needs as possible and then send the pattern and stock blank off for profiling.

File Shapes and Choices

Square, round, and triangular files each have their place when dealing with metal parts fitting.

A $^3/_{16}$-inch parallel round smooth cut file is just the ticket when fitting a new barrel link on a 1911-style pistol. The radius on the barrel lugs of these style pistols is another place that needs attention when fitting a new barrel so that the slide stop pin rides over it allowing proper barrel lockup.

If you need to cut a dovetail for a sight but do not have access to a milling machine, spending less than $20 for a quarter-inch square file and sight base file will get you through this task. The square quarter-inch file is used to remove the bulk of the metal, keeping the bottom of the future dovetail flat, level and perpendicular to the bore.

The sight base file is triangular shaped and has two safe sides that are used to undercut each end of the dovetail until the sight fits snugly in place. As the safe sides do not have teeth they are employed as guides to ride in the bottom of the dovetail while the side with teeth cuts. There are plenty of gun craftsmen who still use this method of installing sight dovetails and do a reputable job of it.

Needle files are hard to beat when the need for getting into tight places arises. These files are small enough so their size does not obliterate your ability to see what you are doing. Putting a slight chamfer on an extractor or the radiusing of the underside of a 1911-style extractor for case head clearance is where these files shine.

Of most use are the smaller 4- to 5-inch overall length files with 2 to $2^1/_2$ inches of cutting surface. The Swiss pattern files offer

Power Files

Using rotary files and burr bits in a motor-driven hand tool can add speed to your filing, especially on softer materials such as wood, but they also have application on metal.

A round, coarse burr bit, for instance, removes wood from a gunstock quickly in preparation for a glass bedding job.

Also, the cylinder and tapered carbide burr bits are handy for shaving metal, especially in hard-to-get-at areas. This works well when installing and blending flared magazine-well extensions on 1911s.

Additionally, small carbide ball burr bits are handy to use when a screw slot is butchered up, and you need to get the screw out for replacement. The little ball will cut a good enough slot so that the battered screw can be turned out.

The rat-tail file is quite handy for getting into small curved areas like those behind a grip cap.

more grades of cut in the file teeth. For me, the #1 medium coarse, #2 medium, #3 medium fine, and the #4 fine serve particularly well.

When dealing with the harder heat-treated steels sometimes found in gun parts, the fine-cut diamond needle files have enough stamina to remove burrs and sharp edges where a normal file wouldn't cut it.

File Sizes and Thicknesses

Just as there are many different styles of files, there are different schools of thought on what sizes of files should be used. Control of

Pushing a file over a flat-topped vise will keep the edges of the part from rounding over.

the file becomes a factor, and for that reason my preference is for files with lengths of 4, 6, and 8 inches.

For me, it's much easier to feel what the file is doing when I'm using a size I can control. There are those who do quite well using the 10-, 12-, and 14-inch files.

For most of the part fitting I encounter, I find myself reaching most often for the pillar files in my rack. This type of file has a thicker body and therefore has less tendency to flex than some of the thinner files. The thicker, smaller files are also an asset when you need to keep the cut flat. Because most pillar files have safe sides, you don't have to worry when getting up against 90-degree shoulders that don't need undercutting.

When involving yourself with striking or draw filing barrels for tool mark removal or eliminating the pits caused by rust, a bigger file should get the call, mainly because you can get both hands on the file. This type of filing usually calls for much longer stokes with the determined effort to keep the work piece flat. Chalk the file to keep the file teeth from pinning or clogging up with the metal being removed and use a file card or brush to keep the file clean so it doesn't score the work.

When dealing with the roughing of stock shapes, I move up to the larger files. The 10-, 12-, and 14-inch rasps and files afford more width and length to hang onto when shaping a forearm or rounding the toe and heel on the butt.

Working Flat

One of the difficulties involved with filing is keeping the file flat and not rounding off edges. Whenever possible use a vise with square, flat, smooth faced jaws. I use one of the cheaply made drill press vises that has had the top of the vise jaws surface ground so that they are now true to one another. The inside faces have also been surface ground so that they too are flat. When a part that needs to be dressed with a file is placed between these jaws, the file moves across the jaws and keeps the outside edges of the part from rounding over. Flatness is extremely important when dealing with sear surfaces and other parts that need to mate squarely.

File teeth are pitched forward and only cut when pushed forward.

Tip

If you need to remove an excessive amount of material, don't start with a file. Instead, scribe a line at the necessary depth and hacksaw the material above this scribed line. There isn't much sense wearing your arms out filing when there are quicker ways to remove the material.

Working with Pins and Punches

Pins find their way into many different sections of a gun, and you need to know how to remove and install a variety of them.

By Chip Todd

ONE OF THE THINGS some gun owners—engineers or fairly well-educated hobbyists who have a good grasp of mechanical things—ask about is how to handle the different kinds of pins in their guns. Particularly, they often want to know if their punches are the right ones, or if they can use a slightly different one without damaging their pins. Gunsmiths who have worked for years with different kinds of pins take the varied shapes, uses, and special punches needed to work on these items for granted, but there are a few intricacies about dealing with them that aren't common knowledge among either serious hobbyists or 'smiths.

Below, I'll discuss some of the more frequently found pins, their uses, the special punches for them, and then how to use the pins. It is also helpful to know how to modify pins without spoiling their usefulness, and you'll benefit from knowing several methods of making them stay in place.

The Straight-Ended Pin

The straight-ended pin is the most commonly used type. Its shape is strictly cylindrical and is usually annealed (unhardened). It may be made of almost any material, but it is usually carbon steel in most firearms. Its fit can be either slip-fit or interference-fit (see sidebar), depending upon the use of the pin. But even when it is used as a slave pin, it's still called a straight pin.

Standard pin punches, drift punches, and small steel rods all serve well in dealing with straight pins. There are times when just a piece of rod, a nail, or a small screwdriver will suffice in removing a pin. Be that as it may, it is always better to use the most impressive punch you can when the owner is looking on. The impression of using the right punch is usually as important, if not more so, than the results achieved with it.

Dowel Pins

Dowel pins are usually hardened steel with slightly chamfered ends that aid in starting the pins into holes. The ends are not usually finished to a smooth surface, but the sides of the cylindrical body of the pins are most often ground to a very fine finish. With their hardness, any irregularity in the sides would broach metal along with the pin when it was installed, causing galling and sticking when the pin needs to be removed.

The distinctions between dowel pins and straight pins are somewhat blurred, as there are often dowel pins with only one end chamfered and also some straight pins which have had the ends deburred by blending the sharp edges away.

As with straight pins, dowel pins respond well to being driven with pin punches and drift punches. The choice of punch will be determined by the tenacity of the pin in its hole. Drift punches are stronger than most pin punches, and tend to be used with more force; therefore, they will likely leave scarred pin ends. This can play havoc with good-looking pins in highly visible places.

Roll Pins

Roll pins, or spring pins, are commonly used where two or more pieces are to be held together, but not pivoting in relation to each other. The pins are split longitudinally, with the edges of the split opening sticking out from the diameter of the pin. This gives two edges that bite into the part's hole, keeping the pin in place. They are usually tempered blue-violet like a spring and made of spring steel, hence the name spring pin. The hole forces the two edges of the split in, causing the pin to achieve a round shape with quite a bit of outward force against the hole's walls. With these edges biting into the walls, seldom do roll pins come out without some persuasion.

Still, I have embellished their holding power by scoring their edges with diagonal pliers. This should be done only with pins that

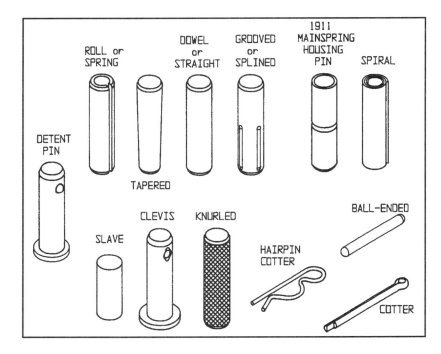

Various types of pins you might encounter when working on firearms. Most aren't hardened, with the exceptions of the roll pins, grooved or splined, and spiral pins.

are to remain in the holes and are not in a place where the edges of the hole will show. I do this when the hole has become too large for the pin and the pin's slit edges cannot be forced wider with a sharp wood chisel.

Roll pins are used almost everywhere pins can be found and have good holding power and strength. They should not, however, be used where there would be something turning on the pin. The length-wise split would quickly enlarge the hole in the rotating piece and render it useless.

When using them, they should be started into their holes with a roll-pin-starting punch. In spite of the obvious naming, it is pretty hard to find something like this in the local hardware store. I get mine from Brownells stock and find they are much better and safer than trying to hold the pin with a pair of long-nosed pliers while driving the pin into the hole. This punch is identified by the hole in its end, into which the roll pin is placed. The punch makes it easy to hold the pin in line with the hole and drive it far enough in to establish the direction it will need to go. The roll-pin starting punch need not be limited to just roll pins, but one must realize its limitations and not use it to force tight, solid pins into a hole with a healthy interference fit. This will just break a good punch.

As soon as the pin has started, usually about one fourth of its length, it is safe to change to the other type of roll-pin punch. I usually continue with the starting punch, though, until the punch nears the top surface of the hole. There is almost no chance of slipping the punch off the pin as there would be with any other type of punch.

The main roll-pin punch is used in seating the roll pin and in driving it out of the hole. This punch is identified by its ball right in the middle of the face of what looks like a regular drift punch. It is this punch that gets abused the most in my shop. I have many friends and students using my tools, and in their enthusiasm to work on their own guns, they often don't notice the little ball on the end and flatten it out against a straight-ended pin. Accordingly, I keep these two roll-pin punches in plastic 22 cartridge boxes with a large "NO!" printed on the top. This has been effective in keeping the punches from being damaged.

Spiral Pins

Spiral pins, the most popular brand-name being named "Spirol" pin, are pins made of rolled-up spring-steel flat stock that takes on a spiraled look when viewed from the end. For the pin to compress, it must have enough force exerted against it in an inward radial direction to overcome the friction of the stock rubbing against itself when the spiral is tightened. They are very tough pins and can be used for some rotational situations without their hurting the hole they are in. They are hard to get started, but drive well when they are in the hole over one quarter of their length. They are somewhat finicky about having the right-sized hole. They do nothing that a straight pin won't, but they retain their position well if they are put in a hole near the right size.

They should be installed and removed in the same manner as roll pins and with the same punches. You may need to use a smaller punch than the outside diameter suggests, because different pins will have more spirals depending upon how much holding power they possess.

Tapered Pins

Tapered pins are just straight pins with one end smaller than the other. They are used to drive gears and locate parts, but never to have an object rotate about them. Tapered pins are designed to be installed into tapered holes and should always have a small through-hole in the bottom of their receiving hole to facilitate their removal. They most always have domed ends, but the domes vary

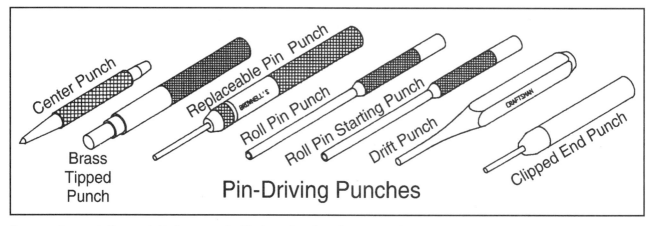

Some punches most often needed in firearm repairs. The brass-tipped punch represents those with aluminum or nylon tips also.

so much that there are no punch sets that I know of for these pins. Because they are hardened, use standard pin or drift punches to install or remove them.

Ball-End Pins

These pins have ends that are hemispherical and polished, as they are usually ball ended for aesthetic reasons. Few things look as bad as ball-end pins that have been abused by being driven with other than cup-ended punches. As far as destroying a gun's cosmetics, marred ball-end springs rank right up there with boogered-up screw-head slots on firearms.

One of the most common uses of this type of pin would have to be the barrel pin on Smith & Wesson pistols. It takes a very small cupped-head punch to drive these small pins out without either flattening the ball end or scoring the receiver around the pin's hole.

Grooved Pins

Grooved pins are the invention of Groov-Pin Corporation, hence their name, but they are manufactured by a number of companies.

These pins are generally dowel pin-like in nature, with some chiseled grooves around them to raise up ribs that bite into the hole's sides. The raised lands are sharp and can be either at 90- or 120-degree intervals around the pin. The splines, lands, or whatever a particular company calls them, are from one quarter, one half, or up to the full length of the pin. The lands are formed by impact—not rolling as are the splines of splined pins.

Grooved pins are usually tapered on the ends and can be easily driven with a hammer. I choose to refer to my hammers as high-speed presses, as this draws more sympathy when I happen to compress the end of my thumb. Work with pins and you'll, sooner or later, need the euphemism to save your pride.

Splined Pins

Splined pins are the pins with straight or crisscross grooves that are rolled into the metal in a continuous pattern. The rolling causes the metal to be raised between the grooves by almost the same height as the grooves are in depth. This displacing of the metal

cold-works the grain structure and hardens it to some degree, making for great holding power.

The pins are installed and removed with pin punches like the straight pins and are nearly always made of high-carbon steel, but are not hardened. They make very good pivot pins for triggers, hammers, and other gun parts, but they are usually confined to the lower-priced guns. They do not stand much removal and re-installation, because the splines cut into the hole are either destroyed after several installations or they are deepened so that the pin goes farther into the hole than it was intended.

When they find splined pins on a handgun, many consumers want to throw the gun away. But there is nothing wrong with these pins, as their use on military weapons suggests: for instance, the M-16 contains them. They should be put in by hand, and the 'smith should remove them by bending the bent end straight and pulling the ring-shaped head away from the hole.

Due to their very nature, splined pins must be driven in with quite some force, or they will not do what they are designed to do. That is, they must displace some metal, cutting grooves into which the raised splines will stick. Start them with a hammer and only change to a drift punch when they are mostly into the hole.

Cotter & Detent Pins

Cotter, or detent, pins are so reliable and low cost that they are used extensively on airplanes. Most cotter pins are made of a fairly soft steel, but there are some stainless, spring steel, and brass ones to be found. I never replace those made of spring steel or non-ferrous metals.

One of the guns which uses detent pins is the MAC 10. Its front pin is either a hollow pin with a barbed pin to retain it, or the detent pin of recent years. The hollow pin is just like a hollow rivet with a hole for the barb of the retaining pin. The latest MACs have used detent pins, as they are easier for the uninitiated to use. You just push until it is installed and pull until it is removed.

The ball is really a plunger, as the detent is the dent that the ball was intended to fall into. In the case of the MACs, the plunger ball pops out just outside of the hole and the universe acts like the detent (dent). The ball is a hardened bearing with a coil spring under it, and the top of the hole is staked to retain the ball and spring. I rate these pins pretty high, although they ensure that there will be some of the pin sticking out farther than I would like for it to. This is the reason the pin is usually relegated to the military-style weapon.

Another pin in this family, the hairpin cotter is familiar to those who have worked on cars. They are fairly reliable. They are used both in grooves around a pin, and with a hole in the pin and the straight leg sticking through the hole.

A second cousin of the hairpin cotter is that even more active pin with the curved leg on both sides. This one almost always is mounted in a groove cut around a shaft or pin. Shadetree mechanics call them "Jesus Clips," for the number of times they have had to say, "Jesus, where'd that sucker go?" If you take them off with a pair of long-nosed pliers, instead of prying them off with a screwdriver, you can control them better.

Knurled Pins

Knurled pins are soft straight pins that have been rolled with knurling rollers to offset metal into either straight or diamond-shaped lands or raised points. These pins are usually hardened after the knurling so that their barbs can bite into hard metals for retention in the hole. The knurled area may be the full length or even as little as one-quarter of the length of the pin.

Clevis Pin

The clevis pin is quite handy, and it is usually used in conjunction with cotter pins or hairpin cotters. They have a round head with radiused edges and a countersunk hole in the shaft near the end. The use of the clevis pin is about the same as the detent pin; it is more suited to military looks than the sleek look preferred on consumer firearms.

Sometimes, a clevis-like pin is used with its head in a counterbore and the proximity of another part retaining it. This is true on some models of lever-action rifles. It is a most useful type of pin, and, used correctly, is practically infallible. They should not take any amount of tapping or hammering to remove them, just a stiff wire or welding rod in most cases.

The most famous cupped-end pin found on firearms would have to be the mainspring housing pin on the 1911 automatic pistol. It is really a combination of a ball-end and a cupped-end pin, as it is meant to be driven in one side and out the other. The cupped end is usually found on the left side of this weapon but functions equally as well on either side. This pin has a circumferential groove in the middle that serves as a retainer when the mainspring's lower plunger point is in it. I rarely run into other uses for it.

John Browning used it on the 1911 because a good military weapon should be able to be dismantled with only a cartridge. But, you say, the 45 ACP has a round nose? Well, nobody's perfect.

I use an ordinary pin punch to remove the 1911 mainspring housing pin, but I only push on the punch and don't hammer the pin out. When the gun is a pristine, glossy-blue new one, I use a brass punch with a ball-shaped end to push the pin past the mainspring axis. This should always be done with the hammer in the uncocked position to minimize the pressure on the retaining pin when you are trying to remove it.

Terminology For Fitting Pins

There are a couple of terms relevant to how pins fit in the holes provided for them, and it's helpful for you to understand the difference.

When a pin has an *interference fit,* the pin either has the same diameter as the hole in which it rests, or the pin is slightly larger (one or two thousandths of an inch) than the hole. This fit is more accurate, and the pin is less likely to come out than is the slip fit. In extreme cases, where high pressures are to be encountered, the pin may be three or four thousandths of an inch larger than the hole, and the pin will require contraction before installation. This is accomplished by placing the pin on dry ice before driving it into the hole. Upon reaching its final resting place, it expands as it assumes the temperature of the pinned metal and achieves a very tight hold.

In a *slip fit,* the pin is one or more thousandths of an inch smaller than the hole it will occupy so that it can be easily installed or taken out. This fit will require that the pin be retained by some method or geometry. Often, pressure from one of the two or more parts being pinned together will suffice to hold the pin in place. It may also be held in place with another part placed to prevent axial movement of the pin.

More often, you will encounter a combination of both of these two fits such as in the pivot pin of some pistols when the pin is driven through the frame in an interference fit, through the trigger in a slip fit, and then through the frame, again, in an interference fit. For ease and time's sake, we often call a pin with an interference fit a tight fit. Conversely, a slip-fit pin can be referred to as a loose-fitting pin.

The other pin on the 1911's mainspring housing is the flathead retaining pin that holds the mainspring and its end in the housing. It is a small pin that is straight on one end and has a head like a slotless flathead screw. The head is designed to go into a countersunk hole in the front side of the mainspring housing. The 1911 sear pin and hammer pin are similar, but with a much shallower angle to the countersunk head. They have such a slight head that it is difficult to see it if you're tired or in a hurry. These should be slip-fit and

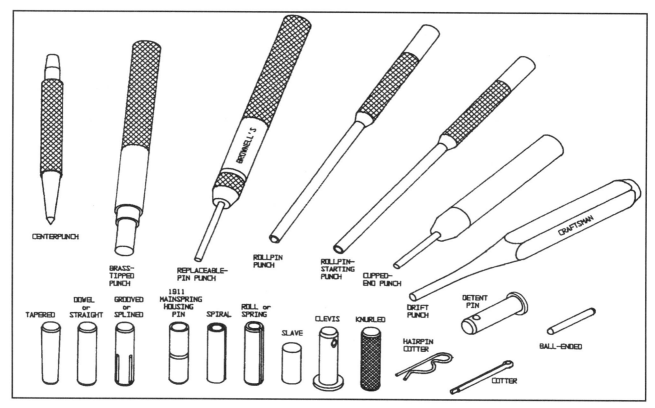

Punches and pins most often used on firearms and reloading equipment. Each pin requires very definite punch consideration.

require no installation or removal tools, while the mainspring plunger retaining pin will usually take a pin punch to push the pin out while the plunger is depressed.

Other Pin Tips

There must be some cases where you shouldn't use lubrication on a pin when you're re-installing it, but I cannot think of one. I prefer to use some good oil with a few drops of STP in it so that the oil will stay on the pin no matter how long the firearm is inactive or how much pressure I must use to install the pin.

I highly recommend the use of a Dremel cutoff wheel when cutting pins, because it only produces a small amount of heat to change the temper of a pin, and it can cut any steel pin, no matter how hard it is. Cutting pins with diagonal pliers or bolt cutters calls for a serious secondary operation to remove the squashed end. The cutoff wheel cuts with a good square end which can easily be blended smooth with a Scotchbrite wheel in a few seconds.

Most pins are removed with the punches that put them in, only there are some cases where a pin may be above the surface and can be "rolled out" with end-cutting pliers. I find this a good way to remove pins that have been driven into a blind hole, but is still sticking out enough to be grabbed with the end cutters.

There are several good ways to make pins stay where you put them. They can be bent slightly so they will exert pressure on both

ends of the hole, or the end(s) can be flattened with a hard hammer, or they can be staked with a centerpunch. I also use medium-torque thread-locking compound, such as Locktite, Staylok, or other products to hold them fast. Which method you use should be dictated by the situation and how visible the pin is. It would not do to flatten the end of a high-priced pistol's hammer pin if it is prominently in view.

Some pin situations call for setscrews in a perpendicular hole to lock the pin in place. This can also be accomplished with the top of the pin's hole being threaded for a locking screw.

Along with the bending and egg-shaping the pins, you will run into cases where you will have to straighten out bent pins. I just roll them on a flat steel surface while hammering them with a smooth-faced hammer. Be aware that this will often cause the length of the pin to increase. This method can be used to intentionally lengthen pins, as well as score them with diagonal pliers.

As long as the pin is out of view, and there isn't a bending force on it, there are many ways you can get away with tightening, stretching, and locking them into their holes. Some are better left to be done when the proud owner isn't there to see, as most non-technical types don't understand the existence of tolerances and the growth of holes when exposed to stress. If there is a persistent owner in view, I'd suggest the use of a thread-locking compound, even though this isn't usually as secure as the mechanical methods of securing pins.

Tips For Choosing— And Using—Abrasive Stones

From the hand-held Arkansas stone to the high-dollar ScotchBrite wheel, your options for smoothing metal are wide open.

By Chip Todd

SMOOTHING METAL with abrasive stones is one of the most important operations a gunsmith can perform. It also has ranked right up there with dental surgery on my list of favorite entertainments.

I always considered "stoning" one of the necessary evils associated with metalworking and went to great lengths to minimize my association with stones. My subconscious might be partially responsible for my attitude, as I really hate to put out my hard-earned money for something that vanishes while I'm expending so much energy. I forced myself to overcome this attitude when stoning saved some lengthy projects from the "frustration container" I line with garbage bags.

Before we get into their different uses, let's first look at some of the types, shapes and compositions of abrasive stones, along with some do's and don'ts concerning their use. We have to know which stones do what to choose the right one for the job. Learning the correct use of the different types and shapes of stones didn't come easily, but the experience has repaid me many times over.

Composition and Cost

Stoning is, by definition, the use of abrasive pieces of synthetic or natural stones which have been shaped for particular jobs. The larger the granules, the coarser the cut of the stone. The shape of the granules is also important in determining the smoothness of the finish left by stoning. Also, the hardness of the stone is as important as its cutting ability, for hardness determines the formability of the stone, including influencing how the stone resists forming when you don't want it to.

There are times when files just cannot do the smoothing required in gunsmithing; yet, seemingly less precise stones can do the job. Even diamond files, the only ones that can cut into hardened steel, are really stones with a steel core. You cannot cut dead-hard steel with common files, yet almost any abrasive stone will do so easily.

Natural stones come from the earth, having undergone great heat and pressure over a long period of time. The grade of the stone is determined by the amount of foreign minerals present. Coarseness is determined by the loose proximity of the granules with respect to

Arkansas was known for its abrasives well before the 1992 election, including, far left, a flat Arkansas stone. Other abrasives include, from left, a round India, a square Carborundum and a triangular ceramic alumina stone. Lower right, the author holds a flexible stone suitable for working on curved surfaces or in hard-to-reach places. They are made of aluminum oxide bonded to a flexible spine.

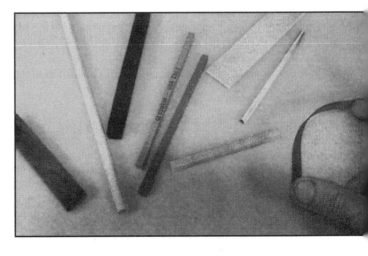

each other, while hardness is a matter of chemical makeup and physical structure.

Arkansas stones, as they are known in the trade, are actually novaculite stone. Per their name, they are usually found in and around Arkansas and are the most widely used natural stones. Arkansas stones are fine-cutting and are usually white, resembling white marble. The gunsmith can easily feel an Arkansas stone's smoothness, and he can predict the finish to be correspondingly smooth. These stones are fairly highly priced, because they require a lot of energy to be expended in their shaping. For instance, a 6-inch-long, 2-inch-wide, 1-inch-deep Arkansas stone costs $17.36 in Brownells catalog.

In contrast, India and Washita stones are generally dark and coarse and remove larger amounts of material than the Arkansas stone. I have heard of the Washita stones, but I haven't used one. They have been so overshadowed by the India stones that little is written about them. Most of the softer stones are India. Found in black and a red, sand color, India stones are natural aluminum oxide and are usually subjected to a man-made process called sintering to form them into useful shapes. Available in fine, medium, and coarse grades, they generally cut faster than hard Arkansas stones. I like these stones for smoothing curved surfaces and for forming a stone with which to get into crevices. These, like most natural stones, are also somewhat expensive compared to artificial stones. But the modern processes of sintering them into shapes reduces the cost below that of Arkansas and polycrystalline Ruby stones. For example, a 6-inch-long, $1/2$-inch-wide, $1/2$-inch-deep India stone from Brownells costs $6.29.

More expensive than the India stones, super-hard polycrystalline Ruby Stones are especially suited for working hard metals like tungsten carbide and hardened tool steels. They come in three grits, all relatively finer than those grades in other stones. With the advent of ceramic alumina stones, I find it hard to pay for high-priced Ruby Stones. A 4-inch-long, $5/16$-inch-wide, $1/4$-inch-deep Ruby Stone in fine grade costs $33.10 from Brownells. But they will give a beautiful finish.

Further along the finish scale is the ceramic alumina material spawned by the U.S. space program. This ceramic material was developed for use in the thrust nozzles of rocket exhausts due to its great heat tolerance. It was also required to withstand the incredibly corrosive effects of the fuel, unsymmetrical dimethyl-hydrazine, (UDH2). All fuel lines, valves, and other components that come into contact with this fuel need to be gold plated to withstand its corrosive effects. The final finish obtained from these synthetic stones is phenomenal, but compared to what other natural or artificial stones do, they remove a minuscule amount of material.

Carborundum is the trade name of a material and the manufacturing process of abrasives manufactured by Union Carbide Corporation. Used for most grinding wheels and inexpensive sharpening stones, it is easily formed into precise shapes by pressure and heat. Thus, it does not require the expensive carving necessary when shaping natural stones. This material is usually fairly coarse and cannot compete with the finish left by the natural Arkansas stone or the space-age ceramic alumina material. Its main attractions are its relatively low cost, the amount of material it can remove, and its ease of manufacture.

Diamond stones are a cross between natural and artificial stones, in that real diamond particles are embedded into a nickel coating on an unbreakable plastic or metal base. They are used with water, not oil, and should last indefinitely because they don't get dull. They cut faster than other stones and are generally available in two textures, coarse (325 grit), and fine (600 grit), and in the form of bench stones, laps, or files. Their cost makes me keep them locked away so that they will not be used in place of regular, cheaper stones. A fine bench diamond stone, measuring 6 inches by 2 inches by $3/4$-inch, costs $47.50 from Brownells.

How to Buy and Use Stones

Because stones come in so many shapes and sizes, the hobbyist or gunsmith can be confused when he starts buying stones for the shop. I would recommend buying the following shapes in this

The Dremel Moto-Tool, shown with an assortment of mounted stones, Cratex, cutoff wheel and sanding drum, is a favorite in the author's gunsmith shop. Of course, gunsmiths should always wear eye protection when working with rotary power tools.

When stoning the inside of a flared magazine well with a coarse, soft stone, move the stone linearly and axially and use water liberally to remove fouling. Using a coarse stone, of course, removes more metal, but it also reduces your stoning time.

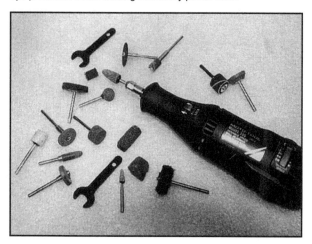

order: a sharp-cornered square of about $1/4$-inch per side, a triangular stick of about the same size, and a flat stone $3/4$- by $3/16$-inch in cross-section. I find sticks about 5 inches long easiest to handle, while those used to level a larger flat surface need be around 6 inches in length.

Starting gunsmithing requires more of the fine-cutting stones than coarse ones, since the type of jobs a starting gunsmith would take on don't usually require removing any significant amount of metal. I use the coarser stones more than most gunsmiths because I hate filing; then I use moto-tools with Cratex to do quite a lot of my finish work. I often use fine or medium stones that have wide, flat surfaces to level out flat planes such as the sides of 1911 slides. I also have found that it is economical to glue sandpaper to a stick and save wear on the more expensive stones. I would suggest that a starting gunsmith start out with some Arkansas stones of the proper shape for trigger jobs and a couple of Carborundum stones for quick metal-removal chores.

I avoided soft stones when I saw them crumble away so rapidly, but soon found them of as much value as the harder, flat stones. That they crumble away allows them to conform to an irregular surface and be contoured into the proper shape with which to work in corners more readily than harder stones.

Harder stones hold their shapes better and retain the perfect angle cut into them by the manufacturer. They excel in leveling surfaces in a way that allows the 'smith to see the surface approaching flatness. For this work, it is handy to have a hard India stone with a sharp 90-degree corner for making sear notches and other critical angles true.

However, the wide, flat stones get most of my attention, because a lot of my work involves leveling surfaces. For this, I use the medium-hard Carborundum stone, or when features allow, stearite sandpaper on a flat surface. The sandpaper is more economical than the stones, and I can follow the sandpaper with a finer stone if necessary. I have also found the white stearite paper cuts faster and finishes smoother than the grade indicated on it. It is also longer lasting than other types of papers.

I recommend this type of sandpaper for applications requiring 100-grit to 320-grit metal removal—and I recommend 3M papers exclusively. Having owned automotive body shops and run manufacturing plants in the past, I have found an appreciable difference in the papers made by 3M and those by Bear-Manning, Norton, and Bay State. My sandpaper bills were reduced by almost 50 percent when I changed to 3M; the workers noted the reduced energy required to do their jobs; and the quality-control examiners lauded a corresponding increase in finish quality when we used 3M papers.

Motor Tools and Stones

There aren't many tools that come into use around a gunsmithing shop more than the small, hand-held rotary grinder, generically called a motor tool. The thing most of the brands have in common is their $1/8$-inch shaft size, which keeps gunsmiths from being limited to only those tools made for particular grinders.

There are many brands of motor tools on the market, including one you can charge on the Sears card, but I have found the Dremel Moto-Tool to be the best. The Moto-Tool, Dremel's copyrighted name for its motor tool, is the most widely used and for good reason. Dremel has been building hobby handgrinders longer than anyone else on the market. Foredom has been making hand-held flexible-shaft tools for a long time, but they just don't lend themselves to gunsmith use as well as does the Dremel tool. In my opinion, gunsmiths should celebrate Mr. Dremel's birthday, because there is no end to the chores a motor tool can perform. For stoning jobs in my shop, the Dremel gets fewer days off than a priest.

The gunsmith may buy Dremel Moto-Tools as stand-alone products or in several types and sizes of kits. There are motors with bushings, ball-bearings, single speeds, two speeds and variable speeds. Dremel also offers a kit with a flexible shaft and handpiece. There are some interesting accessories also offered, such as the router attachment, drill press and other fixtures not really aimed at the gunsmith. The router attachment is well suited for woodworking and hobby use, however.

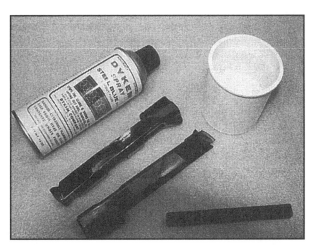

Dykem steel dye is often used to identify high areas when stoning with a flat stone. For the gunsmith on a budget, dark permanent-felt markers serve as well. Use a wide, flat, hard stone such as a medium-hard Carborundum to level flat surfaces.

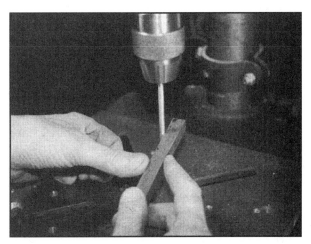

Stoning a cylindrical piece of metal in a drill press requires the gunsmith to use light strokes with the wet stone to avoid bending or possibly breaking the rod. To avoid busting your knuckles, always pay careful attention when stoning on a rotary device.

Stoning the inside of a trigger guard and the finger grooves on the frontstrap with a rocking boat motion are good ways to use a soft stone. Strokes along a curved surface tend to cause less trouble than trying to rock against the curve.

A soft stone is used when cleaning up after silversoldering on a custom front sight, so that it will contour into the square joint. Using a crisscross motion keeps you from wearing in flat spots on round surfaces.

The Dremel-type rotary stones can be shaped with the rectangular, gray stone found in the kits by spinning the rotary stone at a high speed and holding a corner or edge of the shaping block against the stone. This technique is much like using a wood lathe, in that the workpiece is spinning and the shape of it is influenced by manually holding a cutting implement against it judiciously.

I keep my rotary stones separated into two distinct groups, the hard and the soft. It is apparent at a glance which stones are coarse and which are fine so they can be mixed together without wasting your time searching for the proper stone for a job. More often than not, I gravitate to the one nearest the desired grit and hardness and in the best condition. Nearing the end of the life of my sampler collection, I have quite a few stubs in the bottom of the box, and I try to use them when I can bear the extra strain it places on already tired hands. Handling small pieces of abrasive does little for the skin or the muscles of the fingers and hands. I find myself buying new stones the day after I have made myself use up the bits and pieces of stones.

Of course, all power tools should be used only when wearing safety glasses or a face shield. In hand stoning, this isn't necessary unless you happen to be incredibly fast.

Using Popular Stones

The most commonly used stone in your workshop will be the flat, hard, fine stone with a 90-degree corner to be used for sear and sear-notch work. I also use diamond-coated files because they cut harder metal and leave a fairly smooth surface that can be touched up with Cratex wheels. (Note: Take care to use water with diamond files. They are expensive, and the diamond coating will be quickly removed without water to lube the way.) When I must use a stone for sear or sear-notch work, I usually choose an ceramic alumina stone for its hardness and fineness of cut. If the sear or notch is rough enough to require a coarser stone, you should consider case-hardening the surface.

Another popular stone is the 3/4-inch-wide, 1/8-inch-thick medi-

um-cut stone used with plenty of water to flatten a surface. I use this whenever I am unable to level a surface with flat-glued sandpaper. There might be some protrusion that prevents the use of a large, flat abrasive surface, so this stone is a must. I wash stones like this with a good hand cleaner and a fingernail brush under running warm water. It would be a good idea not to use the spouse's vegetable or nail brush because the stone tends to work well on bristles, also.

I keep several grades of fine-cutting round stones around to use inside shotgun bores after installing a bead sight near the muzzle. Marks from these are much easier to polish out than those from a Dremel sanding drum. The sanding drums, wrapped with a tissue liberally laced with semi-chrome polish, are good for the final polishing of the shotgun muzzle's interior.

Another good use for abrasive stones is against rotating parts. This confines their use on round surfaces that are concentric about an axis which can be chucked up. I use the stones to give a final finish to many of the parts which I make with my lathe, and even use the stones with my drill press projects. As with filing, caution must be exercised when using a handheld object against a rotating part; not only with respect with the workpiece, but with the spinning chuck as well. Letting the end of the file or stone be hit with one of the chuck's jaws can cause it to effortlessly ventilate one palm or knock a thumb out of joint. Either is bound to leave an impression on even the most unimpressionable gunsmith.

It is imperative to use water or oil as lubricant and anti-filling agent when stoning a rotating part. Use normal filing motions; the stone will load up immediately if you don't. Also be aware of the surface speed because the rotating part increases the relative speed between the stone and the surface of the workpiece by several magnitudes. The larger the workpiece diameter, the greater the difference of the relative surface speed. I use this technique when dressing the end of a threaded part made in the lathe or in breaking the sharpness of an edge cut on the lathe.

Brownells sells some useful items called Flex-Stones, which can be used in quite a few applications that call for curved surfaces and hard-to-reach places. They are aluminum-oxide particles bonded to a flexible spine that conforms to curved shapes yet is stiff enough to transmit the pressure needed to remove material. They are 1 millimeter thick (0.039-inch) and last well if not subjected to sharp edges or solvents.

When fitting parts or trying to achieve a perfectly flat surface, it is useful to dye the surface to be stoned with an minute coating of color to readily show the low spots. The mainstay in the machining industry is a dye named Dykem. It is so well entrenched that the generic name for surface dyes is "dikem."

In the abrasive stones section of the catalog, Brownells offers a "Prussian Blue," a paste used mainly to check the fit between parts. It also can be used to locate low areas of a flat surface, but Dykem is better for this purpose. Dykem comes in many hues, but intense blue is the standard of the metalworking industry. It is an alcohol-based lacquer that smells good and gives you a high if you aren't careful. Being a lacquer, it is waterproof and needs acetone or Dykem Remover to remove it. It comes in either spray can or liquid in poly bottles with a squeeze-bulbed brush applicator/cap.

For those of us who are stingy to a fault, a good felt marker in appropriate color is almost as good as the relatively low-priced Dykem, even though they ultimately cost a lot more. The advantage of felt markers is their small initial cost for those just getting their feet wet in the business.

Coat the part to be stoned flat with whichever dye method you choose and commence stoning. A moment should be taken to think out which direction the abrasive tracks (scratches) should be oriented in order to lessen the chance that they will be visible after stoning. For instance, on semi-auto pistol slides, the stoning should be from end-to-end with the stone parallel to the length of the slide. This is the direction in which any unevenness of the surface will show up. After several strokes with the stone, the bright metal colored areas will give away the low area's hiding places at a glance.

Stoning, with water, should continue until the high areas are reduced to the level of the last remaining dye spot. You might then follow this with some final stoning with a smoother stone or a trip to the ScotchBrite wheel. This wheel and its use will be described later.

The same technique is used on curved surfaces. Just think out what the stone will do at its worst and orient it in such a way to lessen the effect. Strokes along a curved surface tend to cause me less trouble than trying to rock across the curve. These minute flat planes are easily eliminated, while low spots caused by the edges of the stone while rocking across a curved surface can be murder to eliminate. Again, just close is enough if you have a good buffer equipped with a ScotchBrite wheel.

When using the dye method to find interference between mating parts, you should put the dye on the part that seems to need the metal removed. After examining the interference mark(s), it is more easily determined how one should go about removing the offending metal. A scratch all along the marked part would indicate to me that I had dyed the wrong part. It also indicates a spot or area on the mating part would be the culprit which needed rubbing out. Remember, the dye is so thin that it doesn't really enter into the picture, fitwise. Remove the dye from the first dyed part, and dye the

When Not To Use Stones

There are situations in which you should avoid using stones if there is any other way to do the job:

● I usually try not to use stones around the muzzle for fear they are too coarse, too hard or too anything which could alter the shape or surface condition of the muzzle.

However, I do use long, thin stones to touch up the inside of the bore at the bottom of the ported holes when using a mill or a drill with which to make gas ports. In this case, it is important to use a hard, fine stone to keep from damaging the rifling. I force a copper-jacketed slug past the ports before stoning to remove what burrs I can.

● Stones, unless they are very coarse, aren't used very often on wood. Not only will the stone develop heat that will burn the wood, the wood will likely load up the stone, make it stop cutting, and start burning anyway. A rotary stone can usually be cleaned of wood by heating it with a propane torch or the low flame of a welding torch. This turns the wood into ash, which can easily be scrubbed out of the grain of the stone.

● Aluminum, pewter, magnesium, lead, tin, or zinc alloys will load up a stone permanently.

● Aluminum is the worst offender of the non-ferrous metals, bonding with such ferocity that it takes re-dressing the stone to remove the clumps of aluminum embedded in the work surface. These aluminum clumps tend to scratch steel badly and can ruin some otherwise good work in the blink of an eye.

● Similarly, magnesium fouls up a grindstone, and it also flashes off or explodes when steel or iron are used on the wheel afterward. In essence, the wheel is just a large flashbulb without a housing. The same goes for buffing magnesium. It causes so many explosions in the buffing industry that few companies making automotive racing equipment can find shops that will risk working with the metal.

mating part in the suspected area. Repeat the mating action between the parts and notice the interfering area or spot now. Stoning where there is an interference between parts should be done with the stoning marks diagonal to the action of the reciprocating or rotating part. This enables you to spot any rub marks and allows the marks to carry lubrication.

A Stone in the Hand

There is a natural way almost everybody finds to hold abrasive stones, but this might not always be the best way.

It seems as if the natural way to hold them always results in their being broken into shorter pieces that defy further use. The best way for me to combat finger and hand fatigue is to hold the stone through the palm and little finger with the tips of the next three fingers resting on the stone, and the index finger pushing the stone into the workpiece. With this hold, you should only apply maximum pressure to the stone when the index finger is over the point of contact with the pressure lessening with the reduced proximity to that point. Retaining the same pressure throughout the stroke will result in broken stones.

The preferred motion depends on the type of stoning and the shape of the work surface. When stoning a surface like the inside of a trigger guard, it helps to add a slight rocking motion to the natural back and forth stroke because most trigger guards have cross sections similar to that of a football. If the trigger guard has flats across the inside, the rocking motion would not be appropriate.

Instead, this is a good place to use the soft, shape-conforming stones that will crumble until they match the contour of the work-

piece before really working. Some soft India stone about a $1/2$-inch across and a $1/4$-inch thick is particularly well suited to the task. The thickness is for strength and to give the stone some material with which to conform to the trigger guard shape.

On large, flat surfaces, there are spots where stoning marks parallel to the long direction of the flat would suffice. But just as often, you will want to apply the stone in circular motions much smaller than half of the distance across the flat. These circular motions should orbit around the flat area in another, larger circular path with an ever-descending radius.

This ensures that the stone attacks the metal from a different direction each time it comes back to the same place. The path should overlap a different portion of the circle with each reduced circular path.

The arch on the tops of slides makes me want to stone in a criss-cross pattern so I am compromising a linear path and an arched path. As mentioned before, the linear paths would cause small flats to develop along the length of the slide and stoning across the radius of the top might induce some edge marks from the stone. The criss-cross pattern is a good way to prepare for final surface treatment.

One Other Abrasive Tool

There is no other single tool in my gunsmith shop more appreciated by my students than the buffing motor with its ScotchBrite wheel.

I'm afraid that I concur and might be guilty of overusing it. Since its cost rivals the national debt, I cringe every time I hear the Baldor buffing motor bog down even the slightest. This wheel is an adaptation of the kitchen scouring pad but is firmer and more tightly secured. It does the same thing, just in an accelerated manner.

There is nothing in my experience that will remove irregularities, burrs, blueing and rust, silversolder overruns, and a host of other maladies as well as the ScotchBrite wheel. It also deburrs the ends of threaded devices, blends in faceted stoning, and prepares parts for buffing better than anything else available. The bad news is the wheel's cost. I was paying $38 for a 6-inch by $3/4$-inch wheel in Los Angeles and now pay about $32 at a good industrial hardware store in San Diego. I've tried several different wheel brands but have found none that suit me as well as the ScotchBrite. The pads, however, are not much different from the abrasive-impregnated pads of other manufacturers, in my view.

I use them for everything from re-brushing brushed stainless guns to finally smoothing things on a lathe or drillpress prior to buffing. The grit, denoted by the color of the pad, most used around my shop is the maroon ScotchBrite material, approximately equivalent to 320-grit white sandpaper. It gets impregnated with the metal it has contacted, so I cut it into small pieces dedicated to a particular material's use. The cost of the impregnated pads is not much more than the cost of sandpaper, and it lasts longer. It does not work well with any liquid, as it tends to overcut when wet.

Abrasives suppliers: Brownells, Inc., Rt. 2, Box 1, Montezuma, Iowa 50171; Frank Mittermeier, 3577 E. Tremont, New York, N.Y. 10465; and A.G. Russel, 1705 Hwy. 71 N., Springdale, AZ 72764.

The Not-So-Simple Drill Bit

They may be familiar to some, but not everyone knows the ins and outs of drill bits. Here are some basics you can use or pass on.

By Chip Todd

DRILLING IS ONE of the simplest forms of machining, yet it is also one of the least understood of the machine arts. Perhaps it is so visually familiar to us, that we take drilling for granted and don't look into it further. My gunsmithing students made me aware of how much I have neglected this in their education: I had assumed that what had become second nature to me was obvious to others without the same experience. Therefore, I'll share with you some of the things I've picked up about this handiest of the machine shop tools in 36 years of working in and owning machine shops.

When the average person hears the words "drill bit," the most common image brought to mind is that of the "twist" drill. The name is no mystery, as it looks every bit (pun intended) like it had been gripped by a giant and twisted. In fact, substituting a machine for the giant, and adding a slight pull while twisting, is exactly how drill bits are given their spiraled configuration. Drill bits are first machined with two grooves running longitudinally, and are then twisted under heat. The tempering process is applied after the twisting.

Common twist drills are nothing more than two sharp edges which shave the surface of the workpiece, and lift off the shaved material with inclined planes (flutes). Estimating the torque of a drilling action requires the use of engineering equations for the friction of a wedge (the cutting edge) and the lifting action of an inclined plane. You have probably seen an auger used for digging post holes—somewhat like a curly French fry on a pencil. It also has broken more arms than a Model T crank. This little reminder from the past still lurks in the handles of the common auger and even a little bit in a good half-inch drill.

This danger can be lessened by using a lower angle of the inclined plane, or what is commonly referred to as a "fast-spiral bit." In this way, torque is traded off for more mechanical advantage in the form of lifting and separating the material being drilled. This is most evident in the post-hole digging auger; they employ a "fast" spiral to make the auger manageable. Lifting has a direct relation to energy (heat), and so it follows that a fast-spiraled drill bit creates less heat since it is not lifting the material shaved off quite so violently as a bit with a slow spiral (or fast lift).

Fast-spiral bits have flutes that make more turns around the shaft of the bit per unit of shaft length. The fast spiral is also known as a "high" spiral, although I've never heard of a "low" spiral bit. Slow-spiral bits have a pitch which circles around the shaft less than it tends to progress along the shaft. Most drill bits fall somewhere in between the two extremes, with cheaper bits leaning more toward the slow spiral. Conventional bits have two flutes, as these are stronger than bits with three or more flutes. Three- and four-flute bits are usually finishing bits used to cut less and give a smoother finish.

The optimum drill-point angle is mainly dependent on the type and hardness of the material being drilled. Woods and plastics require a more pointed tip—with its sharper angles—than do harder materials such as steel. The type of steel can often call for a more shallow point angle to reduce tip heat and premature edge failure. A general rule of thumb when buying bits is to look at the finish of the metal, the tip angle, and the spiraling of the flutes; a sharply-pointed tip with a fairly rough finish usually indicates a cheaply made bit aimed at the woodworker. Conversely, a fast spiral and shallow tip angle usually means the bit is made to handle the rigors of drilling metals. I steer clear of bits with an exaggerated rib along the flutes, as this is usually a defense against a poor material's heating and often indicates a weaker bit.

Drilling speeds vary with bit diameter and the material being drilled, with smaller bits generally requiring more speed for an optimum surface. In my experience, most machinists use much slower speeds than they should when using the smaller sizes of drill bits. Drilling-speed formulas are dependent upon feed rates, which means

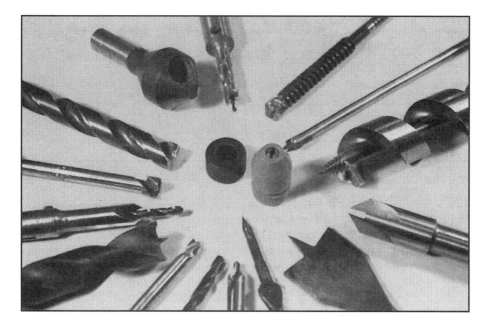

Various types of drill bits, clockwise from top: Carbide-tipped masonry, changeable spade, self-feeding auger, four-fluted countersink, spade, countersinking spade, countersinking centerdrill, stub twist, undercut brad, bradpoint, metal countersinking step, Forstner, sheet metal, pierced (anti-chatter) countersink, counterboring step. In the center, drill stops of the collar and chuck types.

little when feeding by hand. Automatic feeding, used almost entirely for production work, is rarely encountered in a gunsmith's shop.

The formula for drill speed is used for relative speeds only; it is difficult to estimate the feed rate of a spindle lowered by hand. Softer materials such as wood require higher rotational speeds. Plastics, on the other hand, tend to heat and smear with speed. Hard steels require slower speeds and feeds to minimize heat generation. The most-used formula for approximating the proper drill speed is taken from Machinery's Handbook, the bible of machine shops:

$$\text{Drill Speed} = (C \times 12) / (3.1416 \times D)$$

In this formula, C is the cutting speed in feet per minute (typically 50 to 100 fpm for steel), and D is the diameter of the drill. This formula yields optimum speeds from 14,706 to 29,412 rpm for a #80 drill bit, and 764 to 1528 rpm for a $1/4$-inch drill in steel.

Speeds also vary with the style of the bit, the shape of its cutting edges, and the material of which the bit is made. Excessive heat from over-speed can cause a drill bit to drill a hole smaller than its diameter by heating up the metal being drilled. After cooling back down, the hole is often left smaller than it was when the bit passed through it in its expanded condition. The opposite occurs when a dull drill bit is expanded from heat and cuts oversize. It is difficult to predict which will happen when the drill becomes dull, but more often than not, the bit will drill an oversized hole. Drilling holes deeper than three times the diameter of the bit can cause a buildup of chips between the flutes of the bit, resulting in elevated temperatures and, hence, oversized and rough-walled holes.

Proper drilling lubricants, formulated to reduce heat, are beneficial on all metals—and necessary with some like copper and stainless steel. There are lubricants made especially for drilling and tapping aluminum, as some of the best lubricants for steel cause aluminum to actually burn with a chemical reaction that is difficult to extinguish. I have caused aluminum to burn—producing an acrid, brown smoke—impervious to the use of water or the fire extinguisher I keep in my shop. Heed the warning, "not for alu-

minum" found on quite a few machining and tapping fluids.

Boeing, the company that dabbles in airplanes, developed a synthetic sperm whale oil which is many times better than the genuine thing (my apologies to the 747s of the deep). It actually makes "dull" bits cut again, and prolongs the useful life of a cutting edge by several times or more, a point which helps lessen the sting of a drill bit's high price. To its credit, just a hint of Boeing's oil on a drill will last for an hour or more. Look for it by the name "Boelube"; even rival aircraft manufacturers use it for their drilling operations.

There are so many specialized types of drill bits, that it would take an entire volume to describe and illustrate them. A few of the ones you're likely to encounter are shown in an accompanying illustration. Here are brief descriptions of some of the types of bits, points, and terms you most often find when dealing with drills:

Deming Drill: Also called a Silvering drill, this is a short, rigid bit which is good for most general work.

Sheet-Metal Point: Zero-degree cutting edges with point in center. The point is just large enough to hold the bit in the same place; the cut is perfectly flat-bottomed.

Counterboring Bit: A sheet-metal type without the pointed tip, but with a guide; cuts flat-bottomed holes for flush screw heads.

Brad Point: Much like a sheet-metal bit with small, vertical, cutting tips added to the outside end of the cutting edges.

Reduced-Shank Bit: A bit in which a portion of the shank's diameter has been reduced to facilitate use in a smaller-capacity drill chuck.

Split-Point Bit: One in which the center portion of the cutting edge's trailing edge is notched to enable a bit with a thicker center web to cut into material without a pilot hole.

Pilot Hole: A hole drilled to guide and provide clearance for the central web of a larger size bit.

High Speed: A description not referring to a bit's rotational capabilities, but to the type of steel of which it is made.

Cobalt: Drill made of a very tough and hard cobalt steel.

Carbide: Refers to tungsten-carbide. This is an ultra-hard material of which the hardest bits are made. It is, however, a very brittle alloy and cannot be used for drilling regular steels (it will break).

Titanium Nitride/Titanium Carbide: Very hard coatings for steel surfaces which act like case-hardening, in that the surface is extremely hard but the metal under it remains softer and less brittle. This coating is approximately 0.0002- to 0.0004-inch thick, so it doesn't add appreciable dimension to the bit's diameter.

Other Tips

One thing I've seen many experienced machinists do wrong is to cool a hot drill in water when they are sharpening the bit on a grindstone. I used to do this also, but learned from Darex—the company that makes fine drill- and cutter-sharpening fixtures and machines—that to do so makes the edge brittle, breaks it off easily, and quickly dulls the tool again. Cooling even carbide-tipped bits in water isn't wise. Although the carbide isn't affected by the sudden cooling, the tips are silver-soldered onto the bit and the quenching can crystallize the silver solder and cause the tip to come off. Let the bit cool at room temperature.

There is no way that even the most experienced machinist can hand-sharpen a drill bit as evenly as a good fixture can. There are jigs which move the bit across the grindstone with a swinging motion, leaving the relief-angle surface flat. This isn't the optimum, as it just doesn't support the cutting edge as well as a generated point. A generated point is one in which the bit is rotated and cammed longitudinally to curve the relieved surface in a radius. This offers the maximum support to the cutting edge without dragging on the material being drilled.

Over the years, I have had many different brands and types of drill-sharpening fixtures and machines, and have formed opinions for several different situations. I have run production and been a tinkerer, and a machine-shop owner—three different scenarios calling for different drilling needs. I have found as a gun tinkerer that Sears, General, or Black and Decker drill-sharpening fixtures will suffice. As a serious gunsmith and small machine-shop owner, I need the superior sharpening obtained with a point-generating fixture, such as that produced by the Darex fixture. This fixture works with a regular bench grinder and has no limitations. For production work, there is no choice but to use a good, self-contained machine from which you can get generated points quickly. One must weigh the cost of replacing drill bits against getting them sharpened by a commercial concern or buying a sharpening fixture.

I started my children out using tools when they were knee-high, as there are always little jobs around the house that require the use of hand tools. My daughter has her own tools, now that she's off at college, and she takes delight in being able to fix things herself. Of course, drilling is one of the tool skills upon which she depends the most. I wouldn't have it any other way.

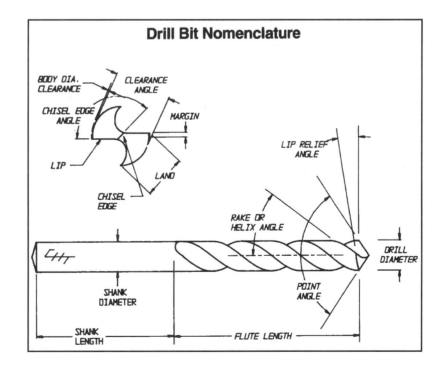

Drill Bit Nomenclature

Polishing Tools and Techniques

A good polishing job can save a gun from the junk heap, but a bad job can send it there quickly. Here's a review of the basics the old pros use.

By Frank Fry

ALL GUNSMITHS and hobbists eventually get involved with some type of metal refinishing. If not directly in your own workshop, you may be dealing with a specialist who does it for you. Even though you might deal with blueing on a day-to-day basis, sometimes it's good to be reminded of the basics. Our concern here is with polishing itself, rather than the actual coloring of metal.

There are as many ways to ruin a firearm through improper polishing techniques as there are firearms to ruin. Potential problems include rounded corners, dished screw holes, wavy barrels, dings and gouges that are not polished out, blueing over rust, pulled letters and numbers, and bead- or sandblasting in an attempt to cover poor polishing techniques. The results? The destruction of firearm value.

By using proper techniques, however, many common firearms, ready for the junk heap, can be reblued to "like new" condition after proper and careful polishing. Note that rare or valuable firearms should not be reblued, as their collector value may be higher in original and untouched condition. Such arms, if they are to be refinished, should be "restored" by restoration experts—and that process is beyond the scope of this discussion.

Of course, polishing a firearm for blueing takes a little more time than just using a wire brush on the barrel and then rubbing it on a loose muslin polishing wheel. It is more ignorance than laziness that prevents good polishing.

Polishing tools you'll use include a file, emery cloth, stones, and a file card.

The purpose of polishing is to prepare the metal for whatever final finish is to be applied. Firearms can be blued, anodized, or even left "white." No matter what material you are working with—steel, aluminum, brass, wood—all exposed surfaces must be prepared in a manner pleasing to the customer's eye. Some of these finishes will:

● Give the surface of the work the same homogeneous polish.
● Vary the finish to present a pleasing contrast of smooth to rough.
● Engrave or etch the surface in pleasing patterns.
● Contrast blue to "white."

There are other techniques that can be used to produce a customer-pleasing finish. But the ultimate goal is always customer satisfaction.

There are generally two accepted types of blueing in use today. Both give a blue-black or black finish to ferrous material, and both are mildly rust resistant.

Rust blueing is an actual rusting process which requires careful monitoring. It is slow, etches the work, will not attack solder, and is more rust resistant than the chemical hot blues. Rust blueing is very pleasing and is found on high-grade over/under or double guns. Hot chemical blues attack solder and chemically oxidize the surface. Hot chemical blueing is quick and easy, however, and is generally used on commercial production-grade guns. Browning is another controlled-rust process which ultimately produces a brown finish to ferrous materials. It, too, is mildly rust resistant.

Plating is the addition of another metal to the surface of the material by electrical means. The process can be used for rust resistance as well as to give hardness, lubrication, or any other property of the material which is being used for plating.

Exotic finishes such as Magnaflux are very rust-resistant and can perform a variety of tasks in keeping guns in good condition. Anodizing is a method of coloring aluminum which actually dyes the metal. Other processes can react with and dissolve aluminum. All of these finishes require careful polishing of the base metal to give the desired final result, and any step which is neglected in leading up to the final finish is detrimental.

There are two basic metal preparation processes—hand and machine. Hand finishing is done in a number of successive steps. It is the mark of the professional gun bluer and finisher. The steps involved are to:

1. Remove machine marks with files.
2. Remove file marks with abrasive cloth (80/120 grit).
3. Remove polishing marks made by previous polishing with successively finer grades of cloth until final finish is reached. (180-grit up through crocus cloth if desired.)

Hand Polishing

The polishing cloth should be used with a backer that has no sharp edges to scratch or gouge should it accidentally come in contact with the work. The backer must conform to the shape or radius of the work being polished. Cutting oil may be used to keep the cloth from clogging with polishing debris. It should be noted here that abrasive polishing stones may also be used. They are available in a variety of grits from fairly rough down to "India Hard," which will produce a very shiny finish. As these stones are not flexible like cloth, they will help produce the ripple-free, waveless finish needed for an ultra-high polish. Stones may also help for getting into corners and crannies inaccessible to cloth.

Each successively finer grit of polishing paper must be used at a 45-degree angle from the previous. Use the same 45-degree angle as for machine polishing. This will enable you to see when the previous polishing marks have been completely removed. (If all polishing is done in the same direction, it will be difficult or impossible to see when the removal of the marks of the previous grit is complete.) Some gunsmiths feel that the last and finest grit of polish should be done perpendicular to the longest flat surface being polished, and that polishing should follow the round surfaces. Thus, a barrel will have

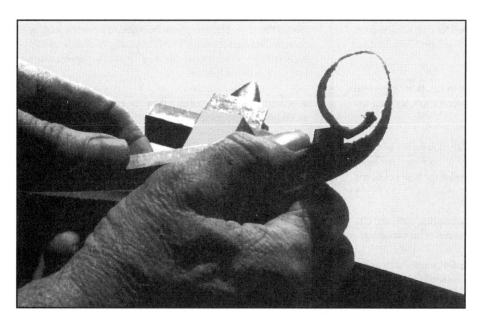

Emery cloth used with the backer produces a good surface.

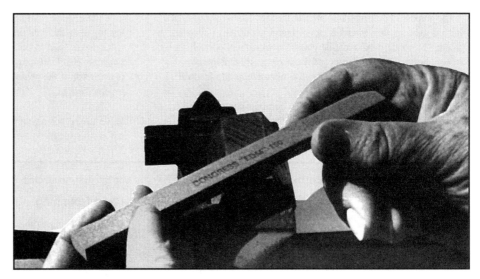

Using a polishing stone at 90 degrees removes previous marks.

the final polishing applied in shoe-shine strokes, rather than strokes end to end (unless it is an octagonal barrel). The final luster found in the best hand polishes may be applied with ScotchBrite, crocus cloth, jewelers rouge, or some other material of your choice. (We'll have more to say about final finishes in a moment.)

Machine Polishing

Machine polishing has probably ruined more guns than it has saved. It is quicker than hand work, but much more care is required to do it correctly. Everyone seems to have a method of machine polishing that works best for them, and you'll probably discover a technique that works best for you. Just remember that polishing wheels cut much more quickly than hand polishing, and can ruin your work before you realize what is happening.

There are several basic wheels used in machine polishing, and each has its detractors and proponents. Here are some of them:

● Hard Felt. Cuts very fast! Hard felt is good for flats when used in the same manner you would use a surface grinder. Excellent for polishing up to final finishes.

● Spiral Sewn Muslin. Does not cut as fast as felt. Best for general polishing, but will dish out holes, round over corners, and pull letters and numbers.

● Loose Muslin. Used for final polish. Cuts slowly, but will dish holes and pull letters and numbers rapidly. With rouge, the loose wheel will produce a "mirror" finish (provided the base polish has been done correctly).

● Wire Wheels. Used for removing loose surface rust, scale, and dirt. Wire wheels in various grades can be very useful in final finishing.

● Other Wheels. Air bladders, flappers, and machines such as the square-wheel grinder are available. These are sometimes useful for difficult surfaces and unusual applications.

The actual technique of machine polishing is much the same as hand polishing. First, file out any machining marks, then polish with successively finer grits until the desired polish is reached. Finally, use the same 45-degree process as used in hand polishing for removing all previous marks before moving on to the next finer grade of polish. Caution: Do not mix wheels and polish grit grades. Have one wheel for each grade of polish.

Polishing Pointers

Here are some pointers gleaned from gunsmiths across the country:

● The work must be kept moving under the wheel; a "scoop" will be polished into the work if it is stopped under the wheel. A scoop will have to be removed by filing or hand polishing, because any attempt to get it out with a polishing wheel will only make it worse.

● When polishing flat surfaces, polish from the center of the flat toward the edge. This will allow the wheel to leave the work without rounding over the edge. This is especially necessary on octagonal barrels where additional care must be used to prevent waviness in the edges of the flats.

● Around screw holes, polish toward the edge, and rotate the work around the hole to prevent dishing.

● On round work, polish from the center toward the edge to prevent the wheel from rounding over any edges which follow the contour of the work.

● Always polish so the wheel leaves the work—never so the edge is introduced to the wheel first.

● Small wheels, or specially shaped "bobs," are useful in getting into areas a large wheel can't, such as the flutes in cylinders. Make the bob smaller than the shape to be polished so it polishes half the area at a time. Reversing the work and polishing the other half

Draw filing helps to remove pits from the work.

allows the bob to polish toward the edges, helping to keep them from becoming rounded off.

● Letters and numbers will be "pulled" if sewn or loose wheels are used. A hard wheel will not pull the letters, but may polish them away. Such areas are best done by hand and then blended into the final machine finish.

Another caution: Wheels can grab and throw material being polished with some violence. This is hard on parts, and hard on you if you are in the way. Always be aware that this can occur, especially with small parts which can be almost impossible to find. And always polish on the lower half of the wheel. Always polish with sharp edges pointing in the same direction the wheel is turning.

Polishing wheels are not designed for cutting or removing metal, but for polishing the surface as the name implies. Any attempt to use a polishing wheel to remove a pit will only result in an ugly depression. The edges of the pit will be pulled out, making the flaw more obvious.

Special Considerations

Deep pits or gouges can be welded and cut back down to the surface. The possibility always exists that the metal used in welding may not exactly match the base metal, and the blue of the weld may not match the blue on the remainder of the work. Gouges can be removed by draw-filing. When draw-filing a gouge, blend the filing area into the metal around it. The deeper the gouge, the larger the blending area. On octagonal barrels, this blending may have to be full length to preserve the points where the flats join. Because of this, the width of the flats may vary slightly. This difference is usually not noticeable.

Letters and numbers must be hand polished if their sharp impressions are to be preserved. File and polish up to the stamping, but not the stamping itself. If rust pitting, dinging, or damage to the stamping has occurred, it may be better to leave this imperfection in the stamping area rather than to try to remove it. Most minor flaws will be unnoticed when mixed in with letters and numbers, and this is certainly less noticeable than having half the letters and numbers polished away. A very light touch with your final wheel will blend this area into the surrounding finish without damage to letters or numbers. Another important point to remember is the BATF rule. It is illegal to "remove, alter, or obliterate" the serial number!

Of course, any firearm polishing is likely to be a combination of both hand and machine work. Use machines where possible for speed, and use hand work for detail. There is no need to spend hours laboriously removing machine marks on a barrel when a barrel spinner and square wheel can do a really good job in minutes. Likewise, there is no need to round off edges, ruin letters and numbers, or dish out holes—not when a few minutes of extra care will keep them sharp, clean, and square.

Final Finishing Techniques

Bead- or sandblasting is not a polishing technique. It will not hide imperfect or sloppy polishing, and, in fact, will bring these imperfections out and make them more visible. Blasting is also an indication of lazy or incompetent work. This type of final finish has its place, but it should not be used to hide sloppy workmanship.

A light beadblast will give a "rust blue" appearance to a well-polished gun and enhance the appearance. Sandblasting will give sharp contrast between high polish and dull surfaces. Bead- or sandblasting will kill glare on sighting surfaces, add contrast to otherwise boring blueing jobs, and can give the customer a unique-appearing firearm he can be proud to show.

Wire wheels can also give unusual finishes to a final polish. A soft wire wheel, when lightly run over a barrel (crossing at 45-degree angles), can give a good approximation of some factory finishes. A rough wire wheel used at intersecting 90-degree angles will give an entirely different finish. ScotchBrite will give yet another.

No one person has the patent on metal finishes. What you find to work best for you will be what you use. Nevertheless, the excuse that "it's what my customer wants" will not hold water if it is used to cover laziness or sloppy polishing. •

A substrate showing polished sides against unpolished metal is a good tool for demonstrating your polishing work.

Selling the Service

If you get good enough, you might try selling your work to others. In selling a blueing job, a badly rusted barrel can be used as a demonstration piece. Mask off several sections and apply several grades of polish to those areas. The contrast between the untouched rusted metal and a mirror finish is impressive, and does the selling for you. The section of hexagonal stock shown in the photograph is polished in varying finishes on three flats, and left "ugly" on the remainder for contrast. Be sure to price the various grades of polish realistically, and refuse to lower your standards to please a customer who only wants his firearm "dipped." It is far better to lose the quick buck than to have him demonstrate to all who will listen and look, that this is the quality blueing you put out.

How do you determine what to charge for this service? Is the charge for a cheap 22 single shot the same as for a Browning over/under? With the understanding that your time is all that you have to sell, is it unfair to charge the 22 owner as much as the Browning owner? Use your sample blueing piece and explain to the Browning owner that much more care will be required in handling his fine firearm than in handling a cheap rimfire. Most owners of firearms over $800 are understanding, and will opt for the higher quality job. If your 22 owner also wants that quality of finish, be up front and tell him the price may exceed the value of the firearm. If he insists (it might have great sentimental value), get a healthy deposit before starting the work. Then deliver what you promised! Pricing must reflect the economy of the area of the country you work in, the amount of time needed to prepare the work, the quality of the firearm involved, and any extra care required to produce the type of finish requested.

Note that the time required to polish a firearm will vary from worker to worker, and some polishing jobs will require more time than others. As you become more proficient in the techniques of pol-

ishing, time requirements generally decrease. Be sure to recognize that an additional charge is customarily made when draw-filing is needed to remove deep pitting or gouges in the metal. Depending on the degree of work needed, $25 to $50 is not unreasonable. Be sure to mention this to the customer so there are no surprises later.

Most gunsmiths have three grades of finish to offer their customers, a "factory" finish which approximates an original finish, an intermediate grade with more luster and more polish, and a super polish to a mirror finish. Some readers may note that I have not mentioned beadblasted finishes. All I will say about that is that a beadblasted finish by itself would not even be considered by a professional, except in the final stage of polishing for special effects. The blasted finish alone, without base metal preparation, is amateurish, in my opinion, and should be rejected whether the customer requests it or not.

A "factory" type of finish includes removing the old finish, either by polishing or by chemical means. The metal is then machine polished with several grades of polishing grit, starting with 180 and ending at about 240. Remember the wire wheel may also be used to produce a good factory finish. The process should take from about 45 minutes up to several hours, depending on the firearm being polished and the disassembly and reassembly required. The time needed for blueing is not included. The cost of a "factory" blue should be in the neighborhood of $40 to around $125. Your pricing should be graduated so that the largest and most complicated jobs command the highest price.

A higher grade of machine polishing will require more grades of polishing grit, probably going from 240 to as fine as 400. It will also take much more time, probably half again as much as required for the factory-type finish, and the cost will be accordingly higher. The cost of this intermediate finish usually starts at around $55 and up to the same general range as the factory finish. Be sure to maintain all sharp edges and screw holes.

The super-high-grade finish will require still more time. With a finish of this type, any imperfection will be highly obvious, and considerably more hand work is needed to prevent waves, ripples, and other machine-induced flaws. My suggestion would be to do the major polishing by hand, after filing out all the pits and imperfections in the base metal. Any corners or areas which show wear can be renewed at this time. Use polishing cloth in successively finer grades to work the polish down to 400. The wheel can now be used to bring up the mirror-like surface we expect from this high-grade finish. The final polishing will be done with 550-grit or even jewelers rouge. Time needed will be about double that required for a factory finish, and the cost will also be approximately twice that of the factory finish, or in the range of $80 to $200. Corners should remain sharp, screw-hole edges clean, and the surface uniformly and highly glossy with no ripples.

Note that a Belgian or "cold" blue process may not take as long as the super glossy finish in metal preparation, but the application time for the blue will be longer. The cost for this process is similar to the super-glossy finish, in the $50 to $200 range.

The reputation of many gunsmiths is built on the quality of the polish beneath the blue. So take the extra few minutes to produce the polish necessary to have your work stand out as superior.

Sear and Hammer Fixtures

If you want to get into trigger work, here's some tooling that makes your job easier and your quality more consistent.

By Chick Blood

IT DOESN'T MATTER which pistol or revolver you happen to be working with, reducing a trigger pull puts you face-to-face with hammer and sear modifications.

I use the term "modification" cautiously. There are many handguns on the market where any modification of the hammer/sear interface that goes beyond polishing should not be attempted. Most guns that fall into this category are self-loaders in 9mm, 40 Smith & Wesson or 10mm calibers. They were never designed for any purpose other than law enforcement or personal protection. When they are used in competition, it is usually at an action shooting event. Even then, most have been overhauled for teams or contract shooters by factory custom shops or nationally-recognized master pistolsmiths and are no longer considered purely defensive weapons .

Thanks to realizations that they couldn't perform every trigger job in the world and that there were some extra bucks to be made by sharing at least some of their ideas, a few of those 'smiths have kept you in the picture. They've done it by marketing the tooling they've developed to make their own work easier and of consistently high quality.

Among this tooling are fixtures dedicated to a single pistol or revolver. Perhaps the most notable, and most specialized of these were developed by Tom Wilson. His individual hammer/sear jigs for the M1911, High Standard, S&W Model 41, Browning Hi-Power, Ruger 22 auto and New Model Ruger Blackhawk are each cut from solid bar stock, precision machined to exact dimensions and adjustable to compensate for any slight differences that might occur in otherwise identical pistols. So are his hammer/trigger jigs for Ruger Security, Speed and Service Six model revolvers.

Each of Wilson's jigs is accompanied by the necessary shims, pins and instructions that are meticulous in their detail when describing how that fixture should be used.

For example, the M1911 sear jig instructions are specific in telling you to use good quality honing oil and a fine India stone to give the sear 50 strokes with about $2^{1}/_{2}$ pounds of downward pressure. You are then to switch to a hard, white Arkansas stone for at least 200 light strokes, defined as $^{1}/_{2}$- to 1-pound of downward pressure, and to bring the surface to a mirror finish with 300 to 400 strokes of a hard, black Arkansas stone.

Instructions for Ruger revolvers are equally specific, walking you very deliberately through such things as stoning for double-action pull, checking your progress in a partially reassembled gun and correcting any problems that turn up before putting you to work on the single action, full cock notch. It's good stuff. Too bad it doesn't seem to be available without the fixtures, which list from $23.69 for single jigs to $91.67 for sets in Brownells' catalog.

The newest dedicated sear fixture to find its way to my bench lets you adjust cutting angles and examine hammer/sear engagements through a built-in 25-power microscope. Listed at $46.90 by Brownells, it was developed at Yavapai College for use in their gunsmithing program as a student aid to achieving match quality triggers on M1911 autos. Instructions accompanying the tool begin by telling you how to prep the hammer, which the tool doesn't do. If I recall my military armorer's manual correctly, the instructions follow it very closely. So should you. I'll repeat them here for those who don't have, and may never want, a dedicated M1911 hammer fixture.

The hammer's full-cock notch should be lowered to a height of 0.018-inch to 0.020-inch. To cut it, secure the hammer in a padded vise with its hooks facing upward. Place an 0.018- or 0.020-inch shim or feeler gauge on top of the notch and bring the shim's edge flush up against the face of the hooks. With a mild cut file, bring down the hooks until they are even with the shim. Next, use perfectly square, sharp-edged stones to polish the face of the full-cock notch and the face of the hooks to a mirror finish. While filing and stoning, make sure your strokes are square to the surface being

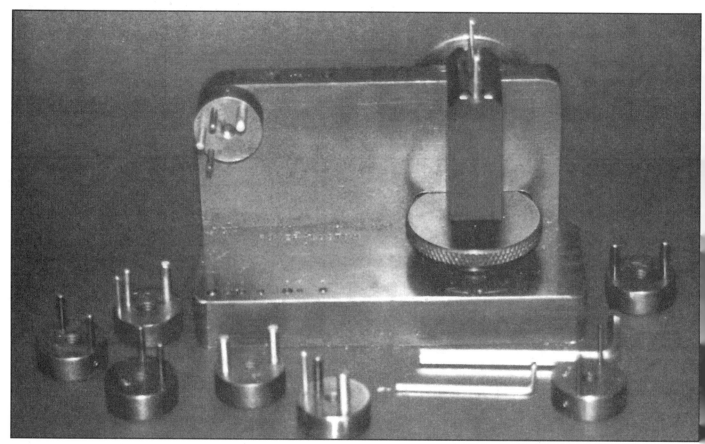

Above: Ron Power's Universal Sear Fixture makes it possible to rework triggers on 24 different firearms by means of adapters. Note the hammer, sear and trigger pin holes in the body of the tool enable you to check relationships between the parts before reassembly.

Below: Three sets of Wilson's jigs. The distinct differences from tool to tool are that each is specifically designed and manufactured to service an individual firearm. Wilson goes so far as to include the proper height shim to achieve a smooth, crisp trigger pull along with highly detailed instructions

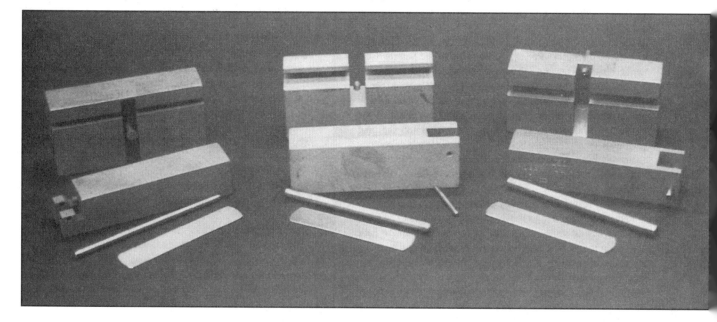

reworked and make absolutely certain you maintain the 90-degree angle of the cocking notch. If you decrease the angle, you'll end up with a heavy trigger pull. If you increase it, the hammer will follow forward when the slide is released and the gun could go full auto. Bad idea.

You then install the finished hammer and the untouched sear on the pins provided with the Yavapai fixture and take a close-up look at their relationship through the microscope. Now remove the sear, coat its primary hammer notch contact surface with a black magic marker, position it back on its pin, then work it and the hammer back and forth against each other to simulate their function in the pistol. When you again remove the sear from the fixture, you'll be able to see rub marks on its primary contact surface and these are your clues for positioning the sear in the jig for stoning.

The jig has a slot at one end and a roller permanently mounted in the other. It also has built-in adjusting screws used to position the sear so that when a 6-inch square stone is placed on the roller and the sear's primary surface, the stone will cut on the same plane as the rub marks. Once that position is assured, the sear is locked in the jig and more magic marker is applied to cover up the rub marks. The stoning begins first with a medium India stone, then a medium fine ceramic stone and finally, an extra fine ceramic for a mirror finish.

The sear's secondary contact surface is cut by flipping the sear over in the jig, readjusting the screws to line everything up and using a fine India stone to cut the secondary angle to approximately one-third the width of the primary surface. The microscope comes into regular use during these sear/hammer mating operations as a quick, accurate means of checking your progress. It sure beats wearing an optivisor or frequently reaching for a magnifying glass and makes this tool unique. Frankly, I wish I'd thought of it first.

The only alternatives to dedicated fixtures I'd recommend were both designed by Ron Power. One of his tools makes it possible, through the use of adapters, to perform sear/hammer or hammer/trigger work on a total of twenty-four pistols, revolvers and rifles.

The adapters fit on one end of a heavy steel, L-shaped bench block and hold the sear, hammer or trigger. On the other end is a lockable elevation wheel to allow for variations in stoning angles and a roller between two, vertical guide pins. This arrangement maintains the stone's relationship to the surface being worked and makes achieving exact angles just about foolproof.

The versatility of this tool is remarkable. By lowering the elevation wheel, the tool can be used to increase sear angle and correct triggers that are too light. Raising the wheel, you can reduce the angle to correct a heavy pull or you can take the angle down to match quality by raising the wheel further. It can be used to do the same with triggers. It can be used to lower hammer hooks. Its top is drilled to accept new model Ruger single-action hammer and trigger pins for check-out of all-important engagement angles. Its base is drilled for Ruger double action, M1911, Ruger MK I, MK II and 10/22 pins.

In Brownells' catalog, it carries the title "Powers Universal Sear Stoning Fixture," but it really isn't. Not quite. Ron has designed another stoning fixture, the Series II, that serves semi-auto pistols and rifles his Universal model doesn't. These are the Beretta 92 and

its clones, the M16, AR15s of current manufacture, Ruger's P series, the Sig 226 and Tanfoglio's EA-9, P9 and TZ. Though it also employs adapters, they are not interchangeable with those of the Universal. If you invested in both fixtures plus all the adapters though, you'd be able to rework with considerable confidence trigger pulls on the vast majority of pistols, rifles and revolvers that

Strictly for reworking M1911 sears, the Yavapai fixture includes a built-in microscope for taking a real, close look at the hammer/sear interface. It was developed to assist students at the Yavapai School of Gunsmithing.

might come your way. How big an investment? The Universal lists at $114.29; its adapters at $16.65 each. The Series II lists at $145.75 with adapters at $22.86 each. You figure it out.

A final word about trigger jobs should you decide to undertake them. And if I'm repeating myself on these pages, I mean to.

If you go too far reducing the pull on a target revolver, misfires may cost a competitor a point, two points or a match. If you go too far on a target pistol, it can spit out a full magazine in a couple of seconds, punch holes in a range's ceiling as the barrel climbs out of control and cause a rapidly widening puddle at the feet of the shooter. If you are ever asked to reduce the pull below factory spec on a police or personal defense gun of any kind, don't.

Chamber Identification With Cerrosafe

With the aid of a couple of cartridge books, this method will help you identify that unknown chamber.

By Chip Todd

THERE WILL ALWAYS be a need to identify chamberings of firearms that have been inherited or bought at yard sales. The lure of buying for bottom dollar and discovering a real jewel is ingrained in most of us, so a little thing like no chambering marks on a rifle or handgun is no deterrent to a gun fancier.

This gives rise to a gunsmithing technique for which little experience is necessary. Anyone can become proficient at identifying firearm chamberings with the help of one or two good cartridge books, along with a little knowledge from which to extend the cartridge drawings to chamber dimensions.

Chamber identification is done with a lead-like metal which has an extremely low melting point and is called Cerrosafe in the firearms industry. It is the safest known way to make moulds of chambers and can easily be taken from the chamber and measured. This metal fills the chamber when hot, but shrinks during the first 30 minutes of cooling to allow its removal from the chamber. Cerrosafe then expands back to the chamber's size for about 200 hours, allowing the casting to be measured with great accuracy. After about 200 hours, the metal expands approximately 0.25 percent, a negligible amount for most uses. Reamer manufacturers and tool-makers are used to working with this slightly expanded metal and know how to take that factor into account.

The metal was originally developed to be used as fuse links in fire sprinkler heads and other heat-sensitive applications; it melts between 158 and 190 degrees Fahrenheit. This means that it will melt in boiling water and can therefore be melted in a double-boiler system.

Another early use for this fascinating metal was the casting of draft-free spaces for machine shop usage. This practice was what led directly to Cerrosafe's use with firearms, because it doesn't solder itself to the base metal like lead and tin do. It can also be used to measure the bore of a firearm which has an uneven number of grooves in the rifling (although I usually just use a soft lead bullet for this).

Cerrosafe is lead-like in color and softness and shines like smoothed lead. It casts into ingots very easily, but I don't do that because I don't want to get it mixed up in my bullet-casting supply. The density is almost that of lead as is its melted viscosity, further adding to the difficulty of keeping them separated. In spite of its similarity to lead, it doesn't seem to wick its way through coffee can seams the way lead does. It could be that the lead is occupying all the space in the seam and will not allow the Cerrosafe through. In any case, we can make use of this factor, and utilize a small coffee or other can for our heating and pouring container.

The equipment required to identify chambers falls into six groups: heat source, container, cleaning, safety, measuring, and literature. Almost any heat source such as an electric hot plate, stove, propane or acetylene torch, or even a heat-shrink gun will suffice. I use an inexpensive electric hot plate that I also use for tempering springs.

The containing/pouring utensil choice is wide open. I use an "International Coffee" can, a rectangular can about 5 inches by 3 inches, by 3 inches tall. I always make sure that one corner is bent properly—to facilitate pouring the molten metal—before I start melting the Cerrosafe. This offers an advantage over a double boiler; wives view gunsmith activities differently than do the 'smiths themselves. A bullet-casting ladle or melting pot might also serve well, although this would be inviting a bullet-casting catastrophe.

The firearm to be identified must be clean before casting, and cleaned again after the casting for safety. Therefore, a well-equipped chamber-identifying bench will need a cleaning rod, bore brushes, mops or cleaning patches, and bore oil. Along with the cleaning things, you may need to have the tools necessary to disassemble and reassemble the firearms.

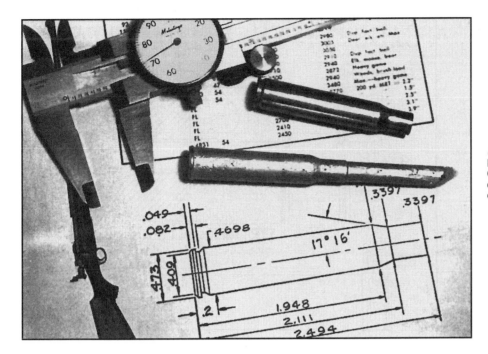

Cartridges of the World, by Frank Barnes, is a good tool for your Cerrosafe use. Photo shows a chamber casting lying on one of the pages.

I recommend the use of eye protection, an apron, and gloves, as there is always the possibility of a spill or splash of the molten metal. Even though the metal melts well below the smoldering point of cloth, it is nearly impossible to get the metal out of clothing. I'll admit to owning a couple of shirts with metallic spots.

Once the casting is made, you will need some method of measuring the casting in several different places. These measurements will need to be taken to three decimal places in inches or two decimal points in metric. Dial calipers reduce the incidence of errors and are much quicker to read, making them superior to Vernier calipers for this use. I sometimes use my electronic calipers because they quickly convert to metric with the push of a button, but these are not necessary. (One millimeter is equal to 0.03937-inch or about 39 thousandths of an inch. Multiplying a metric number in millimeters by the number 0.03937 gives you the same reading in inches. Dividing inch measurements by the same number [0.03937], gives you the reading in millimeters.)

You will also need a reference book or other literature with which to compare the casting's measurements in order to make a good judgment. Most reloading manuals only give the dimensions needed to reload cartridges. The Sierra, Hornady, and Speer reloading manuals give some cartridge dimensions, but are not intended to be used for identification purposes. The most common authority on cartridges is the book written by Frank Barnes called *Cartridges of the World,* now in its 8th edition. It is very complete and you will definitely need it. It can be found in most gun shops and places where firearms manuals are sold. Additionally, *Metallic Cartridge Reloading,3rd Edition,* also from DBI Books, carries cartridge dimensions. However, if you can afford it and want to get direct chamber drawings as well as cartridge dimensions, order the RCBS's *Cartridge and Chamber Drawings,* sold in a ring binder. These are complete design engineering drawings of both the car-

tridges and chambers, showing the allowable tolerance deviations. I also started collecting sample cartridges, removing the primers where possible, to actually test-fit into the chambers after analysis.

One of the nice things about this endeavor is that there is no need for vast experience before starting. In most cases, no experience will be required, and nothing more than some assembly/disassembly manuals will be needed in more complicated cases. I highly recommend *The Gun Digest Firearms Assembly/Disassembly* line of books, the NRA's *Firearms Assembly* books, and the *Gun Digest Book of Exploded Handgun* and *Long Gun Drawings* for any level of gunsmithing. The last two books give more models for the buck but only exploded views, while the others are superior in the details involved in the separate steps of disassembly. I find an unfortunate lack of complete firearm reassembly instructions in the available books. Careful notice of the spatial relationships between adjacent parts should answer your reassembly questions for you.

In preparing the area for the casting work, choose a clear space on a table or bench with an electrical outlet nearby. It helps if there is good ventilation—most metals in their molten form give off vapors which can be harmful. Brownells, the source of Cerrosafe, doesn't list any dangers from the fumes, but it is always a good practice when melting metals to have plenty of fresh air.

Disassemble the firearm so there aren't any extra parts with nooks and crannies into which the molten metal might flow and harden. It is important to think the process through to the end before starting, eliminating rude surprises. This means determining how the casting will be removed from the chamber without having any undercuts or obstructions upon which to hang. Because the shell must go in and out of the chamber, it should be easy to duplicate this. However, it is easy to overlook a seemingly insignificant undercut in some firearms. Also, look to see if there is any danger of the molten metal running into the trigger mechanism. (Just in case it

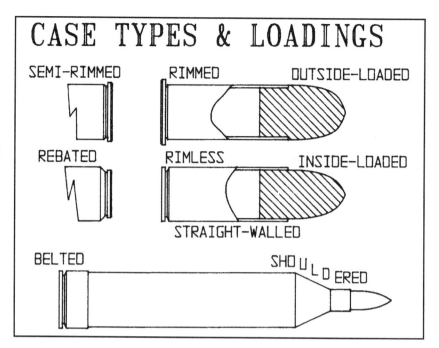

CASE TYPES & LOADINGS

SEMI-RIMMED   RIMMED   OUTSIDE-LOADED

REBATED   RIMLESS   INSIDE-LOADED

STRAIGHT-WALLED

BELTED   SHOULDERED

Learn the types of cases and loadings and you'll be ahead of the game when it comes to identifying that unmarked chamber.

does, we will go through the method of recovering from this later.)

Plug the bore by pushing a small piece of felt, cotton, or rubber into it, stopping just into the rifling near the chamber. This will allow you to capture a small part of the rifling, and also inspect for erosion at the start of the rifling. If there is very much erosion, you may have to go to the section on recovery.

Place the barrel, cylinder, or receiver in a vertical attitude with the muzzle end down, and secure it. Then begin heating the Cerrosafe.

Precautions to take when heating any hot metal or liquid include making certain that nothing is near the edge of the workbench, that the heat source is steady and the cord isn't in the way, and that the heating container is steady on the heat source. If you heat with a torch of any kind, see that the heating container is held even more securely. Heat the Cerrosafe in a reasonably slow fashion, as this is usually safer until you get used to how the metal behaves. Be ready for the metal to melt much sooner than you would expect—158 degrees F isn't very hot. Don't use any more heat than necessary to melt the metal; I have found no literature which tells me at what temperature Cerrosafe vaporizes. The metal will turn the prettiest chrome-like color when it is melted and can be poured as soon as it is all molten.

Pour the molten metal carefully to avoid getting it anywhere you don't want it, but pour fast enough to be sure that it isn't solidifying prematurely and layering in the casting. The only way I know to do it your first time is to proceed as rapidly as you can safely pour the hot metal. Watch carefully so that the level of the casting does not reach the location of the breechface of the bolt or receiver. There can be no Cerrosafe in an area with a diameter larger than that through which the casting must be removed. If the Cerrosafe is left in the casting for more than 20 minutes or so, it can be very difficult to remove, and the integrity of the casting's dimensions may be lost from scuffing.

Remove the casting by pushing a cleaning rod through the bore or the front of the cylinder, tapping lightly if necessary to aid it along. When removed, inspect the casting for scuff marks or scrapes which may affect the dimensions. Set the casting aside to cool for 30 minutes to one hour. (The casting will have shrunk from the chamber dimensions, and must have time to return to the exact size of the chamber. This is a fortunate characteristic, as it allows easy removal from the chamber and then returns to the as-cast size.)

What if the casting refuses to release from the firearm? Believe me, this will happen sooner or later. As they say, fall back to "plan B." This involves slowly heating the chamber area of the firearm with something like a heat gun, hair dryer, or other heat source that does not produce a flame that can affect the firearm's blueing or mechanical parts. I strongly recommend the hair dryer, using it with the gun barrel up and the chamber down over some container. With a hair dryer, it is fairly easy to heat something up to about 170 degrees F, so don't overdo it.

When the metal is recovered, determine what held the casting in place and repour, taking more care in that area. One stuck casting is usually enough to make the next attempt better.

After the casting has cooled and "re-grown," measure the bore diameter first. This can be difficult if the number of lands and grooves is odd, but we must start somewhere. The groove diameter will tell us generally where to look in the cartridge information at our disposal. The next measurement should be the body diameter or case length. If these don't give you a definite clue, jot down all the measurements such as the neck diameter, neck length, head diameter, and shoulder location and angle. You might notice whether the firing pin hits the breechface in the center or at the edge, narrowing the search if the cartridge is deemed to be a rimfire.

The charts at the back of each chapter in *Cartridges of the World* give these dimensions for each cartridge in that chapter, and are by far the handiest of any of the sources which I have. When you have found the caliber which most closely matches your chamber measurements, settle on this as the most probable. There will almost always be some dimension in the charts which will eliminate the cartridge if it isn't the correct one. Remembering that the chamber must be slightly larger than the cartridge in order to allow the insertion and removal of the case, your measurements should be larger than those in the charts by several thousandths of an inch. Chambers need some length to allow for shell length variation, and the diameter includes a tolerance for the shell to expand when it is heated and thousands of pounds of pressure hit it at the same time.

If the casting shows irregularities on the walls of the chamber, look into the chamber to see if there is an area matching the blemish on the casting. If there is, and you are not experienced enough to determine the safety of the firearm, take it to a gunsmith for a safety check before shooting it. I would hesitate to make a blanket safety assurance without more thoroughly checking by Magnafluxing or with an x-ray.

The firearm must now be cleaned and reassembled before returning to use. Take care to look into recesses and other places where some of the Cerrosafe could be hiding. Nothing is more embarrassing than going out to shoot with a gun that doesn't work because of something you overlooked.

One of the most valuable things you will learn as a gunsmith, is how to learn from your mistakes and how to recover from difficult situations. The most common mistake in using Cerrosafe is failing to disassemble the firearm enough before pouring the chamber full of molten metal. It took me a solid trigger group before I learned to slow down when pouring Cerrosafe into a partially disassembled rifle. I would not attempt an identification job until you have the opportunity to see what the Cerrosafe does and how you handle it.

Brownells charges $8.61 for a half-pound ingot of Cerrosafe and $13.76 for a one-pound ingot, which should last forever. The metal doesn't wear out, and you should lose very little each time you work with it.

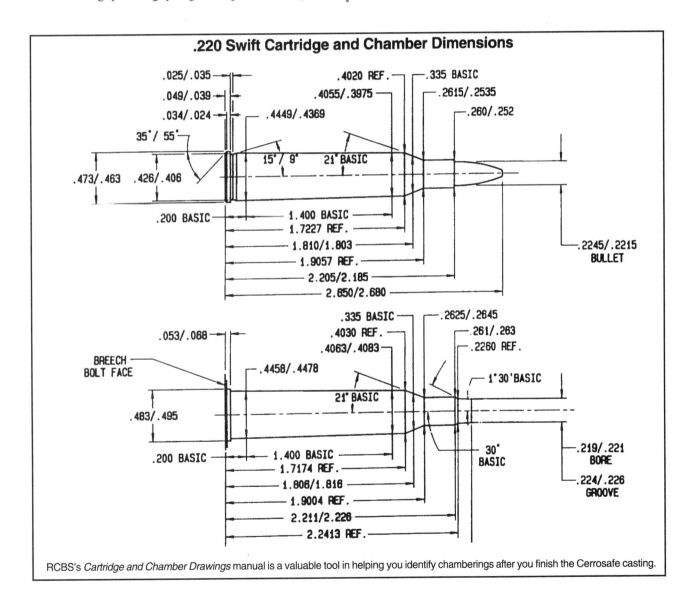

.220 Swift Cartridge and Chamber Dimensions

RCBS's *Cartridge and Chamber Drawings* manual is a valuable tool in helping you identify chamberings after you finish the Cerrosafe casting.

Tapping and Die-Cutting Threads

More manufacturers are using pins instead of threaded holes on their guns, but the odds are we'll be tapping for years to come.

By Chip Todd

IT IS A GIVEN in the firearms industry that manufacturers have to find ways to cut costs to compete with foreign gunmakers. One of the areas, small as it may seem, that is being cut back is the use of threaded holes. If a pin can do the job, that's the route gun makers take.

The need for threaded holes probably won't diminish on the better firearms we see, mainly because of customer perceptions. They equate threads with quality, even though straight pins might do the job just as well. That was certainly evident in the great hue and cry that went up when Winchester replaced screws with pins on one of its rifles years ago.

I wouldn't stake my life on threaded devices being with us from now on, but I submit that no one has shown us anything that even comes close to replacing them. After all, a screw is just a wedge around an axis and is incredibly efficient. Its efficiency is attested to by the proven engineering fact that over 99 percent of the load against a screw is taken by the first three threads, and the fifth thread is always relaxed. The other threads only serve to introduce the screw into the threaded hole and to keep it aligned during tightening. For this reason, sheet metal screws hold almost as much of a load as a machine screw in a threaded hole.

Suffice it to say, chances are we'll be using tapped holes on

firearms for some time to come, so it can't hurt to learn as much about tapping and die-cutting threads as we can.

Threads are identified in the English/Inch system by number sizes and fractions of inches and a dash separating the diameter designation from the thread pitch, which is expressed in threads per inch. The more common household sizes also have UNC and UNF designations, which mean standard coarse- or fine-thread pitches. These are not very useful designations to a gunsmith, because he must pay very close attention to the exact size of a thread anyway.

Drafting standards organizations are pushing the use of decimal designations instead of the usual number sizes for threads. The American National Standards Institute uses .138-32 THD. for what we more commonly know as a #8-32 thread. The idea of renaming threads meets resistance from almost all quarters from mechanical engineers to the machine shops with which they deal.

There are three generally recognized ways to obtain threads on a shaft: You can cut the threads, roll the threads, or cold-head them. Grinding and die-casting threads are too expensive and too cheap, respectively, and are not often-used methods. There are some electronic connectors that make use of die-cast threads, but this has no application to firearms. Taps and dies are commonly made by grinding their threads, but for now we'll concentrate this discussion on using, not making, them.

Cut threads are the cheapest and the most common in use today. However, cutting into the metal severs its grain structure and causes some weakening of the material that makes up the threads.

Rolling metal into shape is a more expensive way to thread a device but results in much stronger threads. Think of rolling threads as compacting the metal structure like you would in a forging operation, but using rolled pressure instead of impact. The metal is mashed into the shape by the tap sliding over its surface. This method not only keeps the grain structure intact, but also "cold works" the metal, a process that actually strengthens it. As a result, rolled threads don't have the acute stress risers and natural split at the extreme of the thread groove caused by cutting threads. Thread-rolling taps are readily available from machine-shop supply houses and only cost slightly more than cutting taps. But the gunsmith should be aware that they require a different set of rules when tapping, which we'll touch on shortly.

Cold-heading threads is similar to forging, where the metal is compressed into the threaded shape by an impact between two dies, but the metal isn't heated before stamping. This is the commercial method used to make the heads on most screws. The metal is stamped under great pressure, filling the cavity of the cold-heading die in the desired shape. Neither the pressure nor the dies are avail-

Various types of threading equipment include tapping/cutting fluids, tap wrench, thread restorer, die and die wrench, die, bottom tap, tap guides, taps (straight and pipe), die wrench, t-tap wrench, die and crescent wrench.

able to the average gunsmith, so we'll pass over this method with just this mention.

Types of Taps

Thread-cutting taps used to cut female threads into a hole come in three common configurations: taper, plug and bottom. These should do just about anything you'll need to do.

The taper tap is pointed at the cutting end and gradually tapers to full diameter about a quarter of the way back. The cutting edges are slightly increasing in diameter to shave metal instead of pushing it out of the way with brute force.

The taper tap is used to tap holes where the threads are meant to go all the way through a workpiece, or to start threads in a deep or blind hole. Its shape slightly enlarges the hole to the right size and aligns the tap by seeking center all the time. In blind holes, the threads are just started with the taper tap, and the gunsmith may switch to a plug tap later. The taper is the easier-cutting tap and should be used where possible.

Plug taps are more blunt on the end and have a steeper angle of taper. These taps require more force because they shave the metal off in thicker chips and their bite becomes full more quickly. Use these in holes in which the depth doesn't allow the use of a taper tap, or as a good compromise, if you can only justify one tap per thread size. Since I use left-hand threads so infrequently, I nearly always buy plug taps in the left-hand version of the thread size unless it is for a specific chore that is to be repeated many times.

The blunt-ended bottom tap is used to cut threads to the bottom of a blind hole or to make full threads go a certain depth without threading any farther. I seldom buy this type of tap because I eventually break the others and just square up the ends to make bottoming taps. I sometimes chamfer the end like the commercial bottom taps, but in most cases I leave the thread-cutting flutes full to the

very end to reach nearer the bottom of holes. I use a plug tap before my homemade bottom tap to give it every advantage that I can.

Pipe threads are similar to standard 60-degree threads, the exception being that the threads are in a tapered hole and at an angle with the axis of the hole. With the threads tapered, it is obvious that the depth to which you tap would determine the size of the opening of the threaded hole. While it is possible to cut pipe threads into a straight hole, it is better and makes the tap last longer to cut the threads into a properly tapered hole. The pilot hole for tapping pipe threads is first drilled, then cut to a taper with a tapered pipe reamer. Keeping a pipe fitting of the intended size on hand is a good way to gauge the results.

At its best, tapping tapered threads is not as exact a science as normal straight threading because it is harder to tell when one is through. It is an operation highly dependent upon a good tapping oil to counteract the wedging action of the thread's taper. I use a good sulfurated cutting oil like that preferred in heavy-metal machine shops to prolong the life of my pipe taps. Pipe threads, by virtue of their normal use, must be more exact and void-free than machine threads to seal off pressure or liquids.

There are almost as many distinct shapes of taps as there are drill bits. Some even have passages in the flutes that allow cutting fluid to flow through and lubricate, cool the cutting edges and flush out the chips. Flute designs fall into four main categories: straight fluted, spiral fluted, two flutes and three flutes.

The straight-fluted taps have cutting edges in straight columns. Others have the flutes spiraled around the core, but this design isn't as strong and inherently has a weaker core because the tap's grooves are deeper. This is to allow the cuttings to flow out in long, curly pieces. Three-fluted taps are stronger than two-fluted taps.

If you are just starting out and can't afford or don't want to buy all the taps you might need, here's what you ought to start with. I

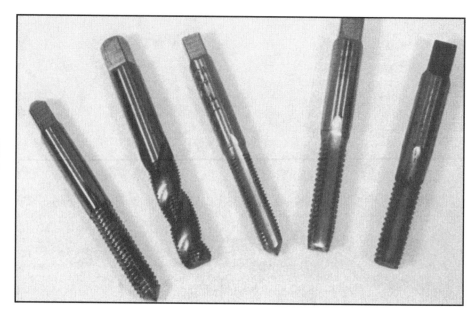

Interrupted roll, spiral-fluted, taper, plug, and bottoming are the main types of taps.

would buy plug taps in 4-40, 6-32, 6-48, 8-32 and 10-32 sizes to handle threads most common to everyday utility work. Plug taps are a good compromise when you cannot afford to get taper and bottoming taps in all the sizes. It takes a little more care to start plug taps, but a little hard work is necessary without the best of tools.

About a dozen taps and matching dies, taper and bottoming taps so that blind holes can be tapped within a thread's pitch of the bottom of the hole, will handle most jobs. The sizes I suggest are 4-48, 5-40, 5-44, 6-40, 6-48 and 8-40. The 5-44 tap will come in handy on Smith & Wesson revolver sideplate screws and Redfield scope rings. Quite a few sights and scope mounting bases use the 6-48 size, and some shotgun front sights use the 8-40 thread. It would pay to check some parts books to see what is most common on guns you're likely to see before deciding which taps would serve you best. I would get these taps in three-flute styles only.

Options

No matter how many taps you have, there will be times you won't have the size required. There are just too many threads out there waiting to ruin your budget. When this comes up, I check my self-tapping screws for a possible match. If I find one, I'm in good shape unless the hole has to be threaded very deeply. A good self-tapping screw will do a fair tapping job in most steels and in nearly all of the other metals. If you can't find a match or the hole must be threaded too deeply, put the job away and call all the machine-shop supply houses in the area.

If all else fails, make a tap for yourself. This isn't as hard as it sounds if you have a lathe handy and a large enough commercial tap to follow. I make a threaded shaft of drill rod with a major diameter of 0.002-inch larger than the screw measured, and cut some flute grooves in it with a stone on a Dremel grinder. I polish the edges with a Cratex wheel and usually grind some relief angle to the trailing edges of the interrupted threads so that the tap won't drag. That isn't really necessary if the tap doesn't have to last.

Your finished tap must be heated to a bright red color and quenched in either water or oil. I prefer oil because I don't want any cutting teeth to break off and possibly get caught in the threads and ruin the job.

Different metals call for specific types of taps so, while each gunsmith has his own theories and prejudices about processes and tools, we'll talk about what has and has not worked for me over the past 30 years.

I wouldn't use the spiral-fluted tap for any metal harder than aluminum, brass or mild steel less than 0.125 in thickness. Copper and stainless are both gummy to machine. The spiral tap is inherently weaker than straight-fluted taps and, I promise, will break at the least opportune time. Straight-fluted taps are best for almost all cases. The spiral-fluted tap is good where the metal is soft and the hole deep because it sends the cut metal out in long streamers and is less likely to pack tightly with cuttings.

Pilot Holes

The pilot hole for cutting threads is, depending on which machinists' manual you're reading, very near or exactly the size of the minor diameter of the thread. The idea is to remove only the metal occupying the space where the thread grooves will need to be, meaning the tap isn't expected to enlarge the hole at all or there will be unnecessary drag and torque on the tap. Most supply houses have drill size/tapping pilot hole charts available for free. I keep one in my tap drawer, my drill drawer and one on my drill press.

Rolled threads can be induced in almost any malleable metal. You just cannot roll threads into a piece of dead-hard steel.

Since rolling threads moves, instead of cuts, metal around until it looks like threads without disturbing the grain's continuity, its pilot hole must be of a different size than that used to cut threads. As the grooves are pushed into the sides of the hole, the displaced material must have somewhere to go. The larger pilot hole leaves room for the material to fill. The recommended pilot hole size is usually

Drill press tapping uses a tap guide, tap, and wrench. The spring-loaded tap guide is in the press' chuck and the crescent wrench is driving the square end of the tap.

about the pitch diameter of the thread, a diameter almost halfway between the minor and major diameters of a thread.

Fluids

I use whatever tapping fluid I find on hand when threading steels other than stainless or hardened. In situations like the threading of aluminum, I use special fluids designed for aluminum. There are some brands of tapping fluids that will, believe it or not, make freshly cut aluminum smolder. I learned the hard way when a solid block of aluminum started billowing brown, choking smoke and would not go out with water. I finally had to tap farther and flush out the burning metal. Heed the cautions on tapping-fluid cans when they state "not for aluminum."

I have successfully used many of the water-thin fluids, but I find myself returning to the thicker sulfurated types when threads really matter to me. The exception to that rule is when I work with stainless steel. Stainless is a bear to machine with any smoothness, and I like my threads smooth. Then I use the creamy stainless-steel tapping pastes like Westlube and Anchorlube. Both are noticeably better than most of the thinner liquids when tapping a stainless or hardened steel.

Last, but not the least effective, is the old standard of machine shops, sulfurated cutting oil, the oil which gives old machine shops their distinct smell.

Tap Handles

You can drive a tap with many different types of handles. What you use is a matter of personal preference and will usually depend on the job at hand.

I like the T-handle types with a double-stepped chuck that accepts different sized square tap drives. Most of these have handles that slide back and forth to clear objects that always seem to be in the way. These sometimes come with ratcheting chucks, but I begrudge the extra space needed for these chuck's size. Another commonly used aid is the straight tap wrench. This has two handles that stick out straight, one to each side, with either two opposing, notched blocks and offset handles or sliding blocks inside a closed yoke. These will serve you well and give good mechanical advantage.

Accessories

When the job permits, a good gunsmith will use a tap guide to produce threads that are in line with the pilot hole. These guides can be handy when drilling and tapping in a press or milling machine.

I don't use a tapping fixture, as it is more suited to larger pieces than a gunsmith usually encounters. I just utilize the press with which I drilled the pilot hole in the workpiece and align the tap with that.

A small spring-loaded device called a tap guide is useful for this. After drilling the pilot hole and before moving the workpiece, replace the drill bit with the tap guide. Place the tap into the pilot hole and bring the tap guide down until its spring is mostly compressed by this. There are taps with pointed drive ends and those which are center-drilled to accept a tap guide. The tap guide will usually have a reversible plunger to allow it to be used with either pointed or countersunk taps.

I use the tap guide to ensure that I won't ruin a good firearm by starting a tap into a pilot hole at a misaligned attitude. This small item might pay for itself dozens of times by saving you the expensive embarrassment of replacing a firearm. I just don't buy any taps that don't have accommodations for a tap guide, as I rarely tap without one.

After spring-loading the tap with the tap guide, a small Crescent wrench or a tappet wrench can be used to turn the tap. The tap guide will keep the tap coaxial while loading it with force to aid its advance.

The most popular type has a reversible, spring-loaded plunger with a point on one end and a cup on the other. This guide is used after drilling the pilot hole for the tapping operation and, without moving the drill press head or the workpiece, installing the tap guide into the drill press chuck. The quill is then extended, compressing the drill guide onto the tap in the hole. The spring-loaded plunger keeps pressure on the tap while also keeping it aligned with the axis of the hole.

Another worthwhile tapping accessory is a tap extension for times you just cannot get an ordinary tap wrench close enough to the area you need to tap.

This is the time you get your money's worth out of the tap extension you bought. Those I have liked most are just about the opposite of an automotive socket-wrench extension. They have a square socket on the tap end, sometimes with a set screw in it or sometimes with a spring-loaded ball. The drive end is usually square so it can be driven by the same types of tap wrenches that would be used in an easy application.

There are some delightful devices on the market. Most are designed to help tap either more closely to perpendicular, which isn't particularly applicable to gunsmithing, or to do a lot of tapping more easily, which is. The latter is production work, which we don't often get, but it helps to have something to hold the tapping end up perpendicular to the surface.

Tips and Techniques

There are widely accepted techniques that have proven themselves over the years and might prevent tap breakage for you.

Taps, while quite hard, nevertheless have some torsional springiness to them. If they didn't, it would be much more difficult to tap small holes without breaking the tap. It is this torsional feel which guides the amount of pressure you'll use. Depending on the material, the cutting fluid used and the size of the hole, the tap should be turned about 30 degrees and reversed about the same amount to clear the threads. If the cuttings jam the tap's way, the resulting threads will look as if they were cut by Lizzie Borden. With each reversal of the tap, advance it to the solid metal again and cut about another 30 degrees and reverse. In all threading with hand tools, be it cutting male threads with a die or female threads with a tap, interrupted advance with some short reversing will help clear the chips and minimize grief caused by trapped particles. This is safer than trying to cut the threads with continuous forward pressure.

I even use roll-thread taps in this manner. If the job is worth my using a roll tap, I feel that I shouldn't take any chances with it. The very reason I use roll taps dictates that I take unusual precautions in tapping. This brings me to the main difference in the tapping techniques of cutting threads and rolling threads.

While rolled threading is more adapted to power tapping, it can also be done by hand. Roll taps are designed for continuous feeding, but will be lubricated better if you use them like ordinary taps.

There is no advantage in using the lathe to thread a hole unless the hole is in the center of the lathe's spindle and the piece can be spun about that hole. Otherwise, it is much easier to use a drill press. I find that there are quite a few times when shafts require a threaded hole in their ends coaxial with the shaft.

Lathe Tricks

The safest way to cut female threads on the lathe is to use the lathe as an aligning device and a tap guide as with a drill press. The

The die for an autopistol is located on the barrel-threading guide just before starting on the barrel. Note the drive indention on the outside of the die by which the die wrench is to grip and drive the die.

tap guide should be put into the tailstock's drill chuck and the tap placed between the workpiece and the tap guide. The rest is like the method described for a drill press.

The desire to eliminate the tap guide and use the tailstock to align the tap will come when you get more experience with the lathe. This also leads to wanting to use the lathe's power to start the tap. I really don't recommend this, but I'll admit to being lazy enough to do it fairly often. I also have had to start over on some jobs because I left part of a tap in the metal.

I advise power-cutting threads on a lathe only after considering the consequences if things hit the fan. In power-cutting female threads on a lathe, I usually consider the threads' function and determine if the pilot hole can stand to be drilled slightly oversize without adversely affecting their integrity. You have to do this because the rotation of the chuck on the lathe cannot stop the way you can when hand-tapping. If the threads are to be utilized to their fullest, I use the recommended pilot-hole size and take more care to keep from breaking the tap.

Install the tap into a three-jaw chuck on the tailstock and firmly tighten the jaws. This operation is not advisable if you have a keyless chuck on the tailstock because they usually self-tighten, and the tap needs to be able to freewheel when it is subjected to overload. Leave the tailstock loose and positioned with the tap close to the hole to be tapped. Keeping a hand on the power switch, turn the lathe on and push the tap into the pilot hole. Watch the tap's advance and turn the power off when the tap starts spinning in the chuck. If the tap has gotten a good start into the hole, you can be assured that the tap is aligned coaxially with the pilot hole.

Now, lock the headstock spindle and finish turning the tap with a regular tap wrench. The tapped hole is bound to be centered and straight with the axis of the workpiece.

Also, the lathe can be used to quite an advantage to cut male threads onto a shaft using regular tapping dies.

First, taper the end of the rod to be tapped and install a good-sized chuck into the tailpiece of your lathe. Put the tapping die into a straight-handled die wrench and center the die onto the end of the rod. With the die in place, manually push the tailstock toward the die and tighten it down when the chuck face touches the die wrench.

You must be absolutely sure that the drill chuck's jaws are not sticking out to catch in the die. Turn the die wrench in the proper direction and crank in on the tailstock's advance crank, using the tailstock to apply pressure onto the die through the die wrench. When you have cut threads for more than five turns, it would be safe to move the tailstock back since the die should have established a straight path along the centerline of the rod.

If threads are to be cut close to a shoulder on a rod, first cut with the die turned the conventional direction, then turn it around to cut close to the shoulder. Remember, the die has a slight funneled side to the thread-cutting teeth and will likely have cutting edges right up flush with the back side of the die. These cutting teeth, which are even with the side of the die, will be able to cut closer to the shoulder. Since the threads cannot be cut exactly up to the shoulder, an undercut is often made next to it at the same depth as the minor diameter of the threading. This will make it possible for the nut or female-threaded part to butt up against the shoulder without having to counterbore the female threads.

Thread-Cutting Dies

While external male threads can be cut onto a shaft with a lathe, the most common method is to use thread-cutting dies. These are cylindrical metal pieces with cutting teeth in the center and relief holes to allow the exit of chips. The thread-cutting teeth are tapered on the starting side of the die to give it a chance to align and gradually start cutting the thread grooves. It is handy to remember that the threads aren't being cut, but rather the grooves are cut, leaving the threads on a male-threaded piece to fill the grooves in a nut or in a piece with female threads.

Cutting threads with a die isn't much different from tapping threads into a hole except the threads are out in the open when they clear the die. As with the tap, it is essential to keep the die handles 90 degrees to the axis of the rod being threaded. If the die is started at a different angle, it will often ignore efforts to re-align it and cut deeper and deeper into one side of the rod until you just cannot turn it anymore.

After getting the die started, advance and reverse it after every 30 degrees of rotation to interrupt the cutting and to help clear the relief holes. It is often necessary to back up the die until you can get the relief holes positioned to allow their clearance by air pressure or a pick. If you are using air pressure, it is as important as ever to keep your eyes protected with safety glasses.

Back the die off when finished and chalk up the new threads with regular blackboard chalk, then run the die over the threads again before cleaning them the last time. They will feel smoother in use.

Special Sizes

Some special sizes of threads common to the gun fraternity should be mentioned here. A $^7/_8$-14 thread used on reloading dies is important to anyone making special devices for reloading. I also keep a $^7/_8$-14 tap and die around to clean and true threads, and I use both at least once a month. This particular size isn't limited to reloading, but since it is not the common household size, the supply houses don't sell many. That means they are expensive.

Brownells sells barrel-threading dies and receiver tapping taps for replacing or making barrels for the more popular firearms. If you have a lathe and know how to cut threads with a threading tool bit, you won't really need the dies for revolver- or rifle-barrel threading. However, there may come a time when a receiver tap for Colt, S&W, or Ruger barrel threads in the receiver will come in handy.

My favorite S&W Model 19 had a tight thread in the receiver that made the bore tight through the leaded area. I first noticed this when I ran a range rod through the bore to check its alignment with the chambers. The rod head got pretty tight when it had to go through that area ahead of the forcing cone, so the bullet was swaged smaller than specification and was traversing the forward portion of the barrel. I knew this couldn't be helping the gun's accuracy, so I chose to change that fit.

I removed the barrel and cleaned the threads in the receiver. They weren't very dirty, so I knew the thread diameter must have been the culprit. Using my most prized Boelube ($60 a gallon), I ran the K-frame tap through the front end of the receiver and it came out with some fine high-carbon cuttings on it. Putting the barrel back on, I ran the same range rod through the bore again. What a good feeling. There was about 0.002-inch difference in the diameter of the bullet pushed through after the operation compared to the bullet pushed through the bore previously. I watch for that in all revolvers now.

If you must install a compensator on an automatic pistol, you will need a die to thread the muzzle end of the barrel. The most common threads for the 1911 are either .575-40 or .581-40. The .575 size is known mainly because it is used by Clark, while the .581 is known because of Brown's and Wilson's comps. The taps cost approximately $20 to $23 and the dies (which are more often needed by gunsmiths) run approximately $30 to $39,

Not even the luckiest machinist could get by without using some type of guide when threading the muzzle of a barrel for a compensator. If the barrel were tapered on the lathe and the die held plumb to the bore with the tailstock, it would be possible to get the threads aligned on the barrel. But I wouldn't want to risk it on any barrel worthy of a compensator.

Brownells sells a two-ended barrel-threading guide for 45s and 38s that doesn't cost an arm or leg. I made mine out of stubbornness, but because I had to make one for my 10mm Omega, anyway, one more couldn't hurt. If you make your own, I suggest it either be hardened to dead-hard and oiled thoroughly or made soft enough not to damage your die and replace it if it got cut. I chose the ultra-hard route and am careful not to force the die over it. The barrel-threading die is turned to a diameter that will fit into the muzzle for about an inch and a middle diameter over which the die will just barely slide. This center portion ensures that the die will cut threads coaxial with the bore of the barrel.

Cold Blueing Tips and Techniques

While not as good as a hot-blue job, sometimes cold blueing is a necessity. Here are some ways to get a finish that'll make you proud.

By Chip Todd

These are the primary tools you'll need to start a cold-blueing project.

ANYONE CAN DISCOLOR METAL, but it takes effort and care to get a cold-blued finish of which you can be proud. First, recognize the fact that no method of cold blueing can match the durability and beauty of a hot-blueing job done by an experienced gun refinisher. Blueing is the final state of the oxidation process of steel, and requires very caustic chemicals and heat to penetrate the metal surface deeply. In short, it takes money; a well-ventilated room; and a will to fight city hall, the EPA, and OSHA to have a decent hot-blueing operation.

The main difference between hot blueing and cold blueing is in the salts that are used. For hot blueing, alkaline salts are used at approximately 290 degrees Fahrenheit, while most cold-blueing solutions are acidic and used at room temperature. A third method of blueing is called Nitre-blueing which is almost neutral, but must be used above 540 degrees F. I won't touch on the Nitre-blueing process here, as it is used to a much lesser degree than the other two. The boundary "ring or haze" you have gotten when trying to touch up factory blueing is caused by the neutral area formed between the two types of blueing. This is

why it can be so hard to get the "invisible" spot touch-up job.

The advantages of the cold-blueing method are apparent when one checks out the prices of heated tanks, the inherent dangers of dealing with caustic and/or hot chemicals, and the great difficulty in disposing of depleted or dirty chemicals. My favorite blueing craftsman has his setup next to his swimming pool as a safety precaution in case he gets seriously splashed with the caustic solution. I didn't want to use caustic chemicals around my children when they were young, and I have since seen no reason to change. Therefore, I suggest leaving the hot solutions to the experienced gunsmiths who are used to dealing with the harsh chemicals, and who are willing to put up with rigid EPA requirements.

"Murphy's Law" of reblueing: The results are inversely proportional to the cost of the firearm, added to the pickiness of the owner. Remember, you will probably be dealing with someone who has no idea of the difficulty of your task; he thinks you just "dip it."

Now that I've shown why you might opt for the less durable cold blueing, let's get into how you can get reasonable results with some consistency. To do the work you have to have a high-interest level, a garage-type shop, and an adequate source of clean water.

Suggested Equipment

To get started in cold blueing, I suggest you have the following equipment on hand:
- Small stainless-steel or polyethylene mixing bowl
- Plastic rectangular container (Tupperware type, pistol size)
- Face shield/eye protection
- Apron (chemical resistant)
- Cotton gloves (latex gloves usually leave prints in the finish)
- Dremel or other rotary grinder
- Forceps, tweezers, or clamps
- Good lighting

The following equipment is not necessary, but it will make the work easier and more trouble free:

- Air pressure and nozzle
- ScotchBrite wheel and/or buffing wheel
- Sand-blasting or bead-blasting equipment

Supplies

The supplies you will need include:
- Cotton swabs, Q-tips, clean rags
- Oil (water displacing)
- Blueing chemical
- Water, fresh and running, if possible
- Vinegar (white) or dilute muriatic acid
- Cratex wheels or lots of elbow grease
- #0000 steel wool
- Sandpaper (320, 400, and 600 grit)
- ScotchBrite pads

There are some things you shouldn't use at all, including newspapers, because the ink has residual chemicals which may ruin the results of your labors. And don't use WD-40 or other rust-preventing oils because they will eat away blueing.

The Cold Blueing Process

The first thing you should do is inspect the gun you're going to work on for scratches, dents, and dings, which will have to be removed during the reblueing process. (I used a revolver for this demonstration.) Decide how they will affect the appearance of the finished pistol, and decide whether the gun should be glossy or matte (dull). Glossy finishes tend to draw one's eye to the defects and are sure to displease if these defects are more prominent than before. The answer is often to make selected parts matte and others glossy.

Gloss is usually obtained by buffing the metal to a chrome surface, but this can be done manually if one has the time and energy to spare. In such a case, use finer and finer grit sandpaper until you reach 600 grit, and then polish with a good metal polish, such as SimiChrome polish (found at most motorcycle shops). Parts requiring a dull finish will need to be bead-blasted, sand-blasted (extreme

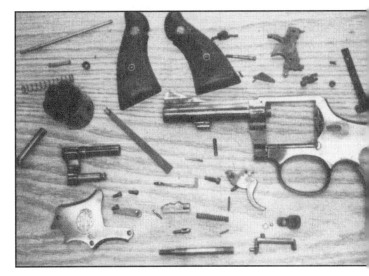

The author used a Smith & Wesson revolver for this project. The gun needs to be fully disassembled before blueing.

cases), or dulled with ScotchBrite pads. I find that the maroon colored ScotchBrite pads are about like 320-grit sandpaper and work fairly well for this. (These are also good for taking out scratches on brushed stainless-steel guns.) Most of the interior parts will not need to be blued; it's only done when I think the owner won't take care in oiling the weapon at regular intervals.

Disassemble the firearm and store the parts that don't need blueing. I use a Seal-A-Meal machine which seals the parts in a plastic bag where they can't get easily lost. The parts which are to be blued are then degreased with Trichlorethylene 1,1,1 or other such degreaser. A handy source of this chemical is Berryman's Brake Cleaner which comes in a spray can from your local auto-parts

If you bead-blast the gun you're going to blue, be sure to mask off any bearing areas that don't need to be roughened. After blasting, the gun is ready for the cold blueing.

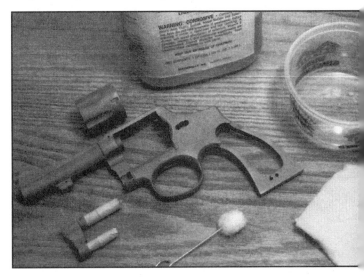

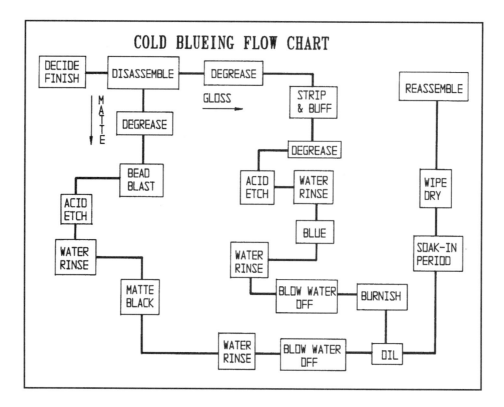

COLD BLUEING FLOW CHART

store. Granted, this isn't the most economical form of degreasing, but it certainly is handy.

After the decision of dull vs. gloss has been made, you will either buff and polish the gun and parts, or bead blast it to a satin gray. Be sure to tape off the surfaces with masking tape that don't show and shouldn't be roughened up before blasting the pieces. I also suggest you blast the receiver with the sideplate in place, as it is easier to obtain an evenness between pieces. I chose the matte finish for this article because it is the one that I'd recommend for one's first blueing job. The only difference in difficulty between the two finishes is that it's harder to get a grease-free metal surface after buffing with the waxy compound. The heat generated by buffing causes the wax to permeate the metal, and the wax is more difficult to remove than the glass powder from bead-blasting.

The main cause of most cold blueing miseries is the lack of proper and complete degreasing of the parts. Even degreasers, which seem to have taken all of the grease from a part, usually fail to get all of the contaminants out of the pores of the metal. Formula 409 cleaner seemed to be the answer for a while, but I got several bad jobs in a row and started the search for something better. It just wouldn't get the worse cases of grease out and was useless against rust pits.

Firearms that have pitting will always need an acid bath in order to get the rust out of the pits. I've found I can get most contaminants and rust out of the metal by using either white vinegar (acetic acid) or dilute muriatic acid (hydrochloric acid). Soak stubborn parts in a very weak muriatic acid solution for about 30 minutes. Always pour the acid slowly into the water, not the water into the acid. You must also keep an eye on the part while it's soaking, as

you don't want this process to eat any of the metal away, just get the rust and grease out of the pores. The part will develop an etched, gray surface, but this will not affect the gloss, unless taken to an extreme. The acid bath leaves the metal susceptible to immediate rusting (three minutes or less), so you must use caution and be observant. When you see the gun emitting a host of small bubbles while in the acid bath, don't be alarmed that the metal is getting eaten away in a rush. The acid is just breaking down the glass powder that is in the pores of the metal from bead- or sand-blasting. While the workpiece is in the acid bath, you may want to spend that time getting your blueing setup ready.

There are several good types and brands of blueing chemicals. Among them are Birchwood Casey's PermaBlue or SuperBlue; and Brownells' Dicropan IM, Oxpho-Blue, Dicropan T, and G-96 Gun Blue. Although any of these will give excellent results, for this article, I used Brownells' Oxpho-Blue, as I have had good results with this for quite a few years.

Pour the blueing liquid into the bowl that you will use, and place it and some clean swabs on a clean area of your workbench. This spot must be free of both the acid you just mixed and any grease that may have accumulated on the bench.

Take the firearm directly from the acid bath and rinse it thoroughly with clean running water for about 3 minutes. It often helps to bathe the piece with baking soda and water, and then rinse with water. Do not touch the metal with your hands, as that will ensure your place in history (or at least the gun's history) by leaving a print in the finish.

Still being careful not to touch the metal, swab the blueing solution onto the gun or gun part as evenly as you possibly can, and

After blueing, give the gun a water displacing oil bath.

continue doing so until you can see no change in the color or darkness. In the case of a bead- or sand-blasted gun, the developing color will be a good matte black. The buffed or otherwise polished gun will go through several stages of blue, black, and iridescent colors. If the color isn't fairly even, lightly acid wash it again, rinse, and reblue. It's important that the blueing goes as far as it can, or you won't get an even color or darkness. A brown color may form on the surface and this must be swabbed over with more of the solution. Remember, this is really rust that you're putting on the gun, and, therefore, you should expect to see some rust color. You must keep swabbing the brown film off so that fresh blueing solution can continue its work on the steel. Alter you can see no further change in the color, rinse the piece in running water and brush the brown discoloration off of its surface. I would also use a good detergent or soap to ensure that all of the discoloring rust and black particles are sloughed off with the rinse water.

Any silver solder or brass which shows after blueing can be treated at this stage with Brownells' "Solder Black" or Birchwood Casey's "Brass Black." These chemicals give the silver solder or brazing a black color that is good enough to hide the seam of either brass or silver solder. Brownells also has a soft-solder blackening agent. Rinse again after using any of these.

If air pressure is available, blow all the water off the piece and out of the threaded holes. If not, then a good water-displacing oil such as that offered by Brownells or a water-soluble oil like that used in most machine shops will work. The latter is a milky-looking emulsion after it is introduced to water. Either will work well.

Oil must be used in any case. It's not good enough to just get the water off and the surfaces oiled. The firearm or part will need to be covered with an oily or greasy film for a while if it's to remain rust-free for long. You may oil the whole piece and return to it in an hour and find it bone-dry. The new surface, especially in the case of sand-blasted or bead-blasted finishes, will absorb oil like you can't imagine. It still amazes me how much a matte finish will digest,

I really don't know enough theory to explain why, but it's readily apparent that the blued finish is harder alter 24 hours than immediately after the process. I have found that wiping the gun with an oily rag shortly after blueing tends to leave a lot of black on the rag and thin places in the color. I have also found that leaving the real wiping off for later, say after 24 or 36 hours, will work a lot better. Reassemble the gun and let it "age" overnight or longer, and then wipe it well with a soft cloth. It may need oiling after the wipedown, but this should be with a cleaner oil than that which you just removed.

One way to get a real gloss without buffing is to use a stainless-steel burnishing brush on your drill press at the lowest speed available. This brush head is covered with 0.003-inch or finer stainless-steel wires which gently burnish the surface to a luster. XXXX-grade steel wool will do nearly as well if you have patience. It is essential that there be no moisture or shiny oil on the surfaces being burnished, or the brush or steel wool will do more than burnish the finish—it will really thin it out. This burnishing will not leave you the black-black of the matte blueing, so don't do it if you want the black to remain. The good dull black will change to a sheen of a gunmetal-gray color. I know of no reliable chemical which will give a truly glossy black without resorting to a hot process.

One last thing before you show off the gun: Cleanup all of the screw heads. Nothing ruins the looks of a newly refinished gun more than damaged screw slots.

I put the offending screw in a drill chuck on which I installed a handle and peen the burrs of the ruined screw slot back in place.

ScotchBrite wheel, or fine sandpaper before blueing the heads will do wonders. The screw heads usually don't have to go through the acid bath if they have been degreased and sanded or ScotchBrite cleaned. Buffing helps the looks of them, but will require acid before taking the blueing well. Oil and reinstall the screws, and the gun should make you proud.

I would suggest that you take before and after pictures of each gun you blue until you gain confidence. I always show the owner the before and after pictures when he picks up the gun. If I know there won't be time for that, I often take a quick Polaroid shot of the gun as it was brought in so that I will have a subtle reminder.

I'm sure there are other good methods of cold blueing, but I've had good results with this method and believe you will, too. And when you develop twists of your own, I hope that you'll share them with all of us.

Chip Todd owns Charles Todd Gunsmithing in Ramona, California. He specializes in combat handguns, custom firearms, and teaching young gunsmiths.

Silversoldering—Useful, But Frustrating

Silversoldering can save you time and money, but if you're just beginning, it can be very frustrating. Here are some tips to help get you started.

By Chip Todd

SILVERSOLDERING IS A most useful process around the gunshop—quick, decorative, and utilitarian—though it can cause problems for the beginning gunsmith. The process is similar to lead/tin soldering, except that silver and brass make up the largest part of the solder, and the results are much stronger. The strength of a silversoldered joint is a function of the percentage of silver, and of the gunsmith's skill in applying it.

I prefer 85-percent silver content to all other alloys, as it has a shear strength of 85,000 psi (approximately that of mild steel). It melts between 158 and 190 degrees Fahrenheit, and flows and wicks as well as any other alloy. Silversolder produces a color much like that of stainless steel, and it resists corrosion better than brass. It takes electroplating well, and can be colored a near-black by using a special blackening solution.

Some gun owners will have difficulty relating to the strength of silversolder. In that case, I find it handy to use the information in Brownells catalog to convince the set-in-his-belief owner of the strength and durability of the 85-percent alloy.

Silversoldering should be used when joining two different types of metals that can't be welded with conventional methods, or when the heat of welding would destroy something in the vicinity of the weld. Also, there are times when welding will change the temper of a part and therefore its strength or durability.

Commonly used metals which lend themselves to silversoldering are brass, steel, copper, silver, stainless steel, iron, and tungsten carbide. Due to the varied nature of these materials, it is important to know which metals react to and conduct heat best. Knowing which parts are the conductors can ensure the success of your work.

Metals which will not accept silversolder are soft, such as aluminum, zinc, and lead. These metals melt at a lower temperature than silversolder, bringing to mind the strange laws of alloys: All alloys melt at a temperature lower than the melting point of any of the alloying components.

Silversoldering should not be used when the joint being soldered is subjected to either high pressure or stress. This would include, but not be limited to, revolver cylinders, structural members of receivers, high-wear points, sears or sear notches, and high-stress areas of slides.

There are many types of flux and alloys, many of which are so similar as to be confusing to the uninitiated. Of the solders, I would recommend the high silver-content alloy; somewhere in the 80- to 85-percent silver range. This flows easily and will wick into the tightest interface. It will be available in stick, wire, flat ribbon, and paste forms, and can be found in almost any good industrial hardware supply house.

The wire form is used most often, as it is the most easily controlled of the four shapes. The flat ribbon will be best to sandwich two parts together with clamp pressure. Stick solder is primarily used when filling is needed, and is more often found with a lower silver content. The paste form is good for soldering in tight places or in the bottom of a hole. The paste is the least economical of the four.

Flux is the paste or liquid which cleans the surfaces of oxidation and entices the base metals to accept a bond with the silversolder. The flux should be spread over the parts to be soldered, cleaning the area for approximately 1/4-inch beyond the joint in all directions. The characteristic color of steel which has been cleaned by the flux is a dull, clean gray.

To use the normal paste flux, brush large areas with an acid brush dipped into the flux. For small areas, I just dip a wooden swab stick into the paste, extract a small amount, and apply it on the

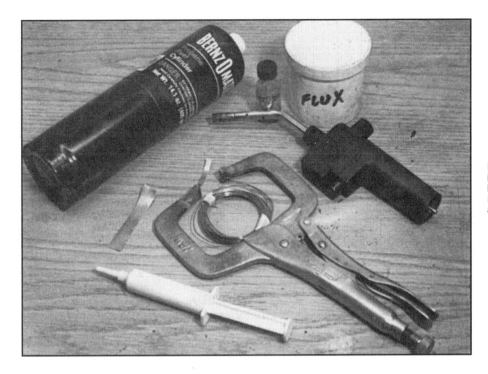

Equipment most used in silversoldering includes propane, flux, torch heads, clamps, silversolder wire, silver ribbon, a silversolder paste syringe, and solder-masking liquid.

area to be soldered. Heating the metal around the flux will cause it to spread out, cleaning as it goes.

Liquid flux is applied with a swab or an acid brush, and is the easiest to use. However, it is more likely to run off when you need it the most. A Boraxo-type cleaner can be used in place of flux in a pinch, but is harder to manage than either of the other two forms.

Silversoldering can be done with very little equipment. All one needs is some silversolder, flux, sandpaper or stones, and a heat source. In industrial environments, silverbrazing can be done in ovens which allows more pieces to be done at one time, and is a more controlled method. However, most wives would object to their ovens being used, even if they were able to get that hot.

The flame method has the advantage of localizing the heat, so that other areas are not affected. The flame of an acetylene torch is very handy for soldering, but is not the most cost-effective within the average shop. In some cases, it might be better to use propane, since that flame isn't so concentrated and forces the beginner to work at a slower rate. It is more difficult to prevent the heat from transferring throughout the piece when using a propane flame, however. Since OSHA has taken most of the asbestos away from us, there have been some fine insulating cloths developed (and I jealously guard the piece I have). I find that most welding supply houses carry some sort of insulating cloth which will help contain the heat from an otherwise inadequate heat source. Clamping the work in a vise is advantageous when you don't want the heat to spread to sensitive parts. I often place metal clamps on the part to act as heat sinks, protecting the temper of hardened areas.

The propane flame will be controlled by the type of tip that comes with the torch. If you are using an acetylene flame, adjust the flame to produce some feather coming off the cone part of the flame. A pure, neutral flame is difficult to maintain and is usually

too hot. Also, an oxidizing flame is death to a silversolder joint, so maintain a slightly rich acetylene flame. The size of the flame can be varied during the process, so you will have to judge for yourself by using as little as possible to melt the silversolder and get it to flow into the joint.

I prepare the joint before deciding which type of clamping method I will use. The joint should be fitted with as much contact surface as possible, and clamped together as tightly as possible. Good silversolder will wick into a joint, no matter how tightly it is fitted and clamped. The thinner the layer of solder between the two workpieces, the stronger the joint will be.

It is difficult to get the stronger silversolders to fill much, as the higher silver content tends to make them wick too well to bridge gaps. I also keep some cheaper silversolder around to use when the joint will not be stressed or if a fill is required.

There are many types of solder-masking compounds on the market, and the ones I have used all seem to work about the same. This masking compound is useful in protecting a surface which you want to stay free of silversolder. The flux will clean off all the area around the mask, but the mask will keep the flux from cleaning the area it covers. A small bottle of mask will last the average gunsmith for quite some time, as it will be used sparingly. A jar of flux will last me for over a year.

The preparation of the metal surfaces is one of the most important parts of any soldering job, whether it be lead solder or silversolder. All oxidation in any form, blueing or rust, must be removed. The flux will usually remove blueing to give a clean surface, but it won't do the same for rust. In some cases, where there is pitting, the pieces should be sand- or bead-blasted to remove all of the rust. Any remaining rust will ruin the joint by either weakening it or discoloring it. High-silver content solders tend to be easier to smooth

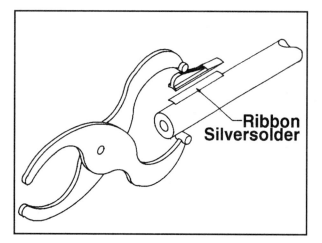

Ribbon silversolder is used for sweating on rifle and pistol sights.

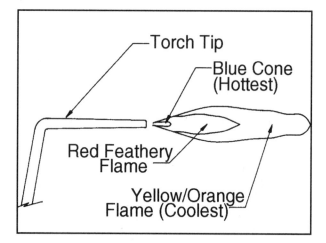

The red feathery part of the flame usually works fine for silversoldering.

out afterwards, so that's another reason to use the best solder that you can get. Joint interfaces should be planned, when possible, so that there is as little solder visible as possible. This will make it harder to see the joint, and will lessen the visual effect of having slightly different colors between metals.

To begin a silversolder joint, fit the pieces, spread a very thin coating of flux over the joint, and align the pieces together with good clamping pressure. This varies depending upon the type of solder being used. When possible, I use the thin ribbon strips between the two pieces to be joined, and choose a clamp which will flex slightly when clamped so that it will not become loose when the thin layer of solder ribbon melts and flows throughout the joint.

If the pieces are such that they can be evenly heated, the soldering process is much easier to control. Heat which has to be contained to a small location always reduces the window between the time the pieces reach flow temperature and the time when the joint has become overworked. Overworking a joint—heating it too much or too long—makes the silversolder crystallize or bubble, neither of which is tolerable. Both weaken the joint and make rough surfaces. To avoid these problems, apply the heat as near to the interface between the parts as possible, making a journey around the joint and trying to heat it evenly. Try to ensure that the silversolder flows throughout the entire joint at the same time. This is the only way to get a joint if ribbon solder is used. Wire or stick solder must be fed into the joint as it is wicked into the interface between the pieces.

When using wire or stick solder, apply it from one side and watch for it to appear in the interface on the opposite side of the joint. This is a guarantee that the solder has flowed throughout the joint and has spread evenly. The same technique should be used with ribbon, but you will need to watch all the way around the joint to be sure it has flowed everywhere it should. This will be obvious when the surface around the joint is suddenly silver in color. The flux will spread ahead of the solder. Don't use too much flux. An excess of flux will form a glass-like substance over the joint, and will spread to areas best left alone.

After soldering, let the joint cool naturally; forcing it by quenching will tend to crystallize it and weaken the braze. If the piece is such that I can't wait, I slowly lower it into water, cool end first, allowing it to sink slowly enough that I get only mild sizzling and not bubbling on the water. This ensures that the metal is not quenched enough to hurt its temper, and that the solder is contracting at the same rate as the pieces of steel or other metal.

The soldered pieces may now be blended together or shaped as needed by any method available. Remember the solder may be as strong as mild steel, but it is much softer and will be eroded or dished out when sanding with a soft backing. This is even more prevalent in the buffing stage. I use ScotchBrite wheels for blending after soldering, but only with much care. They will gouge out the silversolder faster than the steel. I find that stoning a joint is the safest and most desirable of the smoothing methods. Though I hate using files, hacksaws, and stones, I can't argue with the superior results they achieve.

The last step is to clean up and color-blend the work you just did. Any good cold-blueing solution will usually do well if the solder joint isn't too wide (see "Cold Blueing Tips and Techniques" elsewhere in this edition). In cases where the joint is at such a slight angle that there is a lot of solder showing, I cold blue and follow it with Birchwood Casey Silversolder Black. This appears to do funny things while it is working, but the results are good. Nothing, however, beats producing a hairline joint in the first place.

I like to plate some things like triggers and hammers. The Texas Plater's nickel kit is the only way I've found to hide silversolder joints on stainless-steel firearms. It will not stick on the stainless, but will plate the solder very well. I then lightly brush the joint with a Dremel wire wheel to make the nickel look like stainless steel.

I trust these tips will help you get started in silversoldering. You'll find, as I have, that you learn a new twist each time. And that's what keeps gunsmithing interesting; it would be drudgery if we ever learned all there was to learn.

Diamonds Are a Gun's Best Friend

Checkering has both aesthetic and functional values. Here's all you need to know to create your own design.

CHECKERING IS THE process of cutting diamond-like patterns on the grips and forends of gunstocks and also on handgun grips. The diamonds are usually formed by cutting crossing lines into the wood with hand tools or electrically powered checkering tools.

Three basic styles of checkering dominate the field:

● American checkering

● English checkering

● French checkering

You will find variations of these, but nearly all patterns used on firearms since the turn of the century can be identified by one of these three basic styles.

English checkering: In this type of checkering, master guidelines are first laid out to the proper angle to each other, and then scored lightly with a special woodcutting tool. The tool consists of two edges, one to "ride" in the groove previously cut, while the other cuts a new groove. Perfectly shaped diamonds are formed in this manner. The cut lines may be gone over several times to deepen them, but in English checkering, the diamonds are left flat.

American checkering: This type of checkering is similar to English checkering, except the basic lines are gone over again with a V tool which deepens the cuts and bevels the edges of the diamonds. It is the checkering most often used on gunstocks made in the United States.

French checkering: This type of checkering is also known as the skip-a-line checkering, since the final pattern is achieved by skipping cut lines at predetermined intervals. French checkering has traditionally been used on only high-quality guns, but this pattern has also been used on some burnt-in patterns on Remington guns.

Checkering Tools

The beginner can save a lot of confusion and time by buying one of the checkering kits available. Many of the basic kits start out under $20 and usually have three cutters. Each of these cutters is actually a miniature rasp that will quickly cut sharp, true diamonds once you have gained some practice. Most basic kits contain a single-line cutter, a two-line cutter, and a bent cutter designed to cut on the backward stroke. The basic kit alone will allow you to get start-

The most commonly found checkering styles are (from left to right) American, English, and French—the latter sometimes referred to as "skip-a-line."

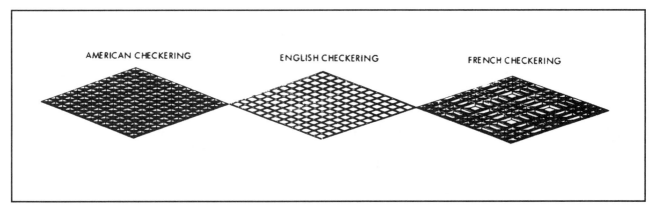

AMERICAN CHECKERING　　　ENGLISH CHECKERING　　　FRENCH CHECKERING

Three types of checkering cutters—the ones most often found in checkering kits. From left to right, single-line cutting tool, two-line cutting tool, and border cutter.

ed in checkering gunstocks and usually will suffice for any job you are likely to encounter.

Before starting to checker a gunstock, the stock must be secured firmly, yet allowed to rotate as the pattern is cut, keeping the work area at the most comfortable, controlled position. A checkering cradle is the answer.

Brownells Inc. offers a reasonably priced checkering cradle, a very simple design that will handle stocks up to about 33 inches long without marring the finish, yet will permit turning the stock as the work progresses. This cradle is also handy for inletting, sanding, staining, and finishing gunstocks, allowing you to work with both hands free. While this cradle may be bolted directly to a workbench, it is recommended that it be secured in a sturdy bench vise. By doing so, you can adjust the height and angle to better suit the situation at hand.

If you are handy with tools and you have a scrap bin that contains a few odds and ends, you might want to build a cradle in your shop. Many different designs have been devised over the years, but in general, most take on the same basic form. Plans and specifications for building your own are readily available.

Checkering Cutters

Checkering patterns on gunstocks require a minimum of three tools to cut the patterns. First, a single-line cutting tool is used to lay out the pattern; that is, the borders and the initial angular master cuts. This same tool is also used for deepening and cleaning the shallow cuts, once the pattern has been cut. The second tool needed is a two-line cutting tool designed to cut the two sets of intersecting parallel lines within the pattern. The third tool is a bordering tool used for cutting the border around the pattern. You will eventually want to add other helpful tools to these three, to make the work go smoother. Checkering tools are available in kits from gunsmithing supply houses.

W. E. Brownell (1852 Alessandro Trail, Vista, CA) produces what is known as the Full-View checkering tool. The accompanying cutters are considered to be the sharpest on the market and the combination of the Full-View handle and Brownell's cutters can be highly recommended to beginner and professional alike. The following information is furnished with the tools and is reprinted here for your information in selecting additional checkering tools and cutters.

"Those who have never done any checkering before will find either the size 18 or 20 a good size to start out with. Decide what size you want and then order cutters in that size only. If you are only going to checker one gun, a good selection would be to get W. E. Brownell's special kit in the size of your choice. This kit consists of one handle (which is the same thing as a holder); one single line finishing cutter (any angle); one bordering a cutter (small, medium, or large); one two-line spacer; one three-line spacer; and one skip-a-line spacer. The two-, three-, and skip-a-line spacers should always be ordered in the same size.

"If you are going to checker only one gun, you can get by with one handle; but if you intend to checker more than one gunstock, it might be better to have more handles so that you will not waste a lot of time changing cutters. A four-line cutter and a super-fine cutter might also be good investments.

"All regular Full-View cutters have nine double-edged teeth, which cut while moving the tool either forward or backward. Thus, it is a double-action tool.

"In order for Brownell's Full-View cutters to give the maximum amount of service before they become dull, chromium steel is used which has been heat-treated and tempered to such a toughness and hardness that they outwear any cutter made with ordinary steel. You may find it difficult to resharpen them because this hardness has a tendency to wear out files. However, some have resharpened the cutters by using a small four-inch knife file having a fine Number 4 cut, filing a couple of light strokes in between the teeth, crosswise of the cutter. Usually, three or four guns can be checkered with the same set of cutters before having to replace them.

"The single-line finishing cutters come in three different angles: 60-degree, 75-degree. and 90-degree. These cutters are used to finish up or sharpen the diamonds after the two-, three-, or four-line spacing cutters have spaced the diamonds to the correct size and have them about 75 to 90 percent completed. If the wood is soft or has large pores, or if you are cutting large diamonds such as size 6 or 18, or if you want the strongest and most durable diamonds, then use the 90-degree finishing cutter; it will produce the most durable diamond possible. On the other hand, if you are cutting in a small-sized diamond (size 24 or smaller), and the wood is hard and small-pored, then you can use the 60-degree finishing cutter to finish the job. These 60-degree diamonds afford a better gripping surface for the hand, but they are more easily broken off. Now, if your wood is medium-hard with medium-sized pores and you are checkering in size 20 or 22, you can finish up with a 75-degree finishing cutter

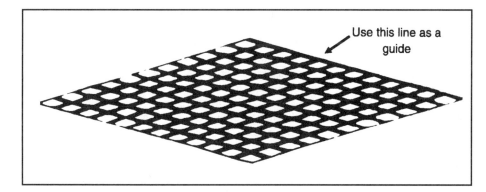

Use this line as a guide

Sample full-size practice checkering pattern. Transfer this pattern to the wood. score the outside lines with a single-line cutter or V tool, and then make parallel cuts in one direction; then cut in the opposite direction.

and produce a nice medium diamond in size and sharpness.

"The single-line super-fine finishing cutters also come in 60-, 75-, and 90-degree included angle. Instead of having nine double-edged teeth like the regular single-line cutters, they have many small teeth like a fine file; this gives a super-fine finish just as a fine, bent file would give. As far as we know, this is the first time a super-fine finishing cutter has been put on the market. It is used in place of a three-square bent file to smooth up the surfaces of the diamonds after your checkering is finished. However, it works better than a file because you can work up closer to the borders without running over. Conserve the use of this cutter for putting on a final super-smooth finish to your checkering job, unless you use it to straighten a line that has run off course when spacing in new lines. It would not be practical to resharpen this super-fine cutter as it would have to be annealed and rehardened and this would cost as much as a new cutter. The teeth on these cutters are cut in by hand and this makes them more costly.

"The bordering cutters are made in small, medium, and large sizes. The large size is generally used on coarse checkering such as 16 lines per inch, although a lot of gunsmiths use the medium-size bordering cutters on everything from 16 to 22 lines per inch. The small-size bordering cutter is generally used on 24, 26, 28, and 32 lines-per-inch checkering.

"Full-View spacing cutters consist of two-line cutters, three-line cutters, four-line cutters, and skip-line cutters. All of these spacing cutters come in sizes 16, 18, 20, 22, 24, 26, 28, and 32 lines per inch. All of these cutters, with the exception of the corner tools, are interchangeable.

"Power checkering tools: Most of the better checkering jobs have been done with hand-checkering tools. However, there are several types of power-checkering tools on the market that will make the work go faster and are especially helpful when a large volume of work is to be done.

"Power tools are expensive—many costing from $300 upward—so they really can't be justified unless a large volume of work is encountered. An individual or a gunshop that has only a few stocks a year—or even a month—would be better off sticking to the hand tools."

Getting Started

Once you have obtained a checkering cradle and a set of checkering tools, you are ready to start practicing. Note the word practic-

ing, because you are going to need a lot of this before you are ready to start on your first good gunstock. Start off with flat pieces of hardwood, then see if you can find an old wooden baseball bat or a damaged gunstock. The curved surfaces of a baseball bat will give you good practice for the rounded portions of gunstocks that will come later.

First use a straightedge to lay out one single line. Then, use the single- cutting tool to score this line, and finally, use the two-line cutter to make a series of parallel lines, side-by-side, by using a back-and-forth sawing motion.

The first attempt will convince you that a certain degree of care is necessary to obtain a regular action in the two strokes, to insure uniformity in the evenness and depth of the lines being cut. Continue to practice these strokes until the forward and backward strokes are regular in timing, and the tool advances about the same distance on each forward thrust. Always keep the lines straight, which should be about four inches long.

During practice, observe the effect of the cutting tool carefully. Try tipping the tool up or down as it passes the wood surface. If the handle is raised, the point will dig in, making the cut too deep, which will also result in tearing the wood and leaving fuzzy lines. The same will apply if the heel of the tool is brought to bear with too much pressure caused by the handle being held too low. When nearing the end of the cut, shorten the sawing motion and bring slightly more pressure on the point of the cutting tool. This will insure cutting the lines deeply enough at this point, and also prevent the cutting from going beyond the edges of the pattern.

You may want to hasten this practice session and get on to actual checkering, but you must first master cutting good, clean straight lines if you have any hopes of obtaining a good pattern on a gunstock later.

In cutting these parallel lines with the two-line cutter, once the first line is cut, one of the cutting edges rides in the line previously cut, as a guide, while the new line is cut parallel to the first one. Then move the tool over, using the line cut as a guide, and cut another line next to it, and so forth. Continue to add extra lines to the preceding ones, always endeavoring to keep them all evenly spaced and of equal depth.

When you are satisfied that you are getting good clean lines in one direction, you can start thinking about cutting parallel lines intersecting other parallel lines to form diamonds. Try a simple diamond-shaped pattern on a flat wood surface first. It stands to reason

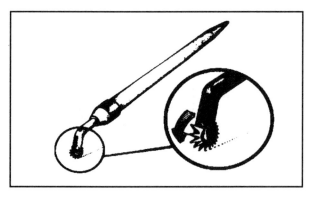

A handy tool for transferring checkering patterns from paper to wood is the pounce wheel; puts a series of deep, fine dots in the wood.

if you use a diamond shape for your outline and guideline, you will have a series of little diamonds inside of the big one when the job is finished.

Use a sheet of tracing paper, or a photocopier, to copy this pattern. Then transfer it to your piece of scrap wood. A pounce wheel (available from Brownells Inc.) is a good tool for transferring checkering patterns. Use the single-line cutter to score the outside border lines, then start on one of these outside lines, using it as a guide with the two-cutter tool, and scribe a new line parallel to it. Now, skip over and scribe another line parallel to the one just cut. Continue to add extra lines to the preceding ones, until you have all lines evenly spaced, straight, and of equal depth.

To cut parallel lines intersecting those already cut, pick another edge that is at an angle with the first one, and proceed as before, cutting parallel lines in this direction. In doing so you will start to form diamonds. Continue this cutting until the opposite side of the pattern has been reached. Pick up the single-line tool and clean and deepen these lines cut with the two-line cutter. When cutting these lines, do not go over the border lines; rather, get as close as possible, but do not go over—even if there are some gaps. We will take care of any gaps later.

Next, use the bordering tool to learn to cut the outside lines of the simple pattern illustrated. The concave bordering tool found in most kits will give a convex border similar to those found in checkering patterns on pre-'64 Winchester Model 70 rifles.

Then start over again with another pattern exactly as you did before. However, try to make this one neater. This practice may be tedious to some, but practice and more practice is a prime requisite in the art of checking gunstocks. You don't need a lot of artistic ability to master gunstock checkering—if you stick to the similar patterns—but you most certainly need the two virtues of patience and perseverance if your patterns are to come out clean and neat.

You will want to practice these simple diamond-shaped patterns until you have done several neat-looking patterns. If you can't obtain good patterns on a flat wood surface, you have no hope of putting them on the more complicated curved surfaces of gunstocks. You don't want to accomplish this in one sitting. If you work past the stage of getting tired, you won't do your best work. Checkering can be fun; don't make it an effort. Work as long as you enjoy it and then stop for a while. When you are refreshed, go back to the project. The main objective is to practice checkering regularly, without becoming too tired.

When you are getting good, clean patterns on a flat wood surface, you will want to lay out these simple diamond-shaped patterns on a curved surface, such as an old wooden baseball bat, and practice cutting them. In doing so, every beginner is going to have a tendency to curve his hand as the tool is pushed back and forth to cut the lines, following the curvature of the surface. This should be avoided, because there is no way the lines will end up straight if cut in this manner. The cutting edge of the tool must be kept flat on the surface, and the hand also kept moving in a flat, even direction, while the rounded surface is turned. Only in this way can you hope to achieve straight lines in the final pattern.

It is best to hold the curved object, such as a baseball bat, in a checkering cradle. However, for practice, a round piece of wood may be laid on a flat surface and rolled with one hand, while the other hand is used to guide the motion of the tool. The movement will be similar to a rolling pin used to roll dough for pie crust; that is, roll the bat toward you as you are cutting forward. Roll it back without cutting, and then roll it toward you again as you cut. Continue this operation until the pattern is complete. When you begin to get good patterns on the curved surface of a baseball bat, or similar object, then you are ready to start thinking about checkering a gunstock.

Checkering Size

The design and layout of a checkering pattern for a rifle or shotgun should be of a size that is practical. Fortunately, good looks and utility may both be incorporated in the overall design of checkering patterns.

Checkering size is identified by the number of parallel lines to the inch in each of the two intersecting sets of lines. For example, parallel lines spaced $1/8$-inch apart (16 lines to the inch) is a very practical size for the beginner to attempt. Parallel lines spaced $1/24$ of an inch apart, intersecting another set of like spacing, are known as 24 lines to the inch. I have seen checkering as coarse as 14 lines to the inch and as fine as 32 lines to the inch, but 18 or 20 lines per inch seems to be the most practical, and best looking.

The size of the checkering should be coarse enough to maintain a definite friction between the shooter's hands and the wood. If the size is too fine, the lines will be shallow and quickly fill with dirt, oil or other objectionable substances, causing the pattern to become smooth; much of the benefits of checkering will then be lost. Patterns with lines spaced closer than 24 to the inch are normally used only on "show" pieces that will never be used in the field. On the other hand, when the size used is less than 16 lines to the inch, the pattern will look somewhat crude and feel uncomfortably rough to the hands.

When selecting the checkering size for a custom rifle, the condition and texture of the stock's grain must be considered with respect to checkering size. Many an amateur will try a 24 line-per-inch pattern on a coarse piece of wood and wonder why his work doesn't look as good as the master stockmakers. In most cases, the masters use a close-grained high-grade wood; otherwise, they could not obtain such quality work.

The wood used in most conventional factory arms made in the

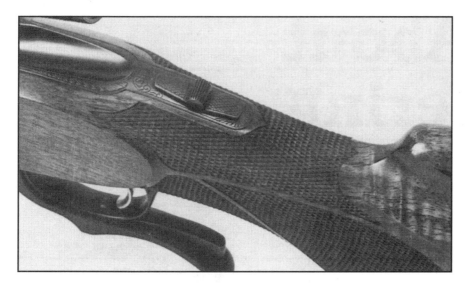

Flawless checkering job by Shane's Gunsmithing of Minocqua, Wisconsin. This is the goal for which every beginner should strive.

United States has straight, fibrous grain that is tough and strong but extremely hard to checker with any size much finer than 18 lines per inch. Wood of this kind seldom cuts cleanly, but has a tendency to tear, especially those that have not been properly dried. The same wood that has been thoroughly seasoned over a long period of time will chip easily. Any attempt to checker with anything over 24 lines per inch is a waste of time. I have had reasonably good luck with 20 lines per inch, but never anything finer. There is little sense in cutting a finer pattern on hunting guns. The coarser checkering will not wear down or become dirt-filled so easily.

Hard, well seasoned, close-grain wood found on the better grade rifles and shotguns can be checkered in patterns running 24 lines per inch, and in wood on extra-fine quality, the lines may run as small as 32 to the inch, or even closer together. I have never seen any checkering smaller than 32 lines per inch. Guns stocked with wood of this quality are generally used more in a gun cabinet than in a field. Under these conditions, fine checkering is useful for appearance, and will remain in good condition indefinitely. Fur-

thermore, most of these guns are elaborately engraved, which in turn demands a certain amount of stock ornamentation in order to match. However, for most of us, a neat-looking checkering pattern of between 18 and 20 lines per inch is all we need, or should have on our firearms.

For the sake of appearance, the size of checkering on a stock should be consistent. Don't use one size on the forearm, and another on the grip. Use the same size throughout.

Some patterns that contain no border lines are known as borderless patterns. Over the years, most of the production models of firearms have their checkering patterns framed within a two- or three-line border. It is believed that bordering is one means of hiding imperfections that go with hurriedly applied hand- or power checkering. This is true to a certain degree; unevenness in ending the criss-crossing lines along the outer extremities of the pattern can be artfully covered up by a border. No one, however, should get the impression that all bordering is for the purpose of hiding imperfections.

More About Checkering

Gunstock checkering has both aesthetic and functional values.

THE FIRST STEP in checkering an actual gunstock is to decide upon a suitable pattern. You can design your own, copy one from an existing stock, or use one of the decals available. Ready-made patterns offered by Stan deTreville are applied directly to the stock, and will follow the contours of the stock perfectly. The pattern may then be transferred to the wood with a pounce wheel, or checkered straight through the decal. About 20 different patterns, from simple designs to highly complicated ones, are offered by deTreville and may be ordered direct or through Brownells, Inc.

If you have an existing pattern on one of your stocks that you would like to transfer to another stock, place a piece of ordinary writing paper over the pattern you wish to copy, and tape it down securely. By rubbing back and forth with a soft charcoal pencil, blacken the paper over the lines of the checkering pattern cut into the stock. You will note that the under lines will show through, being much lighter in the blackened area. The paper can then be removed, and the outline traced with carbon paper onto a piece of hard-surfaced cardboard cut out for use as a pattern for laying out the design on the stock to be checkered; or the piece of paper itself may be taped to the new stock and the pattern transferred with a pounce wheel. The same pattern may be used for both sides of the grip, or the forearm.

If the forearm is to be checkered with a pattern that starts on one side and continues on around the bottom to the other side (one piece), some method must be used to insure uniformity. First, establish the exact center on the underside of the forearm and draw a line running lengthwise along this established center; starting at this point in your layout, cut the outline for one side of the forearm checkering pattern. Do not cut in the centerline. Then fold and tightly crease a sheet of writing paper; open up the sheet and place the line of the fold on the centerline marked on the stock. Now blacken that section of the paper that extends over the pattern outline cut into the stock. Remove and refold the paper. Then with scissors, cut out along the light line showing on the darkened half of the paper. When the paper is again unfolded, the sheet will spread

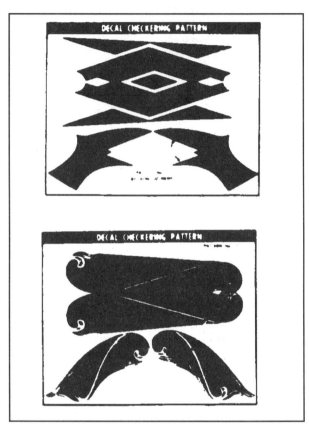

Many ready-to-use checkering patterns are available from Stan deTreville, Box 33021, San Diego, CA 92103.

out into the overall design of the entire forearm's pattern. Now transfer the patterns on the paper to a sheet of thin cardboard, and match it to the forearm cut that you made previously. Bend the rest of the pattern around the stock. The remaining design can be laid out with a lead pencil for cutting in with the single-line tool or veiner. Some stockers also use an X-acto knife for this operation.

Cutting the Pattern

The shape of the small diamonds that go into the pattern will vary to some extent, depending upon the angle used for the guidelines. In general, however, if an angle of 30 degrees is used for the intersecting lines, the patterns will look good and provide a satisfactory grip. Stockmakers often lay out their work, so that the small

The veining tool has many uses for the checkerer, from laying out guidelines for new patterns to re-cutting existing ones.

diamonds have dimensions that are one-third as wide as they are long, for a cut of three to one. Some even cut $3^1/_2$ to 1, but this is about the limit, or much of the desired effect will be lost.

To establish the angle of cuts within the checkering pattern, it is recommended that a template be used made from cardboard, plastic, or thin sheet metal (the latter is the most desirable). Such a template should be laid out in the form of a large diamond, a good size being three inches in length to one inch in width.

By placing this template in position within the overall pattern, the initial (master) guidelines for checkering may be first scribed with a pencil and then cut in with a single-line tool or veiner. After the master lines have been cut into the wood, the remaining parallel lines are cut with the two-line spacing tool. Before the pattern is cut, however, the stock should be firmly positioned in a good checkering cradle. Some stockmakers build their own, while others purchase ready-made checkering cradles. Brownells offers a simple design that will work well and is reasonably priced. Another elaborate design is available from B-Square Co. Any design will work, as long as it holds the stock firmly, and allows turning as you checker curved surfaces.

Some stockmakers prefer a three-line cutter over the conventional two-line type, claiming that the three-line type makes it easier for two of the three rows of teeth to follow in the already cut grooves to keep the new line made a uniform distance from the others. While this is true, the three-line cutter is harder to learn to use correctly than the two-line cutter. For this reason, it is recommended that the two-line cutter be used to learn on; then switch to the three-line cutter if you find it better. The one that is easier for you to produce the best checkering patterns is the one you should use.

After the first set of lines have been scored over the entire pattern in both directions, the entire pattern should be deepened and cleaned with a single cutting tool. This last operation will level all four sides of the small diamonds, causing them to become pointed and sharp.

To border, use the original lines cut for laying out the outside shape of the pattern, and place the inside row of teeth of the bordering tool in these, using this line as a guide for the borderline that will be cut parallel to it. Work around the pattern in much the same manner as you would when using the two-line tool for cutting the inside diamonds. A sharp bordering tool cuts deeply and cleanly, and requires no following up with a single-line tool, although you may want to use a toothbrush to clean out the grooves.

Once the entire pattern has been cut, use a stiff brush to clean out all grooves before dipping the brush into some light gunstock oil and polishing the grooves with the brush and oil. Don't use conventional stock finishing oil in the checkering itself; this will gum up the diamonds. One of the favorite finishes for checkering is Dem-Bart Finishing Oil applied without filler. If the entire stock is to be finished, use the filler on all areas of the stock, except around the checkering pattern. Then, when the oil finish is applied to the entire stock, use a toothbrush to get in between the grooves of the checkering with a back-and-forth motion so as to polish them. In doing so, make certain that all excess oil is removed, so as not to fill the grooves.

French Checkering

The basic principles of French checkering are essentially the same as the type already described, except that lines are skipped at various intervals to form a pleasing pattern. For example, a regular two-line cutting tool is used to cut, say, three lines; then a spacing tool with twice the width is used to cut one line; then three more regular lines are cut; another is cut with the spacing tool, and so on until the pattern is completed. The effect may be varied by changing the number of regular lines cut, the number of lines skipped, or both.

In laying out this type of checkering, care must be taken to use a pleasing pattern. For the first tries, cut a sample pattern or two on a piece of scrap wood, just to see how the lines will work out. Using these samples, you should be able to obtain good matching lines that correspond to the shape of the pattern you are using on the stock.

Correcting Mistakes

Should your first pattern have perfectly straight lines, with no overlaps, and also perfectly pointed diamonds, then you did much better than me. However, in most cases, you are going to make mistakes during the checkering job, and if you are aware of them when you make them, so much the better; most can be corrected. At the outset, carefully check every line before cutting the next one. If the line is not straight, it must be corrected immediately if the remaining lines are to be straight and evenly spaced; otherwise you are going to have a sloppy job.

One of the best tools for straightening out checkering lines is the Kennedy Jointer, and is available from Brownells. While its main purpose is to straighten out checkering lines that have gone astray, it can also be used to make layout and other lines used in straight patterns. The long length of this tool almost automatically straight-

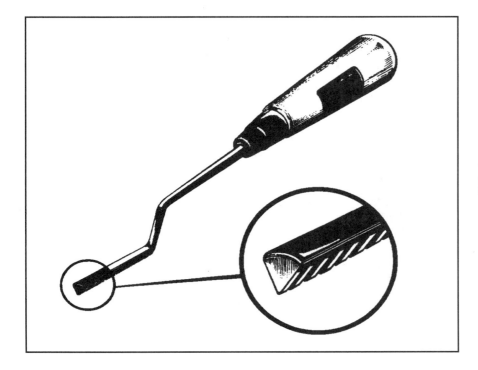

The Kennedy Jointer is one of the best checkering tools for straightening out crooked lines.

ens up the lines if it is pushed back and forth over the crooked line, with a slight downward pressure on the handle.

Another useful tool is Dem-Bart's Special S-1 tool. It cuts with a pulling motion, rather than a pushing motion, and is ideal for getting right up to the border and other tight places.

As you gain more experience in checkering gunstocks, you will find many other useful tools that will make the work go much easier. Some of these tools include bent needle files for final pointing of diamonds; a veiner for outlining and tight corner work; a checkering pounce wheel for transferring patterns, and dual cutters for laying out work.

When a large volume of work is encountered, you may even want to take a look at MMC's electric checkering tool that makes checkering a breeze once you get the feel of the tool. The only problem is the cost, which is around $500 for a complete outfit; this is too much to spend on a tool that will only be used infrequently. Virtually every professional shop doing any significant amount of checkering uses one of these power checkering tools to save time. In examining checkering patterns cut both by hand and with this power checkering tool, there is little difference between the two.

The main points are to lay out an appropriate pattern carefully, use good sharp tools, take your time, correct all mistakes as soon as they occur, and do a good job.

When you get tired, or find yourself making more mistakes than you should, stop and take a rest, even if you only cut one or two lines. When you do this, all you need is more practice to become an expert at checkering gunstocks.

Recutting Old Checkering

In refinishing gunstocks, you will eventually come across a stock that needs refinishing and has checkering that needs restoring.

Refinish the stock, using only a toothbrush with finish remover on it to clean the old checkering pattern; do not sand the areas that are checkered. A wire brush can be used to remove some of the old finish between the diamonds.

When the patterns are as clean as possible, use a bent three-square file to point up and further clean the old checkering pattern. Apply just enough pressure (and it will not take much) to keep the cutting edge of the file centered. Advance the tool in a push-pull motion keeping the arm close to the body to maintain straight lines. Keep the grooves free of dust by blowing or brushing. Then clean the entire recut pattern with a toothbrush and apply two coats of Dem-Bart Stock Finish, again with a toothbrush.

Since the 1960s (and probably before), many firearms came from the factory with pressed or burnt-in checkering patterns...falsies, if you will. These patterns may be recut with checkering tools—using the existing patterns as a guide—to obtain a better looking job.

There are at least two ways to go about it. In most cases, the "lines" forming the diamonds are raised while the diamonds themselves are recessed—just the opposite from regular checkering. Therefore, if the "lines" are used as your guide to cut the pattern, your cut will have to be relatively deep to get below the recessed diamonds. An easier way is to use the diamond points as a guide for your cut and completely reverse the existing pattern. Before attempting this technique on a good gunstock, try to find a damaged stock to practice on.

There will be many times when you may want a gunstock checkered combined with a few little simple carvings such as an oak leaf or two. To be a competent gunsmith, you should at least have the knowledge and the ability to perform these simple carvings... and you can do it; all it takes is practice.

Checkering Metal Parts

This job taxes tools and patience but you can get a better grip on your gun because you did it.

By Dennis A. Wood

TODAY'S FIREARMS MANUFACTURERS are turning out precision arms with the latest technology in manufacturing equipment. Most companies are using computer numerical controlled machinery loaded with pallets of rough steel stock. These machines turn out clone after clone of parts that would make Eli Whitney gloat, almost 170 years after his death.

Investment casting is another technique used in the manufacturing of firearms. This process brings frames and other parts out of a mould with very little machining left to perform on them. Ruger is one such company that has taken investment casting to the pinnacle of success with their revolvers, pistols, shotgun and rifle actions. The savings in the cost of manufacturing is passed along to customers.

Can you imagine the price of firearms if each frame had to be milled, drilled and hand fit with the cost of today's labor? Check out the prices for a custom 45 semi-auto comp gun or the custom rifle metalsmiths' charges and you'll soon see the value of a hand fit and finished firearm. Some folks are purchasing factory firearms and then getting custom touches added as their budgets allow, in stages, a little at a time. One of the few custom touches that can give parts of a firearm a non-slip surface is metal checkering. Straight-line serrating can be done by the investment casting process or machined via the CNC method as long as the metal surfaces are relatively straight and flat. When the surfaces are curved, machining becomes more difficult to perform. This gets expensive as far as machining is concerned because multiple articulating axis machines are extremely expensive.

Serrating long surfaces such as the top of a 45 semi-auto slide

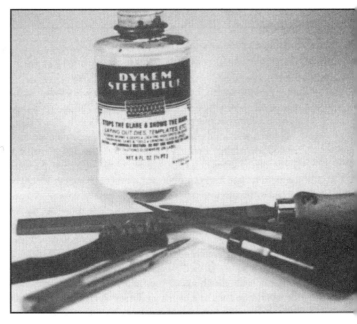

Layout dye, scribe, steel brush, file for spacing checkering and finish files.

can be done in a basic milling machine with a serrating cutter. Achieving the cross-hatch pattern as used in metal checkering can be done with an articulating vise and some very basic hand tools. About the only way to get checkering done on some of the curved parts found on firearms is to do it by hand. The purpose of checkering metal is much the same as the reason checkering is found on a gun stock or handgun grips, the provision of a non-slip surface providing control of the firearm. The difference, of course, is the material. Wood is obviously much softer than steel, so checkering metal is a lot more taxing on tools and patience. Checkering coverage of metal surfaces always involves less area, so the expenditure of time to do the job is much less also.

Metal checkering files can be had in five sizes. The #00 will cut 20 lines per inch, #0 will cut 30 lpi, #1 will cut 40 lpi, the #2 cuts 50 lpi and size #4 will cut 75 lpi. The files are $25 give or take two bucks depending on the spacing selected. Both sides of the $1/2$-inch wide by 6-inch long file have teeth with safe or smooth sides. There are also two line metal checkering files to be had that will come in handy for tight areas that a $1/2$-inch file may not get into. As with any type of file, use a file handle. For practical purposes the #0 at 30 lpi or the #1 at 40 lpi are about the most useful. If metal check-

Bolt release checkered at 30 lines per inch.

ering gets too coarse, it gets too hard on a person's hide. On the other hand if the checkering is too fine, like 75 lpi, it just doesn't provide a good positive purchase.

In preparation of the metal surface prior to checkering you need not polish to a mirror finish. A finish done to 280 or 320 grit will suffice as long as all major scratches or nicks have been removed. Once the metal surface has been smoothed, a coat of layout dye should be applied to the area to eliminate any light glare off the metal. A black permanent ink felt tip marker works well for this also. Once the ink has dried, two master lines will need to be scribed into the surface at 90-degree angles from one another. You may want to experiment with this and try different angles for different effects, but 90 degrees will give a square shaped pyramid. The master lines need to be scribed in deep enough so that your 30 or 40 lpi checkering/spacing file will ride in it without jumping off track. A carbide tipped scribe and a short section from an old steel tape measure works best for me when laying out these master lines. Scratch the master lines several times with the carbide scriber so that you get a good line. Once the master lines are cut, the spacing of lines can be started.

Lay the left or the right edge of the checkering file in one of your master lines and lightly scratch the spacing lines in. It doesn't matter if you cut from left to right or right to left, but with this file you will only be able to cut on the forward stroke. Dragging the file backwards while still in contact with the metal surface is not good for the teeth so this should be avoided. It's not always possible to finish a row from one direction. Swap the part end for end in your vise and finish the rows you started. This will help to keep the lines evenly spaced. Also, only cut or scratch 4 or 5 lines from one direction then swap the part end for end and cut 4 or 5 lines from the other direction. Don't start on the crossing over lines just yet. Finish all the lines in one direction from one master line. Once this has been accomplished and the spacing looks correct, start the procedure in the other direction from the other master line.

If your eyes are getting worn out like mine, an OptiVisor or Magnifocuser set of magnifying glasses at $2^1/_2$-power will help immensely in your line spacing layout and also relieve the close work strain on them. Once all the lines have been laid out in both directions, look them over to see that the spacing looks even. If you have one, a screw thread pitch gage can help determine the correct spacing width.

After inspecting your line spacing layout and deciding you are

happy with how it looks, the next step is to cut the lines deeper. A 60-degree three square needle file in coarse or medium cut takes care of this phase readily enough. Progress from line to line in whichever direction you choose making sure to cut each line as close as you can to the same depth. Here again cut all the lines going in the same direction and then the opposing lines from the other direction. Watch the shape of the little diamonds as they are forming, as we want to maintain uniformity of shape. When the tops of the diamonds have a barely visible amount of layout dye left on them, change to your fine cut 60-degree three square needle file. Use this finishing file for the last few strokes to bring the diamonds up to a point. This file will follow in the previous file's track, just try to maintain a smooth forward stroke. Use a stiff steel wire brush to scrub out the furrows between the diamonds and prepare the part for blueing.

Serrating surfaces involves the scoring of the metal with parallel grooves providing a non-glare, non-slip area. This process can likewise be done by hand with a metal checkering spacing file and then finished with a bent 60-degree three square needle file. Long, wide, flat areas are best done in a milling machine that will do the job much faster than by hand filing. There are a couple of commercially available serrating tools. One of these is a single line cutter much like a woodruff keyseat cutter with the ten teeth ground to a 60-degree included angle. Cost is about $48 for this one. The other serrating tool has a machined steel round shank of $^1/_2$-inch diameter that holds a carbide insert that will cut 20 or 32 lines per inch depending on which insert is selected. This tool with one insert included will run you $105. Replacement spacing inserts are about $46.

A reputable serrating tool can be fashioned from a discarded $^5/_8$-18 or $^9/_{16}$-18 four-flute tap. A bottom cutting tap has a short lead or cutting edge, but a plug tap that has a cutting lead of about seven threads should have the lead end cut off with an abrasive cutting wheel. Taps have very precisely ground teeth at 60-degree included angles and are made of tough M-3 tool steel and can be had for about $6 from Enco Manufacturing in Chicago, Illinois. To use as a serrating tool the tap will need to be altered a bit. Two rows of teeth 180 degrees apart will need to be ground off. The two rows of remaining teeth, 180 degrees apart, will now become your 36-line-per-inch serrating tool. The crown or top of the teeth on one remaining flute will be exactly opposite to the root of the teeth on the other flute. When held stationary in an R-8 collet, in your mill's quill, the 18-tooth tap will now cut 36 lines per inch. If you would like a courser serration, then remove the other row of teeth leaving one flute that will cut 18 lines per inch.

The shank on most all taps is an oddball size so some provision to bring the shank diameter on the tap up or down to a colletable size will need to be made. If you can get someone to grind the outside diameter of the tool shank down to a standard size to fit a standard collet size, this would be the best option. A brass split sleeve bushing can also be made up with the inside diameter that of the tap's shank and the outside diameter that of the collet diameter you plan to use. Using a drill chuck would be the last option unless you have very little runout with your drill chuck. Drill chucks are usually attached by means of a tapered plug going into the back of the drill chuck. The side cutting pressure may be too much for the holding ability of the tapered plug and may let go of the chuck and drop it. So the first two options are the best.

Magazine Repair and Lip-Shaping

Knowing how to identify and solve magazine problems will make your life easier and you happier.

By Chip Todd

NO MATTER WHAT kind of semi-automatic firearm you have, few things about it can spoil your outing as much as a failure to feed rounds properly. In spite of great strides being made to make semi-auto pistols competitive in matches, little has been done to improve the feeding characteristics of their magazines. How important is magazine feeding to the operation an autoloader pistol? With the exception of obvious safety considerations, I can find nothing that causes more trouble than a poorly designed magazine.

The magazine in most semi-autos does more than just hold live rounds; it is usually responsible for orienting the cartridge into the proper height, angle and direction to enter the chamber and then kicking the rear of the cartridge case upward into alignment for insertion. There are some ways to modify other components of the firearm to partially make up for a poor magazine, but nothing takes the place of a well-designed magazine.

Types of Magazines

The magazine that causes the fewest problems is the type integral to the pistol or rifle. Since this magazine type doesn't lend itself to modification, we will not cover it here.

Otherwise, the simplest removable magazine design is the straight magazine with in-line stacking of the cartridges typified by the standard 1911 45 semi-auto pistol magazine. It is a straight, in-line magazine with a notch on the side for retention in the pistol. This is a successful design because it is straight and was designed for a straight-walled, rimless cartridge.

A straight magazine is not suited for rimmed, semi-rimmed, or tapered cartridges. The cartridge rim, which has a larger diameter than the body of the case, causes the ammo to curve when stacked in the magazine. The curved magazine was invented to accommodate a curved stack of cartridges and prevent the rims of rimmed cases from overlapping and interfering with feeding. One of the best examples of this is the good, milled magazine for the AK-47. It has to feed a cartridge that is tapered quite a bit.

The better 22 LR magazines such as the Atchisson 22 conversion for the AR-15 rifle are also curved. This rimfire cartridge has

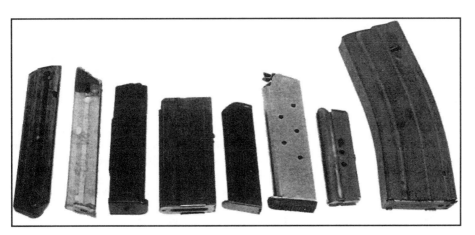

A representative sampling of magazines include: the Luger (straight, wood bottomed), Ramline (clear with constant force spring), Mac 12 (plastic), M1-Carbine (straight, staggered, with removable bottom), Colt M-16 (curved, staggered, removable bottom).

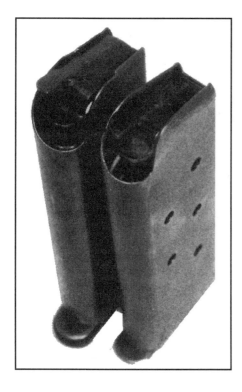

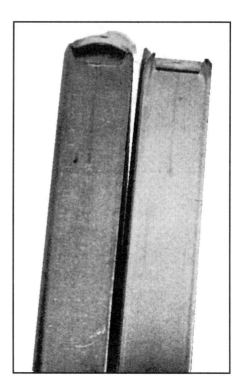

Left—Magazines with rounded and flat followers can easily be seen by looking at the top of each at the rear. This also illustrates the difference between a magazine that releases the cartridge rear earlier, (left), and the stock lip configuration.

Right—This view shows rounded and flat followers from the slide's viewpoint.

a rim that is quite a bit larger in diameter than the body of the shell. To get the shell to feed properly, this magazine has shaped sides to keep tight control over the attitude of the little cases.

Magazines are often wider than a single row of shells would dictate in order to get more shells into a shorter vertical dimension. These magazines arrange the shells in staggered columns to achieve this. One of the most successful of these has been that for the Browning Hi-Power semi-automatic pistol.

The 9mm Parabellum shell is best served with a staggered magazine, as the shell is slightly tapered and its stacking describes a definite arc. Having the shells in a staggered condition, the taper directs the nose of the shell toward the center of the magazine instead of causing trouble by trying to slant the shell above it as in the Luger. John Browning understood this, (and most other facets of gun design), and designed the Hi-Power with the staggered configuration.

Another of the common tapered shells is the 30 Carbine shell. It does fairly well in short, straight magazines, but the magazine must be bent like a banana if more than ten shells are to be held. Thus, larger magazines for this cartridge are commonly called banana clips and were widely used in WWII. The military designed a clipping device to hold two of them together and it was called the "Jungle Clip." The terms "Jungle" and "Banana" are often interchanged.

It was a common practice to add an insert to the front of a magazine to allow the use of shorter shells in a receiver designed for the longer shell. Remington does the opposite with its rifle receivers that are chambered for shells on the shorter end of the scale for that receiver. The 243 Rem. chambering for the Model 700 series rifles have a filler in the rear of the non-removable magazines, for instance. High Standard semi-auto pistols were equipped with magazines of the same exterior dimensions, but with fillers in the front of the units to keep the 22 Short cartridges to the rear of the magazine. This spacer helps relieve the extractors of the greater burden of keeping the front of the cartridge from falling into an attitude that causes a jam.

There are two popular firearms with rotary magazines—the Savage Model 99 and Ruger 10-22 rifles. The former is equipped with a non-removable five-round rotary magazine and the latter with a removable 10-round unit. Both designs function well and have passed the test of time.

One great advantage of the rotary magazine is that the uneven end-to-end configuration is easily addressed in each station or through the design of the rotating drum mechanism. There is also a good rotary hybrid magazine for the 10-22 that has two straight columns side-by-side that take a 180-degree turn to shorten the length. The only drawback to these magazines is the failure of the design to have feed lips or casting that satisfactorily emulates the magazine it replaces. I have had to reshape the upper casting quite a few times in the past to achieve reliable feeding.

There are some few firearms that were designed to use a round-shaped magazine to handle the greatest number of cartridges in the smallest amount of space. The most recognizable of these would have to be the "Tommy Gun" of gangster fame. (The military version of this same gun used a straight stick magazine). These drum magazines are best left to those who specialize in them.

Of the non-removable types of magazines, two of the most common types are often forgotten by most gun owners: the tube magazine used in most shotguns and rimfire rifles. There is an improvement in the in-line tube magazines used on rifles that spirals the trail of the cartridges so that the pointed front of one is canted so that it cannot fire the primer of the next shell. Since tubular magazines are not usually equipped with the feeding mechanism (lips), we will not cover those types here.

Good and Bad Magazines

There are many different ways to make a magazine, and several of them are outstanding.

The nice, heavy AK magazines made in Russia were "milled" of stamped sheet metal. Milled pieces were spot welded to them. Even this small bit of machining would price a magazine out of the market in the West. The finest thing about the AK magazines is that the milled portion is responsible for the feeding of the shells and isn't very easily bent out of shape. Even these milled portions seem to have gone through a secondary stamping step to form the mouth more accurately and consistently.

One of the best magazine manufacturing methods used in the U.S. is using seamless extruded tubing. But this is only practical for straight-sided magazines, so the majority of the magazines have bodies either rolled or stamped and machine-welded for neatness and economy. This calls for some secondary operations that raise the cost somewhat, but assures a good magazine. One of the most common faults of magazines is their feed lips.

There is a cost-effective method of joining magazine sides with tabs and slots for these tabs. This is to be avoided, in my experience, as these joinings aren't stable or slip-free and will only lead to trouble. If the tabs are only used to hold the metal in place for a subsequent spot welding, then they have a legitimate reason to exist.

I view magazines with removable bottoms with mixed emotions. I find nothing wrong with a well-functioning 1911 magazine, and if it isn't functioning well, you can be assured that a removable bottom isn't what is needed to get it working. It doesn't even make it much easier to work on. There are, however, some magazines whose upper-end design doesn't lend itself to the same disassembly as that used with a standard Colt 1911 magazine with its welded bottom plate.

Of those where bottom plates are removable, there are several types that are most often encountered. There is the slip-on to a stop type, the slip on until a plunger pops into a detent or hole type, and the pinned type. These are not the only types, but just the most-often-seen.

Of these, I like those where plates slide on easily and are retained with a plunger and detent. The "slip-on until the drag overcomes your determination" type of removable bottoms should be labeled "installable bottoms." They seem to attract more rust than the similar bottoms which slip on with more clearance and are retained by detents.

A widely-used method of joining the baseplate to the body of the magazine is to flange the bottom of the magazine body and stamp bottom plates with rolled edges to slide on the flanges of the body. I have found some very good Mauser and Walther magazines done this way. To be done right, the tracks formed by the bent metal must have parallel surfaces and not wedge-shaped slots which make the removal and installation of those bottom plates difficult at best.

The WWI Parabellum magazines were rolled steel with pinned bottoms made of walnut, but these were replaced with aluminum bottoms and finally with plastic. While the bottom added nothing to the function of the magazine, the wood was a lot classier and more desirable to the collector.

Some modern 22 firearms have die-cast bottoms and feed lips. Die-casting is sufficient in the case of the bottoms, but less-than-desirable when used for the feed lips. In theory they should be trouble-free, but I have seen many of these come in my shop with feeding problems.

The Orlite magazines for the AR-15s and M-16s are fairly good and may be the wave of the future, but they just give me the feeling of shooting in a county fair shooting gallery. I have not run into any trouble with them, and their feed lips seem to be fairly stable.

Last, there are the hybrid plastic body and metal-headed maga-

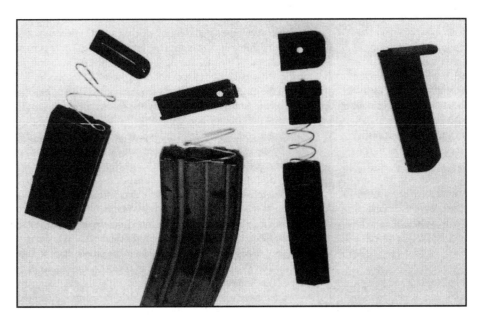

Different types of sliding, removable bottom plates from left to right: bent lip and rolled groove; bottom plug detent; sprung plate detent; and spring plate with dimple.

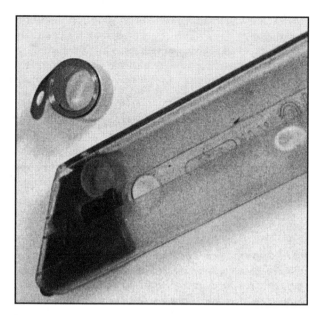

This is a Ramline plastic magazine with a constant-force spring and a similar spring beside it.

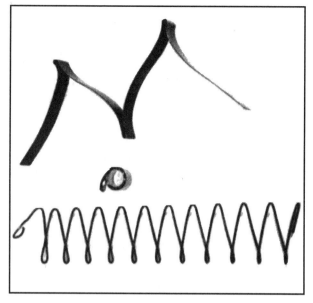

These are three spring types: Folded flat leaf, constant-force, and obround with upper eyelet end bent to aid follower angle.

zines like those found on some of the aftermarket rimfire magazines. These have been very popular with the manufacturers, but they just don't have the same good track record compared to the good all-metal magazines from Colt and High Standard. The best magazines, in my opinion, are those that are thick metal with welded bottom plates. The heavy metal sides make good, stable magazine mouths.

Springs

Magazine springs come mainly in four types: round coil, obround coil, flat folded, and constant-force. The flat-folded is the type found on most rifle magazines, the round coil springs less common, and the obround spring is found in nearly all of the handgun magazines you will see. There is also the more common constant-force spring. This last type is quite a joy when it comes to loading a long column of shells, as the force doesn't increase as more shells are forced into the magazine. It works just like the retractable steel rules used by carpenters and handymen everywhere. The few rotary magazines on the market use a torsional spring similar to that used in watches.

In terms of operation, I rank the constant force spring as causing the least amount of trouble, followed by the torsional, flat folded, and the obround/round (a toss-up) springs.

In the case of staggered magazines, the force on the magazine spring is lessened due to some of the downward force being misdirected into the sides of the magazine. If the insides of such a magazine are rough, the drag against the sides will cause loading to be tougher.

Failures

Let's get into some of the main failures of feeding and how to remedy them. Most that are magazine related can be attributed to

lip failure or the magazine not being in the proper place.

Magazines and firearm actions are made to be cycled at operating speeds, so the feeding of a firearm should always be checked at full speed, excepting the checking done on open-bolt models. Any cycling of any firearm should always be done with non-firing dummy shells. To do otherwise is to invite an accident. It is most important to brightly mark all dummy shells so they can be readily distinguished from other ammo.

The stovepipe jam, the feed ramp jam, and the three-point jam are the most common jams in semi-autos. Other common jams include the failure to extract the empty shell, the slide not picking up the shell from the magazine, and the cartridge dragging on the breechface.

In the stovepipe jam the empty case is caught between the slide and the chamber upright or sticking out to the side. These jams are often caused by the shell hitting the ejection port because of a port that is too small or the ejector not doing its job. If the ejector isn't one of the extended ones, it is more important to have an enlarged port, as the late ejection caused by the shorter ejector makes the timing of the ejection more critical.

Another common cause of this type of jam is the dropping of the case by the extractor before the shell can be struck by the ejector. For these reasons, I usually enlarge the ejection port, slightly extend the ejector, and fit the extractor, if feasible.

In the three-point jam, the bullet's upper front is caught against the top of the chamber with the lower middle of the case bearing against the lower mouth of the chamber, and the upper rim pressed against the breechface. One of its causes can be traced to the magazine not releasing the rear of the shell in the proper place to allow the shell to align with the chamber in time. Another cause of the three-point jam is related to proper throating of the chamber.

I often have guns brought in that have the cartridge jamming when the front of the slug jams into the rear of the barrel at the bottom of the chamber, effectively stopping the slide in its tracks. Proper ramp-to-throat transition is the real cure, but a good magazine follower design often lifts the front of the bullet over this interface, totally eliminating this confrontation. Improper seating of the barrel in the chamber nest in the top of the receiver can cause this jam, whether it be a three-point or slug to the rear of the chamber. Either jam is unrelated to the magazine.

If the three-point jam doesn't respond to other treatment, a problem that I find almost universal with magazines, particularly 1911 magazines, is that the rear of the shell is contained too far forward so that the rear of the shell is held down when the slug strikes the top and the throat of the chamber causes a three-point jam. If it is always the last shell, then look into changing the follower to a rounded-top type so that the last shell's rear is kicked up the same as if it were being raised by another shell.

In lieu of a rounded follower, you must get the rear of the shell up sooner. To do this, the sides of the lips must be formed to hold the case down for about a $1/2$-inch of travel and then to release it quickly so that it can jump up onto the breechface in line with the chamber.

The accompanying CAD illustration shows the difference between the average 1911 magazine's lips and those formed to feed better. The same principle holds true for almost any magazine for either handgun or rifle.

A small amount of work with a Dremel cutoff wheel and duckbill or long-nosed pliers will do wonders for the three-point jam. The same can be accomplished with two sets of pliers and not cutting with a cutoff wheel, but the chances of it not looking very professional are higher. It is a good idea to round-off or blend the sharp edges of the magazine where it was cut so that you won't scratch your hand on the modification.

If the cartridge is getting jammed against the breechface and the middle of the case isn't hitting against the throat of the chamber, then the likely cause is the bullet dragging against the breechface. The rear of the rim of the cartridge case must travel up the breechface as the slide is pushing the shell forward, so the surface finish of

the breechface is important to the smooth transition of the rim against the slide. This is more common in the smaller calibers, although it is also found with the larger ones, too.

This kind of jam can be caused by the rim of the shell getting stopped by either the surface roughness of the breechface or an extrusion around the firing pin hole. Either one can be remedied with an abrasive stone and, obviously, neither of them is related to any fault of the magazine construction or design.

Other Failures

Failure to extract, another common cause of jamming, can usually be traced to either a rough chamber or a problem with the extractor or extractor spring—problems not related to the magazine. I usually check the angle of the underface of the extractor by looking at it while it is extracting, or if this is not possible, I hook a case onto it and feel how well the extractor holds onto it. The angle often needs to be sharpened to slightly more than 90 degrees. A simple pull on the extractor's hook will give you an idea if the spring is stout enough.

The extractor should have a surprising amount of force, but needs to be moved easily enough to allow the extractor to be cammed over the rim of the shell with the recoil spring alone.

When the slide misses the top cartridge, which is not really a jam, the cause can be traced to the magazine being lower than proper, among other problems.

The positioning of the magazine is dictated by whatever mechanism or physical feature is employed to hold the magazine in the firearm. I cannot remember running into any case where the holding scheme doesn't directly affect the magazine's positioning. Be it the bottom of the magazine or a notch in the side of the magazine, if the magazine is too low, something must be added to the magazine to make it come into place.

I have found that a good piece of spring wire, or even a good guitar string silversoldered into place, will cure most improperly-cut or wallowed edges of magazine notches. I just cut a short length of wire of the proper diameter, and silversolder it into the notch or onto the bottom of the magazine to shim the magazine up into the

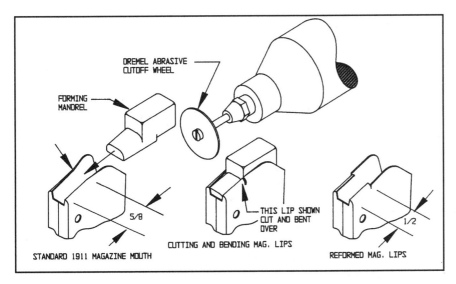

This view shows a stock magazine and forming mandrel; Dremel cutoff blade cutting lip to bend over mandrel;
and finished configuration of modified magazine mouth that allows better case kick-up.

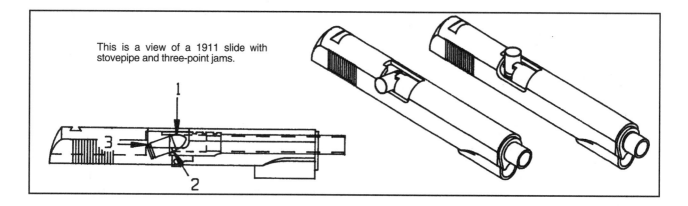

This is a view of a 1911 slide with stovepipe and three-point jams.

proper place. The spring wire (or music wire) is a much harder alloy than any the magazine could be made of, so I have never had to redo one of these shimming jobs. This is only effective if the magazine is loose and can be pushed up into the proper place in the receiver.

If the magazine is seated properly, then the rear of the magazine is most likely at fault. Bending the rear of the mag lips should be approached cautiously, as some magazines have rolled-over rear tops that just cannot be easily bent into a higher configuration. These will require some special consideration beyond the scope of this article. If the construction of the rear of the magazine's mouth can be bent such that the rear of the cartridge is allowed to seat higher, then some duck-billed pliers are exactly the thing to bend the lips wider apart. Care must be exercised to keep the top of the magazine from dragging on, or interfering with, the slide's bottom.

Another situation that is encountered in failure-to-feed problems is the cartridges getting stuck down in the magazine instead of allowing the spring to lift them up into queue. This can be caused by a spring with too little pressure due to length or poor temper, a cartridge that hasn't been sized properly, or an overlength cartridge. The overlength cartridge is easy to spot, as it is jammed tightly against the front of the magazine and resists being moved. It will usually free up if the front of the bullet is raised with a knife or screwdriver blade. After checking the front of the magazine for obvious dents, I would check the overall length of the cartridge against data published in one of the respectable reloading books. If the length checks out all right, the front-to-back dimension of the magazine should be checked against a "known-good" magazine.

If a slight push on the top of the uppermost cartridge moves it down easily, and all of the shells drop toward the mouth of the magazine when the magazine is inverted, the trouble will probably reside in a weak magazine spring. This is assuming that the obvious condition of a stuck follower isn't present. If the follower takes more than a very slight push to move it toward the magazine's base, your problem will most likely be one or more dents in the sides of the magazine or some residue inside such as rust.

Another problem I have seen more than once is the magazine being dented at one of the holes in its side from having a punch stuck through it roughly when removing the follower and spring. This is the correct method of removing the follower and spring, but it must be done gently.

To remove the magazine spring from a magazine with a welded

bottom, use a dowel or punch handle to push the follower about halfway down the magazine and stick a punch, pin, or dowel through the hole in the side of the magazine nearest the underside of the follower and then remove the pressure against the top of the follower. This will capture the magazine spring down in the body of the magazine and usually let the follower fall out of the mouth of the magazine. If it doesn't come out any other way, use some forceps or tweezers to pull the follower out.

The follower's top surface should be angled enough from the back of the follower to hold the cartridges at an angle great enough to keep the nose of a proper length shell from digging into the front of the magazine. This can be checked while the cartridges are still in the magazine. If the angle of the follower cannot be easily bent into a greater angle, then chances are it was also too strong to be bent out of its proper angle.

Too Much Spring Pressure

It is possible for the magazine spring to be exerting so much force on the cartridges that a light recoil spring just doesn't have the oomph to strip the shell out of the magazine and still have enough force left to finish chambering it. This can be easily seen during dry cycling if you look closely. The slide will either stop with the shell partially out of the magazine, or it will stop in a fashion that might be mistaken for an extractor spring that is too strong. The difference can be distinguished if the top cartridge is pushed downward to check its freedom and force. If the magazine spring is too weak, the slide will insert the cartridge into the chamber slowly enough to be noticeably the fault. If the cartridge is run into the chamber rapidly, but the extractor isn't jumping over the rim of the case, then look for a weaker extractor spring or a rough extractor ramp.

I have run into feeding problems where the top of the magazine dragged on the bottom of the slide, causing sluggish cycling. This is most easily checked. The cure is to either get another magazine or to file off the top of the magazine until the slide is allowed to function without dragging on the magazine.

As mentioned earlier, a rounded follower can be indicated if the shell jams when the rear of the case is still held down by the magazine lips. The follower by itself cannot make up for lips that don't want to turn loose of the shell, but I have found no instance where a rounded follower was a detriment. Its function is to emulate the action of a shell on the one above it by lifting the rear of the shell as high as it would be raised if there were to be another cartridge following it.

If it weren't designed well, it could slow the slide down from friction, but that could hardly be more than the rim of another shell would be. I routinely replace flat followers in guns whose rounded followers I can find, as this not only looks good, it improves the functioning of the gun as well.

One of the very few Brownells tools I have not found up to my expectations is the rounded follower forming die. It just bumps an ugly dent in the stock follower. Brownells, however, also offers some beautiful, already-formed round followers that are as good as money can buy. I was satisfied with their previous round followers, but, as they often do, they changed them for some even better-looking ones from Pachmayr. They are available in both 45 and 38 Super sizes and are stainless steel. I have found nothing else to do as much for aligning the last cartridge with the chamber.

Slide release tabs on some magazines, such as the Colt 1911, serve the function of raising the slide catch when the last round is fired and the follower is in its top position. This tab is on the side at the front and engages a boss sticking out from the slide hold-open mechanism.

The most bothersome feature on the Colt 45 and its clones is the propensity of the hold-open tab to miss and ride over the slide release's boss causing the magazine to stick in the gripframe, the slide release to bind, and the slide to return to battery. This is frustrating to even the experienced gunsmith, as it is cumbersome to check with some follower designs.

Everybody making magazines touts the slide hold-open tab on their particular follower, but I have found none better than that on the Pachmayr rounded followers. On those pesky tabs that miss the slide release, the tab can be bent toward the outside of the magazine by gripping the tab from the front and bending it sideways toward the outside of the magazine. Restraint must be used, as the tab can be bent out so that it hangs up or drags on the side of the magazine, though. The essence of this adjustment is to insert the magazine into the receiver watching what the slide release tab on the follower does. If it misses the slide release boss, bend the tab outward slightly until it raises the slide release each time the empty magazine is inserted into the gun. Check the magazine release mechanism each time to insure that the magazine still ejects properly.

If the slide release is hard to push down and it tries to tilt the magazine follower forward, I have often found that the angle of the follower is too slight and the rear vertical member of the follower is being pulled away from the back of the magazine. Having the magazine's obround spring in backwards will most definitely cause this to happen.

The front of the obround spring must be pointed upward and higher than the rear of the spring. If it already is, then try bending the front of the spring up higher. This will usually do the job.

Few things on an automatic pistol are more mysterious to the average shooter than the functioning of the magazine. He knows which magazines work better for him, but usually doesn't know what makes the magazine function better, so he has to buy until he gets one that comes from the factory just right for his pistol. Nothing is really mysterious about the magazine if you just think about what each little feature does and how it can screw up the operation. Magazine work is really quite easy to perform with a little practice.

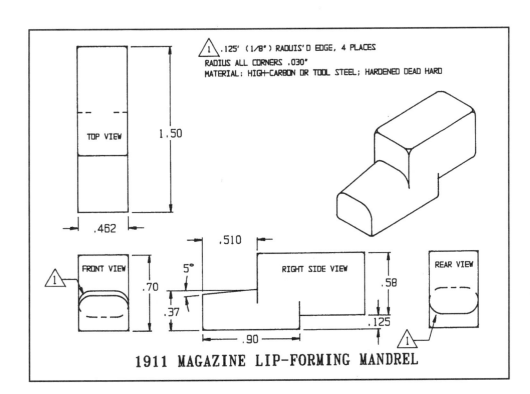

This details Todd's 1911 magazine lip-forming mandrel.

Tricks to the Trade

Every gunsmith has little tricks of the trade that he'd never share. Here are a few you can claim as your own (but don't tell anyone else about them).

By Chip Todd

IN THE SEVERAL YEARS that I've been teaching gunsmithing, it seems like almost all of my students have asked at one time or another for little tips they can use in their day-to-day work.

For some, the question may be a simple thing like: "How important is a vise pad?" For others, it might be: "What do I do about boogered up screw slots?" It really doesn't matter what the question is, because most of us in the trade are actually anxious to help those who want to learn.

None of these items I'll discuss with you are complicated enough or take enough time and experience to devote a full article to, so I decided that I would combine all of my favorite shop tips into one feature.

The Ultimate File Cleaner

Cleaning files with a file card or wire brush is fairly ineffective in many cases and can accelerate the dulling of your best files. Here's a trick I learned years ago from a gunsmith in Inglewood, California.

Flatten the neck of a large-caliber cartridge case and push it against the file's teeth parallel to their cut. Several passes will shape it to that particular file and you will find that it will remove even the most tenacious particles. It will clean down to the bottom of the cuts, and will find its way into your favorite toolbox.

Vise Pads

I've purchased many vise pads from commercial sources and find that they don't last long, or that they aren't suited for the task at hand.

The least hardy are the thin sheets of lead, as they are cleaved in two by clamping anything with a line contact such as a gun barrel. I do keep some lead sheets around, but I'm selective about using them.

Lead ingots, which you have around for your bullet casting, work well, although they aren't as easy to handle as sheets of lead. I often machine reliefs in them to fit the occasion, figuring the worst that could happen is that I would have to melt them into ingot form again. I keep one around to fit oddly-shaped barrels as on the Smith & Wesson Model 19, (with its ejection rod shroud) and Colt Pythons. These special blocks are sacred and don't get used for any other purpose.

Some of Brownells Powdered Rosin makes the ingots grip blued barrels without any damage to the finish. The most "damage" that I've seen to barrels removed this way is some of the lettering on the barrel getting filled with lead. It is easily removed with a sharp pin or the point of an X-acto knife blade.

I often paint on a coat of mold release agent and make Acra-Gel casts of a particular object that has to be clamped repeatedly. As it takes time for the gel to harden, this is only useful when I think ahead.

Powdered Rosin

Powdered rosin is handy around any gun shop for a variety of uses. The main use around my shop is to prevent barrels and other round pieces from slipping when clamped in a vise and subjected to torque. The rosin will provide the friction needed when taking rifle or pistol barrels from their receivers or in screwing them back in. So far, it has always prevented the lead blocks I use between the barrel and vise from scarring the finish.

It can be used as an exceptional flux for melting lead alloys, albeit an expensive one when compared to things like old soldering paste, paraffin wax, or commercial bullet-casting fluxes. It will, of course, act as a good soldering flux when you are out of any other cheaper kind.

Repairing Screw Slots

Peening the burrs and displaced metal on screw heads can effectively renew them to the good appearance essential to any firearm.

To hold the offensive heads while preparing them for restoration, I use a steel block, drilled and tapped for all the common screw threads I use (and some I don't use). I have two of each size; one threaded to the top, and one in which I have drilled a

A flattened cartridge case works well as a file cleaner and won't dull the file the way wire brushes can.

slight counterbore to clear screws not threaded all the way to the head.

Run the offending screw into the proper hole and carefully peen the burrs back into place. Flat-headed screws are the hardest to do, as they require peening the entire top surface of the head and filing it flat. Peening enough to remove irregularities in the head will call for some clean-up of the slot. This is easily accomplished with auto ignition point files or needle files which are available from Brownells. The supply house also sells screw-slot files which have toothed edges and smooth "safe" sides. The screw-slot files are primarily useful in filing new slots when making screws, but they're also helpful in reclaiming slots. Be careful not to widen the slot any more than necessary. This sticks out like a sign around your neck saying "Amateur."

Filing the top of the head back into shape and polishing it will make a stainless steel screw ready to install, or a carbon-steel screw ready to blue. To bring it to its original condition, I usually use my buffer-mounted ScotchBrite wheel on the screw head, followed by the cloth wheel with white rouge. Holding the screw while polishing it is simplified by using a pin vise, or make a much handier tool by installing a handle on a small drill chuck. I use the drill-chuck tool to hold screws and pins while buffing, peening, sandblasting, or other operations around the shop.

Blue the carbon-steel screws with any of the popular blueing solutions. The head will usually take the blueing solution well if you clean it with a degreaser and detergent and water. It's not as hard to get a good blue on a screw head as it is a gun; the area isn't large and flat, and the screw head will respond to brushing with a bristle brush you wouldn't dare use on a firearm that has been just polished.

Making a Hand Vise

I've never seen a hand vise that proved to be as useful as one made from an extra drill chuck. Okay, I know they are for different purposes in most cases, but I've never really used my hand vise much and my students and I use the hand-held drill chucks quite often. I made three sizes which cover everything from pins up to $1/4$-inch-diameter rod stock.

Start by fitting a bolt into the rear threads of the chuck, and cutting the bolt off at about $2^1/2$ or 3 inches total length. Use a lathe to shape a piece of wood into a handle, or use a plain piece of doweling. If a lathe is not available, the handle can be drilled and shaped entirely on a drill press or whittled by hand. If the threaded shaft is installed first, you can often turn the piece in the press while holding a grinder against it to simulate the effects of a lathe.

The same thing can be done for sanding it. I use strips of emery cloth like a shoeshine rag, letting the drill press or lathe do the real work for me. If the wood used is one of the oily types like walnut, teak, or rosewood, you won't have to put a finish on the wood. It will darken with time, however, as it picks up dirt and grease.

The threaded shaft can be glued into the handle with any type of glue, but I prefer Brownells' Acra-Weld or Acra-Gel. If you don't have any cyano-acrylate glue, a drilled hole and roll pin will lock the shaft in just fine.

It is unnecessary to use the key to a keyed chuck since the jobs you'll use this tool for usually don't require such a tight hold. The little chucks sold for use with Dremel tools are just about the right size for your smallest hand chuck, and the ones made for $1/4$-inch drills are the right size for the medium-size vise.

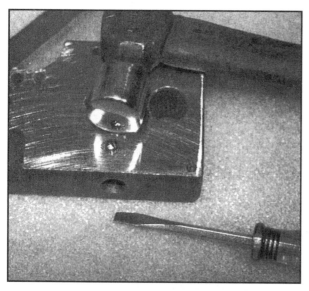

A steel block, drilled and tapped for all sizes of screws, helps restore damaged screw slots to nearly good as new.

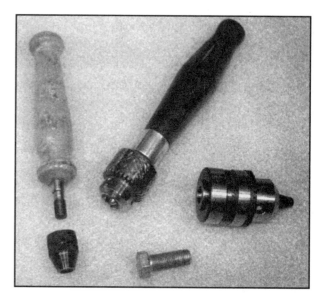

Improvised hand vises made from drill chucks hold the small jobs better than the big vises. They're easy to make as well.

Lengthening Coil Springs

Pulling coil springs in order to lengthen them will only introduce overstressed areas which will collapse and ruin the performance of the spring. The first spot to stretch will be weakened and will continue to be the spot which stretches. This is a no-win situation which is best avoided. So what do you do?

Coil springs can be successfully lengthened by peening them in a controlled manner with a ballpeen hammer. I start by measuring the relaxed length of the spring in order to quantify the growth, then I measure the inside diameter to more easily pick a piece of drill rod or a pin punch to fill the inside of the spring. This "filler rod" is the key to lengthening the spring without exceeding the metal's yield point in any location. You can use the shank end of a drill if you don't have the right size drill rod. I never throw away a broken or used-up drill bit if its shank is in good enough condition to be used for a gun pin or to fill the inside of a coil spring.

You will need a hard steel surface onto which to place the filled spring while rapping it with the flat end of a ballpeen hammer. I make the filler rod fit the inside of the spring as tightly as possible without having to pull hard to remove the rod. Pulling an overtight rod from the spring might negate all your lengthening work if it stretches the spring while coming out.

Place the side of the filled spring on the hard steel surface and rap it sharply with the hammer while rolling the spring and filler rod. Be sure to keep moving the impact point of the hammer up and down the entire length of the spring while rotating it evenly. You should be able to judge the growth of the spring by watching the space between the coils growing. It is essential that you move the hammering about—always seeking the places where the coils are more tightly packed. The spring will grow slightly in diameter, but not enough to matter in 99 percent of the jobs.

This growth will usually be only one or two thousandths of an inch, but will help you by loosening the spring on the filler rod. Removing the rod from the spring frequently to measure the growth, I repeat the process until I have a spring that does the job. I've never had a spring fail that was done this way.

Incidentally, if you don't have a collection of springs, you should start one. I never throw away a spring, because I'll need it as soon as the garbage truck clears the driveway. [T.J. Stuntebeck finds lots of uses for the flint springs in disposable cigarette lighters. -Ed.]

If you collect springs, you will eventually have a collection of tangles. The easiest and fastest way to untangle coil springs is to drop the mess on a hard surface and watch them scatter. At a plant I ran, we had "spring separation boxes," used to contain the overactive members of the spring clumps which tend to run for cover like roaches hearing a light switch. Very few tangles can resist this trick.

Allen Head Screws the Easy Way

Allen head or hex sockets for any purpose can be made easily in the shop. They're quite handy for things like full-length recoil rods, or even your own custom-made hex-socket screws.

Hex sockets are extremely easy to make, but the mere thought of doing it seems to discourage most people. Even most machine shops don't know they can make their own. It's done by forcing a tool called a "broach" into a drilled hole, thereby shaving the corners of the hex down into the bottom of the hole. To my knowledge, broaches for this purpose aren't available over the counter. It just isn't a common practice to do something which we all have left up to some mysterious process by screw companies.

I have made hex-socket broaches from die pins (which are about as hard as steel comes), using a spin indexer on a surface grinder. This was an unnecessary nuisance, as I learned while making spe-

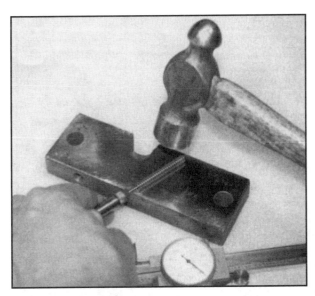

You can lengthen a coil spring without introducing a weak spot by filling the spring with a pin, then rolling and peening it.

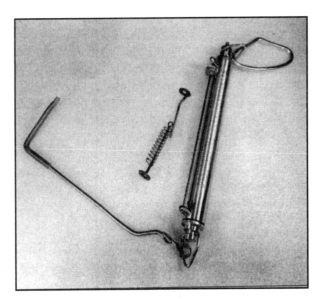

This improvised spring-rate jig can be used with your trigger scale. It's more precise than using a postal scale.

cial wrenches for my handgun-security devices. I needed a hole in the ends of some hex wrenches and couldn't anneal them with normal methods.

Good hex keys are made of air-hardened steel which doesn't cooperate with normal annealing practices, so I decided to simply let that work for me. These hard steel wrenches can be cut with a Dremel cutoff wheel, and be made to serve as excellent broaches. Be sure to make the cut end flat and square to the axis of the hex rod, with all the corners being sharp and clear-cut.

First decide what size hex socket you need, and pick out the hex wrench you'll use for a broach. Measure it across the flats (the shortest measurement) and drill a hole of that size where you want the hex socket, to a depth of about 0.200-inch. I slightly chamfer the top of the hole to help center the broach. This also makes the finished result look like the best hex socket you ever saw.

Place the piece in which you want a hex socket with its other end solidly against an immovable object, or clamp it between two pieces of lead to protect the sides and keep it from moving during some serious hammering. If the hex you choose is very small, you will need to use a very short piece of the hex wrench mounted into a steel rod approximately $1/4$-inch in diameter. You will need only a length equal to about three times the major diameter of the hex sticking out of the holder. This holder should be of a very hard steel like 4140 or better. I use drill rod for this purpose.

Position the hex wrench/broach piece over the hole, align it coaxially with the hole, and tap it into the hole about $1/16$-inch with a steel hammer to get it started. Check the alignment before going in farther and do any straightening required to bring it back into line with the axis of the hole.

By now, you'll need to grip the broach with some type of plier, as the piece you use should not be long enough to invite bending during hammering. With everything aligned, drive the broach in to

the bottom of the hole. You'll know when you reach the bottom.

Pull the broach out and you have a good hex socket. If the broach sticks in the hole, clamp it with Vise-Grip pliers and carefully tap it until the broach comes out. Very few machine shops can make an Allen socket that easily.

Rebound-Rod Fitting

Most law-enforcement agencies will not allow trigger stops on their weapons under the premise that the stop might become unadjusted and prevent the gun from firing.

This leaves the gun without a good-feeling trigger and prompts people to design an innocent-looking stop and name it something else. Smith & Wesson did this for the Model 28 double-action 357 large-frame Highway Patrolman, calling the trigger-stop replacement a "rebound bar" (since it is inside the rebound slide). It's a steel rod that limits how far the rebound slide can move and, subsequently, the trigger's travel. It's a solid piece and can't change—except in a direction favoring the safety of the policeman.

Fitting it can be a study in patience, as the perfect fit with the gun open will keep it from firing when the sideplate is installed. The sideplate has a hole into which the rebound-slide stud fits. With the sideplate off, the stud is flexed toward the rear of the pistol by the rebound spring, and forced back into proper alignment when the sideplate is reinstalled. The stud hole in the sideplate forces the stud back into proper position, and the rod, which fit before, doesn't fit anymore. Solution: File the rod shorter and retry the gun with the sideplate back on. If you have filed off a little too much, peen the rod lightly with a hammer or crimp the rod with a pair of wire cutters. Done prudently, this gives you another chance without having to start over with another rod.

If you remember the fact that the rebound-slide stud is flexed when the sideplate is removed, it makes the job much less frustrat-

Hex broaches of various sizes can be made with a fairly simple process that even a machine shop would be proud of.

ing. There is no way to explain the feel of a properly adjusted trigger stop to one who hasn't experienced a good one. That's one of the subtle touches that highlights the difference between a superb trigger job and an average one.

Compression Spring-Rate Measuring Jig

Making a jig to measure a spring's rate isn't difficult, and can be done with little in the way of tools. There are several good ways that come to mind, and I'll go through them all before you need to make a decision.

The need for a jig disappears if you have a postal-type scale available, as it is no real trick to measure the spring. (Apply downward force, and measure it with that force still applied.) However, if you want to really get down to quality measurement, you will need a jig that allows you to utilize the accuracy of your trigger-pull scales (see photo). Somehow, that seems more like gunsmithing and less like handling mail. The problem boils down to converting a tensile force (pull) into a compression force (push). Nothing new about this; outboard boat steering dampers are a good example of this technology at work.

First, you'll need flat washers and either welding rod or the proper size and weight cotter pins. The only tools needed will be long-nosed pliers and a soldering iron (for the cotter-pin type) or wire cutters and an acetylene torch (for the washer-and-wire type). It is also feasible to make the washer-and-wire type using a soldering technique instead of welding the metal. The size of the coil spring to be tested dictates the size of the jig, so different sizes may have to be added to your toolbox from time-to-time.

Section 2
Handguns

Basic Work on 1911 Pistols 82

Troubleshooting Smith & Wesson
    Revolvers 86

Inside the Kahr K9 93

Smoothing Ruger Single-Action
    Revolvers 97

Fitting 1911 Slides and Frames 101

Mounting Handgun Scopes 103

Handgun Security Devices
    You Can Make 107

Working Colt Single-Action
    Revolvers 110

Repairing Beretta 92 Pistols 114

Smoothing the T/C Contender's
    Trigger Assembly 118

Troubleshooting Browning 9mm
    Hi-Power Pistols 122

Troubleshooting Luger Pistols..........125

Checklist: Charco Revolvers.............130

Lorcin L9mm Pistols.......................131

Easy Revolver Jobs for
    Beginners.....................................134

Working the Glock Pistols................142

Correcting a Taurus Revolver's
    Problems......................................145

Installing Melded Rear Sights 149

Working Charco/Charter Arms
    Revolvers......................................152

Fitting M1911 Extractors 156

Smith & Wesson's Third
    Generation Pistols......................158

Troubleshooting Ruger P-Series
    Pistols 162

Basic Work on 1911 Pistols

The first step in troubleshooting any firearm is understanding how it functions, or how it should function.

By Chick Blood

THE M1911 AND M1911A1 are recoil-operated, magazine-fed, self-loading pistols.

The M1911A1 is a variation of the M1911, but its modifications have no effect on the pistol's operation or maintenance. Specifically, the tang of the grip safety of the M1911A1 is extended to provide better protection for the firing hand; a clearance cut has been made on the receiver (frame) for the trigger finger; the trigger face is knurled and cut back; the mainspring housing is curved instead of flat; the top of the front sight is wider. Outside of these differences, the pistols are identical. Overall length is 8.59 inches. Height of front sight above bore axis is .5597-inch. Weight with a full, seven-round magazine of military ball ammunition is 2.437 pounds.

During loading, a charged magazine is inserted in the receiver well. The slide is hand drawn to the rear, cocking the hammer and compressing both the recoil spring and the mainsprings. The magazine follower, seated above the magazine spring, raises the uppermost cartridge into the path of the slide. When the slide is released, the compressed recoil spring forces it forward and the slide strips

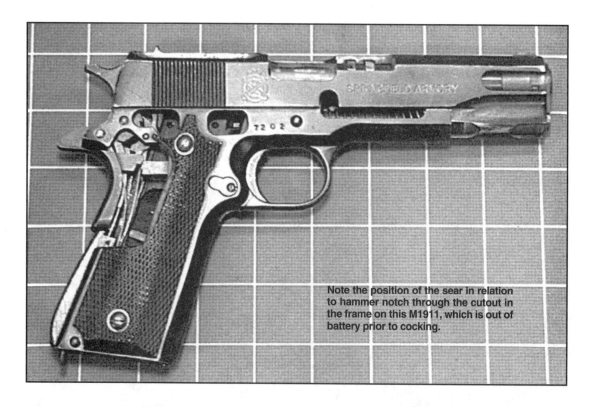

Note the position of the sear in relation to hammer notch through the cutout in the frame on this M1911, which is out of battery prior to cocking.

off the cartridge, carrying it into the barrel's chamber. As the slide nears its forward position during this motion, it contacts the barrel's rear extension (hood) to move the barrel forward. The rear of the barrel then swings up on its link. When both the barrel and slide reach the full-forward position, they are locked into place by the lugs on the upper barrel and lugs inside the slide and are prevented from further forward motion when the lower barrel lug encounters the slide stop pin.

The pistol is now in battery. When the hammer was cocked, the hammer strut moved downward to compress the mainspring. Under pressure from the longest leaf of the sear spring, the nose of the sear has engaged the hammer notch to hold the hammer in the cocked position. The disconnector is seated in its recess under the slide, under pressure from the center leaf of the sear spring, and ready to transmit any motion of the trigger's bow to itself and the sear. Still, before the pistol can be fired, the grip safety must be pressed inward, the thumb safety must be down (unlocked) so the sear is free to release the hammer and the slide is free to move rearward.

In the process of firing, squeezing the trigger disengages the sear from the hammer notch. The hammer, forced forward by the mainspring, strikes the firing pin, causing the pin's front end to hit the primer of the cartridge. The resulting detonation ignites the propellant powder charge that is contained in the case, generating gases that drive the bullet through and out the bore. At the same time, the pressure from these gases drive the slide and barrel to the rear. The barrel moves only about $1/8$-inch before swinging down to disengage its upper lugs with those in the slide and coming to a stop at its lowest position. The slide continues on back to again cock the hammer, extract and eject the empty case and compress the recoil spring. The spring keeps returning the slide forward until the magazine is empty, at which time the follower raises the slide stop into the slide stop notch and locks the slide back. NOTE: The weight of the slide and the barrel significantly exceeds the weight of the bullet, so the latter is out the muzzle before the slide and barrel begin to unlock.

So it goes—and has gone for over 80 years—with the M1911. It is truly simple in design and this makes servicing it simple.

This isn't to suggest that you're not going to encounter problems every so often with one just out of the box. Case in point, a brand new Norinco brought in because the slide wouldn't return fully forward after it had been hand-racked back. After merely field stripping the gun, the cause was immediately obvious. The machining of the slide and frame rails was so crude their surfaces looked like an old-fashioned wash board. A few passes with a slide rail file, along with some serious stoning and polishing, allowed the pistol to function perfectly.

Many of the troubles you will encounter with the M1911 will involve what are called its major moving parts, even though some don't move. Let's discuss what you can to do correct the problems they cause.

Trigger

If the trigger is loose in the frame (we're talking sloppy to the point that the bow may be undersized), you can enlarge the bow on a reforming die or replace the trigger. Whichever you do, insert the trigger in the frame, the magazine in its well and make sure there is clearance between the two. If they make contact, it can cause the

During cocking, the slide pivots the hammer back and the sear engages the hammer's notch to prevent the hammer from falling when the slide is released and until the trigger is pulled. The barrel has moved down to unlock its lugs from those in the slide.

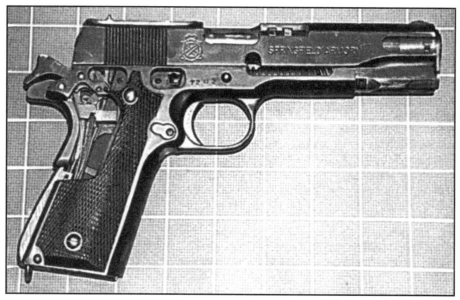

In battery with the hammer and sear engaged and the barrel locked up, the pistol will not fire until the grip safety is depressed and the thumb safety is engaged in its frame notch.

trigger to drag; so can burrs on the trigger, trigger bow and trigger bow channel in the frame. Stone them.

With adjustable triggers, the bow can drag on the disconnector. If you suspect this, correct it by filing the bottom rear of the bow a tad below flush. Stiff triggers can be caused by excess sear spring pressure, uneven hammer hooks, incorrect sear face and break-away engagement angles. You can ease excess pressure by bending the spring toward the rear of the pistol. You might be able to true up the hammer hooks with stoning, but if they're too worn, replace the hammer. If the sear is the culprit, replace and refit it. Creepy triggers may be rough sear, rough sear notch or worn sear/hammer pins related. To correct, replace or refit the sear or hammer and replace the pins as needed.

Hammer

When a hammer fails to cock, whatever is causing it has to be replaced. This includes a hammer that has had its cocking notch broken or lowered to extremes; a broken hammer strut; a damaged sear or sear spring. A hammer that drags when cocked could be rubbing against the frame; the ejector or its strut might be bent.

If drag is due to the strut, replace it. If drag is related to frame-rub and the hammer is not bent, stone the side of the hammer that's making contact. You'll be able to see the marks. However, if the contact is between the hammer and ejector, you may have to create clearance for the ejector or replace it.

Hammers on Series 70 and earlier models have a half-cock notch and can drop when the slide is released if the notch is broken or has been altered. In either case, replace the hammer. Dropping from half-cock on Series 80 and later models is normal. They have no half cock notch.

Sear

It is the sear's job to hold the hammer back until the trigger is pulled. When it fails to do so, there could be several reasons why.

Check out all of them. The sear spring might have become weakened. You can make a field fix by bending its long leaf—the one that contacts the sear—toward the pistol's front. It is better to replace the spring. The sear might have been worked over by someone who didn't know what they were doing and, accordingly, loused up the sear engagement angles. If that's the case, install a new sear. Sears that bind or creep are most likely too short and you'll have to fit the pistol with a new one. Other factors that create bind or creep include a rough hammer notch; worn sear/hammer pins and a rough disconnector bevel. Polishing and replacement are the respective remedies.

A more serious sear malfunction in Series 70 and earlier models is "bounce." This rarely, if ever, occurs when trigger pulls are above $3^{3}/_{4}$ pounds. Sear bounce lurks in the $2^{1}/_{2}$-pound pull range and is due to extremely shallow sear/hammer engagements, light sear spring and light mainspring pressures. The sears in these pistols can literally bounce out of the full cock position and past the half-cock notch. The hammer follows through, the gun fires and keeps right on firing until the magazine is emptied. Believe me, a 45 gone full auto makes an H&K MP5 sound as slow as a pump gun. Watch out for bouncing sears and always test fire any M1911 on which you've touched the sear, hammer, disconnector, sear spring or mainspring before considering the job complete.

Disconnector

All else being in order, a normal disconnector prevents the release of the hammer until the slide and barrel are safely locked together in their full-forward position. Additionally, this prevents firing of more than one shot with each squeeze of the trigger. If the disconnector is too short—new factory disconnectors are 1.28 inches to 1.29 inches overall—it can cause doubling and even full auto fire.

Always replace a disconnector that doesn't mike out to factory spec. Always make it easier for it to do its job by cleaning up any burrs, nicks or dirt in or around the disconnector's port at the top of the slide and inside the frame. When you fit a new disconnector, keep in mind that its being a little too long is okay as long as there's no drag between it and the slide. To operate correctly, this part has to move down far enough to disconnect and up far enough to reconnect. You should check this movement visually, with the slide installed and with a sear spring that has had its right and left leaves clipped off.

I'm sure it has been written here before, but you can test whether or not a disconnector is creating problems before you disassemble the pistol. It's about to be written again. Cock the hammer, pull the slide 1/4-inch to the rear and hold it in that position. Pull the trigger and release the slide without letting up on the trigger. If the hammer falls, the disconnector is worn on top. For another test, pull the slide all the way back and engage the slide stop. Squeeze and hold the trigger back as you disengage the slide stop. The hammer should not fall. Now release the trigger and squeeze it again. This time, the hammer should fall. If it doesn't, check the sear spring for weakness before you make the decision to replace the disconnector.

Barrel

Heavy leading in a barrel is often caused by reloads that are too hot or that employ lead bullets made from too soft an alloy. Reloads that refuse to chamber will usually do so nicely after the slug has been seated to the proper depth and the round has been taper crimped, unless the slugs are semi-wadcutters and the barrel hasn't been throated to accept them. In that case, throat the barrel. You can do this free-hand with a Dremel or Foredom tool and a grinding point. Go slowly if you've never throated a barrel before. The basic rule in throating is to flare the rear of the barrel without deepening the chamber. If you ignore the rule, you could remove too much metal, reduce the required degree of case support and create a condition that will result in blown rounds. Since that's a dangerous condition, and since the cost of replacement barrels starts in the $65-$80 range today, you might want to opt for one of Brownells' barrel throating jigs. It lets you remove a very specific amount of material by degrees and avoid some serious damage: damage to the shooter; damage to your legal defense fund. Admittedly, it has been a while since I've seen a M1911 barrel that wasn't already throated by the factory, but you might come across one that needs to be opened up a tad more one of these days.

An easily-spotted cause for a feeding failure is a barrel ramp that overhangs the frame. When this occurs, the edge of the case mouth can hang up and prevent the round from moving into the chamber. One reason for these overhangs is a lower barrel lug that, for no good reason, has had too much material removed from its rear. This allows the barrel to seat back further than it should. Should the overhang be extreme and correction require welding up the lugs and refitting them, I'd advise investing in a new barrel. If you don't have the gear on hand to perform the welding yourself, and you don't happen to know a good and affordable welder, the cost would be about the same. If the overhang isn't too severe, take your grinding point to the barrel ramp and carefully remove enough material to eliminate it. Ideally, the barrel ramp should rest about 1/64- to 1/32-inch forward of the frame ramp so the nose of the round can move easily from one to the other.

When a barrel is failing to unlock because it has bulged or has a broken lower lug, replace it. If the failure is due to a broken link or

link pin, replace it. When a barrel fails to lock up, it can be caused by excessive crud in the upper lugs, improper bushing clearance, heavily battered upper lugs or a broken bottom lug. I don't have to tell you what to do about the crud. The barrel bushing is about to be discussed and if either of the other two conditions are the source of the problem, replace the barrel.

Bushing and Extractor

If the pistol is flipping empty cases over the head or into the face of the shooter, the bottom angle of the extractor needs to be redressed. If the extractor is failing to pick up the rim of the case, focus on the extractor bevel. If there are repeated failures to extract, and the chamber isn't dirty or pitted, extractor tension needs adjustment. Worn or broken extractors are always replaced.

A bushing that is loose in the slide, assuming there's nothing wrong with the slide, should be expanded. If the bushing is too loose on the barrel, refit the bushing. Loose bushings contribute heavily to inaccuracy, as do bushings that bind. If you feel some drag at the business end of the pistol when the slide is hand-cycled, it could restrict proper lock up. It's caused when the bushing's skirt is too snug. Chamfer it to relieve the binding.

Magazine

While indispensable, this rectangular piece of metal housing a single spring can be the source of 23 problems all by itself—often more than one at a time.

Look for rough or bent lips if there are feeding problems, then dress them smooth with a file or tweak them straight with a pair of long-nose pliers. Look for a weak spring or a spring that has been installed backwards. If the rounds release late, spread the lips. If they release early, close the lips. If the follower is bent, replace it with one of the rounded top variety. They encourage better feeding, whether the ammo is hardball or semi-wadcutter. In my opinion, the best cure for a magazine gone haywire is to reach into a handy box of brand new ones and replace the danged thing.

Most Likely Causes of Problems

Use this as a check-list and refer to it first whenever a M1911 comes your way. It could save you time, trouble and money.

Failure to feed: A dirty or dented magazine; a weak or broken magazine spring; a worn or broken magazine catch; a bent magazine follower.

Failure to chamber: An obstructed, dirty or pitted chamber; poorly made reloads; a weak recoil spring.

Failure to lock: Lack of lubrication; burred or dirty locking lugs; a weak recoil spring.

Failure to fire: A broken barrel link, a broken or worn firing pin; a broken or weak firing-pin spring; a bent or broken hammer strut; a weak mainspring.

Failure to unlock: A broken barrel link; a broken link pin; broken barrel lugs.

Failure to extract: A broken or worn extractor; a burred, dirty or pitted chamber.

Failure to eject: A broken or worn ejector.

Failure to cock: A worn cocking notch; a worn sear; a defective sear spring; a worn or broken disconnector; hammer and sear pins installed from wrong side of frame.

Troubleshooting Smith & Wesson Revolvers

Here are some of the things you can do to cure common problems without creating more problems for yourself.

By Chick Blood

IT DEPENDS ON who's doing the talking but some say Smith & Wesson adopted a lifetime warranty policy as a knee-jerk reaction to Taurus, which had one first. Others suggest the S&W policy was a serious effort to reduce the risk of liability.

I happen to agree with the others who think the policy was aimed at liability. I can't confirm or deny the exact figure, but I have heard that $65 of the retail price for any gun goes to cover the cost of liability insurance. One thing manufacturers can do to keep those rates from rising ever higher is to rein in tighter on repairs performed by unauthorized or improperly trained individuals. This restraint is increasingly manifesting itself by requiring a firearm to be repaired by the factory or an authorized service center and by increasing the number of parts placed on restricted distribution lists.

A further, and justifiable, measure is voiding the warranty on a firearm that has been mechanically altered to the point it no longer meets factory specifications and standards for safety. An example of such alteration would be the reduction of the single-action trigger pull on a S&W K, L, or N-frame revolver to less that $2^1/_2$ pounds. Instantly, the factory may no longer be number one on the list of those to be sued should an accident subsequently occur involving that particular firearm. More than likely, the person who performed the trigger job will enjoy that dubious distinction.

For that reason and others, alterations will not be the subject here. Troubleshooting, and some of the things you can do to correct the trouble without creating more than you can handle, will.

To begin with, all S&W K, L and N frame revolvers are so much alike that what applies to one applies to either or both of the others. After hearing a gun owner's complaint, your approach to diagnosing what ails their gun begins with a check for proper function.

After making sure no live rounds remain in the cylinder, examine all the frame screws to make sure they're tight, then check the cylinder assembly for: (1) cylinder stop engagement in each cylinder notch; (2) free rotation of the cylinder in the frame; (3) easy opening and closing of the cylinder by finger pressure alone; (4) see if the cylinder opens when the hammer is cocked, because it shouldn't; (5) with the cylinder open, keep it from rotating and check for a tight extractor rod by twisting the rod in both directions; (6) check for easy extraction by charging the cylinder with dummy rounds, pointing the gun straight up and pushing rearward on the extractor rod; (7) close the cylinder and push the thumb-piece forward. It should return to its at-rest position; (8) run the same test of the thumb-piece in double action for all the cylinder charge holes; (9) grasp the cylinder and check for end shake—an excess of movement forward and back—then check for slop in the fit between the cylinder bolt and each cylinder notch by rocking the cylinder side to side. There's supposed to be a little wobble, not a lot; (10) pull back on the trigger until the cylinder bolt disengages the cylinder, then give it a spin. You should hear a distinct series of clicks. It's called "singing" and indicates the hand is functioning properly.

Your final pre-check is for mainspring force. To perform it, you'll need a set of NRA-approved trigger weights. After making sure the strain screw located in the frame between the grip panels is screwed in all the way, point the revolver straight up, grab the frame with one hand and the barrel with the other. Dry fire in double action and hold the trigger to the rear while you pull the hammer fully back. Take your hand off the barrel and place the trigger weight arm on the first step of the hammer just below its nose. While the trigger weights stay on the bench, ease the hammer forward to secure the trigger weight arm between it and the frame. Lift the trigger weights off the bench. The hammer should not move rearward under a minimum weight of $3^1/_2$ pounds if the revolver is a 357 magnum, or of $3^1/_2$ pounds if it is 38 caliber.

A little out of order, but appropriate at this moment, is what can be done to correct an out-of-factory-spec mainspring. You never do it by backing off on the strain screw. You always do it by replacing the screw or filing it shorter, whichever is required.

Now let's go back, or forward, to the rest of the pre-check you ran, what it might have turned up and what you can do about it.

Misfires

If nothing appears to be wrong with the trigger or hammer, no primer indent is the complaint and the ammunition is OK, a thorough cleaning may be the cure. Pay special attention to the lockwork and the hammer nose area. The hammer nose should move freely on its pin.

Hammer bind is another possibility, which might clear up after the lockwork has been cleaned, but can also occur due to a high sear pin. This pin secures the sear in its slot in the hammer. I have yet to find a high one in a factory-fresh S&W, but have discovered them as the cause for hammer bind, or drag, in K, L and N frame revolvers someone tried to "make work better." After removing the hammer from the frame, careful stoning of the pin until it was flush with both sides of the hammer erased the problem.

You can also count cylinder end-shake as a cause for misfires. This condition widens the gap between the cylinder's rear and the hammer while narrowing the gap between the cylinder's front and the barrel. It follows that when the rear gap gets too wide, the hammer's nose can't impact the primer, or can't impact it enough to detonate it. The rear gap on a 38 S&W should not exceed 0.068-inch. On a 357 Magnum, it should be no greater than 0.098-inch. The rear gap on a 22 caliber should be no more than 0.014-inch. These dimensions can be readily checked out with feeler gauges.

One simple method for correcting cylinder end-shake requires a yoke liner, a ballpeen hammer on which the flat face has been polished and trued, plus a hard surface or bench block. After removing the yoke from the cylinder and frame, insert the liner in the yoke. Rest the yoke on the bench block and lightly peen all around the yoke about $^1/_{32}$-inch from the end of its barrel to stretch it. Reassemble the yoke and cylinder, check again for end-shake and repeat the peening if needed. If you overpeen, the cylinder can bind. If it does, carefully remove material from the peened area of the yoke by rotating it against a file until the bind is relieved.

During your pre-check, you may have spotted a loose or distorted hammer nose bushing. It can cause light primer hits or no primer hits at all. So can a damaged hammer nose. If the former is present, return the revolver to the factory. If the latter, replace the hammer's nose yourself.

You're not through with causes for misfires just yet. If the cylinder stop remains down and doesn't pop up through its slot in the frame to engage the notches, the stop's spring might need replacing. On the other hand, you may have to replace and refit the cylinder stop itself. If so, detail strip the revolver, throw away the old stop and slide a new stop into all the cylinder's notches to find out which one is the narrowest. That's the one you'll file the stop to fit.

If the ball of the stop is too thick, file it thinner on the plate side of the revolver. (Looking down on the top strap, that would be the stop's right side.) Stone the edges of the ball and contour it to remove burrs, but do not deform it. Invert the ball into the frame's cylinder stop slot to check the fit. If it's tight, do no further filing of the stop. Lightly file the frame side of the slot itself. (That's the left side as you look down at the revolver.)

With the trigger held fully back, the cylinder should have a slight side play when the stop is engaged in the notches. If it doesn't, the ball is too thick and you must carefully, very carefully, thin it down further. If the ball doesn't engage the cylinder notches at all, place the stop in a vise and judiciously file down the adjustment step sur-

At least 40 things can go wrong with Smith & Wesson revolvers, most of which can be identified and fixed by the knowledgeable gunsmith. It is important to know when to do the work and when to send the gun to the factory.

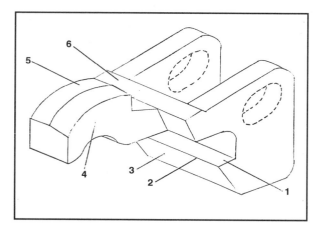

Anatomy of a S&W cylinder stop: (1) recovery surface, (2) point of stop, (3) bevel, (4) side plate side, (5) ball, (6) adjustment step.

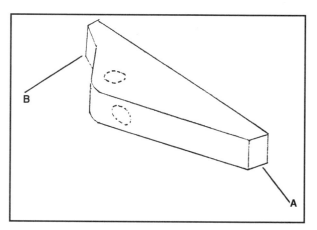

When fitting a sear, concern yourself with two areas: (A) the area to file to change the bevel, (B) the seat to let out the sear. If you file the bevel at an improper angle, the gun will fail to fire.

face at its top. This will allow the stop to rise higher through its slot in the frame. Next, install the trigger, then cycle it to see if the stop moves down, up, forward and backward without once completely leaving the slot. If it does so, file the bevel and the point of the stop. Make one stroke across the point, then file the bevel from its bottom to its top to sharpen the point you just dulled up. When the cylinder stop fails to move rearward during this check, file its recovery surface. A ball that is too long for the slot should be filed on its flat, or front, end. Your ultimate objective is to center the stop in its frame slot to assure a smooth, four-way action. Much disassembly and reassembly goes along with adjusting a cylinder stop. Get used to it.

Normally, the width of a cylinder stop ball is .102-inch. With older guns, the cylinder notches may be worn to a point where no amount of fitting and adjusting will do. In these cases, give up the thought of replacing the cylinder. It's a factory-only job. Ordering in an oversize stop, whose ball width is .105-inch, may enable you to complete the repair.

Slow/Hesitant Trigger Recovery

One cause for this is a broken or modified rebound spring. "Modified" usually means someone has cut more than two coils off the factory's 17-coil spring in an attempt to improve the trigger pull. The fix is simple. Replace the spring. Also, some modifications may have been attempted on the hammer or the hammer/rebound seat. There are two remedies: replace and realign the rebound or replace the hammer. To accomplish the first, polish both sides and bottom of a new rebound to avoid drag between it and the frame. Deburr each side of the tongue at its front to avoid trigger interference and stone the hammer seat at its top—16 strokes should do it. Do not drastically alter the height of the seat in the process. It should mike out between 0.308- and 0.312-inch when you're finished. If it is too high, drag may occur between the hammer tail and the hammer stop. If it is too low, drag can be created against the hammer block because the gap between the frame and hammer's face is too small.

Speaking of gaps, there is a place you need one to prevent the

hammer from hitting or dragging on the rebound. To see if it exists, hold the hammer forward and the trigger back. A little play, so little it's called a "wink," should be evident between the back of the hammer and the front of the rebound. If it's not there, file the front of the rebound's hammer seat and break its upper corner. Besides contributing to sluggish trigger recovery, this is also a cause of misfires. I decided to cover the matter of rebounds and hammers here since both are major safety factors in S&W revolvers.

A third cause for poor trigger recovery is trigger binding. This can be corrected by lightly stoning and polishing the top of the trigger hook. Finally, here's that cylinder stop again, this time causing interference with the trigger hook. Best cure: replace the stop.

Trigger Pull Too Light

You check this out in double action with the cylinder closed. The cause may be a loose strain screw, which you either replace or tighten. If it is due to light mainspring force, replace the spring and the strain screw. If a broken or butchered rebound spring is creating the problem, replace it. Then there are "knuckles," which you can feel by pulling the hammer back to detect roughness. If present, you may be able to smooth them out by tightening the strain screw, but replacing the screw and mainspring should eliminate them.

Rough Double Action

Dirt in the lockwork, high pins on the trigger or hammer, cylinder end-shake, extractor rod runout, a worn sear and cylinder bind are all possible causes here. Since the first three were discussed earlier, let's focus on the last three. Extractor rod runout is due to a bent extractor rod and makes its presence pretty obvious if you open the cylinder and spin it rapidly. If the cylinder wobbles during its rotations, the extractor rod is bent. To straighten it, specialized tooling is recommended. Ever since it became generally available, the basic ingredient for all my rod straightening work has been Ron Powers' extractor rod alignment tool. The handle supplied with it has holes at each end. The end with the smaller hole is used to straighten extractor rods. We're going to get into yoke alignment a little later because it's something that has to be done before you set to work truing an extractor rod. For now, let's proceed under the assumption that step has been accomplished.

With the cylinder secured in the tool according to Powers' instructions, slip the small hole end of the handle over the rod. Rotate the cylinder by hand and watch the free end of the handle to determine the highest position it reaches during rotation. Grasp the handle at its free end and press downward. Don't lean on it and don't use the opportunity to pump up your biceps. Press a little, check the run out, then press a little more until the handle rotates with minimum, or no, wobble.

The sear, if worn or damaged, will need replacing and refitting. If you don't feel your skills are up to the task, send the revolver to the factory or an authorized service center. This is one of those parts that is critical to the revolver's safe operation, and you're asking for all kinds of trouble you don't need if you undertake fitting one and end up doing it wrong. Material must be removed from surfaces in miniscule degrees, with progress to the desired end checked constantly. It would be an excellent idea to closely examine the hammer/sear assembly on a factory-fresh S&W before you ever take a file in hand. Take special notice of the angle at the sear's bottom, where it travels over the trigger, and how far its lower tip extends out from the hammer body.

All cautions being said, remove the old sear from the hammer by drifting out the sear pin with a $1/16$-inch punch. The sear and sear spring will fall free. Reinstall the spring and new sear into the hammer and secure the assembly in a padded vise with hammer surface "A" (see photo) parallel to the vise jaws. The dotted line shown indicates the correct angle on which to file the sear and allow it to travel easily over the surface of the trigger. This cut is made with a Barret file on a slight bevel while removing a little bit more material from the sear's lower surface than from its top.

If the lower tip of the sear extends out less from the hammer's body than the one on a factory-fitted sear, you have to let out the sear by filing its seat. As it was with cutting the base of the sear, this is a matter of file a little, try the action and maybe file a little again.

Once you've done it several times, fitting up a sear right the first time gets easier, but never automatic. Don't try talking yourself into believing that it ever will.

Among other things that can cause a cylinder to bind is lead buildup between it and the breech face. The Lewis Lead Remover, an admirable enemy of lead, gets rid of it with no danger of damage to a revolver's vital parts. To lead buildup add a burr on the yoke, a yoke screw that is too tight and a yoke that is out of alignment, to reasons why a cylinder binds. A yoke screw can get overly tight if it's thrown up a burr between the yoke stud and button. You can stone a burr. You correct a misaligned yoke with a Brownells yoke alignment tool and a wooden or plastic wedge.

Remove the cylinder from the yoke and insert the tool inside the yoke's barrel. With the yoke installed in the gun in its closed position, see if the end of the tool is lined up with the center-pin hole in the frame. If the tool is out of line on the high side, the yoke must be lowered. If out of line on the low side, it must be raised. If it's out of line to the frame side, it must be moved to the plate side. And vice versa. To raise the yoke, insert the wedge between it and the lower part of the frame and tap the wedge. To lower it, the wedge is inserted between the yoke and the top strap. To move the yoke to the plate side, leave it in its closed position and tap it toward the plate side. To move it to the frame side, open the yoke and tap downward on its barrel. Never attempt to align the yoke when the tool is in contact with the center-pin hole and never, never bash it regardless of which

To file a sear bevel, hammer surface "A" is parallel to the vise jaws indicated by the solid line. The dotted line serves as an indication of the proper bevel angle. Check the exact angle against a factory-fresh S&W hammer/sear assembly.

Two areas of the rebound that may require reworking are (A) the hammer seat, (B) the tongue. Since this is one of the major safety factors in K, L and N frame revolvers, go easy and check your progress often.

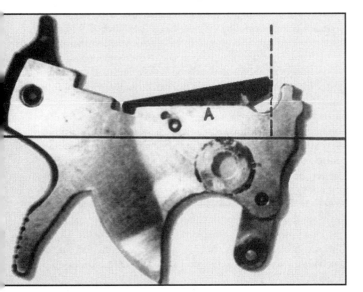

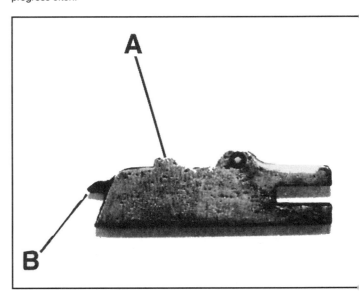

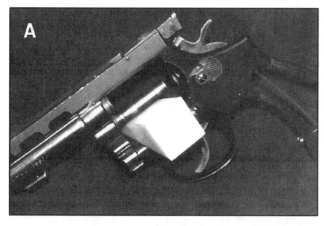

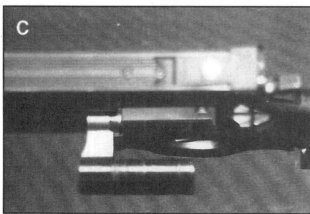

To realign a yoke: (A) To move upward, insert the wedge between yoke and frame; (B) To move down, insert the wedge between yoke and top strap; (C) To move to left, open the yoke and tap downward, (D) To move right, close the yoke and tap toward the plate side of revolver. The yoke alignment tool, omitted here for clarity, should be in the yoke for support during adjustments, but not in contact with the frame.

direction it is being moved. A few gentle taps will do it, or... eventually.

Heavy Trigger Pull

This may be caused by ammunition in the cylinder rubbing the frame, dirt under the extractor, lead buildup between the barrel and cylinder, dirt in the lockwork, heavy mainspring force or long ratchets.

Fortunately, everything except long ratchets have already been covered and it's a good thing they have, because long ratchets have to be filed with extreme care. If they're overdone, the cylinder stop will be prevented from entering a notch before the hammer is fully cocked. This results in poor or no alignment between the cylinder, barrel and hammer nose.

At Smith & Wesson, all ratchets are cut at the same time with an ingenious hand tool designed by the factory's assembly workers. Unfortunately, it has never been made available to anyone who doesn't work on the line, not even to old graduates of the S&W armorer's school. Equally unfortunate, as clever as the concept may be, the tool doesn't cut each and every ratchet to the perfect length 100 percent of the time. The good news is, you'll rarely if ever come across a long ratchet. The bad news is if you do, there are

very stringent rules for very cautious use of a Barret file to bring it into specs. Follow them religiously.

The surest test for a long ratchet is to cock the hammer in single action and pull the trigger. If the hammer fails to fall on any given cylinder charge hole, that cylinder has a long ratchet. With the charge hole of that cylinder at 12 o'clock, place your left hand over the frame with your thumb on one side of the cylinder and your middle finger on the other. Slowly open the cylinder and put your index finger on the cylinder notch that was under the top strap. The ratchet to be filed will be the one to the right of the chamber directly under the notch. Mark it with a felt-tip pen and roll the cylinder counterclockwise to give yourself some working room. Next, push the extractor rod rearward towards the thumbpiece, place the middle of the file on the top (pointed area) of the ratchet you're going to cut and be sure the edge of the file is slid under the ratchet above the one to be cut. The file should be positioned upward, toward the rear sight. Keep the file parallel to the notch you're cutting as you swing its rear edge to almost contact the extractor's arms and lever its point upwards to avoid marking up the extractor collar. Draw the file backwards two strokes—no more. Rerun the single action/hammer fails to fall test and reduce any more necessary filing to a stroke at a time.

There's a rehearsal drill I frequently put myself through to get a feel for filing ratchets before I actually took a file to one. The revolver was real, but I sanded a tongue depressor into the shape of a Barret file and faked every step in the process over and over again. All those dry runs had great therapeutic value at reducing the pucker factor when I got around to the real thing, and I recommend them to you.

No Double Action

You can't miss this one because you can't pull the trigger at all. Look to the ammunition first. A frequently reloaded, improperly trimmed case may have stretched so much its head is jammed between the cylinder and the frame. A primer may not be seated to its proper depth or may have flowed back due to excessive pressure.

Other causes to consider are the sear, a worn trigger cam, a catching cylinder stop, a bent extractor rod and a misaligned yoke. Guilty sears, triggers and cylinder stops should be replaced. The rod and the yoke you can repair as described under the rough double action section. However, if the trouble is due to damaged studs in the frame, the repairs are for the factory only and not for you.

No Single Action

Take a look at the hammer spur. Has the gun been dropped or hit? If it has, and the spur is bent, it may hit the frame before the trigger bevel drops into the hammer's single-action cocking notch. Replace the hammer. Don't try to fix it. This particular malfunction can also be traced to a worn single-action cocking notch or a worn trigger bevel. Replace the hammer, the trigger, or both, as required. If the problem is caused by a bent extractor rod or misaligned yoke, you already know what to do about it. If it's attributable to the bolt not returning with the cylinder closed, replace the center-pin spring.

Rough Extraction

Reasons for this such as bad ammo, a bent extractor rod and dirt, you've already heard about. Additional possibilities are a loose extractor rod, a bent or damaged extractor spring, burrs in cylinder charge holes and bent extractor pins. You can remove burrs with a precision chamber reamer and bent pins are restricted to factory replacement, so I'll discuss the remaining two.

To tighten a loose extractor rod, first hand tighten it and insert six dummy rounds into the cylinder. Clamp the rod in a padded vise behind its knurled end and turn the cylinder counter-clockwise or clockwise, depending on the threads. You don't repair a bent or damaged extractor spring. You replace it.

Cylinder Doesn't Open or Close Smoothly

There is a long list of probable causes for the cylinder to be a bit stubborn when it's opened or closed. Among them are dirt under the extractor, ammunition rubbing the frame, primer flow, a loose extractor rod, a bent extractor rod, an out-of-alignment yoke and cylinder end-shake. Corrective measures for all of those have been covered. Causes not yet covered include a worn bolt, a worn yoke button, a worn yoke screw, a short or worn center pin, a worn recoil plate firing pin bushing and a loose thumb-piece nut.

The worn bolt should be replaced, a revolver with a worn recoil plate bushing sent back to the factory and the loose thumb-piece nut tightened. A worn yoke button can be remedied by replacing or refitting the yoke screw. On older style Smith & Wessons, the screw actually leaves a score mark on the button's inside surface. When one of these is replaced, it must be fitted as follows: After installing the screw in the yoke and the yoke in the frame, open and close it slowly a few times. If there's any binding, you'll feel it. Remove the yoke and yoke screw. Noting the score marks on the inside of the button will show you where it's binding. File only those spots by rotating the yoke into your file. If you overfile the button you'll cause cylinder end-shake, but no sweat. You can correct your error by putting the yoke on top of a lead babbitt or piece of soft pine and carefully peening down the end of the button.

Since this same peening procedure can be followed to compensate for a worn yoke screw, I won't expand on it except to mention two things. Yoke screws on newer revolvers have a plunger that applies all-around even pressure to the yoke button. When they're worn, replace them. In cases where the interface between yoke screw, regardless of style, and button is really sloppy, replace the screw with an oversize one. These are available from S&W and can be employed as a cure for yoke end-shake as well.

In clearing up problems with the trigger, the only areas you should put a stone to, aside from burrs you're cleaning, are (A) the bevel and (B) the hook. In doing so, maintain original angles.

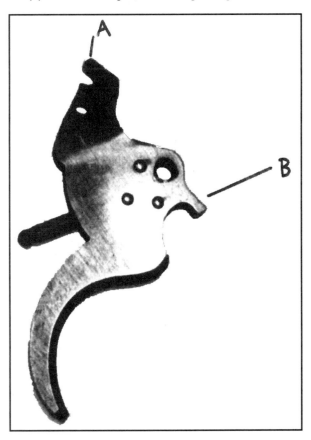

The center pin that runs through the middle of the cylinder serves multiple purposes. It is the axis upon which the cylinder revolves, the means of extracting spent shells from charging holes and the means by which the cylinder is locked into the frame at two points: the bolt at the rear of the cylinder and the locking bolt which is pinned into the barrel lug. When a short or worn center pin fails to make these engagements, the pin must be replaced. Most center pins start out life on the long side, which also prevents lockup, and must be fitted to the revolver. To do this, assemble the center pin, center pin spring, extractor spring, extractor rod and extractor rod collar to the cylinder/extractor and hand tighten. Use a flat-ended punch to depress the extractor end of the center pin flush with the extractor's collar and take a look at the knurled end of the extractor rod. If the center pin protrudes, mark the amount of its excess, disassemble, and carefully grind off the excess. The objective is to achieve a flush fit between the pin, the extractor collar and the end of the extractor rod when the pin is depressed.

Timing

Improper timing is a way of saying something's wrong because the cylinder fails to index as it should. Another, "DCU," means "doesn't carry up."

At times, this is caused by cylinder cramping, which can be cleared up by deburring or realigning a yoke, straightening an extractor rod or replacing a center pin. This assumes, of course, that one of them is the source of the pain. A worn ratchet or ratchets could be the problem.

Installing a hand thicker than the factory original can usually make up the difference, but putting one in may require you to open the hand's slot in the frame by filing it. Hands in a new gun will mike out to between 0.093-inch and 0.095-inch. Oversize hands will be between 0.095-inch and 0.097-inch.

A worn hand, on the other hand, often creates a DCU problem on all charging holes. If it is worn enough, the cylinder won't rotate at all but before you get into replacing it, see if the hand torsion spring is broken. If you're not lucky, it won't be.

A replacement hand should mike out at "new gun" dimensions and the first thing to do is install it in the trigger. Lock that assembly in a padded vise, deburr the high side of the hand with two light strokes with a stone, then re-install the trigger, rebound, rebound spring, hammer, hammer block and mainspring in the frame. With the hammer down, check to see if the hand protrudes beyond the face of its slot. If it does, remove the trigger from the frame and carefully file or stone the end of the hand down until it is even with the slot's bottom.

Push Off

You should check for this from the get-go by cocking the hammer to its single-action position, taking your finger off the trigger and putting no more than 6 pounds of forward pressure on the hammer spur. If the hammer falls, that's push off caused by a worn/broken

trigger bevel or a chipped/broken cocking notch on the hammer.

You never do anything to a hammer except replace it. Any repairs you make for push off must be performed on the trigger. For a broken bevel, the repair is replacement. For a worn one, place the trigger on a bench, bevel end up and to the right, and hold it firmly in place. Place one end of a 6-inch square stone on the bench, lower the stone into contact with the bevel and, using the bench surface to keep your strokes true, give the bevel eight or 10 light ones to sharpen it. Reassemble the gun, check for push off and repeat the stoning—four or five strokes maximum—if necessary.

Spitting Lead

This is a common complaint with both common and uncommon causes. Among the common causes are lead buildup on the breech face and all things that prevent correct cylinder/barrel alignment, including a worn cylinder stop, yoke out of alignment, cylinder end-shake, and yoke end-shake. Among those not yet discussed are a worn cylinder notch and a worn forcing cone.

Worn cylinder notches can be remedied by fitting the gun with an oversize cylinder stop or sending it back to the factory for a new cylinder. I strongly suggest you choose the latter course in cases where all the cylinder notches aren't worn to similar degrees. Though fitting an oversize cylinder stop differs little from fitting a normal one, making a perfect marriage between it and six diversified notches is masochistic, if not impossible. The factory would also prefer that worn forcing cones be strictly their business as well but unless the cone is a pitted, ragged shambles, anything they can do you can do. However, the job calls for some hand tooling that has been made specifically for the purpose. It is used without removing the barrel from the frame. A rod to which you attach a facing cutter is slipped into the barrel . A centering cone and handle are then fitted to the rod's free end. A few light turns with back pressure exerted trues the breech. Notice I said light turns. Shaving off too much material can increase the gap between the cylinder and the breech to a No-Go dimension, which can only be corrected by setting the barrel back.

After truing, replace the facing cutter with a chamfering cutter to reform the cone. Again, easy does it. Though these chamfering cutters do a clean, chatter-free job, a prime finish is secured by replacing the one you've used with a brass lap machined to the same angle as the cutter and some fine abrasive.

Lifetime warranty or no lifetime warranty, it's quite likely a great deal of the revolver work you do will be done on Smith & Wessons. Since it is likely you'll never attend the factory's armorer's school or work on the assembly line, some additional reading can do you no harm. I recommend three books to continue your education: *The S&W Revolver*—VSP Publishers, P.O. Box 1966, Tustin, CA 92681; *Firearms Assembly/Disassembly, Part II Revolvers, Revised Edition*—DBI Books, Inc., 4092 Commercial Avenue, Northbrook, IL 60062; *Brownells Catalog,* Brownells, Inc., 200 South Front Street, Montezuma, IA 50171.

Inside The Kahr K9

Field-stripping is as far as the factory wants anyone to go with this mini-9mm, but here's the story on how to work it.

By Chick Blood

THE KAHR K9, produced by New York-based Kahr Arms, is a pistol you've likely not come across before, but because it features a number of proprietary designs that allow it to feed and shoot 9mm ammo (and may soon be able to digest +P and +P+ loads) in a handgun only slightly bigger than a standard 380, it's worth taking a look inside it to see how it works.

The K9 pistol, a recoil-operated and mechanically locked John M. Browning-style gun, has a number of patentable features and a simple design that allow it shoot 9mm ammo in a compact piece, but the K9 isn't a cut-down version of an existing pistol. Every part was made from scratch to create the smallest 9mm autoloader available, and the highly compact, 25-ounce package uses no alloys or plastics to achieve its light weight. It measures 6 inches from the front of its slide to the back of its receiver, and stands 4.4 inches high. Its barrel is 3.5 inches in length, and it has a magazine capacity of seven rounds. It is fashioned all from ordnance steel, and is trigger cocked and double action only. The striker is automatically held under partial tension after each round and is fully secured by a passive firing-pin block until the trigger is fully depressed

The Kahr's uncommon safety/shooting features are one of the things that make it worth examining. When you rack back and release the slide of a K9, it only semi-cocks the pistol. When you start pulling the trigger rearward, it contacts a protrusion on the cocking cam which lifts the firing-pin block. Simultaneous with this action, the cocking cam pulls the striker back from half to full cock and puts it under maximum spring tension. Completing the trigger pull allows the cocking cam to release the striker, which is now free to move forward and fire the chambered round. During recoil, a ramp in the slide rails disengages the trigger bar from the cocking cam, allowing the cam to reset itself and reactivating the firing pin block.

The K9 is the smallest pistol made to digest full-power 9mm ammunition. It should have 200 rounds fired through it to achieve fully reliable feeding and functioning.

There is no conventional, externally located safety lever on the K9. Due to its design, it simply cannot be fired until and unless the trigger is pulled completely to the rear. However, the function of its firing pin block should be checked before the pistol is first used and regularly thereafter. If you encounter a K9, you should first check its function with the slide off and the barrel out. To begin, draw the striker back manually about 1/4-inch and ease it fully forward. As long as the firing pin doesn't project beyond the breech face of the slide, the pistol is working properly. If it does protrude, you've either accidentally depressed the firing pin block while running the test or the pistol must be returned to the factory for repair.

The sights are unconventional, too. At first glance, both front and rear sights appear to be drift-adjustable, but this is only true for the rear sight. By loosening the rear sight set screw, you can drift the rear sight in either direction. However, there's no way to drift the front sight without wrecking it. Sooner or later though, some K9 owner who hasn't digested his owner's manual is going to try a front sight adjustment and bring his banged up pistol in for you to fix.

To accomplish this, remove the slide, barrel, recoil spring, and guide. Turn the slide upside down and locate the little hole inside the top of the slide near its front. Inside the hole is the spring-loaded front-sight pin. By depressing the pin with a small punch, the front sight can be slid out of its channel and replaced. I suggest you start the sight out, then turn the slide right side up and cup one hand over it before pushing the sight out the rest of the way. A really tiny spring puts pressure on the sight's pin, and if it takes off, you're never going to see it again. To install a new front sight, start the sight in its channel, insert the pin and the spring and depress both until the sight is in far enough to capture the spring. Once it has, you can concentrate on centering it.

Other Kahr Tricks

To field strip and reassemble the K9, remove its magazine and make sure the gun is empty by visually checking the chamber. Draw the slide back so its relief cut is aligned with the slide lock pin. Push or tap the pin out from right to left and ease the slide forward under recoil spring tension. Pull the trigger to release the striker, then push the slide further forward past the cocking cam. You can now relax pressure on the trigger and remove the slide. Push the rear of the recoil spring guide slightly forward with your thumb and lift it clear of the recoil lug while keeping control of the recoil spring. Carefully lift up the back end of the spring and guide and remove them to the rear. Grasp the barrel by its recoil lug, push it slightly forward, then lift and pull it rearward out of the slide.

You reassemble the K9 in reverse order, but with a few caveats.

(1) The trigger should not be depressed.

(2) Before remarrying the slide to the frame, make sure the recoil

Field stripping is as far as the factory wants anyone to go in disassembling the K9, and Kahr will void the warranty if a gun is damaged or malfunctions due to improper reassembly.

guide rod and spring are parallel to the slide rails and not off to one side or the other.

(3) Make sure the smaller end of the recoil spring is against the flange of the spring's guide.

(4) You may have to depress the ejector at the rear of the frame to allow the slide to slip on. If the slide doesn't go smoothly onto the frame, don't force it. Go back over the reassembly steps to see if you missed anything. Trying to overpower a stubborn K9 slide can damage the pistol and void the warranty.

Detail Stripping The Slide

To detail strip the slide, turn the slide upside down and insert a small tool in the notch on the underside of the slide's back plate. Slip the tool in between the plate and the rear of the striker spring guide. Push the guide forward to compress the spring and clear the guide from its recess in the plate. Leave the tool in place to hold the guide forward.

The right rear of the slide has a semi-circular cut in it about halfway up. The extractor's rear pin rides in that cut. You'll have

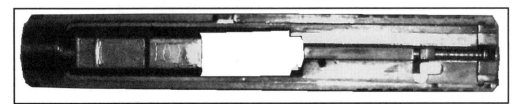

This inverted view of the Kahr's slide clearly shows the slide back plate, striker assembly and safety.

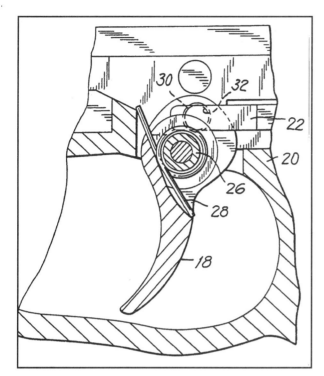

This drawing from the K9 patent papers gives you a better idea of how the trigger spring is positioned. You'll need a special tool, which may be manufactured from a small, slot-head screwdriver, to get the spring seated properly.

to reach in there with a very small jeweler's screwdriver to depress the extractor pin, then start the back plate up a fraction toward the top of the slide. Once you have it started, cover the plate with your thumb before removing the jeweler's screwdriver and the tool you used to compress the striker spring guide. Make very certain to keep that back plate under control. The extractor and striker springs are very strong, and if they get away from you, you may never find them again. Besides, either one of those springs can put a nasty dent in your face, not to mention the danger they represent to your eyes.

As you look down on the slide, the safety is located a little forward of the back plate's slot. Depress the safety and slide out the striker by pulling rearward on its tang. Tilt the rear of the slide down and tap it on the bench to remove the extractor's forward pin, spring, and rear pin. If they don't fall out, depress the safety again and give the slide another rap or two as before. Turn the slide right side up, rap it against the bench one more time, and the safety will fall free.

If the parts that are supposed to come out as a result of all this

rapping don't come out, it probably means you have a K9 that is long overdue for a good cleaning.

Detail Stripping The Frame

To detail strip the frame, take the K9's grips off and remove the trigger-bar spring by reaching under it with a dental pick and carefully freeing it from its position in the frame. The trigger is retained by a pin that drifts left to right and is removed downward to either side of the trigger guard. The trigger spring and trigger spacer will probably free up when the trigger pin is driven out. If they don't, now is the time to lift them clear of the trigger bar. Next, remove the bar rearward from the right side of the frame.

At this writing, the ejector is not an integral part of the frame's back, which is not an integral part of the K9's frame. If you must remove the ejector, pry it upward from its two dowel pins while being extremely careful not to bend it. When and if the K9 ejector will become one with the frame's back I can't say, so if you have any doubts at all, either leave it alone or call Kahr.

By the same token, the frame's back may one day become part of the frame. Right now, it isn't. It is held in by two pins. The forward one is the cocking-cam pivot pin, the one to the rear is the frame back pin. They are both tapered and must be driven out right to left. Once they are, the cocking cam, cocking cam spring, and frame back will drop free.

The magazine catch comes apart and goes together like a M1911. In fact, the K9's locking pin and spring interchange with a M1911's.

The cocking cam has a small hole on one side. The end of the cocking cam spring must be inserted into that hole. If it isn't, you won't be able to get the gun back together without damaging the spring. The shorter of the two pins you removed to free the frame's back is the cocking cam's pivot pin. When you've positioned the cam for reassembly, you'll have to maneuver it a bit by lifting it up so you can push the pin through. Since the pin came out right to left, remember to put it back in from left to right. The same is true for the frame back pin.

To reinstall the trigger, insert it up through the trigger guard and position it in the frame. You'll have to hold it there while you insert the trigger bar boss through the frame and into its hole in the trigger. Next, install one leg of the trigger bar spring under the end of the trigger bar, the other leg into its slot in the frame and hold everything in place by re-attaching the right grip. Don't expect this step, or the one that follows, to be easy on your first attempt. They both take some practice.

More Reassembly Tips

Before moving on, you will need a special tool, which you can make from a small, flat-blade screwdriver.

In this top view of the receiver, you can see the installed cocking cam on the right side, about an inch forward of the frame back.

Grind or file a radius in the screwdriver's blade that matches the radius of the trigger spacer. Secure the frame in a padded vise and, working from the top, insert the trigger spring over the spacer and into its position on the trigger. The accompanying patent papers drawings provide a reference to show you exactly how the spring is to be seated. Now press down on the spacer to line it up and insert the trigger pin.

The safety is reinstalled before the extractor assembly and held in place by the extractor assembly and the striker. When you install that front extractor pin, its beveled end must face away from the slide's right side.

Final Note

The K9 comes with a warranty the manufacturer will void if anyone dismantles the gun beyond the field-stripping stage, or either damages it or causes it to malfunction due to improper reassembly. Though the parts list in the owner's manual carries no asterisks to indicate a restricted part, the only one openly offered is a recoil spring, which should be replaced every 3000 rounds. This, the manuals says, is "to assure reliable function and maintain the warranty of the K9." Guess you can't be too careful these days.

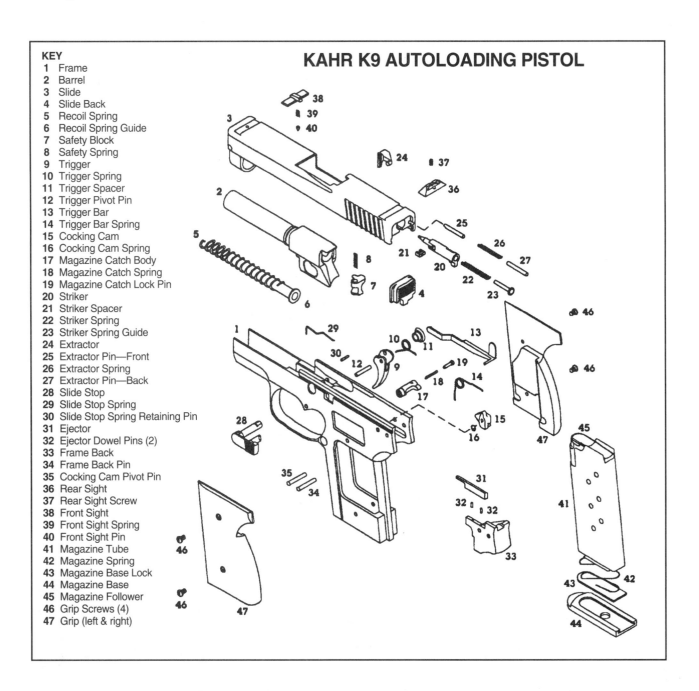

KAHR K9 AUTOLOADING PISTOL

KEY
1 Frame
2 Barrel
3 Slide
4 Slide Back
5 Recoil Spring
6 Recoil Spring Guide
7 Safety Block
8 Safety Spring
9 Trigger
10 Trigger Spring
11 Trigger Spacer
12 Trigger Pivot Pin
13 Trigger Bar
14 Trigger Bar Spring
15 Cocking Cam
16 Cocking Cam Spring
17 Magazine Catch Body
18 Magazine Catch Spring
19 Magazine Catch Lock Pin
20 Striker
21 Striker Spacer
22 Striker Spring
23 Striker Spring Guide
24 Extractor
25 Extractor Pin—Front
26 Extractor Spring
27 Extractor Pin—Back
28 Slide Stop
29 Slide Stop Spring
30 Slide Stop Spring Retaining Pin
31 Ejector
32 Ejector Dowel Pins (2)
33 Frame Back
34 Frame Back Pin
35 Cocking Cam Pivot Pin
36 Rear Sight
37 Rear Sight Screw
38 Front Sight
39 Front Sight Spring
40 Front Sight Pin
41 Magazine Tube
42 Magazine Spring
43 Magazine Base Lock
44 Magazine Base
45 Magazine Follower
46 Grip Screws (4)
47 Grip (left & right)

Smoothing Ruger Single-Action Revolvers

Smoothing the actions is one way to make single-action shooters happy. We look here at Ruger revolvers.

By Thomas J. Stuntebeck

I'VE BEEN INVOLVED in one form or other of the shooting game since the summer of 1948. That may not remove me from the "Johnny-come-lately" category where many of our numbers are concerned, but it's been long enough to allow me to form a few rather definite opinions and conclusions. Among them is one that says shooting should be a pleasure, not a chore! Another says I do not crave a great deal of self-inflicted pain!

For those who choose to fight a gun for every shot, or feel that having the heck beat out of them with every pull of the trigger is a validation of their manhood, what I have to say will be of no interest. For those who believe almost any gun's action can be better than what comes out of the box, I may have some useful advice.

The fact that I do not reload to the "red line" is not meant as an indictment of those who need to load hot. I tailor my ammunition to what the gun will shoot best and to what I can tolerate for an extended period of time. I've seen many cases of "combat fatigue" coming off our local range from an afternoon of doing 100 rounds or so of the "good stuff." Many of these cases were as much the result of fighting a gun with a lawyer-friendly action as the result of the earthshaking loads that had been fired. Here, we will attempt to alleviate at least one part of that problem.

Among all the action types, probably the least-discussed, in a

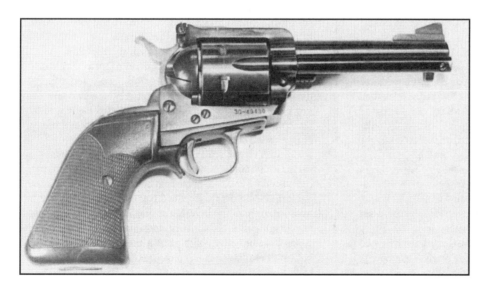

The Ruger three-screw-action revolver is close to the old Colt in terms of action and trigger. The newer two-screw actions are a bit more complicated.

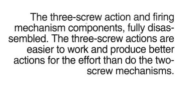
The three-screw action and firing mechanism components, fully disassembled. The three-screw actions are easier to work and produce better actions for the effort than do the two-screw mechanisms.

technical sense, is the single-action revolver. Generally speaking, they are the strongest of the action types, albeit the slowest to load and unload. They do not cock themselves, and they do not hold a large quantity of ammunition, either. But they are—or can be—extremely accurate at some awesome distances, and are the gun of choice for many silhouette shooters and handgun hunters.

I suppose we've all heard it said that an action wouldn't be so stiff or heavy if it wasn't necessary. In 1873, when the Colt Single Action Army revolver made its debut, the priming used at the time may have dictated the stiff springs found on most of the older guns—as well as their modern counterparts. However, the technology used in making primers today pretty well negates the need for those extremes of hammer impact. For lack of a better way to put it, today's primers are softer, the priming compounds in them are hotter and more consistent, and good ignition requires considerably less striking force.

In this article, we will deal only with the Ruger actions. Although its looks tend to say "cowboy gun," its innards don't, so I feel it better to deal with the Ruger as a separate entity from the Colt and its modern clones. (The legendary Colt SAA is discussed elsewhere in this book.)

The three-screw Ruger is close to the old Colt in that it has the three-position hammer and a trigger of much the same style. The two-screw (or two-pin) models made today are just a tad more complicated and have additional parts. The engineering that accomplished this was masterful, though I'm sorry that any change was necessary. This is a shame because, in my opinion, the older model was more easily worked and produced a better action for the effort.

And so, with personal philosophies out of the way, we can begin to examine the whys and wherefores of what some might call gilding a lily. Smoothing an action does not always mean lightening it, but, in most cases, it is difficult to gain a smooth feel even when polished parts are under an excess of spring tension.

What's excessive? In my view, excessive is any amount beyond what is required to allow a part to function safely and properly.

Today, that leaves a lot of room to run. I am not talking about building a hair trigger, just actions that don't require all the strength of Samson to be cocked and fired. What you get is strictly up to your good judgment.

When the primary work is done, the Ruger single action revolver can be taken to weights that are unbelievably light, yet still function reliably. And note that many new shooters come along faster if they don't have to fight a stiff action, though I won't go so far as to recommend a very light action for use by a novice shooter.

Disassembly and reassembly for the old-timers among us will be routine, and for those unfamiliar with this action type, I would suggest getting one of the NRA books on firearms assemblies or any of the series of Assembly/Disassembly books put out by DBI Books, Inc. If you intend to do any amount of work on guns, they are invaluable. I have to admit to falling back on mine for something new to me, or something I have forgotten over the years. In any case, don't be in a hurry.

Since the object of all this is to create an action that operates smoother, we need to create smoother-operating parts, especially those that rub on each other in their functioning. It's the combination of rough, or at least unpolished, surfaces throughout the action that contributes to the gritty feel of many mechanisms. What we can do in a few minutes with stones, emery paper, and the high-speed buffing wheel or hand grinder would take many years of use to reproduce. Even then, an action likely would not reach the same degree of smoothness before one or more parts break or wear out.

On either type of action, smooth out the sides of the hammer and trigger with an India stone, followed by fine emery on a file. Concentrate on the areas around the pin holes of these parts.

Next, smooth out the front and rear edges of the arm that protrudes from the rear of the cylinder stop. Do just enough to remove any irregularities on the part, and burnish the areas with an Arkansas stone before polishing on a rouge wheel. Also polish the bottom where the spring and plunger contact.

Remove the irregularities on the front and rear of the hand with a fine file. Remove just a bit more from the front below the lower tooth and blend into it before finishing it out with an India stone, front and rear, and polishing on the rouge wheel. Don't change the dimensions of the top of the hand unless absolutely necessary.

Polish the cylinder pin except for the part that shows in the front of the frame. Burnish the front cylinder bearing and, using a 60-degree chamfering tool, bevel the front of the pin hole. Burnish the face of the cylinder ratchet with fine emery paper and thoroughly wash both parts. (Note: In rare instances I have used very fine red rouge in oil to lap these two parts together. While I prefer not doing it this way as the wear on each part can get away from you too easily, it works in a pinch.)

When dry, relubricate and mount them in the stripped frame. Spin the cylinder to insure a free-running rotation. I usually spin the cylinder to a very high speed with compressed air and let it slow down by itself while I watch for any "stuttering" in the rotation pattern.

In the two-screw action, the transfer bar is the most obvious of those new parts. It should be smoothed out with emery paper on the front, back, and the side opposite its pivot pin, then polished on the rouge wheel.

The transfer bar rides on the extended arm on the trigger. The bearing point on that arm should also be India stoned, burnished with emery, and touched to the rouge wheel. A slight countersink on this hole will clear any small burrs away and leave a small lube reservoir as well.

The back of the trigger below the sear contact should also be cleaned up and polished. This is where the hammer toe makes contact and cams the trigger into cocked position. The toe of the hammer should also be polished, but avoid any serious amount of wear on the engagement area.

Reducing the depth of the cock notch on either action type is, in my judgment, unnecessary, and in most cases, ill advised. If the trigger still feels gritty, polish the face of the cock notch and the mating area of the trigger and try it again. Use an Arkansas stone for this work.

Although chamfering the ends of the pin holes of the working parts may not be totally necessary, it will clean up any minor burrs or roughness in these areas and, as with the transfer bar arm on the trigger, provide a small reservoir for lubricant.

Having deburred, smoothed, and polished the major moving parts of these actions, it's time to reduce some of the spring tension on them to insure reduced wear and increased ease of operation.

The early three-screw actions had a spring with coils that wrapped around the cylinder-stop pin, with arms that hooked over the stop and into the inside wall of the frame. Spring weight on this part can be relieved by camming the leg that hooks over the stop back off the stop, while the parts are in place. When finished, the stop should rest firmly against the top of the frame recess no matter what position the frame is held, and should present noticeably less resistance to finger pressure. Keep in mind that this part has to hold the cylinder in line with the barrel with some potentially powerful loads being fired from it.

This system was changed to a simple spring and plunger, and remains so in the two-screw actions built today. Polish the hollow plunger on the rouge wheel and trim back the spring until the conditions described above are in effect. I feel these two procedures are best done in stages and matched to the overall feel you are trying to create.

Polish the hand plunger on the rouge wheel and, with the major parts in the frame, put the spring and plunger into the frame and cock the hammer. The hand should be fully forward and resting on the cylinder ratchet. Cut off all the spring material that protrudes from the frame except one full coil, making sure the plunger is resting solidly on the hand. The hand must make solid contact with the ratchet from the beginning movement until the hammer is in the full-cocked position.

On the early frame, the trigger spring and plunger are in the grip frame at the rear of the trigger-guard opening. Polish the plunger and grind off the coils at the rear of the spring until you have reached the weight or feel you want. This might also be a good time to fit up a trigger stop, if this is desired. Replace the plunger with one of your own manufacture that has a longer tail on it to bottom out in the spring well. This is another "cut and try" operation, but the feel of the finished trigger is worth the effort and could add significantly to your final shooting enjoyment.

Left—The first place to start is to polish the face of the hammer hooks and hammer toe. This applies to old or new Ruger actions. Right—The rear of the trigger beneath the sear area must be polished as well.

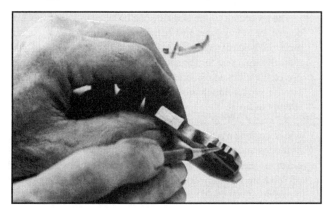
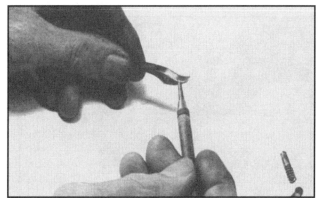

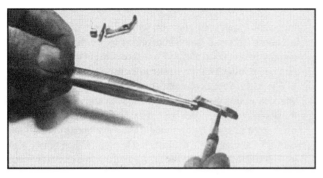 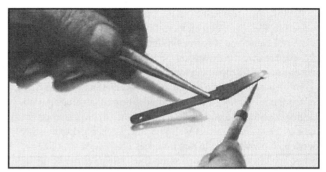

Above left: Polish the rear of the hand and the front below the lower tooth. Don't change the dimensions of the top. Above right: The head of the hammer strut should be polished. You should also deburr and polish the shank of the hammer strut that runs through the hammer spring and seat/retainer.

Unfortunately, the same thing cannot be done to the two-screw action, because the trigger needs to go as far back as it can to ensure that the transfer bar is covering the head of the firing pin. I suppose the top of the transfer bar could be lengthened, but I'm not sure it would be worth the effort.

The trigger spring in the two-screw frame can be worked in two areas. Start by bending the two rear legs up until they are almost touching the top of the hammer spring when they are rehooked on their retaining pin, with the hammer and spring in the rest position. I then remove and polish the loop on the bottom where it contacts the trigger. I also bevel and polish the area on the trigger where the springs rest. If any further reduction in weight is desired, carefully pry up on the looped end with the spring installed in the grip frame. This is another of those bend-and-try operations until you have a feel that is satisfactory. The final trigger weight will be determined by the combination of this spring and the hammer spring working together.

Highly polish the head of the hammer-spring strut. Then bevel and polish the shank that runs through the spring and the spring seat.

Drive out the hammer-plunger retaining pin and remove the plunger and spring. This piece actuates the cylinder latch and does not need all the spring tension it has, out of the box. Chase out the

If the loading gate on the revolver is a "nail breaker," break the corner of the two flats and polish it along with the flats on the gate's pivot pin.

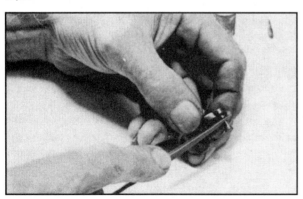

spring well with an appropriately sized drill. Older guns may have rust and crud in there, and the newer ones may have burrs or metal chips left by the manufacturer. Clean up or replace rusty springs and trim them down to a point where the area on the plunger just above the pin relief barely shows in the retaining hole, with the spring in place. Polish the sides and end of the plunger, but do not reduce its overall length. Oil the plunger hole and reassemble the parts in the hammer.

Wash all the parts to get rid of any rouge or carborundum dust that might cause unwanted wear. (Mixed with oil, this is just like lapping compound.) Relube all parts, especially the pivot points and spring cavities. Finally, reassemble the gun. Try the action and weigh the trigger to see if anything needs to be done to the hammer spring.

You will no doubt notice a much freer-running action for your efforts. Some shooters, though they are in the minority, like the feel enough to leave the hammer with its original tension. As a matter of form, I square up the ends of the hammer spring and thereby reduce the length by about one full coil.

I polish the hammer spring on a straw rouge wheel as it spins on a steel mandrel to burnish the inside of the coils as well. Any further reductions of weight and size are up to you. Keep in mind who will be using the gun and the purpose for which it will be used, as well as the fact that the two-screw model will need to be a bit heavier in its final form because of the transfer bar.

Conclusion

The procedures discussed here can be taken to almost any safe degree, or to any point just before a part will cease to function properly. You can go from a smooth-out job for the novice to the radically light one for the shootist. Again, be sure of the expertise of the ultimate owner. By all means, check out the firearm for the proper functioning of all safety features before you attempt to fire it.

No matter to what degree you use these techniques, I believe you will be creating a better item that will last longer because of the lack of friction and tension on the parts. It will be an item that will be a pleasure—not a chore—to shoot, and something you can be proud of. You are basically doing the work the factory custom shop would do, if you could just get them to do it.

Fitting 1911 Slides and Frames

You can accurize a 1911 pistol forever, and it will still be a waste of time unless the barrel locks up the same way every time. Here's a way to be sure that happens.

By Chick Blood

ANY ACCURACY JOB on a Model 1911 or its variants is a waste of time unless the slide is properly fitted to the receiver. Without this step, and pretty much regardless of what else is done, the barrel can't lock up with the mechanical repeatability required to make the pistol truly competitive.

The special tooling required for an operation like this isn't cheap but is necessary to perform the job. Among the things you'll need are an indicator reference plate or slide-rail micrometer, a depth indicator, a pair of frame plates, a slide-rail spreader, a magazine-well insert, a micrometer or dial calipers, and a set of ten precision-ground gauging bars for forming receiver rails. An exception to the expensive items, but just as necessary, is a 4-ounce ballpeen hammer with a highly polished face. It should not be used for anything but slide fitting.

If you were working with a boxful of slides and receivers, you could begin by picking through them to find a pair that already make a good marriage—that is, they have minimal horizontal and

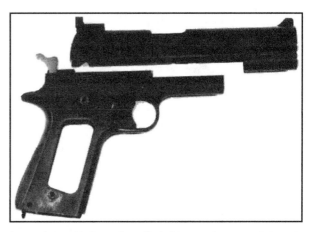

Prior to fitting, this Essex frame/Colt slide mutation was strictly an 8-ring shooter despite a match barrel, trigger job, Group Gripper and a few other add-ons. After slide fitting, it benched six consecutive five-shot groups in the X-ring at 25 yards .

vertical play. However, I'm going to assume you're not part of a military marksmanship unit where such abundance might exist and are limited to re-working the pistol you have on hand.

To get started, strip the receiver completely except for the plunger tube and stock screw bushings. Using a smooth mill file and stones, remove all the finish on the outer edges of the rails and set the receiver aside. Go easy here and maintain parallel between the rails on both sides of the frame. I check progress frequently with a dial caliper from front to rear while spanning the rails.

The initial step in removing vertical play from the slide is to remove all irregularities from its bottom edges. If you're lucky, you need nothing more than a medium stone, followed by a fine one. If you're less than lucky, truing with a smooth file may be needed first. If the slide is very hard, you'll have to rely on a milling machine and carbide end mill for your initial passes. Those passes should be extremely light.

Once the bottom edges have been trued to the point where they appear parallel with the slide-rail slots, polish them. In their newly finished state, they become the basis for adjustment of the frame rails as well as being primary bearing surfaces.

The indicator plate mentioned earlier is now inserted between the rail slots from the rear of the slide to the recoil spring tunnel.

The fit must be snug to ensure accurate slide-rail measurement. These are taken by running a depth indicator the length of the plate with the indicator's shoulders resting on the bottom of the slide.

You'll need some specialized tooling designed for frame-to-slide fitting. Top to bottom and left to right are a set of frame rail bars, a magazine well filler, slide micrometer, slide spreaders, frame side plates and dial calipers, all available from Brownells.

Any irregularities must be stoned out, polished and re-checked until you have slide bottom edges and rail slots that are perfectly parallel with each other. Only then will a measurement of slide-rail thickness (depth) be precise.

You can fabricate an indicator plate if you have basic machining skills. The plate should be made of steel and be drilled and tapped over the breech block area so at least two set screws can elevate it flush with the underside of the top slide rail and be surface ground true. Aside from having to make one, or having one made for you, a reference or indicator plate can pose problems.

If the slide-rail undersurfaces aren't true, and the indicator is elevated up against them, any measurement made will be off accordingly. To avoid this, I use a slide rail micrometer to determine depth. It's a specialized, very precise tool made by Starrett. I take measurements every $1/2$-inch along the length of both rails. If there is more than 0.002- to 0.003-inch of variation in thickness along the length of either rail, I smooth-file or stone the high spots.

The importance of slide-rail thickness can't be overstated since this determines how far the frame rails must be lowered. For example, if rail depth measures 0.114-inch, you have to lower the rails about 0.115-inch. The extra 0.001-inch is for clearance, but as little as 0.0005-inch shouldn't create a problem.

Now place the trued, polished and measured slide in a padded vise. Position it vertically, about 3 inches back from the muzzle end. Working upward, squeeze the slide in 1-inch increments without using excessive pressure. Reposition the slide in the vise aft of the ejection port and squeeze again. (I seldom apply pressure in the port area. The slide is weakest there and can easily crack if I get too ham-handed.) Apply fine lapping compound to the rails, mate the slide to the receiver, and work it back and forth. The fit can be snug, but not to a point that you can't move the slide by hand. There should be no binding. If there is, locate it and stone out the cause. Rinse all lapping compound off with solvent, re-mate the slide fully to the receiv-

er, and check for movement by torquing the assembly in the opposite, east-to-west direction. If necessary, repeat the squeezing/lapping procedure until horizontal play is minimized without any binding. If you go too far with the squeezing, and escape cracking the slide, you can widen the slide with a wooden wedge or a set of spreaders like those shown in the accompanying photo.

With horizontal play out of the picture for the moment, mount the protective plates on both sides of the frame, insert the magazine-well filler, and secure the assembly in a padded vise. Use a smooth mill file and stone to remove any burrs from the rails. Proceed to stone the forward section of the top of the receiver; round the rail ends and the front of the ways below the rails slightly.

Select the gauging bar required to lower the frame rails to the predetermined depth and insert it into the rail slot. Using your polished hammer, tap—do not bash—straight down on the rails every $1/8$-inch fore and aft of the magazine well. Lowering the rails adjacent to the well, the frame's weakest point, will do little or nothing to improve performance. After swaging down the rails one time, check the uniformity of your work with the gauge bar. If tolerances are out, insert the bar at the point or points affected and tap once or twice more. Note that in the lowering process, the rails will spread and serve to reduce side play further.

Relieve the rail edges to remove any burrs or high spots, lap the receiver and slide, clean both with solvent, and check for vertical movement. This is done with the slide in its battery position. Grab it at the muzzle end and wiggle it up and down. If there is too much vertical play, go back to the gauging bars, tapping, lapping, cleaning and checking the results again.

When you think you've got everything just right, it might not mean your job is done. Occasionally, a slide gets lowered so much it creates a whole new set of problems.

The slide could be rubbing the receiver in the recoil-spring plug area. You can correct this with emery cloth wrapped around a dowel to remove metal from the receiver. Another problem could be that the disconnector is now too long and is rubbing the bottom of the breech block. To correct this situation, shorten the disconnector by rounding off and polishing the flat at its top. Insufficient room between the frame and slide for the barrel can be fixed by using a half-round file to deepen the barrel bed until the barrel fits in with the slide in battery.

Finally, brightly polish—do not grind, file or stone—all slide and frame rail surfaces you worked on. A properly fit slide should move smoothly of its own weight when the receiver is tilted up. Also, it should have no vertical or horizontal play in excess of 0.001-inch. If you achieve that kind of fitting on your first try, you have done a lot better than I did on mine.

A final reminder on fitting. The barrel, barrel link and disconnector, each critical to the safe functioning of a M1911, are all affected by the fitting process. So are hammers and sears, especially those that have been reworked. Always, I repeat, always test-fire the pistol before considering the job to be done. When you proof the gun, don't start off with a magazine full of hardball. Stack one live round on top of a couple of dummies for the first few strings, then work your way up to nothing but full loads. It's a great way to avoid the hazards of a 45 that decides to go full auto—the least of which would be damage to your ego.

Mounting Handgun Scopes

Handgun hunting is a popular pastime these days—and it's no longer considered bad taste to have a scope on your gun. Here are some tips for mounting them.

By Chip Todd

THERE WAS A TIME when it was considered either wimpy or pretentious to put a scope on a handgun. Now that handgun hunting has become a more widely embraced form of taking game, that's no longer the case. There has been a steady upswing in requests for gunsmiths to install scopes on handguns, from large-bore revolvers through super-autos and specialty guns such as the Contender and XP-100.

I find that gun owners who would not hesitate to install a scope on their own hunting rifles ask for help to get handgun scopes installed and bore-sighted. Bore-sighting can be tricky with some types of handgun mounting systems, and many shooters are intimidated by the unknown.

If you have already selected the type of mount you want, you have a head start on the job. If not, try to choose the sturdiest type of mounting system available for that handgun. It never hurts to be overly rigid; only insufficiently so. Take into consideration the direction that the handgun will recoil, and select a design which counteracts that expected action. I have had to add a small brass pad to the bottom of several mounts with heavy scopes to eliminate bending of the mount's base under heavy recoil. There is no perfect part which will cover all contingencies, so think through what the effects from recoil will be, and determine if the mount will handle that action adequately. Remember, an object at rest will stay at rest until a force acts upon it to change that state of being. A scope will want to remain in the particular space it occupies, and will resist any force trying to put it into motion. This means that the gun will be recoiling upward and rearward, which makes the scope act as if something has hit it downward from the rear.

There are many different types of scope mounts for handguns, so I'll simply explain several of the more frequently encountered ones:

Weaver Type. The Weaver-type mount is a positive dovetail extrusion, with grooves cut laterally to accommodate the cross screws which clamp it down and take the brunt of the recoil force. The Weaver and some of its clones have rings of sheet metal and an extruded ring base. Tasco has improved this with die-cast metal rings which are both attractive and functional.

Bayonet Type. This is the design the more expensive mounts use, and is usually considered the strongest and most secure. The ring's bottom is shaped like an upright truncated cone with flats on two sides. It is inserted into a hole in the base which is similar, but turned 90 degrees. The scope is installed by placing it 90 degrees from the bore axis, sticking the ring's cone into the base's hole, and rotating the scope 90 degrees.

Sometimes only the front ring is the bayonet type, and the rear one has securing screws on both sides of the rear ring. On other sets, both rings are bayonet, and the scope is added only after the rings are secured to the base.

Conetrol System. In my opinion, the Conetrol scope-mounting rings are the best looking and the most streamlined of all the rings on the market. They're not found on the discount rack at K-Mart, but for sheer beauty and function, they cannot be matched. The machining on these rings is probably a nightmare for a production line foreman, and I suspect that they aren't turned out in large numbers.

B-Square Mounts. B-Square makes mounts that aren't intended to be aesthetically pleasing, but are designed to be simple and sturdy. They're made of strap material and are vertically oriented with

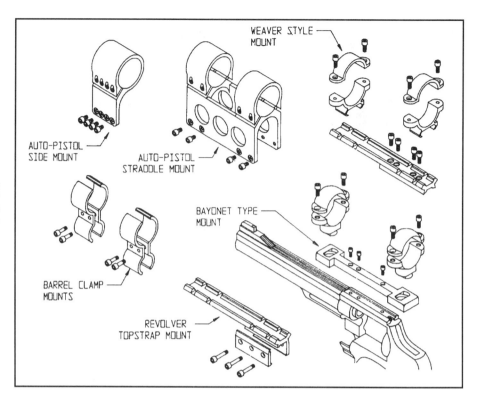

It's no longer considered bad taste to scope your handgun, and the number of mounts available is growing. These are some of the more popular.

shaped radii to hold both the barrel and the scope entrapped between the two sides. They aren't particularly cheap, but they're functional, as are most mounts that clamp onto the barrel. One of their advantages is that they are both mount base and rings in one, saving the cost of a separate base. Another advantage is that they are very rugged and secure.

The other clamp-on type of mount uses the topstrap of the receiver on revolvers as the holding point upon which to clamp. These are fairly nice looking and work well. On carbon steel guns, however, the finish will most likely suffer from the mounting of this type of base.

There are also a few mounts which are made to clamp onto the

To mount a scope, you'll need to have three of the most common taps on hand—tapered, plug, and bottoming.

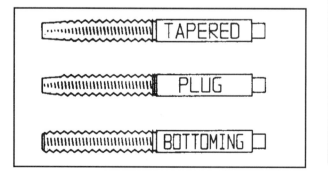

small dovetail often found on 22 rifles and some handguns. These are used with generic extruded dovetail bases. I find these mounts a handy way to mount the T/C Instasight and other dot sights with dovetail type clamps. The Cyclops is another of the passive dot sights which has its own mounting clamps to fit a dovetail.

The process of mounting a scope base on the topstrap of a revolver varies little, no matter what brand of base you use. They usually require that the gunsmith drill and tap the topstrap for the screws. This is easier said than done, as it is a permanent step and one doesn't want to have to replace a receiver or produce a weakened topstrap. Most revolvers, particularly the adjustable-sight Smith and Wesson revolvers, have a sight unit long enough that the scope base screws are hidden under the sights should you wish to remove the scope and return to the stock sighting arrangement. Even on the fixed-sight models, it is easy enough to put plug screws in the tapped holes to fill them if you want to change back to open sighting.

Before starting on a scope-mounting job, use masking tape or duct tape to hold the scope in the approximate position in which the mount will hold it. This may save you some embarrassment if the scope does not have the extended eye relief necessary for handguns, or if the eye relief is not right for the particular shooter. If the intended shooter can hold it in the position in which he is going to shoot and can see the crosshairs with a full background around them, then it's okay to proceed with the job.

For now, let's deal with the mounting of the scope on a revolver or single-shot pistol. Later, we can delve into the different procedures necessary for scoping semi-autos.

First, check to insure that the firearm is unloaded, then disassemble it. Arrange a method of keeping the parts from getting scattered, dirty or lost, by using small jars, magnetic rubber strips, or "borrowing" the Seal-A-Meal long enough to seal up the parts. I use a plastic bag sealer more than almost any other tool in my shop.

Next, remove the rear sight. If the gun has adjustable sights, clean the channel beneath the sight. If the sight base is the type held on with screws, we first need to ascertain where the base will have to sit in order to have the scope in the same position as it was when we checked for proper eye relief. Nothing is more frustrating than trying to shoot a scoped gun that you can't hold far enough away for your eye to see the crosshairs.

Place the base in position and mark the desired location of the screws with a scribe or transfer punch. I recommend that you get some transfer punches if you're serious about gunsmithing. They are graduated sizes of hard steel rod with small points in the center of one end. They are used by choosing the one which just fits through the holes in the mount, and tapping the punch with a hammer. The size of the punch's body centers the small point in the hole and marks the location you need. This is followed by a more substantial punch mark done with a regular center punch. I find it safer to punch the first hole's location, drill and tap it, and then install the mount's base with the first screw before locating the other screw holes. This has saved me lots of grief. (I didn't always do it this way.)

You'll need to devise some method of holding the revolver in the drill press in an upright position for drilling. It's possible to do the drilling with a handheld electric drill, but I'd be very careful to keep the drill bit perpendicular to the surface being drilled. It's quite a disappointment to find that the screws won't thread properly because the holes are tapped at an angle. At the very least, use a vise to ensure that the gun doesn't move while you are drilling. I always use the best bits I can afford, as the guns I drill aren't liable to be of the cheap variety. Come to think of it, I don't remember ever seeing a cheap handgun with a scope on it.

Different metals call for different drilling strategies. Stainless steel is a stringy metal that is more difficult to machine than carbon steel. Therefore, use a slow speed and stainless lube when drilling stainless, and more ordinary lubes when drilling blued steel. You will be able to purchase small cans of special machining lubes at machine-shop supply houses, and the countermen are usually well versed in lubricants. It will also pay to get your taps from a machine-shop supply or order them from Brownells. The sizes required to match the screws supplied with scope bases will not be found in tap assortments or kits, nor do such kits offer the quality you'll need for serious machining. The most often used size for scope mounts is 6-48 (a number 6 screw with 48 threads per inch).

In the locations where you will be drilling through the topstrap, you should use a tapered tap and run the tap to nearly its last thread. However, you will find that there will be times when you will have to drill and tap the front hole over the threaded part of the barrel, a situation where drilling too far can ruin a perfectly good day. This "blind" hole will require that you tap with a plug tap and follow this with a bottoming tap. The bottoming tap has full-depth cutters almost to the tip of the tap. Incidentally, when I break a tapered or plug tap, I grind it flat on the bottom and rename it a "bottoming" tap. I don't know how long it's been since I had to order a real bottoming tap.

After the holes have been tapped, you should file the burrs which have formed on the underside of the topstrap, and slightly countersink the top of the tapped holes. Next, fit the base onto the receiver and install the screws to check their length. They should not protrude below the bottom side of the topstrap, yet they need to come within one thread of the bottom. Overlength screws not only look bad, but can scar or bind the cylinder. A screw which might have to go into a blind hole, one with no opening all the way through, needs

It is easiest to do your drilling with a drill press, but an electric drill can do the job as long as you find a way to keep the gun steady and the drill straight.

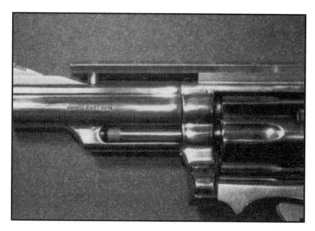

A support foot counteracts the bending of the base on recoil.

to be as long as it can be without bottoming out or running out of threads. An overlength screw in a blind hole can distort rifling or the bore.

It takes some care to shorten screws with threads as fine as 48 per inch so that the threads aren't smeared into each other. I either saw them with a hacksaw or cut them with a set of diagonal-cutting pliers. It is then necessary to grind the end flat and deburr the starting threads. I bevel the end slightly, usually only one thread's width, polish the end, and then blue it with Oxpho-Blue or whatever blueing solution is closest at hand. Be sure to rinse it with water, dry, and oil it again.

Clean the mounting base, its screws, and the threaded holes in the receiver to remove grease and tapping fluids, and decide what type of thread-locking compound you will use. Most 'smiths use either Loctite or Sta-Lok compounds, but most any will do. I have found that firearms which recoil fiercely will fracture the seal of any of the rigid locking compounds. Therefore, I often use RTV or other silicone rubber compounds which are sold as bathtub caulk. The flexible nature of the rubber ensures that it will not fracture and will give the proper locking action. I also use it like a flexible seal between the base and the receiver on the larger calibers.

Pistols

Scoping semi-automatic pistols is another ball game with a different set of umpires. The slide must be free to recoil as designed, a limitation which precludes mounting the scope on the slide, and the larger calibers put serious G-forces on the scope. There are several answers; the correct one is that with which you are the most comfortable shooting.

There are arrangements which use a special grip panel on one side, with a vertical mounting strap to support a scope over the slide. This keeps the scope from experiencing the thrills and agonies of a slide ride. They aren't as popular as the frame mounts because they aren't generally perceived as things of beauty.

The most popular semi-auto scope mounts are those which mount to the frame; either they cantilever the scope over the bore, or straddle the slide in a bridge fashion to give a sturdier and more

symmetrical appearance. One of the drawbacks of these two styles is the necessity of drilling and tapping the receiver. Even if the owner doesn't mind the holes being punched in his favorite weapon, many receivers aren't thick enough in the right places to allow more than two threads in the holes. This means that there must be more holes for more screws to make up for the deficiency in thickness. To deal with this, the newer combat guns tend to have thicker walls in the proper places to accept mounts.

If the receiver is a hardened variety, you will need to drill the pilot hole for tapping one size over that which is normally recommended. When tapping 6-48 holes, I use a No. 31 and $1/8$-inch bits for regular and hard metals, respectively. The latter gives very little thread engagement and good screws must be used. Here again, I use the silicone rubber to lock them without fracturing.

Side mounts, such as the CPMi mount for the CZ-75 and its clones, are held stable with Allen screws, since they hold the scope from a single point, albeit a ring which is almost a tube. I find that mount to be very stable and fairly easy to install—after I got past the problem of the hardened receiver. The instructions called for a 0 to 1 degree down slant in relation to the bore. This was the only part which was the least bit uncomfortable about the installation. I find myself glad I have one of the SmartLevels, which is a digital inclinometer of great accuracy, since I'm certain that I would have aimed for a 0-degree installation if I didn't have the digital meter. A straightedge is something that all of us know how to use, so I'd suggest that for this type of installation.

You will find some semi-autos with the barrel exposed in such a way as to lend a stable platform for the scope mount. This is more often found in the rimfire pistols which operate with a simple blow-back action, such as the High Standard and Ruger.

I lock the threads in the same fashion as those of the revolver's base. The scope is inserted into the ring(s) and tightened very tightly before proceeding to the zeroing-in stage. This is the same for scopes, dot-sights, and electronic wonder sights. On the harder-recoiling calibers I also use the silicone rubber around the inside of the rings before setting the scope into the rings.

Sighting-in a scoped pistol is made easier by using a bore sight such as the Bushnell or Tasco models, which come with good instructions. The bore-sights will not zero the scopes well enough to be dependable for hunting, but will at least get you onto the target at 200 yards. In lieu of a bore sight, I would hold the gun in a vise and find a way to sight through the bore from the firing pin hole. Pick out an object about 20 or 25 feet away and center it in the bore at the muzzle end. Then, very carefully adjust the crosshairs of the scope to that object.

This is as much as one can do without shooting the pistol. Even laser sighting devices only give line-of-bore sighting at best. Each shooter holds the handgun differently with varying degrees of wrist rigidity, so the shooter needs to have this pointed out to him. I steer away from "sighting in" a gun for them, as they usually don't know how many factors are working against the possibility of a universal sight adjustment. By all means, request that the gun not be shot until the next day, as the thread-sealing compound needs time to set properly.

Handgun Security Devices You Can Make

Here are some effective but inexpensive handgun locks you can make in your shop.

By Chip Todd

THERE HAS ALWAYS been a need for a device which will allow easy access to a firearm yet keep it safe from youngsters. The problem can be easily solved by throwing money at it—or by sacrificing quick and easy access to the gun by adults.

In spite of its overprotective and restrictive ways, California has finally passed a gun law that makes sense. How they handle it remains to be seen. The law provides for felony charges against the owner of a firearm who leaves that gun within easy access of a child if that child has an accident with it. (Florida and other states have similar measures on the books.) I think that the law, taken at face value, is a good one, because we all have a moral obligation to see that something of ours isn't harmful to others.

It has been shown that within a very few minutes of picking up a handgun, a toddler will have it aimed straight at his face with his thumb on the trigger. There's apparently a natural tendency to look down the barrel; this is just a baby's way.

The problems with the design of existing handgun locks are the cost of the better systems, the poor looks on collectible firearms, and systems which are relatively easy for teenagers (and even six-year-olds) to defeat. Some of the designs are also awkward, and tend to damage the finishes of high-priced guns. Any one of these reasons is enough to eliminate them from faithful use.

To be effective, the safety lock must reach all the way to the breech; it shouldn't be easily removed with common tools found around the house; and it must be quickly removable in time of need.

One approach manufacturers have used is making the lock require a manual dexterity that youngsters don't yet possess. This might work with toddlers, but its not an effective approach with teenagers, who have as much dexterity as most adults.

In my opinion, a unique "key" is the solution to the problem—one which can't be readily made by a teenager. To prevent a round from being chambered and the gun exploded by accident, the lock cannot block the barrel without also blocking the chamber. Now, if the firearm were to be safe from damage to its finish and could be left loaded and still be safe, we would have all the bases covered.

Bruce Farmer and I have designed a gun lock that satisfies all

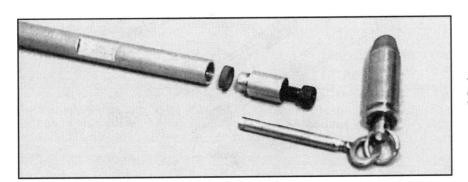

The Todd/Farmer handgun security device can be produced by almost anyone with only a few simple tools.

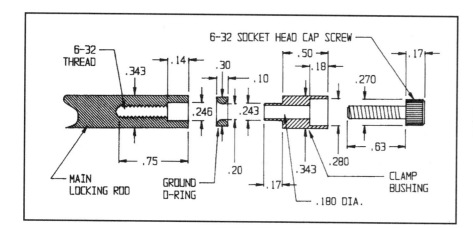

6-32 SOCKET HEAD CAP SCREW

6-32 THREAD

MAIN LOCKING ROD

GROUND O-RING

CLAMP BUSHING

.180 DIA.

Sectional drawing of the gun lock with dimensions. The simpler version uses the same dimensions.

these requirements. Plus, it can be made by the average handyman or apprentice gunsmith with very few tools. The easier of the two models put forth here could be made with a drill press, or even just a hand drill and file. The "deluxe" model would be better made on a lathe. A third one, which I have drawn, is better than either of the others, but takes a slitting saw which most people don't have available. I will explain the two easier locks so that you can make your own decision should you choose to make one. Actually, there are really more than three models, as semi-automatic pistols, rifles and shotguns would use a chamber-only type, while revolvers would be able to use the through-the-chamber-and-bore type.

The accompanying drawings really tell the story of the gun lock's construction, so I'll simply add some additional instructions that may prove helpful. I used brass for my prototype locks because, being softer than steel, it can't damage the bore. Brass is also cheaper than stainless steel and more readily available in the sizes needed to approximate the diameter of popular bores. You could probably use a plated metal, but I can't see going to the trouble when brass will do just as well without that expense.

The size I chose to use for 357 and 9mm bores is 0.344 or $^{11}/_{32}$-inch. This was determined by snugging the minor diameter of a 357 bore with a small hole gauge and measuring the results with a dial caliper. I then subtracted 0.005-inch so that the same rod stock would be useful for 9mm handguns as well. I would use the same 0.005-inch clearance for other calibers, since that's enough to allow easy insertion, and the O-ring can easily expand that much under the compression of a 32-pitch thread. An easier calculation would be to try to find some round stock between 0.008- and 0.013-inch

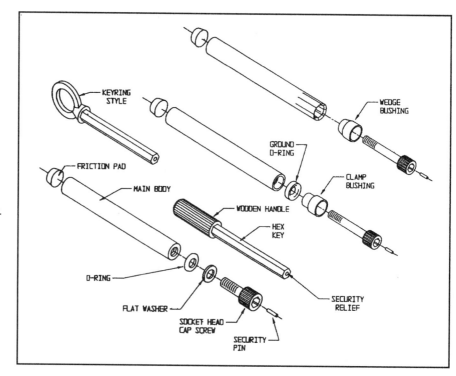

Exploded parts view of the gun lock.

KEYRING STYLE

FRICTION PAD

MAIN BODY

O-RING

FLAT WASHER

SOCKET HEAD CAP SCREW

SECURITY PIN

WOODEN HANDLE

HEX KEY

SECURITY RELIEF

GROUND O-RING

WEDGE BUSHING

CLAMP BUSHING

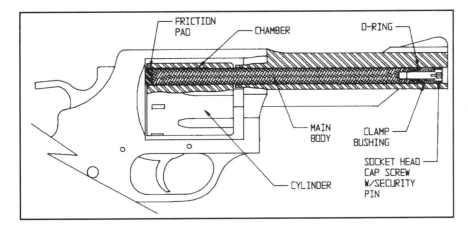

The gun lock is easily installed and removed, as this cutaway drawing shows.

less than the nominal bullet size for the caliber.

The inside diameter of the O-ring should be from 0.020-inch under to 0.020 over the diameter of the screw used. The cross-section of the O-ring should be about $1/8$-inch diameter, so that it can be ground to leave a flat surface at the diameter of the gun-lock rod.

You will need most of the equipment listed below, although, with a bit of ingenuity, you might do without a couple of items listed:

- Drill motor or drill press
- Drill bit(s)
- File
- Sandpaper or ScotchBrite pad
- Allen wrench
- Contact cement or "crazy" glue
- Dremel grinder (not absolutely necessary)

I choose the soft stock, either neoprene or other oil-resistant material, with a high coefficient of friction before I do any cutting of the metal. This allows me to know how much to subtract from the length from the muzzle to the breechface. I measure the distance from the muzzle to the breechface, subtract the thickness of the friction disk plus another inch for the section nearest the muzzle. Both ends of this rod must be fairly smooth and perpendicular to the length of the rod. A hacksaw or cutoff tool (in the lathe) are sufficient for cutting the stock, and a file and drill press or lathe tool do well in squaring the ends.

Drill first with a starting drill like a center drill and follow that with a drill of the proper size for the tap you are to use. In a drill press, centering the drill can be a challenge for a beginning gunsmith. This is fairly easy when you know the trick. Chuck up the end of the rod you want to drill, and lower the rod through the drill press vise. Clamp the rod in the vise with the vise free to move on its own, and then secure the vise in the position it finds. Loosening the drill chuck, install a center drill and drill the center of the rod in the vise. The drilled hole should be in the center of the rod.

Drill the tap drill size about $1/2$-inch deep and tap the threads in it. I used an 8-32 thread, but a 6-32 socket-head cap screw will suffice for even a 22 caliber, as the head can be thinned down to 0.177-inch in diameter without any trouble. Smaller screw heads have hex sockets too small on which to reliably put security posts. I would really hate to try to drill a hole in a $1/16$-inch hex socket and

install such a security post, much less try to drill the Allen wrench for the post.

The method of using a washer and not a counterbored section of rod is much easier to do and is just as good. It doesn't have the professional looks when out of the firearm, but is just as secure as the other. The washer's outside diameter can be reduced by installing it on a screw with a nut, and then spinning it in a drill press with a file against it. The washer should be filed down to the diameter of the gun-lock rod.

Install the O-ring onto the gun-lock with the washer or clamping sleeve, and tighten the screw about one-half turn after it starts clamping the O-ring. Reinstall the unit in the drill press or lathe with the breech end in the chuck. While spinning the unit in the lathe or drill press, hold a Dremel tool with drum sander or drum-shaped grinding stone against the O-ring, thereby reducing the outside diameter of the O-ring to the diameter of the main rod. This will, of course, shape the outside to a flatness which will be just what we want. Tighten the screw more tightly and measure the O-ring's diameter to ascertain that it will put pressure on the inside of the bore. The ones I do easily expand over 0.025-inch in diameter with only minimal tightening. This is more than enough to lock the rod into the bore.

The friction pad can now be cemented onto the breech end of the rod and the rod reinstalled in the drill press or lathe. Repeating what we did with the O-ring, we can shape the friction pad to a shape which has the end slightly smaller than the rod end. Now we should be ready to try it for size. Push the rod against the breech with the Allen wrench, and tighten the screw slightly until the rod cannot be pulled out of the barrel by slanting the wrench and pulling. Over-tightening could cut the O-ring in such a way that it would prove difficult to remove.

A good variation on this design would be to have the main rod of the gun lock countersunk on the end and split into several fingers by slitting with a slitting saw back about $1/2$-inch. The clamping sleeve would then need a cone-shaped end to force the split fingers out to clamp the bore.

Clean up the gun lock in a suitable solvent which won't dissolve the cement used for the friction pad. I usually clean the brass rod with either fine steel wool or ScotchBrite pads before cleaning with the solvent.

Working Colt Single-Action Revolvers

European copies of this type of revolver are enjoying renewed popularity. Here is how to make them more "user friendly."

By Thomas J. Stuntebeck

The Colt SAA Model 1873 is the basis from which almost all of today's single actions are derived.

SAMUEL COLT IS generally considered to be the father of the revolving-cylinder handgun. It was rumored that he "borrowed" the idea from an English gunmaker, but apparently he was never challenged on it and turned out his first revolver, the Paterson model, in 1837. The company he founded went through many financial ups and downs for the next 10 years. In 1847, however, the Walker Colt put him on a solid footing and he and his company did extremely well until his death at age 48 in 1862.

Colt Patent Firearms Co. continued upgrading the basic concept, and 11 years after Colt's death, the first fixed-ammunition revolver made its appearance. The Model of 1873 is the parent gun of most single-action revolvers made up to today, 123 years later. Remington made three models, the 1858 percussion and the 1875 and 1890 centerfire revolvers, though they never did as well commercially as the Colt. Their mechanisms are similar to the Colt's, but since the 1873 type is the most common, we will be dealing with it in much greater depth. The 1873 is one of the most imitated guns in existence, with modern copies coming from Italy and Germany. In addition, domestic companies like Ruger used it as a base for many mechanisms of their own design.

SAA revolvers made by Uberti of Italy and imported under a number of banners seem to be the most accurate reproductions, and are probably the most used by western re-enactors and cowboy shooting groups around the country. Fast-draw clubs, though not as active as they were a few years ago, still do their part with these same guns. Tuning fast-draw guns is another discipline by itself. For now, we'll concern ourselves with making the old hawgleg/thumbuster just a bit more "user friendly" than it is when it comes out of the box.

I was among those who went along with the idea that a hard-heavy action was meant to be that way or the factory would not have made it. Back in 1873, the historical need for a heavy hammer strike went back to the percussion guns and into the flintlock era. The primers used in the first centerfire ammunition no doubt needed a very sound blow as well.

Primers made today are hotter, more consistent, and have softer cup material in them. Today, a factory hard-heavy action is bowing to either tradition or a potential product-liability suit. In either case, the weights found on most triggers are unnecessarily heavy and probably account for most of the premature wear and breakage found on these guns.

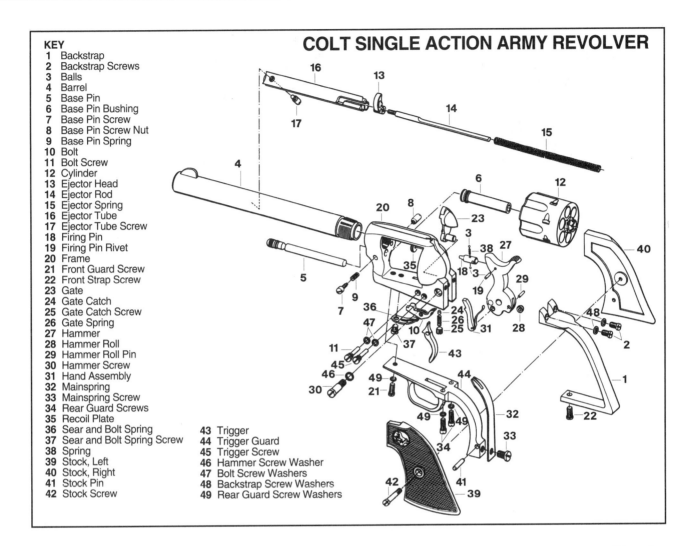

COLT SINGLE ACTION ARMY REVOLVER

KEY
1 Backstrap
2 Backstrap Screws
3 Balls
4 Barrel
5 Base Pin
6 Base Pin Bushing
7 Base Pin Screw
8 Base Pin Screw Nut
9 Base Pin Spring
10 Bolt
11 Bolt Screw
12 Cylinder
13 Ejector Head
14 Ejector Rod
15 Ejector Spring
16 Ejector Tube
17 Ejector Tube Screw
18 Firing Pin
19 Firing Pin Rivet
20 Frame
21 Front Guard Screw
22 Front Strap Screw
23 Gate
24 Gate Catch
25 Gate Catch Screw
26 Gate Spring
27 Hammer
28 Hammer Roll
29 Hammer Roll Pin
30 Hammer Screw
31 Hand Assembly
32 Mainspring
33 Mainspring Screw
34 Rear Guard Screws
35 Recoil Plate
36 Sear and Bolt Spring
37 Sear and Bolt Spring Screw
38 Spring
39 Stock, Left
40 Stock, Right
41 Stock Pin
42 Stock Screw
43 Trigger
44 Trigger Guard
45 Trigger Screw
46 Hammer Screw Washer
47 Bolt Screw Washers
48 Backstrap Screw Washers
49 Rear Guard Screw Washers

My circa-1915 P-frame Colt has a $6^1/_2$-pound cocking weight and a $2^1/_4$-pound trigger pull. My Uberti Sheriff's Model P-frame has a 7-pound cocking weight and a $2^3/_4$-pound trigger weight. Both, in 45 Colt caliber, have never failed to fire a live round of ammunition. Both actions may be considered too light for the average shooter, but I built them this way to make a statement. The techniques we will discuss here should permit you to adjust an action to almost any degree, while assuring that it will safely do what it was intended to do.

To begin work on the revolver, clear and disassemble the gun completely. Scrub all parts thoroughly in a good solvent, whether the gun is new or old. Smooth out the sides of the hammer with an India stone and fine emery paper, concentrating on the area around the pivot-pin hole. On a rouge wheel, polish the hammer roller and the bottom-rear of the hammer where it is mounted. Holding the hammer with the notches facing down, polish that area, but be careful not to thin the webs of the safety and half-cock notches any more than it takes to get a high polish. Draw the hammer up and away from the wheel so as to not roll the edge of the cock notch.

With the same grits, smooth up the sides of the trigger. Highly polish the rear of the trigger in the curved area just below the sear contact point. Avoid disturbing the contact point if possible. A Cratex bob on a Dremel tool works well in this area for me.

Polish the side of the cylinder bolt with fine emery paper. Don't take an appreciable amount off the locking lug itself unless it is needed. Polish, to a rather high degree, the bottom of the piece where the spring makes contact. On the rouge wheel, polish the beveled area that makes contact with the camming bevel on the hammer. I also like to smooth out the face of that particular part of the hammer and polishing it.

Starting with an India stone and finishing up with fine emery cloth, smooth out the sides and front of the hand. Stay below the lower tooth of the hand on the front, and do not change the dimensions at the top unless it proves to be necessary. Carefully polish the front area on the rouge wheel and, being extremely careful, polish the rear curve of the hand spring.

In some guns, the pin holes on these parts have already been chamfered. If this has not been done, use a small cone-shaped carbide cutter to do the work. I use it in an "eggbeater" drill to avoid taking too much material out of the hole. This process removes any small burrs or irregularities on the piece and creates a small reservoir for lubricants, making it worth the extra effort.

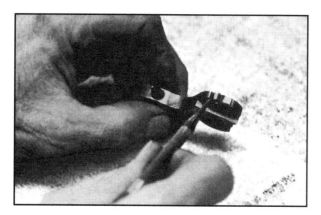

Polishing the front of the hammer hooks and hammer toe gets you started toward a smoother action.

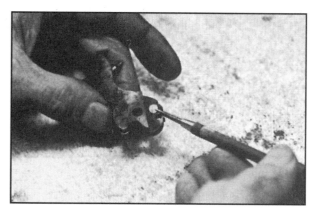

Stoning and polishing the cylinder-stop cam bevel eases the revolver's operation and prevents breakage of the stop legs.

Examine the hammer, trigger, and cylinder bolt screws for any roughness. If any smoothing is necessary, wrap fine emery paper around the pivotal area and turn the screw until a smooth finish is produced. Be careful not to make any large dimensional changes to these pins, as their parts can easily become misaligned, with an adverse affect on functioning.

Polish the full length of the cylinder pin, except that part showing through the front of the frame. Chamfer the front of the pin bushing in the cylinder, and check the rotation of the cylinder on the pin with those pieces installed in the bare frame. The bushing is a separate piece in the Colt SAA, but if it is in the cylinder solidly, I would not try to remove it. Instead, treat it as one piece. Giving the cylinder a brief, high-speed spin with compressed air will help detect any roughness inside the bushing and, if minor, will do the burnishing needed to smooth it out. Be cautious if you plan to lap these pieces together, because the wear can get away from you very easily!

With fine emery and an Arkansas stone, burnish the faces of the cylinder ratchet and the cylinder bushing. Be careful not to remove a significant amount of material or excess cylinder end-play will result, which could affect the gun's headspacing.

If the gun you are working has excess play and faulty headspacing, now might be a good time to make up a new bushing. I have used sections of a 22 barrel turned between centers. I make them approximately 0.050-inch longer in overall length to allow for a good final fitting. The added length is in the front bearing area, with the original measurements from the shoulder to the rear remaining the same.

In-house manufacture of both a bushing and cylinder pin might be considered if these parts have worn excessively in an older gun. An inordinate amount of movement in the cylinder—fore and aft as well as side to side—can affect timing, ranging, headspace, and the ultimate safety and reliability of this firearm. If you don't want to make the parts, they are available from EMF Corp., Gun Parts Inc., and more than likely from Dixie Gun Works. As a courtesy to gun owners, I always keep the old parts and offer to return them, especially in the case of an old, original arm.

If you are working a gun that has a "nail-breaker" loading gate, freeing it up is a relatively simple matter. Smooth and polish the top of the loading-gate catch (plunger), and round the corner of the two flats on the gate-pivot pin. Arkansas stone the area and polish on the

rouge wheel for a final finish. If it is still too stout, clip half a coil off the spring at a time, and try it after each cutting. Be sure the catch screw is set flush with the bottom of the frame. When finished, the gate should still snap open and closed with some authority. It should swing open with only moderate thumb pressure, however.

Having covered those areas that affect the smooth operation of the firearm, we'll deal with what some may consider sacred ground— the action weight. If an old P-frame is to remain "original," I would do no more than polish the contact points of the hammer spring, trigger and bolt spring, and the rear curve of the hand spring. On a new reproduction, I would do the same for starters, then carefully bend the legs of the trigger and bolt spring in the appropriate direction to reduce their tension until a satisfactory weight or feel has been reached. Most of the new flat springs are not as brittle as the old ones, and will tolerate some careful recontouring.

If bending springs is not your cup of tea, a shim under the trigger and bolt spring may work just as well. The thickness of the shim will determine how far away the legs will sit from the two parts, controlling how much tension is applied to them. I have used leather, neoprene, steel or aluminum shims under this spring, depending on the desired softness or crispness of movement. A try with all of these materials might be in order before the job is called finished.

By this time, the hand spring has been polished. Now we can address the tension this spring applies to the hand to keep it in contact with the cylinder ratchet. The hand is one of the high-wear parts on this gun, not so much from rotating the cylinder as from being dragged over the ratchet as the cylinder is spun for loading and unloading. The extreme tension of the hand spring is the main culprit. Going into the hand recess of the frame with a 1/4- by 1/4-inch India stone and cleaning up the back and side well, helps to ease the hand's operation noticeably. Nevertheless, the spring tension will eventually have to be addressed.

With small, flat-jawed pliers, carefully bend the spring toward the hand in short movements, trying the feel with the hand and hammer together in the frame after each bend. At the same time you are trying these parts for feel and function, check the action of the cylinder bolt. It should release the cylinder just before the hand begins to rotate the cylinder. If things were working properly before you bent anything, but now give you trouble, put a slight bit

This photo shows the relationship of the hammer to the cylinder-stop legs as the hammer is being cocked.

The hammer roller, the bottom rear of the hammer, and the hammer-spring contact area must be polished.

of tension back into the hand spring. The hand may not have been going deep enough into the ratchet to start it out properly. The timing of these two parts is critical to the good operation of this revolver.

There are many schools of thought on the treatment of the hammer spring. The oldest involves placing a leather shim between the frontstrap and the spring, with the mounting screw going through both pieces. This acts like a shock absorber and gives the feel of weight reduction. You can't go back much more with the shim than a $3/16$-inch thickness, or you will lose contact with the hammer roller. Depending on its hardness, a $3/16$-inch shim will compress to about $1/8$-inch under screw tension. That does it where I am concerned. If the gun has one-piece grips, you may have to do some relief work to fit them again. As long as the shim is shaved down flush with the frame, two-piece grips should give you no trouble.

Next to bending, probably the most controversial method of reducing a hammer spring's tension is thinning the spring by planing, grinding it on a rotary stone, band sander, or file. This is a permanent alteration to the part and should be approached with a good deal of thought and caution. Bending carefully might be better for your purposes if you go at it slowly.

If you opt to grind, I'd recommend you use a band sander with a very fine grit tape. This prevents the rapid removal of material from a single spot along the length of the spring that might become a breakage point. Keep the spring moving as you grind. Come off the grinder in a straight line to keep from dubbing over the ends or leaving a lump. Hold the spring with bare fingers. This helps you determine how hot it is getting so you don't draw the temper out of it. If it turns blue while you are holding it with gloves or a vise-grip plier, you may have lost the battle. Bare is better; you'll drop it long before any heat can hurt it.

Take the time between grinding sessions to put it in the frame and weigh the trigger and, if possible, the cocking weight. It would be a good idea to test it on empty cases with rifle primers in them, too. As long as you are busting them, you know the pistol primers will work. Where you stop is largely up to you, but you may want to keep the trigger weight around the 4- to $4^1/2$-pound mark for starters.

Depending on how far you took the grind, you may have to deep-

en the hammer-roller notch at the top of the spring. For looks more than anything else, I polish the spring over its full length before I reassemble. Note: If you are not well-versed in grinding springs like this, I'd suggest you ensure that there is a replacement item available.

Do not decrease the depth of the cock notch. It's very shallow—even though it may feel like it's half a foot wide. Burnish its face with a square Arkansas stone, doing the same on the contact surface at the top of the trigger. Color the two areas with black magic marker and work them together a couple of times to see if they are making contact all the way across. I prefer to make any adjustments to this condition on the trigger. It's the least expensive of the two items, in case it has to be replaced!

Tear it down again and give all the parts a good scrubbing in solvent. There will be carborundum dust and rouge in every nook and cranny, and it will wear the gun out like valve-grinding compound when it's combined with oil. Dry everything off and lubricate again. I like to use a silicone spray when all the parts are laid out on the bench. It gets into places I might miss after it's back together. Be sure all the pivot points get a drop or two of a good grade of gun oil before you close it up.

Hand cycle the action a number of times. You may want to make a few more adjustments up or down, but the base work is there. As with all work of this kind, safety is paramount! Check all the safety features for proper operation before you take the gun out to the range. Of course, a test firing is in order—just to be sure it all works together the way you set it up. I begin with milder handloads and work my way up.

Most of these techniques will also work on single-action percussion revolvers since their actions are the basis for the 1873. You should bear in mind that, although the percussion caps are a bit more sensitive today, the hammer weight will still need to be somewhat heavier to ensure positive ignition on all different manufacturers' caps. This takes very little away from the job, though it will probably not have the overall slickness of the Model 73 and its imitators.

What remains, then, is waiting for the look on the face of whoever tries it as he thumbs back the hammer for the first time. If you let someone shoot it, you may have to fight him off if he wants to buy the gun from you. You'll have a gun you can be proud of for two reasons—it's a lot slicker and it shoots better, too.

Repairing Beretta 92 Pistols

Following a few simple guidelines about what should and shouldn't be done to the Beretta will make its repairs go smoothly.

By Butch Thomson

IT HAS ALWAYS been said that consumer sales will boom on any given gun if it gets into the movies, wins a military contract, or is a choice of law enforcement agencies. Beretta Model 92 pistols have done all three of those things and, sure enough, their sales have been as strong as any handgun's in the country for the last several years.

Most buyers think handguns with such impressive credentials should and will perform perfectly every time and are very disappointed the first time it has to make a trip to the shop. It doesn't make them feel any better to hear that even good guns must be worked on from time to time.

In that respect, the Beretta 92 is no different from a lot of less-famous guns: it's good, but it makes frequent visits to the repair shop.

The pistol's basic problems usually stem from failures in feeding, extraction. or ejection and misfires. We'll discuss these first, looking at their common causes and the most obvious solutions. As we get into the disassembly process, we'll examine the individual parts' role in all this and how they are affected by the problems.

Feeding difficulties. Of the four leading factors that lead to this problem, bad ammunition is probably the leading contributor. You'd be amazed how many times people will try to shoot bent, indented, or otherwise faulty cartridges. Replacing the ammo often corrects everything, even if it is the simplest solution. Most of us take it for granted, but cleaning a pistol is something a lot of shooters don't think of or do. Their feeding problems are caused by dirty chambers and actions, and solved by a good cleaning. The third cause, related to the second, is a dirty or sticky magazine. Many people who are sticklers for keeping their guns clean have never disassembled and cleaned a magazine. Damaged magazines, whether they are indented, burred, have bent lips or other blemishes, are the fourth cause of feeding woes and must be replaced or repaired.

Extraction failures. These are also caused by four major factors, the most common of which is a jammed extractor. The Beretta's exposed extractor is easily fouled by powder residue, dirt and other foreign matter and must be cleaned thoroughly and often to prevent the problem. A dirty chamber will hold a fired case just long enough to stop the extraction. Cleaning and lightly oiling the chamber will cure this sticky problem. Bad ammunition, which may not be powerful enough to get everything moving, or might even have a faulty rim, causes extraction problems more often than people would think. Short recoil is the fourth cause but one of the trickiest to trace. This condition is often ammunition-related. A short stroke caused by underpowered ammo could mean a bullet is stuck inside the barrel, an extremely dangerous condition. Many guns have been blown up as someone attempted to fire a second round through a plugged barrel. Anytime a gun is reported to have had a short recoil, always inspect the barrel for any sign of swelling inside.

Ejection failures. Every factor that affects extraction can cause ejection problems, as can a damaged ejector. The common belief has always been that as long as good ammunition is used and the gun is kept clean, the ejector should not cause any problems, but that's more theory than fact. In the real world, they have to be replaced from time to time for a variety of reasons. The ejector on one 92 that came in for repairs had literally been ground off the pistol. The owner just said he thought that would make it work better.

Misfires. This condition can be blamed not only on bad ammunition or the pistol being dirty, but such factors as the safety not being fully turned to the off/fire position, improper work on the action, the action's not fully closing, firing pin damage, or an impaired mainspring. Check out everything you can think of in this area before opening up the action.

Now let's take a more detailed look at the Beretta's magazine, the role it plays in the gun's feeding problems, and some ways to correct the condition.

BERETTA MODEL 92F AND 92F COMPACT AUTO

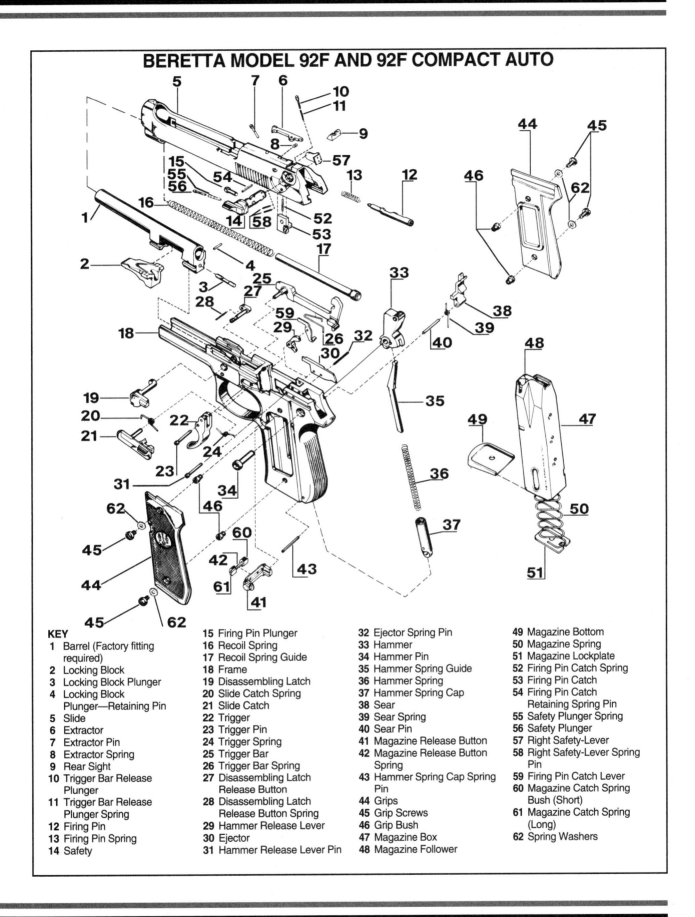

KEY

1 Barrel (Factory fitting required)
2 Locking Block
3 Locking Block Plunger
4 Locking Block Plunger—Retaining Pin
5 Slide
6 Extractor
7 Extractor Pin
8 Extractor Spring
9 Rear Sight
10 Trigger Bar Release Plunger
11 Trigger Bar Release Plunger Spring
12 Firing Pin
13 Firing Pin Spring
14 Safety

15 Firing Pin Plunger
16 Recoil Spring
17 Recoil Spring Guide
18 Frame
19 Disassembling Latch
20 Slide Catch Spring
21 Slide Catch
22 Trigger
23 Trigger Pin
24 Trigger Spring
25 Trigger Bar
26 Trigger Bar Spring
27 Disassembling Latch Release Button
28 Disassembling Latch Release Button Spring
29 Hammer Release Lever
30 Ejector
31 Hammer Release Lever Pin

32 Ejector Spring Pin
33 Hammer
34 Hammer Pin
35 Hammer Spring Guide
36 Hammer Spring
37 Hammer Spring Cap
38 Sear
39 Sear Spring
40 Sear Pin
41 Magazine Release Button
42 Magazine Release Button Spring
43 Hammer Spring Cap Spring Pin
44 Grips
45 Grip Screws
46 Grip Bush
47 Magazine Box
48 Magazine Follower

49 Magazine Bottom
50 Magazine Spring
51 Magazine Lockplate
52 Firing Pin Catch Spring
53 Firing Pin Catch
54 Firing Pin Catch Retaining Spring Pin
55 Safety Plunger Spring
56 Safety Plunger
57 Right Safety-Lever
58 Right Safety-Lever Spring Pin
59 Firing Pin Catch Lever
60 Magazine Catch Spring Bush (Short)
61 Magazine Catch Spring (Long)
62 Spring Washers

If you find out your gun won't feed correctly, try to discover what the gun is doing. If it is jamming a military-type full-metal-jacketed cartridge against the feed throat or is feeding too high, more than likely it is the magazine and not the pistol. You will also find that the cartridges sometimes ride too high in the magazine, a condition that prompts an extracting cartridge's rim to catch on the lip of the next round in the magazine. This can cause a stovepipe jam or a short stroke of the action and failure to feed the next round.

With the gun closed and empty, try to jiggle the magazine around. It will have some play but the movement should be minimal. When the magazine is latched, you should not be able to pull down on it at all and, when pushed, it should move upward less than a millimeter. Now open the breech and let the slide catch. Hold it open and repeat what you just did with it closed. It should feel just the same. If there is greater movement in this case than there was before, the feeding problems can probably be solved by replacing the magazine. However, there is no guarantee that the magazine will be a good one, even if it does fit in the well properly. If the magazine moved up and down, check the latch for wear or indications that someone may have tried to modify it. There is one cut on each side of the magazine, one for right-hand shooters and one for left-hand shooters. Remove the magazine and look at the feed lips. If someone has been trying to adjust them, you can nearly always see the telltale marks of pliers. You might also find that the front edges have been filed or ground down by someone who mistakenly believes this will make his pistol better feed hollowpoints. It won't help, but it will let the next cartridge in the magazine slip too far forward on recoil, which in turn causes the feeding round to rise too high and create the problem that we just talked about. If the magazine has been worked on, starting all over with a new one is preferable to trying to re-shape bent feed lips. Bending and re-bending of the metal takes away its original spring-like capabilities.

The next problem we have with these magazines is internal. A dirty or damaged follower, spring or box will cause feeding problems. Pushing in on the plate nipple that extends through the hole in the magazine bottom allows it to slip forward off the box, freeing the plate, spring and follower. The spring, which is attached to the plate, should extend at least 2 inches below the bottom of the magazine box with the follower fully to the top. If it is not, the spring is either fatigued or has been shortened, and should be replaced. Some shooters clip the spring and grind down the bottom of the follower to make room in the magazine for an extra cartridge. This practice is ill-advised because it makes the magazine, and therefore the pistol, unreliable.

Converting the Beretta's magazine release from its right-handed position to accommodate left-handed shooters is a common and normally very easy job. Remove the grip panels and put the frame in a vise, remembering that the alloy frame is marred easily and must be protected. With a punch about the same size as the magazine release button, push the button in as far as it will go. It should be about two or three millimeters below the surface of the frame, although it sometimes sticks and doesn't want to go in all the way. Holding the button in place, unscrew the other side, remove all the parts, and reassemble them from the opposite side.

All that sounds easy. And it is, until you've used an hour and every trick in the book to make a stubborn button go in far enough

only to find that you can't reassemble from the other side because the magazine release catch is not the same size on both ends. I felt bad about charging our minimum service fee for a five-minute job until I hit three in a row that just refused to work. I learned my lesson—do not quote a cheap price unless you leave room for the troublesome job.

To field-strip the Model 92, depress the latch release on the right side of the frame and rotate the disassembly latch on the left side clockwise until it points down. Pull the slide and barrel assembly forward off the frame. Pushing the recoil spring guide forward releases it from the locking block to be lifted out of the slide. The locking block plunger extends beyond the breech end of the barrel. By pushing it toward the muzzle, the locking block will move away from the barrel, which can then be removed from the slide. The recoil spring is the same on either end, so remembering which end to reassemble onto the guide bar isn't necessary. On the other hand, making a habit of putting a spring back in the same way it came off will help you avoid problems when springs unexpectedly turn out to be directional.

If you need to remove the locking block from the barrel, you must drive out the locking block plunger pin. This pin can be driven out from either side. There are no springs in this unit, so it comes apart with ease. Pull the plunger down from the rear of the barrel lug, and the locking bolt will slide out either side. Beyond cleaning, do not mess with this locking block. Do not attempt polishing, buffing or fitting. This locking block is factory-fitted and any play in it makes the breech insecure, which can be dangerous. Despite the risk, people still grind on these locking blocks in hopes of smoothing the action, which is rough by design.

Never do more than the following to smooth this action: Use a soft buffing wheel and fine jewelers rouge on the sharp edges, polishing just enough to smooth them. Be sure the front rounded edge, which faces the muzzle when assembled, is smooth but never polish it enough that metal is removed. A good rule of thumb is to avoid removing all the blueing from a blued Model 92, while only lightly buffing the stainless steel version. Roughness in the plunger slot can be eliminated with a fine emery cloth rolled over something the size of a toothpick. Again, do not remove all the blueing. You can polish the end of the plunger, but do not change the shape of its round end, and be sure you don't shorten it.

The bearing surface of the barrel lug that faces the bearing surface of the locking block can be lightly buffed, as long as metal is not removed to the point that the locking block is looser than it was when you started.

The Beretta extractor's shape and tight fit does a good job of keeping dirt out while the gun is holstered, but the extractor is vulnerable to fouling from firing. The tight fit also works against it, as even minor build-ups can prevent the extractor from doing its job. This in turn makes the part more susceptible to rust. An extractor pin that can be driven out from the top of the slide secures the extractor. Its spring is very strong, so pay attention when it is released. The extractor claw is large and tough enough to avoid problems under most conditions, but it should be inspected regardless. The claw can and will break, especially if it gets loaded down with dirt or rust.

Disassembly starts by turning the takedown latch—which is

occasionally hard to remove—to its normal carry position and pressing the latch release button as far into the frame as possible. Pull out on the takedown latch while lifting it up, and wiggle it. The latch will slip over the slide rail and can be lifted out of the frame. When the takedown latch separates from the takedown release button, the button and its spring will come out of the right side of the frame. If you have removed the grip screws but the grips are sticking to the frame, reach inside the magazine well and press out on each panel.

At this point, remove the trigger-bar spring by slipping the point of a thin-bladed screwdriver between the bar and the spring. Slide the point of the screwdriver toward the rear of the frame until the spring comes out of the slot cut in the bottom of the trigger bar. By rolling the screwdriver's tip over, you can pop the top of the spring right out of the trigger bar. Now pull the part of the trigger-bar spring that faces the front of the pistol up and out of the slot cut in the frame. Swing the front of the spring out away from the frame and lift the rear of this spring out of the hole that houses the rear part of the trigger-bar spring.

It is now time to remove the trigger bar. After cocking the hammer, pull the front of the bar partially out of the trigger, then move to the rear of the bar and slip the bar out and over the safety as far as it will come. Returning to the front of the trigger bar, pull it out a little more from the trigger. Continue these two steps until the rear of the bar comes free of the safety. At this point, the front will come all the way out. It is important to notice that the end of the trigger spring was hooked over the trigger-bar pin that you have just pulled out of the frame. It has now snapped back into the frame as far as it can. When you reassemble this pistol, don't forget to pull this spring back out and hook it over the trigger-bar pin. This is often forgotten, and the pistol has to be dissembled so the spring could be put back where it belongs. The sharp edges on the trigger bar should not be smoothed or rounded off. This is not a part of the Model 92 that should be changed or modified in any way in an attempt to change the trigger pull.

The trigger can now be removed, and my way is a bit different from the normal method. The trigger pin is held in place by the end of the slide-catch spring. To remove the trigger, this spring has to be pushed up out of the way. This is not difficult to do, but, with these close tolerances, use caution if a sharp tool is used to push this tough little spring out of the way. A sharp tool can scratch the finish on the frame, the end of the trigger pin, or both. Instead of a sharp tool, use a flat-end punch of the same size as the trigger pin. Hold the punch flat against the end of the pin and push the spring up. Hold it there while pushing the other end of the trigger pin, on the opposite side of the frame, until the pin clears the spring latch.

Another way is to push the thumb piece on the slide catch up as high as it will go, and then take a small scribe and reach in under the end of the spring and let the slide catch lift the spring out of the way. Then you can just drop the trigger pin out. Using the latter method, if you do scratch anything, it will be behind the slide catch and will not be seen.

The hammer-spring support is a pin that is driven out from the left to right. This will allow the hammer-spring support, followed by the hammer spring, to come out the bottom of the frame. You are now ready to disassemble the heart of the Model 92. Use a small punch to drive out the pin from the top down, and you will have the whole working assembly on your workbench.

If you want a softer double-action trigger pull, be very much aware that this will increase the chance of misfires. I don't like cutting hammer springs, and would much rather use one of the many aftermarket springs. This will give you a softer trigger pull with greater reliability. I have seen many 92-type handguns with springs that have been cut. Some worked, but many not only jam frequently, but suffer from other problems. Cutting the hammer spring can lead to poor feeding and ejecting, which will often result in damage to the frame. The design of this pistol counts on the pressure of the hammer spring to help hold the action during firing and recoil. Without this recoil pressure, the pistol may seem to be working fine for awhile, but the increased wear on the frame can lead to both slide and frame damage. Removing only a couple of coils might not be too bad but taking three or more is overdoing it.

As long as no one gets carried away, the soft wheel I referred to earlier is great for lightly buffing the sharp edges of the other internal moving parts. Carefully polishing the hammer and sear can make the action much smoother but overdoing it can create excessive play and may make the handgun dangerous. The key to buffing the Beretta is to remove only the rough edges and smooth the surfaces. I cannot overstate how important it is to avoid removing metal or rounding edges.

Work on the mating edges of both the sear and hammer should only be done with good stones and from a jig. If you do not have a jig, restrict your stoning of these sear points to a few light strokes, just enough to polish their edges. Do not attempt to change an angle or amount of bite on these without the proper equipment.

These pistols do not have fixed barrels so, while they shoot well from the box most of the time, tightening and stabilizing the barrels can improve their overall accuracy. Several aftermarket companies produce kits to do this job. It is the muzzle that really needs to be locked up. All the guns have some muzzle movement and many have a lot. Since they do not have barrel bushings, slide attachments that hold these barrels tight are a great aid to their accuracy.

Smoothing the T/C Contender's Trigger Assembly

The trigger on this single shot is easy to refine, and the work you do will almost always pay performance dividends.

By Chip Todd

THE THOMPSON/CENTER Contender single-shot pistol is a favorite among hunters and precision handgun shooters, who like its interchangeable barrels and wide assortment of chamberings. Overall, the pistol is easy to repair and maintain, but one part of the product benefits particularly well from the gunsmith's attention: the trigger.

Unlike many other pistols, the Contender has an indirect method of releasing the hammer. The trigger releases a striker which, in turn, strikes the sear, releasing it from the sear notch on the hammer. The trigger has a notch on it somewhat like a hammer would normally have, and the striker acts like a sear usually found on a trigger. The advantage of this arrangement is that the sear and the hammer's sear notch can overlap for safety without this overlap being felt by the shooter.

With this unusual geometry, the trigger group is complete within itself and can be taken out of the receiver and worked on separately. I would advise working on this trigger group and leaving the regular sear and hammer alone, as extremely good results can be achieved without any work being done on the parts lodged within the receiver. It is also very easy to do all of the stoning and polishing without even disassembling the trigger group, although you might want to do that just for convenient handling, and to be

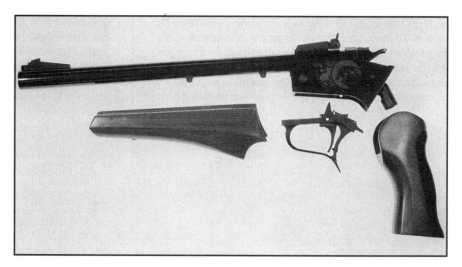

The Contender's unusual geometry allows the complete trigger group to be taken out of the receiver and worked on separately. It's best to work on this trigger group and leave the regular sear and hammer alone, because extremely good results can be achieved without any work being performed on the parts lodged within the receiver.

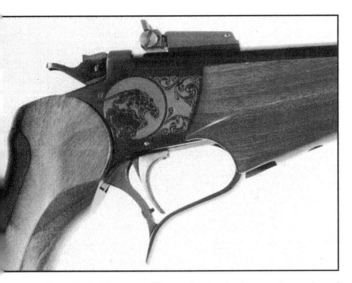

Overall, the Thompson/Center Contender is easy to repair and maintain, but one part of the product benefits particularly well from the gunsmith's attention: the trigger.

able to reduce the amount of return spring pressure on the trigger.

Test First

To start any work on the Contender, begin by checking the firearm for an empty chamber, pulling rearward on the lower portion of the trigger guard to open the action. The barrel snaps downward, opening the chamber. Close the pistol by pivoting the barrel upward, and then measure the gun's trigger pull so you will later be able to judge how effective your work was. I use a Chatillon Model 6 straight-pull spring gauge I got from Brownells, a device which measures 0 to 6 pounds. One Contender I recently worked on reg-

istered a trigger-pull weight of 3 $\frac{3}{8}$ to 3 $\frac{3}{4}$ pounds, much of which was due to roughness of the surface of the sear and sear notch. The trigger overtravel stop was not adjusted, so I planned on setting that after smoothing the trigger group.

Disassemble the Contender by first removing the forearm and grip with two different hex keys. The grip frame capscrew is located under the small plastic plate on the butt. The plastic plate must be removed; it is held in place by three Phillips-head screws. The forearm's hex socket screws are retained in their respective holes with neoprene O-rings, the longer screw toward the rear of the piece. After removing the forearm, squeeze the lower tang of the trigger guard rearward to open the action. This removes stress on the pivot pin. Use a nylon rod or a wooden dowel to push the pin out.

Remove the trigger group from the receiver by pushing out the small pin found directly over the trigger. It is easily punched out because it is retained by a notch in its center, which is captured by a bump in the hollow spiral pin through the trigger housing. A screw in the rear of the trigger guard must be removed before the trigger group can be lowered out of the frame. This screw has a large, flat head, somewhat like a fillister head without the ovaled top surface, and is there to retain the trigger guard stop spring. Removing this part is easier when you press the trigger group back into the receiver without first turning the screwdriver. Because the receiver only has a few threads for this screw, three or four turns of the screwdriver will allow the screw to fall out. The trigger group can then be lowered out of the frame.

Polishing

Accompanying photos show stoning the trigger sear notch and polishing the surface of the striker without taking the trigger and striker out of the trigger housing, but I would suggest that they be

Left—This shows the striker being retained by the trigger notch. The two parts' engagement is seen to the right of the tallest portion of the trigger group. That tall feature guides the trigger group into the receiver. The trigger overtravel and freeplay screws are seen to the lower right and in the middle pointing forward and up, respectively. The trigger return spring cup is above the freeplay adjustment screw. Right—This shows the trigger striker in the released position.

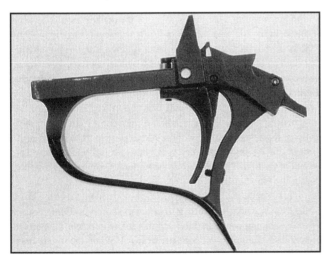
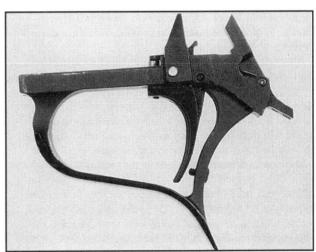

To polish the upper portion of the striker, use a Dremel Moto-Tool in this orientation. This view shows the forked rear of the trigger guard that retains the guard stop spring with the trigger guard stop screw notch.

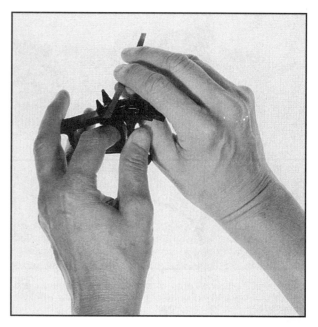

Use a Brownells flexible stone strip to smooth the underside of the trigger notch without disassembling the trigger group. This is done to smooth the trigger's feel without significantly reducing the trigger pull. Be sure to remove all the grit from the action if you perform this work on an assembled trigger group.

taken out so that the trigger return spring can be cut shorter to reduce the amount of trigger pull, if necessary. But be careful not to get carried away and cut too much off before trying it out. It's best to polish where the trigger sear notch and the striker's nose contact each other and then trying the trigger pull before cutting off the return spring.

Polishing the trigger notch can be done in the trigger housing using a fine, flexible stone which Brownells offers, or it can be carefully smoothed with a Cratex knife-edged wheel on a Dremel Moto-Tool if it is taken from the trigger group. I remove the trigger from the housing so I can use the Dremel and Cratex wheel. The Cratex wheel I used for the striker was a straight wheel, a thin cylinder, because the striker's surface to be polished is out in the open. I hold the wheel parallel to the edge of the striker, as illustrated in the photo. This makes it easier to keep the surface flat and parallel to its pivot hole.

After using the fine Cratex wheel, I then buff the area using a cloth wheel and white jeweler's rouge, which produces a mirror finish. Use the cloth wheel perpendicular to the edge with the surface of the wheel hitting the surface of the striker before going over the edge. If the wheel encounters the edge on the way to the surface, it will wash out the sharp edge and make the engagement between the trigger notch and the striker unreliable.

The same technique can be used on the surface of the trigger notch, which contacts the striker's edge. However, I would use a knife-edged Cratex wheel and like-shaped felt wheel for buffing. Be sure not to change the angle of the notch in any plane. The striker nose surface and the trigger's notch must remain tangent to their pivot points to prevent the trigger from having to move the striker

rearward to release it. Or worse, damaging these edges will allow the trigger's sear to release the striker on its own.

Post Polishing

After washing the parts free of rouge, I reassemble the trigger group and try the trigger pull, with an eye toward adjusting freeplay and overtravel. The trigger group doesn't have to be refitted to the frame to make these adjustments.

Adjust the freeplay first with the freeplay adjustment screw. This small setscrew points upward and contacts the trigger guard in the front of the trigger. To adjust the screw, turn it until the trigger releases the striker. Then loosen it about $1/8$-turn. If the striker won't reengage the trigger notch, unscrew the freeplay screw another $1/8$-turn. The engagement of the striker should be very small, but overlapped enough to firmly withstand reasonably sharp jolts from a padded or soft hammer hitting on the trigger guard. When adjusted properly, the freeplay will be as large as possible without being discernible to the finger. At this stage, ensure that the gun won't go off by itself.

When trying the trigger pull with the trigger group out of the gun, hold a thumb near the striker to prevent it from hitting anything. It is less painful to hold the thumb close to the captured striker so that it won't gain much speed before it hits your thumb. The pull of the trigger group will be the same as it is when it is installed into the frame.

Next, set the trigger overtravel screw, located on the rear web of the trigger guard. It is fairly stiff because Thompson/Center uses a screw-holding compound to keep this screw in place. Tighten the screw several turns and cock the striker. Holding the trigger rear-

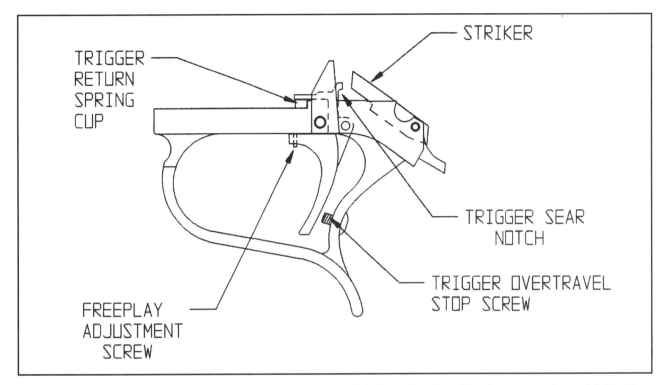

Adjust the freeplay first with the freeplay adjustment screw, a small setscrew in the front of the trigger. The trigger overtravel screw is fairly stiff because Thompson/Center uses a screw-holding compound to keep this screw in place.

ward with enough force to normally release the striker, unscrew the overtravel screw until the trigger notch releases the striker. This is still a point that requires more trigger pull than the notch and striker should require. By loosening the overtravel screw a little further, the trigger pull will feel quite crisp, disengaging without any noticeable creep. Unscrew the trigger overtravel screw until it feels the same as it was prior to adjusting the overtravel screw. The overtravel screw should have several thousandths of clearance when the trigger is its forward position, enough to prevent the screw from adding to the trigger pull, but still close enough to prevent the shooter from being able to feel travel of the trigger after the striker is released.

Trigger Spring, Reassembly

After adjusting the freeplay and overtravel screws, determine if the trigger pull is light enough. If it is still too heavy, you'll need to shorten the trigger return spring.

This is located in a cupped retainer in the front of the trigger. The spring can be removed by taking the trigger pivot pin out again and removing the trigger. Cut off only one coil at a time. Otherwise, you may have to get another spring or lengthen the one you cut. Be

sure to put the cut end up into the cup because the original ends of the spring are closed coiled, and the cutting process leaves an open end.

After the pistol is completely reassembled, it is always a good practice to try the action to ensure the safety engagement hasn't changed. If the hold of the striker doesn't prove to be completely reliable, loosen the freeplay screw until the gun passes any reasonable safety test you can dream up, but tapping on the grip, receiver, barrel, and trigger guard are good tests. If the gun fails to remain cocked through all of this abuse, loosen the freeplay screw slightly and redo the tapping tests. The freeplay screw is easily adjusted with the firearm in working trim, as is the trigger overtravel screw.

I have to know a person's abilities well and respect their judgment before I allow any gun to leave my shop with a trigger pull below $2 \frac{1}{2}$ pounds, but I recently adjusted a friend's competition T/C to a trigger-pull weight of $2 \frac{1}{8}$ pounds. With the current climate in our courts, I don't want to open myself up to a lawsuit if I take the trigger pull below that.

If you or the gun's owner plan to use a T/C in a meet, it's a good idea to try the gun out in practice and leave time for re-adjustment well before a competition.

Troubleshooting Browning 9mm Hi-Power Pistols

The Hi-Power is considered by many to be John Browning's finest pistol, but even the best need help sometimes. Here are some trouble-shooting tips.

By Chick Blood

THE BROWNING Hi-Power preceded all the "wonder nines" by many years, assured the principles upon which 99.9 percent of them operate, and has a high-capacity magazine.

Yet the Hi-Power has never achieved the popularity of the others. Not because of its cost. It costs less than most. Not because it's less reliable or accurate. If anything, it equals or betters the best of the bunch. But because the Browning is a single-action-only pistol, not double-action first or double-action-only, it has been overlooked in recent years. The belief the double-action styles were more serviceable, or safer, came into vogue with the adoption of the Beretta by the U.S. Army. After that, the vogue became dogma and the rush was on.

Browning's pistol came into existence after the military staffs of several nations that were allied against Germany in World War I collectively worked out the specifications for an auto-loading pistol. Its weight couldn't exceed 1 kilogram; it would be compact and well-shaped to the hand; it must carry more than ten cartridges and be terminally effective at 50 meters; the caliber must be no less than 9mm; the bullet must weigh no less than 123 grains and the muzzle speed must exceed 1148 feet per second. Other requirements called for an external hammer to serve as a cocking indicator; the weapon to remain open after the last round has been fired; an easy-to-manipulate manual safety; a magazine safety; assurance the weapon would not discharge if dropped, and could be easily assembled/disassembled without the aid of tools.

Though he rightfully borrowed heavily from his design for the M1911 45ACP, Browning may have outdone even himself in meeting those specifications.

Like the M1911, the Hi-Power has an external hammer with a half-cock notch, a slide stop to hold the slide open after the last shot, and it can't be fired unless the breech is closed and locked. Unlike the M1911, the Hi-Power is fed by a double stack magazine holding thirteen rounds and has a magazine safety which prevents firing of the pistol when the magazine has been removed.

When you pull the trigger of a loaded Hi-Power, it rotates around its pin to lift the trigger lever. The trigger lever contacts the forward end of the sear lever in the slide and causes it to rotate. When it does, the rear of the sear lever moves downward to contact the sear and disengage the hammer. The hammer, driven by the compressed mainspring, rotates forward to strike the firing pin, compress the firing pin spring and fire the chambered round.

During recoil, the unlocking, extraction and ejection functions of a Hi-Power slide are the same as those of a M1911, with an exception. The unlocking of a M1911 barrel is achieved with a slide stop pin, a barrel link and lower barrel lug. The unlocking of a Hi-Power barrel occurs when the barrel lug, found just forward of the feed ramp, contacts a cam located in the frame just above the trigger assembly. When the slide moves forward to chamber another round, the camming action is reversed to raise the barrel into its locked position within the slide.

If the trigger is held to the rear throughout a cycle of firing, extraction and ejection, the forward end of the sear lever comes to rest against the side of the trigger lever. In this position, the trigger lever can't properly engage the sear lever, and won't until the trig-

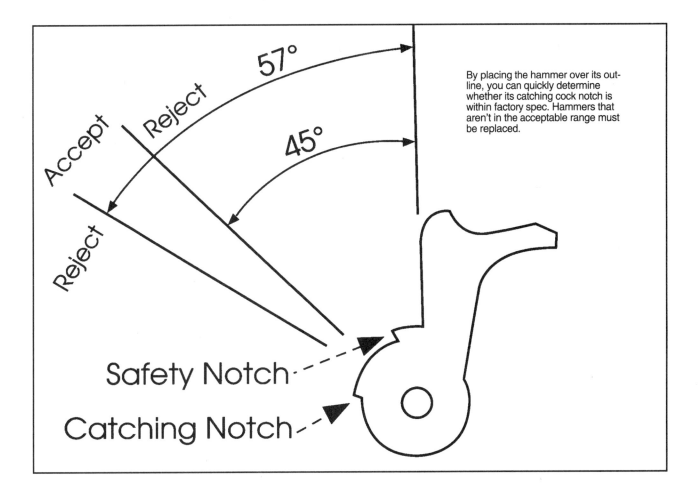

57°

Accept

Reject

45°

Reject

By placing the hammer over its out-line, you can quickly determine whether its catching cock notch is within factory spec. Hammers that aren't in the acceptable range must be replaced.

Safety Notch

Catching Notch

ger has been fully released. This constitutes the disconnect feature of the Hi-Power's fire control system. The trigger has to be released after each shot to allow the firing of the next cartridge. As far as I know, this feature has never failed and no Browning Hi-Power has ever gone full auto. But that's not the gun's only safety feature.

In the "On" position, the manual safety blocks the sear, preventing its rotation and disengagement from the hammer. When the magazine is removed, the magazine safety, under pressure from its spring, rotates the trigger lever forward. This misaligns the trigger and sear levers and prevents their engagement when the trigger is pulled. Even with a round in the chamber and the manual safety in the "Off" position, the Hi-Power cannot be fired unless a magazine is fully inserted.

To service a Hi-Power, the best place to start is the same place you should start with any firearm: a safety function check. With the magazine removed, the hammer fully cocked and the manual safety off, pull the trigger. The hammer should not fall. As a second test, leave the magazine out and simulate firing by racking the slide back and letting it slam forward five or six times. The hammer should not be jarred off its half-cock notch. Insert the magazine after you have fully cocked the hammer by pulling back and releasing the slide. The hammer should fall

when the trigger is pulled. The trigger should let go between 7 and 10 pounds. With the magazine still in, rack back and release the slide to re-cock the hammer and put the manual safety in the "On" position. Pull the trigger as hard as you can with both index fingers. The sear should not disengage or partially disengage the hammer.

You'll find probable causes for failures that show up during this safety check as we get into troubleshooting the Browning Hi-Power.

There are six possible reasons why the hammer falls off its full cock position and is caught by the safety notch:

1. A weak or sprung sear spring.

2. A trigger pull that is too light due to improper sear interface surfaces.

3. Interference with the sear lever at the pivot point with the sear.

4. Interference between the top of the sear and the slide.

5. A worn or bent sear pin.

6. The trigger lever is improperly fitted and extends too high in the frame. This can also cause the hammer to fall from a full cock position when you insert a magazine.

Sear and trigger lever work fall in the factory-only category. Springs and pins are available as replacement parts. If the manual safety is difficult to operate, check the safety spring and plunger for

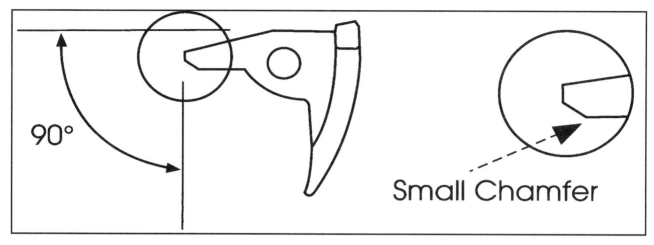

90°

Small Chamfer

This drawing can be used to determine whether or not the engaging surface is perfectly flat and 90 degrees from the sear's flat, upper surface. If it isn't, the sear has to be replaced.

free movement. Also check for smoothness at the end of the safety plunger and the indent hole where it rides in the frame. Remove any burrs that show up there or between the safety and the sear at the tab on the forward, left side of the sear. Do likewise for burrs at the safety and ejector contact point.

If the pistol fires when the hammer falls to half cock, a bent or worn sear pin could be the cause. A worn, broken or altered half-cock notch could also be at fault, as could an out-of-spec sear or a sear whose engagement surface has been filed back. This malfunction only occurs with Hi-Power models having the new type of hammers. Hammers are restricted parts, pins aren't.

Both new and older models of the Hi-Power can experience ejection problems. A common cause is a worn extractor engagement surface. You can sharpen it or replace the extractor. On new models, look for a weak extractor spring or an extractor that is binding on its pin. If it's the spring, replace it. If it is binding, find out where and smooth things up. On older models, the extractor is internal to the slide and, if bent, will affect ejection. Replace it.

There's a difference in how you replace these extractors, too. On newer models, install the large end of the extractor spring in its hole in the slide. Position the extractor for installation and align the holes with a $1/16$-inch punch inserted from the top of the slide. Install the extractor pin from the bottom of the slide and drive it flush. On older models, position the sear lever for installation with its small, slender end toward the front of the slide. The extractor will he held in the slide by the firing pin retaining plate.

Another difference between the old and the new worth noting is the firing pin spring. Until a production change was made in 1972, the Browning's firing pin spring was 0.024-inch in diameter. Newer springs are 0.30-inch in diameter and about $1/8$-inch longer. If the pistol you're working on has a spring of the old configuration, replace it with the newer one.

Save the possibilities of a weak magazine spring or excessive crud, the primary cause for feeding problems with a Browning is poorly made handloads or the wrong kind of factory ammunition. The Hi-Power sometimes malfunctions with 90- and 100-grain hollowpoints. Usually, feeding problems can be eliminated with the use of full-metal-jacket rounds of no less than 115 grains.

Finally, let's go over a few tips on inspecting the hammer and sear to determine whether they're worn or have been overworked to a point that a dangerous condition exists. There are two diagrams here that may help. One serves for inspecting the hammer's catching cock notch. If you position the hammer on the outline, you can quickly see if it is within specification. If the angle of the notch is not within the acceptable range, the hammer must be replaced. Do not attempt to bring it back to spec. You'll only make what's wrong with it worse.

The other diagram is used in sear inspection. The sear must be replaced if it does not meet the criteria shown, no matter how slightly the engaging surface is rounded or has been filed back.

In making these evaluations, it's best to use a five-power eye loupe or an OptiVisor.

Troubleshooting Luger Pistols

You should note that more "shooter Lugers" are showing up in the U.S., because the more that get here, the more that need work. Here are some things to watch for.

By Frank Fry

LUGER CONJURES MORE images of romance, intrigue, and mystery (and more erroneous information) than any other handgun—except, perhaps, the Colt single action. As import laws have relaxed somewhat in recent months, demand for "shooter Lugers"—those which are not collector's items—has increased. Hugo Borchardt, who designed revolvers for Winchester Repeating Arms, never received the credit he deserved for designing, developing, and marketing the forerunner of the Luger. Of the two major handguns used during World Wars I and II (the Colt 45 and 9mm Luger), the Luger was used by more countries and in greater numbers than the GI Colt 45.

For gunsmiths, there are two major types of Lugers, the P-06 and P-08, that concern us. The variants of these two models are endless, and some of these may have high interest and value to collectors. Both models are found in either 9mm and 30 Luger, but most commonly in 9mm.

Some expertise should be developed to determine if the pistol to be worked on has any collector value. If there is collector value, you should be aware of it. You should be aware that any work done to the gun may adversely affect that value. You must make an informed decision regarding possible loss of value.

Both models of Luger operate under the same principle and basic design—that of short recoil and rising toggle. During firing, lines of force against the breech bolt lie below the pivot point of the toggle pin, forcing the toggle to remain closed against the rails of the barrel extension, creating a very strong and positive lock. As the toggle moves to the rear, the toggle knobs strike cams on the frame, lifting the line of force above the center line of the toggle pivot pin, allowing the toggle to rise, opening the action.

The noticeable external difference between the P-06 and P-08 is that the P-06 toggle and extractor are flat, or flush with the frame, while the P-08 toggle and extractor are rounded. The major internal difference between the two is that the P-08 has a coil recoil spring located under grip panels in the rear of the grip, while the earlier P-06 has a leaf spring. The P-08 is considerably more common than the P-06.

Other differences within each model may also be found. It is,

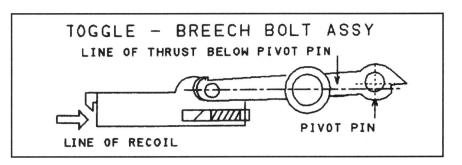

Recoil thrust below the pivot pin forces the toggle down, locking the action closed during firing of a Luger.

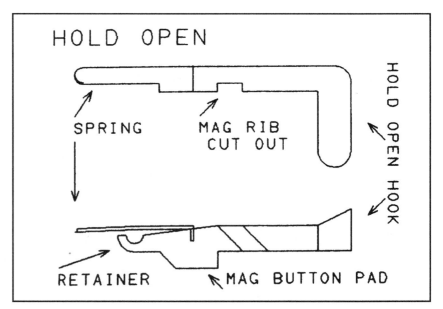

EJECTOR

EJECTOR
POINT

RETAINER
HOOK

RETAINING
PLUG

A locking stud and retaining hook provide pressure for the ejector.

however, not within the scope of this article to identify any of the multitude of model variations.

Many of the moderately priced Lugers being imported today are poor specimens and, although advertised as shooters, they may or may not function properly. The rumors that Lugers are dirt-sensitive and that they jam easily are not necessarily true. These pistols, along with Colt, Savage, and other brands, were considered and recommended for further testing for U.S. military use. They are, however, quite sensitive to mismatched parts, and may have associated malfunction problems. The Lugers were originally made to exacting specifications with major, and many minor, parts serial numbered. Mismatched major parts such as the toggle, bolt, or barrel extension could indicate that the gun may function unreliably.

If the number stamped on the bolt or toggle does not match the barrel and barrel-extension number, a headspace check may well be advised. If headspace problems are found, and bolts or toggles are available, a combination may be found that eliminates the problem. As these parts are not usually available in the average gun shop, the alternatives are that the barrel will either have to be set back a turn or will have to be replaced. The pressure flange on the barrel should be measured to determine if there is sufficient material to allow setback, as not all the flanges are the same thickness. If there is not sufficient flange thickness

to set the barrel back, the only option is barrel replacement.

In disassembling the pistol for cleaning and internal inspection, an easier method than using human power to compress the recoil spring by pressing the muzzle on the bench or holding the barrel extension back with the hands can be used. This lazy man's method is to have the gun do the work for us.

Remember that eye protection is always recommended, and make sure the pistol is free of ammunition.

Check the magazine for live ammunition, insert it in the pistol, and open the action to lock the toggle open. Remove the magazine. After the trigger, or takedown, plate has been removed, the toggle can be released, and the barrel and extension assembly will slide off the front of the frame. The toggle pin can be more easily removed if the toggle is raised about half way. After replacing the toggle/bolt assembly, barrel, and extension assembly, using the magazine to lock the toggle open will make reinstalling the takedown plate just as easy.

Note that these pistols can be fired with the barrel and extension off the frame. If a live round is inadvertently left in the chamber and the sear bar is pressed, it is possible for a discharge to occur. Because of this accidental-discharge possibility while the Luger is partially disassembled, extra caution should be taken in normal safety procedures.

HOLD OPEN

SPRING

MAG RIB
CUT OUT

HOLD OPEN HOOK

RETAINER

MAG BUTTON PAD

The magazine button contacts the bottom of the hold open to lock the Luger action open.

There are only two screws in the entire mechanism—one grip panel screw on each side of the frame. The remainder of the parts are keyed, slotted, or pinned together. The major parts are generally large, sturdy, and resist damage, but care should be exercised, especially with flat springs, as replacement parts may not be easily found. Fabricating any broken parts will be time consuming.

If a Luger shows up in your shop with jamming or malfunction problems, other than the most common extractor, ejector, or firing-pin malfunctions, the problems may seem difficult to diagnose. This is because we are more accustomed to working on Colt 1911-A1 models.

Some of the more common malfunctions, their probable causes, and complaints are:

During firing, failure to load or feed from the magazine. There are two major causes. The more probable cause is a weak magazine spring that does not raise the round fast enough to be picked up. The other cause is short stroking, which prevents the front bottom edge of the bolt from getting behind the base of the round. Both malfunctions have the same symptoms and may not show up on a consistent basis. Other causes can be deformed magazine lips that prevent smooth cartridge stripping.

Several magazines should be used to see if the problem is a weak spring or deformed magazine. If this is the case, it is easily corrected with a new magazine, which is available from Triple-K Mfg. and other sources.

If the problem is short stroking, the problem could well be an ammunition problem. Some U.S. ammunition makers have lightened their loads in recent years, and, as the Luger is ammunition-sensitive, these lighter loads may have insufficient recoil to fully function the action. The result is short stroking. Changing to a more powerful brand of ammunition is a more viable fix than trying to lighten the recoil spring. If an ammunition change does not cure this problem, suspect bent barrel-extension rails. Any misalignment of the rails can cause friction or binding during operation, slowing

down the cycle. The binding action may not be apparent when cycling the action by hand, but can show up and cause difficulties under live conditions.

Action does not fully close during firing. Check for overly tight magazine lips which prevent smooth stripping of the round, or for magazine lips that bind on the bottom of the bolt. The problem may also lie in the mainspring. Check it for rust or loss of compression. If the spring has become weakened, there could be insufficient force to lock the bolt into battery.

Recoil spring removal is accomplished by removing the barrel-extension assembly and removing the grips. Insert a closely fitted pin through the hole in the bottom of the spring guide (at the bottom rear of the grip), and pull the spring guide toward the top of the frame, rotating it to disengage the guide from the toggle link. The spring can now be swiveled out of the side of frame slot. Tension can be released and the spring and guide removed. Reassembly is in reverse order.

Empty case stovepipes or fails to eject. The problem can be short stroking, a weak extractor spring, or a weak ejector spring. If the tail of the ejector is bent, the ejector may not have enough force to extend into the breech block cutout to contact the base of the shell positively. If the problem lies with the extractor, the lip may be damaged, or the spring so weak it does not hold the case firmly.

The firing pin falls, but no ignition occurs. The cause is probably a broken firing pin. The pin is removed from the back of the breech bolt after the bolt-toggle assembly is removed from the barrel extension. Pressing in on the slotted retainer before making a half turn will release the retainer. The firing-pin spring and pin are now withdrawn from the bolt. The firing-pin tip can be rebuilt by drilling and silver soldering a new tip in place. Reshape the new pin to match the contour of the shoulder. Soldering should be done quickly to keep the firing-pin sear from losing its temper.

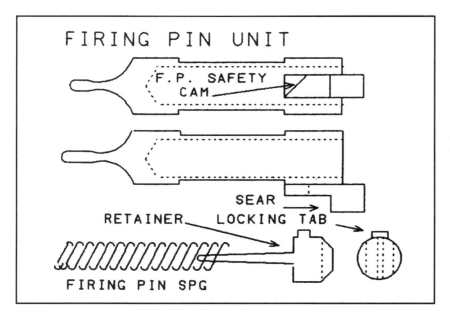

The firing pin is retracted by a safety cam when the Luger's action is open.

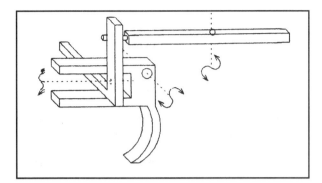

Several changes of force, indicated by the arrows, from the trigger to the sear contribute to the Luger's mushy trigger pull.

All of the sliding parts of the Luger must have minimum clearance (no play), but be free enough to slide smoothly. Bent parts and excessive play can also cause friction and binding that contribute to intermittent malfunctioning, generally during the closing portion of the cycle.

If excessive tolerance is suspected, try to find oversize replacements parts. Welding and recutting parts to eliminate excessive play should be used only as a last resort, and only then with the understanding that the procedure may not cure the problem and in some cases may make it worse.

If parts seem to be fitted too tightly, make sure the problem is not caused by warped or bent parts, which will need to be carefully straightened. If the problem is oversize parts, lap them together until drag is eliminated. Take care not to undersize them.

Trigger pull is too soft. Many customers will want the trigger pull "crisped up" to conform to what they are used to in other semi-automatic handguns. This is a difficult and unrewarding task for the gunsmith. The Luger trigger linkage is considerably different from what we are used to. Study the relationship between the trigger, trigger plate, disconnector, trigger bar, and firing pin. The relationship of these parts results in three changes of directional force from trigger to sear, and contribute to this long, soft, mushy trigger pull.

If an excessive amount of slack is present, some of it can be removed. To prevent visible alterations to the pistol, build up and recut the pad on the top of the trigger bar. Removal of the trigger bar from the takedown plate is recommended before buildup. Trying to get rid of the mushy feeling will not be as easy. Part of that problem lies in some required disconnector-clearance tolerances within the sear bar, and the length of the pivoting arms of the sear bar—neither of which can be eliminated.

Generally speaking, after squeezing all the slack, creep, and squash out of the linkage, the let-off is usually clean. Due to the difficulty in trying to crisp up the trigger, it may be best to let it go at that. Experience has proven that no matter what is done, the results will not be up to expectations.

Poor condition, or barrel replacement necessary. Many of these "shooter" Lugers will be in poor condition, and may need refinishing, or they may have barrels that need to be replaced. Corrosive ammunition, neglect, and improper storage are contributors to these problems. If refinishing or rebarreling is to be done, make sure that the particular pistol has *NO* collector's value. The value of rarer specimens, even in poor shape, can be completely ruined by rebarreling or refinishing.

Checking a collector's guide or publications specifically on the Luger, and being sure of its value before starting any alteration is highly recommended. If the Luger was originally 30 caliber, a caliber change can also be considered at this time. The 30 Luger barrel can be replaced with a 9mm without changing any other action parts. If a considerable amount of shooting is anticipated, ammunition availability and costs can be significant.

Several companies, such as Gun Parts Corp., can provide aftermarket pre-threaded barrels in a variety of lengths. The major difficulty in exchanging barrels will be getting the old barrel off without warping the barrel extension. A block is needed to hold the arms of the barrel extension from becoming crushed or twisted by the receiver wrench. If the breech block is used to prevent damage to the barrel extension ring, be sure to remove the extractor. It extends into a slot in the barrel-extension ring and can be easily overlooked. Removal will prevent damage to the extractor and extension.

If the barrel is frozen or rusted in place, a relief cut made in the barrel flange up to the face of the barrel-extension ring can help relieve thread pressure. It ruins the barrel, but since it was already beyond saving, the loss will be minimal. Any lathe work performed on barrels and barrel-extension assemblies may require a lathe setup which minimizes possible damage to the "tuning fork" portion of the barrel extension. A mandrel can be used to support the breech, helping to keep vibration and shifting of the barrel in the chuck to a minimum.

If you plan on reblueing, the process must be done carefully in areas where parts mate to prevent undersizing and dishing, making them look worse than they already are. Large pitted areas, most commonly found under the grips, can be filled with weld. If weld is to be used to fill pitting in areas that show, the base metal and welding rod may not be of the same composition, and the blue may not be uniform in these built-up areas. Frosting or bead blasting recessed areas to give contrast to highly polished surfaces may help disguise these areas. Remember that heat increases the possibility of warping. MIG or TIG welding is probably the best bet to keep the heat to a minimum.

Try to save the original markings and numbers. Letters and numbers that are dished out and half polished away look worse than sharp markings with pitting. Also be reminded that polishing out the serial number may run you afoul of the Feds. They don't like to have serial numbers altered or obliterated.

Inadequate sights. Unless sights are mounted on the barrel, there is little that can be done to improve the integral rear sight. There are two exceptions to the common fixed rear sight: The 8-inch-barreled Artillery-model sight looks like a miniature Mauser 98 sight, mounted on the barrel in front of the receiver extension ring; the other exception is the 6-inch Navy, with a two-position sight graduated in 100 and 200 meters and mounted on the toggle. Trying to alter the fixed rear sight with aftermarket sights can be a problem, and usually ends up as a genuine certifiable botch job.

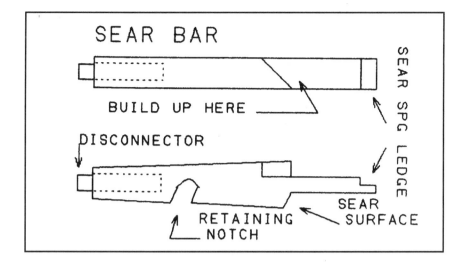

If the Luger's safety doesn't hold, building up the area shown by welding in extra material can fix it.

When replacing a barrel, sight options are greater, as sights can be mounted directly on the barrel. This option is practical only with the longer lengths. If sights are mounted on the barrel, the original rear sight may be removed or left in place as you prefer.

Cleaning necessary. Complete disassembly of all parts is not needed for a thorough cleaning. Those parts that may need to be removed for cleaning are the sear spring and sear bar, ejector, hold open, and safety assembly. There are crevices and recesses under or around these parts that collect dirt. Use care when removing the sear spring; it is keyed into the frame and can be difficult to fabricate if lost of broken. The rear of the hold open must be lifted up far enough for the retainer in the front to clear a pin in the frame, before it can be lifted out. The ejector is lifted at the rear to clear the retaining stud from its recess in the barrel extension. The ejector can now be pivoted inward and lifted out of the barrel extension.

Safety does not prevent firing pin release. After working on the Luger, as with any firearm, test the safety to make sure the sliding safety holds the sear bar and prevents release of the firing pin. If the firing pin falls, welding extra material to the sear bar can eliminate this malfunction. Any welding must be done carefully and be blended into the sear bar to prevent an unsightly glob. The weld should be added to the sear bar, as the safety slides into a slot in the frame, and any significant buildup on the safety slide will bind in this slot.

Remove the safety lever by disassembling the left grip panel and barrel-extension assembly. Drift out the pin found inside the frame in the left side, above the safety-lever pivot. The safety lever and safety slide can be separated and withdrawn from the frame.

If the Luger is a particularly fine and valuable specimen, a careful consideration of the gun's value is again advised to assess any possible risk that would decrease its value during any repair or alteration. Documentation is also advised and should be kept on permanent file.

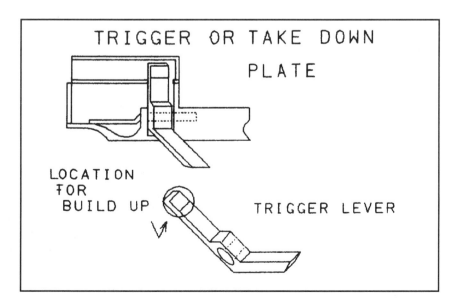

There isn't much you can do to change the trigger's feel, but creep can be removed by building up the lever and refitting it to the sear bar.

Checklist: Charco Revolvers

By Guy G. Lemieux

CHARCO, INC., manufactures small-frame revolvers. All of the company's models use basically the same parts, except for some directly related to the different calibers. That means a variety of trouble spots can be diagnosed and fixed on a number of Charter revolvers fairly quickly.

Here are a few quick pointers to watch for on these handguns:

● **Misfires.** With an empty gun, pull the trigger fully to the rear and hold it there. Push the hammer forward and check the firing pin protrusion. It should fall in a range between 0.035-inch and 0.045-inch. If the firing pin is not too short, the problem may be a "clipped" mainspring, an operation some owners perform to lighten the trigger pull. It the spring has been altered, fit a new main spring and test-fire the gun.

If it still misfires, check the headspace. If the headspace is excessive, a new cylinder must be fitted.

If the firing pin protrusion is too short, the cause is rarely the presence of too short a pin. Instead, the misfire will likely be due to a thin hammer block or a long hammer nose. The cure is to grind a few thousandths off the hammer nose—that portion of the hammer which protrudes above the surface—which strikes the hammer bar. This will usually cure the problem.

If the firing pin protrusion is still too short, the countersink, located in the frame, may have to be deepened. Remove the firing pin and carefully deepen the countersink with a hand reamer.

● **Hard Rotation, Empty.** If the cylinder turns hard when it is empty, the problem is likely due to either a buildup of residue on the crane spindle or lead buildup on the rear of the barrel. Cleaning will cure either problem.

● **Hard Rotation, Loaded.** If the cylinder rotation is hard only when loaded, check the breech face for raised burrs around the firing pin hole and the hand slot. File or stone any burrs flat. If the rotation is still hard, gauge the cylinder with the "go" headspace gauge. Use a hand reamer to deepen the countersink of any chamber which will not close on the "go" gauge. Do not deepen it to the extent that it will close on the "no-go" gauge.

● **Cylinder End Play.** This is ordinarily the result of a thin extractor star. It can be cured by fitting a new extractor.

● **Excessive Barrel Gap.** The gap between the barrel and the cylinder should not exceed 0.012-inch. If there is cylinder end play, the problem should be solved by fitting a new extractor. If cylinder end play is not present, a new cylinder will bring the gap within tolerance.

● **Excessive Headspace.** Excessive headspace in any chamber requires the fitting of a new cylinder.

● **Hard Extraction.** Hard extraction may be due to a rough or galled chamber. This may be cured by polishing the chamber, as long as the finished chamber does not exceed the diameters in the table below. If all the chambers are rough or any exceed maximum diameter, a new cylinder should be fitted. Also note that handloads generating excessive chamber pressures can cause hard extraction. Usually, this will disappear as soon as proper ammunition is used.

Caliber	Maximum Diameter
.38	.385-inch
.32	.344-inch
.22 WMR	.2465-inch
.22 LR	.232-inch

● **Stiff Extraction Stroke.** This is almost always due to the ejector rod return spring's binding in its housing (usually because the spring tip overlaps the following coil). The solution is to replace the return spring.

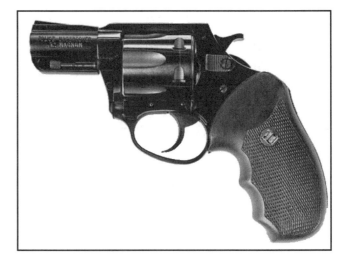

You can troubleshoot most malfunctions on Charco revolvers by knowing a few problem areas.

Lorcin L9mm Pistols

Knowing when to say no is as important as knowing the parts when you work one of these inexpensive pistols.

By Butch Thomson

THE LARGE NUMBER of Americans who want to buy cheaper products has created a whole new market segment of inexpensive cast guns. But if we look at our history as an industry, that should come as no surprise.

It all started with the low-priced 25 autos. After those had been around for a long time, people wanted a more powerful autoloader but still didn't want to pay much. Cheap 32 and 380 ACP pistols flooded the market. This was followed by the cut-rate nine millimeters. The low-priced high capacity 9mm was a natural successor in this progression.

Gunsmiths everywhere have been swamped with repairs on these firearms. To meet the demand for these guns while keeping the price down to what people want to pay, manufacturers have to use simple designs of cast and stamped parts. Such designs often result in parts that are easily broken or deformed. The price structure demands that parts be assembled without hand-fitting, which can lead to feeding, jamming and extraction problems. We come into the picture when the owner wants them fixed.

Like I said, there have always been cheap guns around. Those that were popular in the past were small-caliber revolvers or little 25s. With these inexpensive high capacity 9mm pistols, the theories of fixing them are the same but the problems and risks involved are significantly greater. A 25 ACP cartridge going off in a breech that was not fully closed was not a terrible problem as the round's brass could contain part of the explosive force. But a 9mm that does the same thing can do tremendous damage. These comments apply to all the cheap high-powered autoloaders on the market today. A gunsmith needs to remember what can happen if a pistol he works on has a catastrophic malfunction after it leaves his shop. Before you work on it, the manufacturer shoulders the liability. After you work on it, a large share, if not all, of the liability is yours.

On those "words to the wise," we will discuss repairing and maintaining the Lorcin L9 pistol, as well as several things you should not do because of the potential of safety and liability problems. I'm not singling out the Lorcin. It is no worse than similar pistols on the market today. These same thoughts should be kept in mind while working on any of the cheap high-power pistols.

The Lorcin L9 pistol must be dry-fired and the safety put into the fire position before you attempt disassembly. The takedown latch is a small, square piece of flat metal located in the frame between the grip safety and rear of the slide. The back edge, the only part showing, has a dimple in the center for a small punch. This piece is pushed in with the punch while you pull the slide $1/2$-inch to the rear and lift it straight up. As the rear of the slide is lifted, the takedown button, firing pin spring, and firing pin will be released and, if allowed to, will fall out of the slide. The slide will now go forward and off the frame. Several parts are loose at this point, so do not lose any.

Looking at the slide first, remove the takedown button and the firing pin and firing pin spring. Excessively dry-firing this pistol can cause the firing pin to break, so make sure there is about $1/2$-inch of the thin point extending out from the firing pin body. With the slide off the frame, reinstall the firing pin to make sure it moves freely in its slot and that about $1/4$-inch extends through the slide. This extension is the pistol's only ejector. The gun may still fire if the tip breaks off, but it will not eject. A bent or kinked firing pin spring will not allow this firing pin to move properly, and will cause the occasional misfire. Roll the firing pin on a flat surface to be sure that neither end is bent or wobbles. The pin must be replaced if that condition exists.

You should also be aware that firing 9mm +P or similarly hot loads through this pistol can bend the firing pin. A bent firing pin can stick in the fire position as it extends through the slide, possibly retracting just enough to allow a cartridge to load but with sufficient firing pin extension to slam-fire when the slide closes. Normally, the firing pin will break before doing this, or will stick so far forward that another round will not load. However, if it sticks in just the wrong position, your problems could be extreme. I suppose the gun's going full-auto is a possibility, but the firing pin should prevent ejection.

The only other parts in the slide are the extractor assembly components. Beyond getting dirty and sticking, these parts seldom are problems on the Lorcin. They are held in place by a small retainer pin that is driven in from the top. The pin is removed by driving it out with a punch from the bottom through the top. Remember, this

LORCIN L9 AUTOMATIC PISTOL

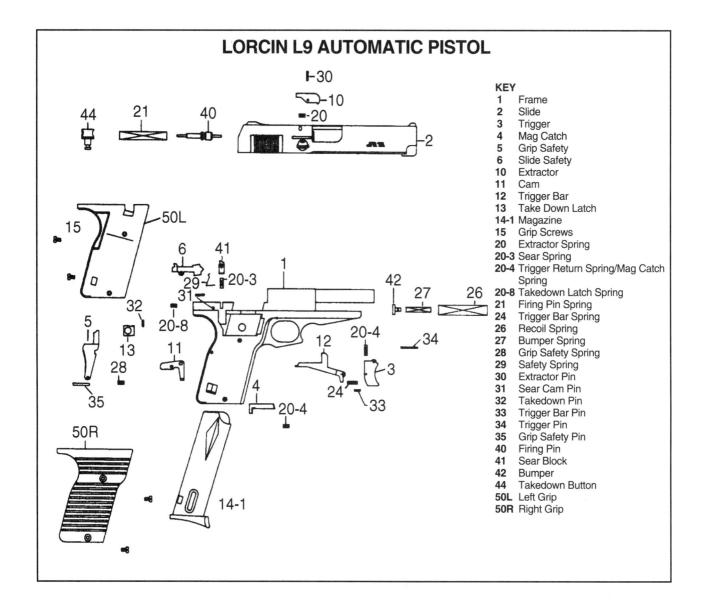

KEY

1	Frame
2	Slide
3	Trigger
4	Mag Catch
5	Grip Safety
6	Slide Safety
10	Extractor
11	Cam
12	Trigger Bar
13	Take Down Latch
14-1	Magazine
15	Grip Screws
20	Extractor Spring
20-3	Sear Spring
20-4	Trigger Return Spring/Mag Catch Spring
20-8	Takedown Latch Spring
21	Firing Pin Spring
24	Trigger Bar Spring
26	Recoil Spring
27	Bumper Spring
28	Grip Safety Spring
29	Safety Spring
30	Extractor Pin
31	Sear Cam Pin
32	Takedown Pin
33	Trigger Bar Pin
34	Trigger Pin
35	Grip Safety Pin
40	Firing Pin
41	Sear Block
42	Bumper
44	Takedown Button
50L	Left Grip
50R	Right Grip

cast slide is easy to chip. The extractor parts are cheap, so replace them if there is a question.

Looking at the frame, we need to check the recoil spring and the bumper spring. This pistol is a simple blowback action that is being asked to handle a 9mm cartridge. The weight of the slide and springs is the entire safety system that keeps the breech closed long enough for the pressure to drop sufficiently. Make sure the recoil spring slides easily over the bumper spring. Roll the recoil spring on a flat surface to make sure it isn't warped. Do not attempt to remove the bumper or its spring.

By placing downward pressure on the top of the sear, you can pull the cam away from the frame and release the sear and sear spring. The sear is made of hardened steel. A hard steel pin running through it works as an operating lever. This pin had broken in the gun we inspected but I am reluctant to say whether this $3.50 part is or is not a weak link in the gun. The same system is used in many firearms without breaking. Inspect both ends of the sear pin to make sure it does not happen to you. The engaging surface of the sear should be smooth and not have any chips. Do not try polishing this sear for a softer trigger pull. You can clean it but do not polish off any of its sharp edges. Any bevel edge at all can allow unintentional discharge.

When the slide is removed from the L9, the safety pops up and allows the safety spring to disengage. This spring pushes forward toward the muzzle to re-engage with the safety lever. The cam that we removed upon releasing the sear assembly can only be damaged outside the pistol. Remove the two screws on the left grip, and take extra care if you have to pry the grip panel off. The panels are made of very thin, easily-broken plastic. Lift out the safety spring before removing the right grip screws. Removing the right grip panel releases the magazine latch and latch spring, which are easily extracted. They can be easily removed.

Now all that is left is the trigger assembly and the grip safety assembly. The grip safety is held in place by a single retaining pin that can be pushed out either side. Do not disconnect or soften the spring on the grip safety.

Although some people do not like grip safeties on their pistols and would prefer them to be disconnected, this must not be done on an L9. The top of the grip safety bar blocks the left end of the sear pin and holds it in place.

The trigger assembly is secured with a directional pin that is driven in from the right-hand side and must be driven out from the left. There are six parts to the trigger assembly, including the two pins. You have the trigger bar and trigger bar spring. Then you have the trigger and the trigger return spring. After the trigger retaining pin has been removed, the trigger assembly can be removed. You should do so only for inspection, cleaning, or replacement. A lightened trigger return spring will occasionally prevent the trigger from returning fully forward, thus keeping the trigger from engaging. The pistol's trigger is marginal and, in the interest of safety, should not be modified. While some L9s have heavier trigger pulls than others, trying to make them lighter is not a good idea.

You can check out all the bearing surfaces in the pistol's frame and smooth the rough edges with light emery or jeweler's rouge. These cast parts chip and break easily, so be gentle. Here are some key areas to examine: If the trigger binds in the frame when all other parts are removed, look for drag marks on the trigger itself. Find the corresponding rough spot in the frame and smooth it down. It is doubtful that you will find rough edges on any of the stamped parts but, with a cheap gun, anything is possible. Take care of the rough-ness but smooth only the non-working edges of the parts. Leave the sharp edges on all working edges. Attempting to remove the barrel from the frame could result in your cracking the thin cast shield around the barrel.

One touchy part of the L9 is the takedown retainer. This three-part assembly consists of the flat steel retainer plate itself, one spring, and its retaining pin. These work well almost all of the time but they must be kept clean. If something gets inside the frame where the retainer plate moves back and forth and blocks its movement, the pistol cannot be field stripped or repaired.

The pistol is reassembled in the reverse order of disassembly. When you assemble the safety bar, first do it without the safety spring in place. Make sure you get the nipple on the back side of the safety into its hole in the frame. Move it up and down to make sure it is working and that the grip safety is not dragging on it. Now you can take it out, put the safety spring in, and then install the safety bar. It must be pushed forward until the nipple slips into place, and held still while the grip panel is replaced.

Most feeding problems can be blamed on the magazine or the way the magazine fits into the firearm. The L9 magazine is well-made and should cause no difficulties unless it has a fitting problem. Some of these pistols do not like anything but full metal jacketed ammunition but there is really no set rule. Some will feed nearly anything and others are very particular. The same thing is true about accuracy, ejection, trigger pull, as well as other items.

What we've said will cover most problems you will encounter but, due to the simple design and loose-fitting parts, you may have to hunt for the right combination.

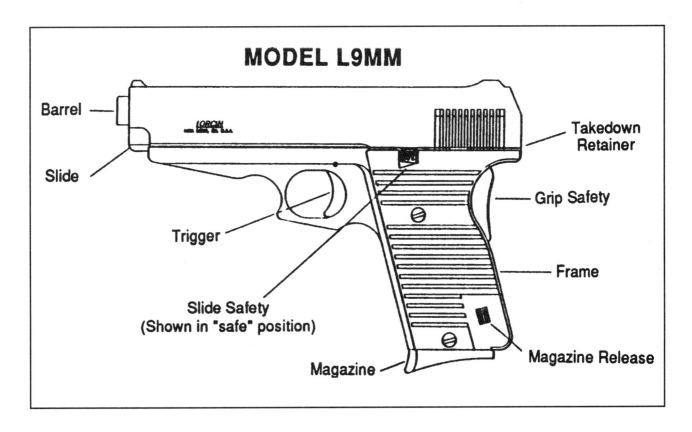

MODEL L9MM

Barrel — Slide — Trigger — Slide Safety (Shown in "safe" position) — Magazine — Takedown Retainer — Grip Safety — Frame — Magazine Release

Easy Revolver Jobs for Beginners

Working with wheelguns allows you to build your confidence while you perfect your skills. Here are some good jobs to start with.

By Chip Todd

IF YOU ARE A beginning gunsmith, the most straightforward handgun to start with would have to be the revolver. Its simplicity of operation is much less frustrating to the inexperienced gun handler than most semi-automatic pistols and their periodically baffling ailments that frequently drive experienced gunsmiths to distraction.

A revolver's malfunctions are also more easily described to you by less experienced handgunners. This factor alone can make learning about handguns easier to digest when you are just starting out.

There is no doubt that patience is a virtue, concerning guns. But it is also a fact that the less patience required; the more fun learning most people will have. Mark up another good reason to start with the simple revolver.

There are several different types of revolver problems you will most likely encounter. The foremost one will be inaccuracy caused by either the handgun or the shooter; either one will seem to the shooter to be the gun's fault, not theirs.

Forcing Cones, Bores

The usual problems attributed to the handgun involve the bullet's action in the bore, the trigger action, and the sights. The least understood of the three is the relationship of the bullet to the axis of the barrel. If the entrance of the bullet into the bore isn't coaxial with the bore, there is not much chance that the bullet will reach

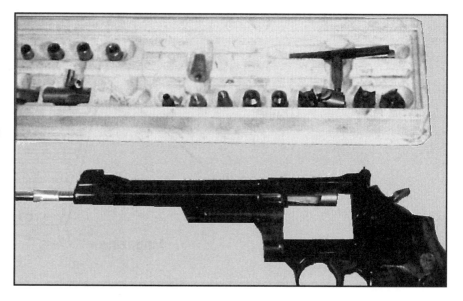

Brownells forcing-cone service kit, shown here with an 11-degree cutter ready to cut into a S&W Model 19, allows the gunsmith to smooth a gun's cone-to-bore angle.

the target's center ring. If the angle of the forcing cone's funneled entrance is shallow, the force required to align the bullet with the centerline of the bore is lessened. The perfect analogy to the forcing-cone situation would be the narrowing down of a highway from four lanes to two. If they did so too abruptly, there would be more friction and cars would change lanes at greater angles. The same holds true in the case of bullets and forcing cones. If the angle of the forcing cone is reduced, there is much less friction and the bullets are much less apt to be forced into the bore in a distorted condition.

There are several types of forcing cones, but you probably will encounter only two in your entire gunsmithing career—the cone cut into permanently attached barrels, and the one on the rear end of a removable barrel like those found on Wesson revolvers. They are the same functionally, but the Wesson style allows the barrel/cylinder gap to be easily adjusted by the shooter with only the handy Wesson tool and feeler gauge. The system lets the shooter screw the barrel in until it bottoms out against the feeler gauge of choice, and is locked into tension by the shroud and threaded sleeve at the muzzle. I am still amazed that the Dan Wesson system works so well in the hands of the neophyte as well as the experienced shooter. It is pretty handy to remove and clean the barrel and forcing cone painlessly.

Cleaning the forcing cone of both conventional and Wesson revolvers is best done with a lead-removing tool like the Lewis Lead Remover, an efficient system for removing leading and fouling of the forcing cone and rifling. It is a simple design, and works well. Many gunsmiths, myself included, believe the bore should have all irregularities filled with something—lead, copper jacket material, just something—to provide the effect of a continuous surface formed by the steel of the bore and the fouling material. Others want all of the fouling out of the bore before shooting the firearm but usually fire a "fouling" round before counting the shots anyway, so the argument may be moot.

At any rate, the Lewis Lead Remover is the most economical

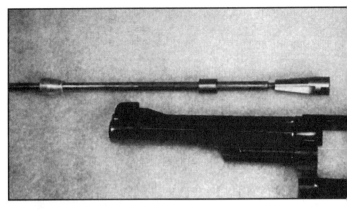

Other implements in Brownells kit include an 11-degree forcing-cone cutter, bushing, rod, and muzzle cone, all of which are shown with the S&W Model 19.

method of smoothing out the bore. One of the only things I find wrong with the Lewis offering is that it is only listed for select calibers. There is no doubt in my mind that it can be used for other than listed calibers, but there is no chart in the catalogs offering the product that says which kit to order for unlisted calibers.

This tool uses common copper-screen wire to scrape off lead in the bore by being dragged through the bore with brute strength. Its best work is done when it is hard to drag the screen through the bore. The circle of screen is about the size of a quarter and has a hole in the center for the screw of the adjustable tip supplied. This tip has a threaded shaft with some gum-rubber tubing on it that expands when the knurled round nut is tightened on the shaft. The shaft is about the length needed to clean a pistol so I had to make a long one to use on rifle barrels. A small rod, which seems too soft to last very long, is supplied with the kit to tighten the expanding tip onto the rod that goes through the barrel.

The process is similar to pulling a cleaning patch through a bore.

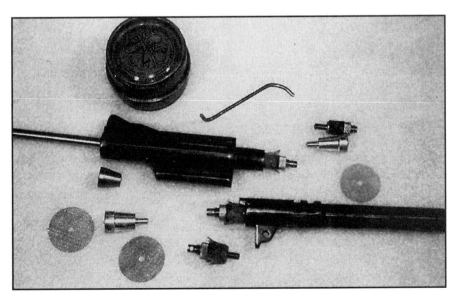

The Lewis Lead Remover kit is shown with two types of barrels and lapping compound. One of the big pluses of this kit is that barrels need not be removed for servicing.

I pull the screen patch through the barrel several times, turning it over if there is very much lead stuck in it. The first time you use the lead remover you'll be amazed at how it can come out with lead all over it, when there wasn't enough to be seen by eye.

A tapered tool for cleaning forcing cones on revolvers uses the same wire-screen circles as the barrel-cleaning tips, but is meant to be rotated to scrape the lead from the forcing cone, not pulled through the bore.

If your desire is more accuracy, less lead spitting, or just plain knowing that your revolver is more precisely adjusted, Brownells, Inc., offers a well-thought-out kit to use on forcing cones.

The angle of the forcing-cone funnel can be changed to a much more accurate shape by using the Brownells forcing-cone tool kit with its full complement of cutters and guides. The cone operation uses a $3/16$-inch rod with a threaded end to secure the cutters. Five facing cutters, two chamfering cutters, an assortment of pilot sleeves, 18- and 11-degree cutters and lapping cones make it a complete cone-transformation tool.

I start by squaring the forcing cone face with the proper size facing cutter, always the largest that will clear the topstrap of the frame without scoring it. The pilot sleeve is marked, but the snuggest one you can get in the bore is the proper one for the caliber. An alu-

minum centering guide is used at the muzzle to center the rod with the bore. Between the pilot bushing and the centering guide, the rod guarantees the forcing cone cutter will be square with the centerline of the bore.

For our purposes here we worked on a Smith & Wesson K-frame revolver, which is one of the most popular. As a result, it is the one I work with the most. The instructions are general enough to be used with almost any revolver, though, because a barrel and forcing cone are virtually alike from one brand to another.

Start by opening the cylinder and removing it from the gun, if possible. This will probably save the cylinder from unsightly marring.

Install the cast-aluminum handle onto the shaft, placing the set screw into the undercut in the unthreaded end of the shaft. Then insert the centering guide onto the shaft with its tapered end toward the threaded end of the shaft. Insert the shaft through the bore and install the proper pilot bushing (untapered cylinder) onto the shaft and push it up into the forcing cone.

Screw the facing cutter onto the threads of the shaft and tighten it with the rectangular bar provided with the kit. Pulling the handle while twisting it clockwise with one hand, push the centering guide against the muzzle with the other. This will cut the face of the forc-

To fix erratic shot placement in revolvers, consider tuning the lockup between the crane and the receiver. This Model 66 S&W pistol has two crane balls installed. The hardest part of the installation was gripping the crane while drilling and staking the top of the hole.

ing cone square to the bore by ensuring that the cutter shaft is concentric with the bore. Use a small amount of cutting pressure, cutting only enough to produce a fresh, bare surface completely across and around the face of the forcing cone. The less the better, as any metal removed increases the gap between the cylinder and the forcing cone.

Smoothing and enlarging the cone's funnel will help the bullet's entry into the bore of the barrel. I would suggest, however, that the factory's 18-degree funnel be changed to 11 degrees to further ease the alignment of the bullet into the rifling. The shallower angle aligns the bullet with less upsetting force. This has more of an effect on the accuracy of lead bullets but also tends to help with jacketed slugs.

The tapered cutter must be held in constant contact with the forcing cone so that it will cut without chattering, something that can be eliminated by turning the cutter fairly slowly. I cut until the mouth of the forcing cone is about .060-inch larger than the bullet diameter. This enlarging of the interior of the forcing cone is helpful in keeping the revolver from spitting lead and the smoothing of the cone's surfaces helps the bullet find the center of the bore in an undistorted condition, most nearly coaxial with the bore. It is essential that the forcing cone interior not be enlarged too much because it can cause the cone rim to be too thin for the strength it needs. I draw the line differently for cones with an 18-degree taper than for an 11-degree taper because the shallower taper carries the thinness further and creates a greater chance of its splitting. Limiting the enlargement of the cone to about the 0.060-inch I mentioned earlier is best for safety. I can never be sure what kinds of reloads might be used.

The forcing-cone kit's lapping tips, made of brass and used with abrasive pastes, are useful in removing any concentric ridges and/or chatter marks caused by the tapered cutter inside the forcing cone. I make it a rule to use each tapered cone tip with the same grit every time because the grit will imbed itself into the brass and could cause deeper scratches than intended. The old Clover Brand lapping compound used by mechanics is still the best I have found. I use only the fine side of the two-sided container and leave the coarse side for other work.

After the lapping operation, there will still be a sharp edge to the forcing cone. This must removed for the job to have a professional appearance. The chamfering cutter supplied with the Brownell's kit is easy to use and comes in two sizes that cover all cones you could encounter. It will only take two or three turns around the edge of the cone to chamfer the edge to a visually pleasing width.

Remember when doing anything to a gun that involves removing metal: The less you remove while still getting the results you want, the safer it will be. It's also economical because it cuts the risk of taking too much off and having to replace a part, or the whole gun.

Rebound Blocks

There is a step on Smith & Wesson revolver's rebound blocks that just must be changed slightly to help them cam the hammer back up onto the block, when the rebound spring has been lightened. The 90-degree step on the stock block should be slanted back another 20 degrees to aid the hammer's climb onto it. Since this is

Custom S&W trigger appears smoothed and polished next to the original serrated trigger.

another safety feature of the revolver's design, it is essential to use restraint in removing material. Removing too much could easily be misinterpreted by a jury if an accident should ever occur with this firearm. Don't avoid thinking about such a possibility. It is very real and one that should be foremost in the gunsmith's mind whenever he is working on any firearm.

The illustration of the rebound block shows the location and amount that can be safely removed to allow a lighter rebound spring in a S&W revolver. The rebound spring is the one called a trigger-return spring by most manufacturers. If the spring is lightened, the act of having to cam the hammer back and up onto the rebound block is often the cause of the trigger not returning all the way forward when it is released.

There are other ways with other revolvers to lighten return-spring pressure, but most others don't need as much work to make it easier for the trigger to return forward. I have found that when all else fails in trying to get the S&W revolver triggers to return to the front when there seems to be enough return-spring pressure, beveling the top edges of the trigger-blocking bar helps.

On most other revolvers, there is a more direct relationship between the trigger-return spring and the trigger. When the trigger spring needs to be weakened and is a flat type, it is often more effective to narrow the spring than it is to thin it. This usually gives the spring more of a chance to last longer.

Sights

Sights could be the most subjective of all reasons for missing the target with handguns, but hearing the interesting excuses shooters often have for their sighting difficulties is one of the more entertaining aspects of gunsmithing. Some are valid and some imagined, and you will have to practice keeping a straight face and nodding in response while trying to determine the real reason for this person's not getting a good sight picture.

One of the first things I look for is a factor—the most obvious is a loose rear or front blade—that might make the sight picture inconsistent or difficult. The next obvious step is to take a look at the shooter's eyes. There is often an awfully good reason for not being able to focus on the target and sights at the same time: the shooter can't see as well as he used to. I'm old enough to qualify for the far-sightedness that comes with age.

Age reduces depth perception, so to compensate for the loss you can use optical trickery and borrow from the original pinhole camera with a device called the Farr-Sighter. This rotary disk clips onto shooting glasses and has an array of graduated pinholes that act as infinite-depth-perception lenses. It will cure all far-sightedness for target-type shooting. I have used one for more years than I want to admit, but I will own up to the dramatic increase in my shooting scores.

Another malady with sights is the sizing of the notch to the blade. The front sight blade is often too thin for the width of the rear-sight notch, a misfit that leaves too much gap on either side of the front blade. If the gap is more than absolutely necessary for easy viewing, the sight picture calls for more judgment than is necessary. This also makes it harder to discern any wiggling of the firearm by the shooter. It can be tested by folding masking tape over the rear sight and cutting a new notch in it with an X-Acto knife. Blacken the tape with a indelible marker, get the shooter to hold the firearm as if he were shooting and have him read the sighting on an object at a normal shooting range to see if the narrower notch allows him to better judge the centering of the front blade. If the narrower gaps on either side between the rear and the front blade don't block out the target, you might suggest he let you install a rear blade with a narrower notch.

The need for a wider notch is easily remedied but troublesome to diagnose, since you can't file the notch wider and return it "like it was." I use the masking-tape dummy here as well, making a slightly narrower front sight above the existing blade. It takes a little more imagination on the shooter's part but if he can give it a fair test, he will be able to tell if the rear- to front-sight relationship is improved.

Ejector Rods

The next few operations can be done without an ejector-rod wrench, but you only have to ruin one to make you want a better method than pliers to remove the ejector rod. Even wrapping the knurled end with leather is risky; you will occasionally mash through the leather or leave the knurling filled with leather. It is also a good idea to be sure which direction the rod is threaded since most aren't strong enough to stand much abuse. It is fairly easy to touch up the knurling on the rod's end with a lathe and knurling tool, but not everyone has a lathe at their disposal.

I make my ejector-rod wrench out of aluminum, which is softer than iron oxide (bluing) and doesn't rust or need oiling. Brownells sells a very nice wrench like this. It probably makes more sense to buy theirs than to make one, but I like to use the lathe and can describe how to make the wrench with only a drill press, a hacksaw and a tap. Some of us just like to use things we've made ourselves.

The wrench is really a clamping collar. The material comes from a $1^{1}/_{2}$-inch-diameter aluminum rod cut off about $^{1}/_{2}$-inch long. Drill a $^{1}/_{4}$-inch hole in the approximate center, and another following the illustration. The two cuts can be made with a hacksaw and need not be as wide as depicted. The collar will close up very little, so an average hacksaw blade will make a wide enough kerf.

After drilling and sawing the holes perpendicular to the collar face, cut the section out for the screw, and drill the hole to pilot the tap. I used a 10-32 x $^{3}/_{4}$-inch socket-head cap screw, but an 8-32 screw would suffice. I had a $^{1}/_{4}$-inch reamer available to me, so I under-drilled the center hole and reamed it out to .250-inch for smoothness.

Knurling is not a necessity, but some type of non-skid surface, perhaps punch stippling or some skateboard non-skid tape, will be handy when your hands are oily. I don't want too much purchase on the wrench. My students use it and I don't want an inexperienced student to have much power in case he turns it the wrong way. The ejector rod shouldn't be on very tightly, nor should it be re-installed with much power. Since it has no appreciable torque on it in operation, it doesn't need to be tightened by a weightlifter.

The steel flat washer is used to prevent the cap screw's head from digging out the aluminum surface. This isn't necessary if the collar wrench is steel, although I would suggest using aluminum or brass because of their softness.

Cylinder and Crane Work

Another cause of erratic shot placement in revolvers is the locking between the crane (yoke) and the receiver. This lockup can be greatly enhanced in most revolvers by installing some type of additional help for the lock system. (Please notice that I use crane and yoke interchangeably, as you will have to in working with different brands of revolvers and in talking to their owners).

There are several types of locking methods of the crane on revolvers, some better than others. The front-locking system used on Wesson revolvers is technically superior for cylinder/barrel alignment but lacks the ergonomic advantage of the more popular Smith & Wesson thumblatch location and direction of operation. The Colt latch is located in the same place as the S&W, but takes an unnatural pull instead of the easier push of the S&Ws.

The best of both worlds is achieved when you add detents and spring-loaded balls to the front of the yoke on the Smith & Wesson and Colt revolvers. This spring-loaded ball and detent lock the front of the cylinder and yoke while the rear is locked by the plunger rod. This has proven helpful in consistently locating the cylinder in the frame. I nearly always install two of the crane-locking balls under the age-old theory, "Anything worth doing is worth overdoing," and the extra ball and detent are not detrimental. In fact, they are superior to a ball with a stronger spring, as that would apply more force to the same point contact between the ball and frame. In time, this would wear, or roll, a groove in the receiver and reduce the detent's effectiveness. The addition of these balls is easy to the point of being almost anticlimactic after getting up the nerve to drill into that irreplaceable crane.

The hardest part of installing crane-locking balls is gripping the crane securely while drilling it and while staking the top of the hole to retain the ball. It is important to be aware that protecting the crane and receiver's finish is the foremost concern when installing crane-locking balls. I use leather to protect the surface from the vise jaws but lead, linotype metal, wood, or tough plastic also make good protectors. You will be hitting the crane with a punch and hammer, so the reliable padding is a necessity.

It is also necessary to tighten the crane in the vise so the hammer blow cannot be transmitted to the pivot shaft of the crane. That

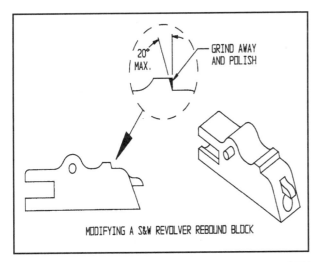

MODIFYING A S&W REVOLVER REBOUND BLOCK

You can take about 20 degrees off the 90-degree step on a S&W revolver, but you must take care that you don't cut too much metal when you're performing the operation.

would destroy the alignment which is necessary to the gun's performance. You will come across gunsmiths who tell you this and other jobs cannot be done well without the crane-holding jig sold by gunsmith-supply houses but that is just not so. The jig only makes it easier to protect and handle the crane. I've installed several hundred crane balls and have yet to spoil a crane. (Does putting it in print jinx you more than just saying it?)

Secure the crane in a small vise as seen in the illustration. Clamp the crane with its lower end clear of the vise bottom, because you will be tapping the upper end with a hammer and punch later. I also use a small machinist's square to be sure the plunger ball holes are perpendicular to the top of the crane. Put a $^1/_8$-inch drill bit into your drill press and lower the bit beside the front end of the crane to determine how deep to place your depth gauge on the drill press. Another way you can mark the depth is to use a drill stop on the bit, (or a piece of masking tape), to indicate the proper depth of the hole. I also use this step to predict if the angle at which the crane is installed in the vise is proper to keep the drill bit in solid metal. It is quite a disappointment to drill into the hole in the yoke reserved for the cylinder's ejector rod, or worse yet, to drill through to the outside of the yoke.

I like the crane ball kits from Brownells, made by Ron Powers, because they work, and it is more trouble than it is worth to hunt up the right-size ball bearings and springs. When I run across ball bearings .124-inch in diameter, I latch onto them to replace those which launch themselves during installation.

The crane ball and spring are to be compressed within the crane to a depth of about $^1/_8$-inch (we'll have to check). This depth is needed to allow the ball to be pushed below the surface when the yoke is being closed. The trick to the installation is staking the ball in hard enough to retain it yet not so hard that the ball is shy enough to only weakly engage the detent. I like to drill the spring and ball hole deep enough to allow the staked metal to be drilled out if I should happen to stake the ball in with too much gusto. If you

haven't gone deep enough to drill it and you need to remove the ball, a little work with an X-Acto knife will remove the staked retaining metal. I suggest drilling a little bit at a time, checking the depth as you go by inserting the spring and ball and using a screwdriver or spatula to press the ball flush with the surface.

Take care, because this phase of the operation is just asking the crane ball to fly across the shop and hide until you give up and get another out. When the ball can be pressed below the surface, the hole is deep enough. Too deep can mean daylight coming through from the bottom. A little daylight will not hurt the handgun's accuracy but owners can get totally bent out of shape at this little breach of cosmetics. Cranes are not on the list of replaceable parts because they are machined for a particular frame, so do whatever is necessary to control the depth of the crane ball hole.

I made my crane-ball punch from a piece of $^3/_{16}$-inch drill rod by filing one end square and drilling it with a small center drill. This indentation discourages the ball from squirting out before the punch has gotten it below the surface. The shape of the tip end isn't critical but it is important to have a small indentation in the end of the staking punch to help keep the ball bearing somewhat controlled when staking it in. The balls are .124-inch in diameter and the drill bit we use is a $^1/_8$-inch (.125) to give clearance for the ball to operate. Given the $^1/_8$-inch hole, the $^3/_{16}$-inch diameter punch swages about $^1/_{32}$-inch on each side of the hole. This small bit of displaced metal is all that is necessary. Staking or swaging the metal like that cold-works it into a harder condition and we only want to use a fairly light hammer stroke at the top of the hole. If the hole is staked or the metal is swaged to an excess, the ball will be retained below the surface or be too shallow for its intended function. I would rather try several times to get the proper stake than to have to cut out the metal and restake it.

The above description of the tool and why it is so sized almost tells how to use it. Placing the spring into the hole, put the ball on top and push the ball and spring down into the hole until the punch stops on the crane surface. I drilled and hardened both ends of my punch so I won't have to take notice which end I use, and I knew the hammer blows would be too light to ruin the ends. I use my brass hammers to do this to avoid mushrooming the end of the punch.

If the crane ball(s) are installed to your satisfaction, use them to locate the spot to drill the detents that hold the balls beneath the barrel. This calls for a well-degreased firearm and a layout fluid such as Dykem. I sometimes, in a fit of stinginess, use a black felt marking pen, but it really doesn't mark the spot as easily as the metal dye does.

It is important to think this through, placing each detent so the ball rests on the first side it encounters, not the back side of the depression. This allows the ball and spring to constantly force the crane into the closed position. Ideally, (and we know that there are no ideals in the real world), we would like to have the ball resting completely in the detent, but the chances of hitting this are not worth the chance of hitting too near the closest side.

I suggest you locate the hole's center about 0.020-inch back past where the ball leaves a mark and then drill the detent to a diameter that gives a good lockup and a push when closed. You may have to buy a long drill bit, about 7 inches, since the chuck can easily rough up the side of the receiver. I like to buy the 7-inch aircraft bits and cut the one I use for crane balls down to about $4^1/_2$ inches. I have chosen a $^3/_{32}$-inch-diameter bit for my detents. The ball cannot stick out of the crane to its full diameter without coming apart. A long-shank center drill would be ideal.

Opening and closing the crane/yoke several times without the cylinder will give you an idea of how the lockup is working, but remember, it doesn't take very much to ensure that the crane stays closed. Remove the felt marker or Dykem discoloration with acetone or a lacquer thinner and you can consider the crane job done.

Checking the alignment of the crane is one of the little jobs I try to work in every time I look over someone's revolver, as it is important to the gun's operation and is so easily done. It is also something most people never consider having done. The tools needed to do this on 90 percent of the higher quality revolvers you encounter will be relatively cheap. You'll need one for the J-frame S&Ws and Rugers and one for K, L, and N-frame S&Ws. You won't run into many others which will be fine-tuned to this level.

The alignment tool is very hard solid tool steel with a small-diameter handle, a larger-diameter central bearing area, and a small nose designed to easily drop into the breechface hole when the crane is aligned properly. Checking the crane's alignment requires removing the cylinder and re-installation of the crane. Swing the crane to its open position and insert the alignment tool into the upper member of the crane. Holding the revolver with its barrel straight up, close the crane and hold it shut. Moving the cylinder-latching mechanism downward, the nose of the alignment tool should readily drop into the breechface's hole.

If the nose hangs up on the side opposite the crane's outward swing, the tool should be retracted into the crane and the crane confined in the closed position. With a soft hammer, strike the crane's member toward the hole in the breechface and keep trying it until it drops easily into the hole. If the tool's nose doesn't swing in enough to drop into the hole, tap in the opposite direction.

Vertical misalignment is handled by using a hardwood wedge and the hammer. My wedge is maple and has about a 30-degree taper. It is used between the crane and the top strap to lower the tool's nose, and between the crane and the bottom of the cylinder pocket to raise the nose. It is a surprisingly good feeling when the tool just drops into the hole when the latching mechanism is moved downward. This tool will also be used for another important job later.

Cylinder end-shake is the movement of the cylinder forward and backward on the crane when the cylinder is in the firing position. With the tolerances necessary to produce a gun most of us can afford, there will probably be some end-shake in most of the revolvers you inspect. This end-shake, while undesirable, is not usually a reason for great inaccuracy. I just like my revolvers to have no excess play.

The two most common ways of eliminating end-shake are by using commercial shims or by lengthening the crane's cylindrical axis. This "axle" is a hollow tube that houses the ejector rod and extractor shaft and rides against the rear of the cylinder's central pocket. This central cavity is slightly larger than the axle of the crane and has front and rear bearing surfaces. The trick is to peen the hollow shaft so it is thinned while you lengthen it. This can be done in a rolling manner rather than by impact.

The easiest way is to buy a small bag of shims from a gunsmith supply house like Brownells or from one of the pistolsmiths such as Ron Powers or Jimmy Clark. The shims attack the problem from the front of the crane by forcing the cylinder toward the rear.

Although the easy way, the cost of the shims is ongoing while the lengthening process eventually pays for the tools and costs nothing after that. I can charge just so much for an end-shake job so I would rather put the money in my pocket instead of elsewhere. For this reason, I don't keep shims around but make them on the lathe when someone just has to have them, which probably costs me ten times what it saves me.

If you use the shimming method and don't have good measuring equipment, there is always the "try, try again" method. The shims are easily put on the crane so that empirically determining the amount required is just as easy to get right as is the accurate measuring needed to do one selection. Put the circular shims on the shaft, slip on the cylinder and try closing the action. The cylinder should turn easily, yet without any added drag. The extreme of too much shimming is that you will be unable to close the action, or the cylinder will bind up solid.

With the cylinder in place, the action closed and the gun held firmly, check for excessive end-shake by gripping the gun and cylinder and trying to run the cylinder back and forth on the crane shaft. When this motion is removed or reduced to being barely discernible and the cylinder rotates freely, oil the piece and put it back together.

To lengthen the cylinder axle on the crane, you need a filler rod, a tubing cutter, and usually a piloted facing tool. The filler rod goes inside the crane's upper tube (the cylinder's axle) and the tubing cutter is rolled around the rear bearing area of the cylinder pivot. It is essential that the tubing-cutter's wheel be dull or it could greatly weaken the axle or actually cut it off. The safest way to approach this is to buy a tubing cutter that has already been modified for this purpose.

The "filler rod" is the same tool you used to determine crane alignment. This tool is put into the empty yoke as you did for that job, and the dulled tubing cutter is mounted onto the rear bearing area of the crane. Turning the cutter, slightly tighten its handle with each revolution to form a shallow indention around the bearing surface. Take the cutter off frequently to check how the crane closes with the cylinder installed. It is unnecessary to completely re-install the ejector rod, but the extractor must be in place to check for end-shake.

There are two situations you definitely want to avoid, in addition to possibly cutting off the end of the crane: lengthening the crane too much or forgetting to put the alignment tool into the crane. Excess lengthening will cause you to have to use a facing tool too much. Forgetting the alignment tool as a filler will cause you to have to drill out the center of the crane. The first is forgivable as it insures that the rear face of the crane is square to the breechface. However, having to drill out the crane to remove the metal mashed into the hollow needed for the ejector rod's spring could cause you to weaken the crane irreparably.

I like the crane to require some effort to close and then square up the end with the piloted face-cutter. If you don't want to buy one,

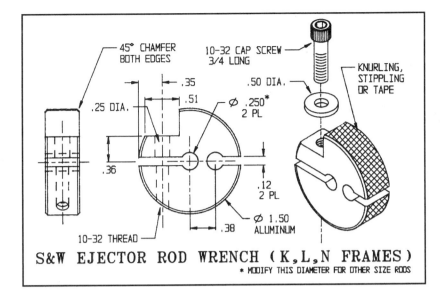

The ejector-rod wrench is really a simple clamping collar.

you should work with the care of a diamond cutter. It is possible to control the lengthening process if you use self-restraint. If this restraint is exercised, there will be no raised metal on the outside to make the cylinder drag, either.

Like the aligning procedure, a cylinder from which you removed the end-shake will give you a good feeling. It might be a good idea to do this several times before you let the gun's owner watch; it tends to make them edgy.

Smoothing Triggers and Hammers

I have been on shooting trips where I found myself shooting a certain gun more than another that I thought would be more fun, and wondered why. Picking up the gun, I found my right index finger wasn't comfortable on that particular trigger. I just can't stand a trigger with pronounced serrations and sharp edges.

For this reason, I often have a shooter dry fire one of my revolvers and ask how their trigger finger felt. I also ask them to compare the pull against another with the factory serrations still on it. Invariably, they guessed the trigger pull on mine was lighter than it actually was, due to the wide and smooth trigger.

It is a rare day when the a shooter doesn't want the serrations removed from his trigger. On the guns I have for protection, I dull the sharpness of the serrations. On my others, I smooth the trigger's surfaces, then polish and plate them. I stopped installing old-style wide triggers for the same reasons S&W stopped: ridiculous jury awards. Anyone who jams a pistol with a wide trigger into a holster should blame himself if he misplaces a toe or two.

If you want to feel a good smooth trigger, get out your Dremel tool, a mounted stone, sanding drum and felt bob. The first thing I do is hold the trigger in a shooting position and see where my finger sits. Any sharp edge, often on the sides of the trigger or up nearer the top of the right side, should be radiused. There is no real rule here; it just has to feel right.

Before I go too far with the edges, I use the cylindrical stone to remove the serrations from the front side. You should have a cup of water nearby—but you know that by now. Friction is heat and nothing has more friction than a good grinding stone. Since the sanding drum is making scratches in line with the serrations, it is often difficult to be sure when the serrations are gone. You just have to notice marks and sand over them. If they move, they weren't the serrations; if they don't, sand some more.

This is one of the best applications for your Cratex wheels, the best intermediate step between sanding drums and the buffing wheels or bobs. Cratex the heck out of the surface, being sure to attack the areas on the move and from a different direction all the time. Staying in one spot can result in low places and weaving reflections when polished.

After the Cratex, a buffing wheel or felt bob with some red polishing rouge will tell you if you need to do more sanding or Cratexing. Polish all you can, then clean the trigger with a solvent. Clean or replace the wheel and polish again with white finishing compound. The trigger should now carry a good reflecting shine.

Along with making the trigger more comfortable, you might check out the serrations on the hammer spur. Those sharp serrations, especially the diamonds on the edges of the spur, become annoying if not painful after shooting for an hour or so.

Use the same tools to knock the tip off the diamonds formed by the checkering or straight serrations. Those will be hard on the Cratex, but what's a single Cratex wheel compared to adding comfort to shooting a particular gun? Please don't do this with the hammer or trigger mounted on the gun. You will get abrasive dust inside your gun as surely as if you'd sandblasted it without disassembling it. Even the polishing compound could do damage if allowed to get inside the gun.

Working the Glock Pistols

The Glock line of pistols may well be the most misunderstood of any on the market. One thing is certain: It ain't easy to tear these guns up.

By Butch Thomson

Your files and emery paper won't do much good on the Glock 20 10mm shown here. All the metal parts have a Tenifer finish, a super-hard treatment that will dull a file before you can mark the gun.

GLOCK PISTOLS ARE A unique breed, with service and repair requirements that, in many respects, are quite different from more traditional handgun lines.

The "plastic" frame has been misunderstood by many, but the fact remains that this polymer frame is one of the strongest there is. In dramatic and highly effective demonstrations, Glock pistols have been dropped more than 300 feet from helicopters, surviving a landing on a sheet-metal roof to feed and fire without any problems. The story of that exercise has been embellished several times since it happened, surfacing along with undocumented stories about Glock pistols literally melting on the dashboard of a car. In reality, the Glock won't start melting until it reaches 392 degrees. But despite all the evidence of durability, Glock pistols can indeed be damaged.

Where the damage comes from is of considerable interest to the "stone and file" fraternity. The majority of problems that occur with the Glock result from taking it apart, putting it back together, or trying to modify it. You don't do trigger jobs on this gun the way you would on a 1911-A1. In fact, this is one gun you don't use a file or emery paper on. The Glock's external metal finish, a non-glare matte called Tenifer, is very hard and will dull your fine files before they can start to cut into the metal. Telling gunsmiths there is any gun in the world that can't be improved with their honing stones is tantamount to high treason, but no one has proven to me that a Glock needs it.

The Glock is designed to shoot and feed any commercial ammunition of the correct caliber, including factory-loaded +P and even machine-gun ammunition. Some reloaders don't like Glock's tight chambers because they won't take cases that aren't sized all the way to the rim. Many of the problems you will see are actually related to the quality of reloads and not the gun itself. Be careful—as some reloaders might not like hearing the suggestion that their reloads might be less than perfect. After all, those same reloads work perfectly every time in that World War II pistol, so it couldn't be the ammunition's fault.

External Work and Sights

The lone exception to the Glock's inherent toughness is the adjustable rear sight, which is optional on some guns in the line. It's very fragile. I don't understand why Glock makes a tough gun and puts a weak sight on it. The adjustable sight is easily decommissioned by simply applying pressure to the back of it, then lifting it straight up and forward. Because the sight extends back so far, this can easily happen inadvertently by drawing it and snagging it on loose clothing, or by merely bumping it while it's in the holster.

The rear half of this adjustable sight is held in place by spring-steel wires extending from the front to the rear. When the rear portion is pushed too far up and over, these wires simply pull out of the rear half.

The *fixed* rear sight, on the other hand, is fine. It's very strong, and slopes so that it does not hang on things. Nevertheless, even the fixed sight is hard to move without damaging it, unless you use Glock's own sight tool. The Glock fixed sight is the best replacement option, followed by a sturdy Millett or other aftermarket adjustable setup.

The front sight is held in place by a small wedge—just like an ax head. To remove it, first remove the wedge by working it up and down with a small thin-blade screwdriver or a pick. (Personally, I use dental picks for a job like this.) Then the sight can be pushed up and out of the slide. If you are going to work on Glocks, you should purchase their sight pusher. This is the best tool to use for changing the rear sight.

As military and police tests have proven, this gun is nearly unstoppable from the outside. The inside does not lend itself to modifications, and much of the damage done to Glocks is caused by amateurish attempts to work on these guns.

Trigger Work

The trigger pull is changed by installing different connectors or "New York" trigger-spring sets. A connector with a "+" stamp creates an 8-pound pull, while an unstamped connector results in a 5-pound trigger. Glock also makes a "-" connector, but it is unavailable in the U.S. unless you buy the entire competition-model pistol. The New York State Police wanted a heavy trigger pull of 11 pounds or more so that officers who were used to the heavy pull on their service revolvers would have a similar feel. This prompted Glock to build the "New York Trigger." These are available in both 11- and 13-pound pulls.

Care should be taken not to install one of the New York assemblies in any Glock with a "+" connector. Doing so can create a binding effect that can lock the action up tight.

Disassembly

The Glock is not too forgiving of anyone doing things any way but the Glock way, up to and including basic disassembly. The slide does not come back but 2 or 3 millimeters to pull down the slide lock. It's imperative that the trigger be fully back in the fired position before the slide comes off straight forward.

Other than broken adjustable rear sights, the most common problems I see on Glock pistols are mangled recoil springs and spring tubes. "Grab and yank" is not the best way to handle these parts, despite what some gun owners think. If the Glock you are working on looks like someone tried to tie the recoil spring in a bow, put in a new one and be sure to replace a 30-coil spring with another 30-coil spring. Always check the recoil-spring tube for chips, dents, or a missing piece of the lip. If the tube is damaged and you do not have another one, just turn it so a new part lines up with the half-moon seat when you reassemble it.

The Glock recoil spring should not be replaced with anything but the correct Glock spring. Glock is now making a captive recoil assembly that will help a great deal. Another problem in this area

occasionally occurs when someone reassembles the Glock with the spring guide too low or too high. For the gun to work properly, the spring guide must be properly seated in the half-moon cut in the bottom of the barrel. It seems to fit both above and below where it really belongs, so check it and make sure it is in the half-moon area.

A $^3/_{32}$-inch punch is all you need to disassemble and reassemble the Glock. You'll find a small screwdriver and a small pair of needle-nose pliers are nice to have.

After removing the slide from the frame following the instructions in the manual, take the slide and hold it straight up and down. Using the tip of your punch, you can lift the firing pin enough to get the punch tip properly seated on the spacer sleeve, avoiding the need to use a sharp tool. The spacer sleeve can be damaged when sharp tools are used to force it down to remove the slide-cover plate. Taking the slide-cover plate off can sometimes be difficult, but if you're holding the spacer sleeve all the way down, it will come. Once it's off, the firing-pin unit and all slide parts will slip right out. Make sure the spring-loaded firing-pin safety does not get away from you at this point, as it is now free.

It's doubtful you'll ever disassemble a firing-pin unit, but if you do, be careful with the spring cups. The first time I looked at one of these, I figured I would be replacing a lot of them, but I have not seen one damaged yet. At this point, you will remove the extractor-depressor plunger set which is in three parts—the plunger, its spring, and its bearing tip. This allows the extractor to slip right out.

Glock slide parts interlock, so make sure everything is all the way in before reinstalling the slide on the frame. Glock says to always test the firing-pin safety. Make sure it works by simply pushing it into the frame, and then try pushing the firing pin through to the fire position. Try this again without pressure on the firing-pin safety before reassembly. Another good idea is to check the extractor. It can be very embarrassing to have the extractor fly off the first time the gun is fired.

Improper disassembly of frame parts results in bent trigger bars and slide locks, as well as damaged frames. Use your punch to remove the trigger pin (both trigger pins on large calibers) and the trigger-housing pin. Taking the Glock apart is very much like disassembling the Nylon 66. After the pins are out, use your punch to lift out the locking block. You should avoid prying it up over the trigger bar, but it's all right to use the opposite side of the frame for a little leverage. Even though you will feel a slight resistance, the trigger pin will come out with reasonable ease. If you're using the slide-stop lever side to pry from, watch the magazine lip of the lever and do not bend it. When the loading block is out, the slide-stop lever can be removed. Next, the trigger-mechanism housing is removed by putting your punch under the ejector and pulling straight up. Trigger, bar, and housing can now all be lifted out together.

To disassemble the trigger, hold the trigger-mechanism housing with the left hand, and pull forward on the trigger bar with the right hand while carefully rotating the trigger bar counterclockwise. As it comes loose, it can be lifted from the frame; small needle-nose pliers will help you disconnect the trigger spring. Remove the connector by prying it out with a small screwdriver. It should come straight out from the housing. Remember, this connector is what sets your Glock's trigger pull. This connector is replaced, not modified, to increase or decrease trigger pull. And remember, it's very important not to install a New York trigger spring with a "+" connector. The New York trigger spring can be installed or removed at this point by slipping it into or out of the trigger-mechanism housing. If you have an early model Glock, the New York trigger may not fit well, and should not be put in. If it's necessary to use the New York trigger, then the work should be done by the Glock factory, or else the entire trigger-mechanism housing should be replaced.

I hear a lot about worn ejectors, though I've never seen one worn down. The 9mm ejector has a slight bend that some have tried to straighten out, only to have it break. These 9mm ejectors must not be put into larger calibers since there is the possibility it could work as a firing pin when extracting a live cartridge. In the same vein, no one should ever hold their hand over the ejection port to keep a live shell in the firearm while yanking a slide open. This can push the cartridge over too far and let the extractor become a firing pin.

There are two types of Glock magazines; one with the traditional reinforcement plate that is disassembled by using a punch through the bottom, and the one that does not have a disassembly hole in the bottom. The latter type of magazine is disassembled by applying enough pressure to the bottom on both sides so the plate can be pulled to the front and removed.

Reassembly of all parts is in the reverse order, but make sure the slide stop snaps down smartly when lifted up. If it does not, its spring is not located right and needs to be redone before reinstalling the slide assembly. The four steel rails inside the polymer frame cannot be removed and must not be rounded off. The sharp edges are part of the design of this handgun and should be left alone.

The Glock comes from the factory with a copper-colored lubricant on portions of the slide. If this is left in place, the gun will last a long time. Glocks require little lubrication. In fact, excessive oiling will defeat its ability to self-clean as it fires.

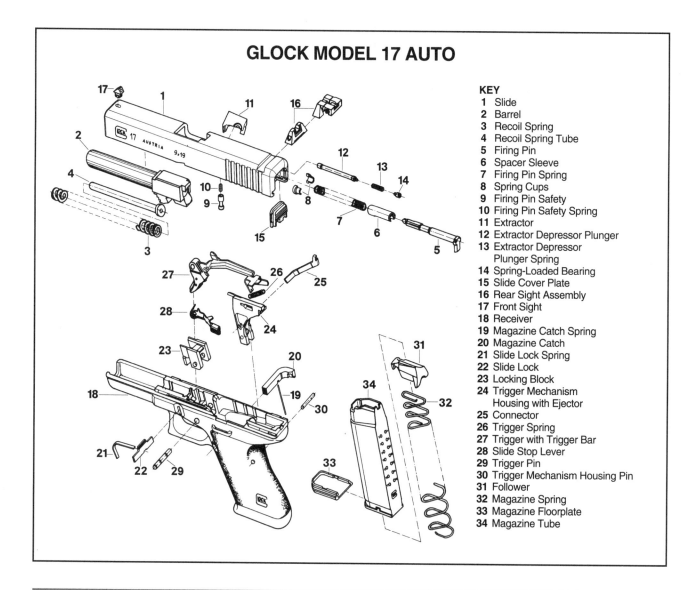

GLOCK MODEL 17 AUTO

KEY
1 Slide
2 Barrel
3 Recoil Spring
4 Recoil Spring Tube
5 Firing Pin
6 Spacer Sleeve
7 Firing Pin Spring
8 Spring Cups
9 Firing Pin Safety
10 Firing Pin Safety Spring
11 Extractor
12 Extractor Depressor Plunger
13 Extractor Depressor
   Plunger Spring
14 Spring-Loaded Bearing
15 Slide Cover Plate
16 Rear Sight Assembly
17 Front Sight
18 Receiver
19 Magazine Catch Spring
20 Magazine Catch
21 Slide Lock Spring
22 Slide Lock
23 Locking Block
24 Trigger Mechanism
   Housing with Ejector
25 Connector
26 Trigger Spring
27 Trigger with Trigger Bar
28 Slide Stop Lever
29 Trigger Pin
30 Trigger Mechanism Housing Pin
31 Follower
32 Magazine Spring
33 Magazine Floorplate
34 Magazine Tube

Correcting a Taurus Revolver's Problems

Looking beyond the obvious when you are examining a Taurus revolver will go a long way toward solving the problems you may encounter.

By Butch Thomson

WORKING ON LATE MODEL Taurus revolvers is reasonably simple in that, most of the time, the problems people complain about are easy to fix. However, I've learned over the years that "most of the time" doesn't translate to "all of the time."

There are times these revolvers prove to be truly difficult, with problems that require much more complicated solutions than they would appear to need at first glance. I hope to be able to cover most of these and show you what to look for.

If you have problems with a Taurus and want to set them right, be advised that some major repairs might be necessary to solve certain complaints, but you won't know for sure until you have the gun apart. There are nine such problem areas, any of which can be easily fixed or might require major repairs and expense:

1. Cylinder is hard to rotate. 2. Misfires. 3 Cylinder does not lock in firing position, or goes past a chamber. 4. Extraction problems. 5. Cylinder is hard to open and/or close. 6. Trigger and/or hammer is hard to move. 7. Trigger does not return fully forward. 8. Will not fire double action. 9. Cylinder does not rotate at all.

It should also be noted here that Taurus offers a limited lifetime warranty on its guns and that any modifications made will nullify both the warranty and the manufacturer's liability.

Before we take this revolver apart, let's look at the most common complaints. Most of these need to be checked out before disassembly. While there are minor variations in the different late-model Taurus revolvers, they are all of the same design, use the same basic types of parts (they are not interchangeable) and thus have the same strong points and weaknesses.

Among double action revolvers presently available, Taurus has one of the best trigger pulls around but that doesn't stop "the trigger is too hard" from being the primary complaint we hear. Cutting the mainspring to soften the trigger pull is so easy and regularly done that misfiring is the second most common complaint. The problem here is that as soon as the gunsmith pulls the trigger and sees that the mainspring has been shortened, he immediately figures that caused the malfunction. That may or may not be true.

There are five other major causes of misfires that should not be overlooked even though the obvious answer is the shortened mainspring. You might have bad ammunition. Short or broken firing pins are rare in the Taurus, but they do occur. When the transfer bar breaks, sticks or has been incorrectly installed, this gun will not fire. From there, you could have two major problems. The cylinder might not be correctly locking into place or the gap between the frame and the cylinder might be excessive. Know the problem and the solution before you tackle the job.

Inaccuracy is the third most common complaint and it might well be the toughest one of all, because 98 percent of the time the fault lies not with the gun but with the shooter.

Eleven Common Problems

The next eleven problems aren't in any particular order of how often they occur, but you will ultimately see them. You should also look beyond the obvious solutions to these problems. The answer may not only be something other than what you first thought, it might be a combination of two or more things. I often find firearms that have been "worked" by someone who did not know what he was doing to have a host of problems to be corrected. It is also true that one broken part can cause others to fail if the firearm continues to be used or if someone tries to force the gun to work.

When a trigger sticks and does not return fully forward, the obvious and most common cause is that foreign matter is jamming up the works. But that isn't the only reason. Among others, the hand sometimes gets stuck against the extractor and must be adjusted. Transfer bars sometimes stick between the hammer and firing pin. Weak or modified trigger springs may have to be replaced. You'll find a similar situation when a cylinder is hard to rotate. The obvious solution is a good cleaning, but at other times, you have a major job on your hands. It is also a condition that could lead to several follow-up difficulties after you've addressed the original complaint.

If the revolver has been fired despite the cylinder's being hard to rotate, several other internal parts may have been damaged. We will look for these when we get inside the revolver. More common causes that lead to the condition include fouling and lead buildup between the face of the cylinder and the barrel. Even if the fouling does not appear excessive, remove it before doing anything else. With the cylinder clean, check all chambers to make sure there is clearance between the barrel and each chamber's face. If the problem continues when all this has been done, swing the cylinder open and hold the thumb-piece back to make sure the action is working properly without the cylinder in place. If it works fine until the cylinder closes, you could have a loose or bent extractor rod, a misaligned yoke, a bent cylinder pin, or an extractor spring rubbing against the yoke. If it doesn't work, the problem is internal and will be covered later on.

I don't know if it is just a quirk or a production problem, but we have had a rash of Taurus revolvers come in with extraction problems. When these guns are not extracting as they should, you can almost always find the cause in one of four areas. Rough chambers do not release expanded brass easily. Correcting this condition may be no more difficult than cleaning out the residue from previously fired rounds. Over-size chambers are normally caused by excessive wear or overly hot reloads. A bad extractor won't sufficiently grip the rims of the fired cartridges to pull them out of the cylinder. Some extractors will slip past one or more fired cartridges, allowing them to remain in the cylinder. Last, but certainly not least, cheap or defective ammunition might be the culprit.

While we are on the subject of cylinders, let's cover those that are hard to open, close, or both. Such conditions are often due to the ejector rod's coming loose and screwing itself out to a point that it will not release. An ejector rod that is too long will cause this, as will a short center pin. As strange as it sounds, the problems can be caused by a bolt that is too short or too long or if the locking bolt itself is stuck.

With the cylinder open, use a punch to push the locking bolt toward the muzzle to see if it is working smoothly and without a tendency to stick. If it is not moving like it should, fix it before doing anything else. Use a small punch to drive out the locking bolt pin, taking care not to damage the blueing. When this pin is removed, the locking bolt should fly out, so do not lose it. If stuck, the pin can be driven out with a small punch inserted through the hole in front of the lug that houses the locking bolt assembly on most models. Some models do not have this hole, so

it may be necessary to soak the locking bolt in penetrating oil to get it loose enough to release. When rusted, they can sometimes be hard to get out. If the entire assembly is rusted, the hole in the barrel lug must be cleared of all rust. It is best to put in a new locking bolt assembly.

Two problems that are seemingly similar have entirely different causes. In cases where the revolver will fire double action but not single action, the cocking arm is normally the problem. The cause of the revolver's firing only in single action must be determined by working the action after you remove the sideplate.

A job often accepted as a simple repair but that can turn into a tough, costly project is when the cylinder does not rotate when the trigger is pulled or the hammer is cocked. When this happens, the first thing to do is make sure the cylinder stop is releasing and that it is doing so in proper time. Try this several times, as it may work fine in most instances and stick only occasionally. If it has stuck, the hand or star may have been damaged and it might be a high-dollar repair. It is possible that the hand is just a little too long, but until you are absolutely positive, do not make the mistake of shortening it.

Solutions

Now that we have found out what needs to be done, let's take a Model 66 revolver apart and look at the repairs as we go.

The grips are held on by a single screw but these semi-wraparound, two-piece grips sometimes are very tightly stuck to the frame. Starting the grip screw into the threads on the outside panel will give you something to hold onto while you wiggle and pull to remove the panel. This will also help you avoid damaging the grip panel's finish by prying it off with a screwdriver. When one panel is off, you can reach through the frame and tap the back side of the second panel until it comes off.

When you cock the revolver, you will see a small hole drilled through the base of the mainspring center pin. Put a small steel wire (a paper clip works) through this hole, pull the trigger while holding the hammer back, then slowly release the hammer. This will take the tension off the mainspring, allowing you to remove the mainspring center pin, mainspring and the mainspring bushing. Use stiff wire for this. A small soft wire that is bent by the pressure of the mainspring could let the spring lock over the wire and make it difficult to remove later. This mainspring is the most "worked on" part found on these revolvers; people are always cutting or grinding them to make the trigger pull softer. One that has been ground on and is too soft will have to be replaced or stretched out to increase pressure. Taurus says replacing the shortened spring is best, especially if more than two coils have been removed. Stretching will work if the springs are not too short, however. These high-quality steel springs will retain their performance when stretched unless it is just overdone.

Remove the three screws that hold the sideplate on the frame. Being careful not to damage any internal parts, put the tip of a screwdriver under the sideplate where the grips were removed. Lifting up gets the sideplate to come off, exposing all the internal parts so you can check out the revolver's action. Before removing any more parts, let's check the internal workings while they are all intact so we can see what is causing our problems. Even though this

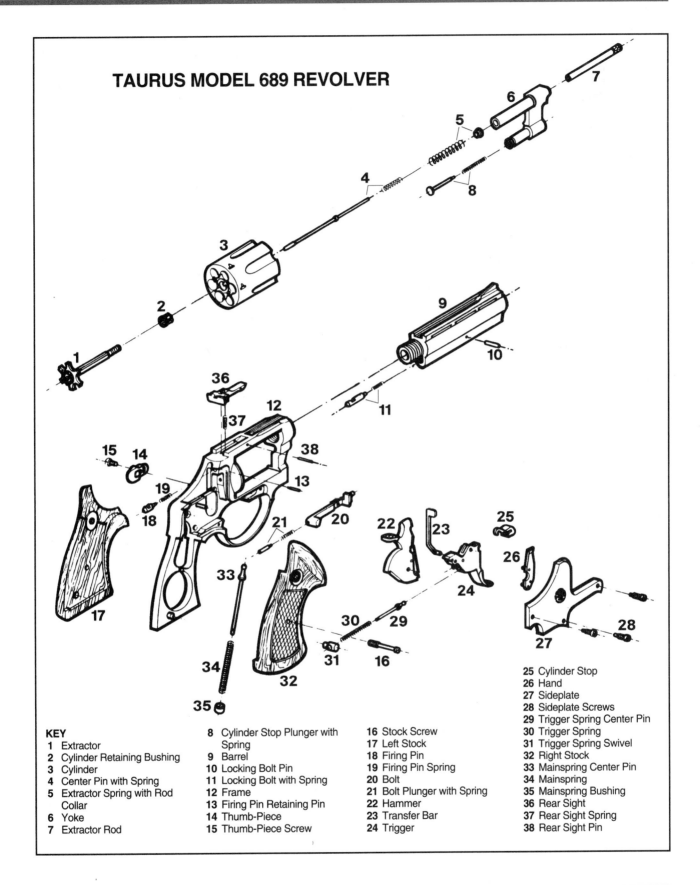

TAURUS MODEL 689 REVOLVER

KEY

1 Extractor
2 Cylinder Retaining Bushing
3 Cylinder
4 Center Pin with Spring
5 Extractor Spring with Rod Collar
6 Yoke
7 Extractor Rod
8 Cylinder Stop Plunger with Spring
9 Barrel
10 Locking Bolt Pin
11 Locking Bolt with Spring
12 Frame
13 Firing Pin Retaining Pin
14 Thumb-Piece
15 Thumb-Piece Screw
16 Stock Screw
17 Left Stock
18 Firing Pin
19 Firing Pin Spring
20 Bolt
21 Bolt Plunger with Spring
22 Hammer
23 Transfer Bar
24 Trigger
25 Cylinder Stop
26 Hand
27 Sideplate
28 Sideplate Screws
29 Trigger Spring Center Pin
30 Trigger Spring
31 Trigger Spring Swivel
32 Right Stock
33 Mainspring Center Pin
34 Mainspring
35 Mainspring Bushing
36 Rear Sight
37 Rear Sight Spring
38 Rear Sight Pin

sounds strange, do not attempt to clean these internal parts until the cause has been determined.

If the cylinder won't rotate, the hand is not pushing the cylinder, the cylinder stop is not allowing the cylinder to move, or, as is often the case, the cylinder stop is not releasing. If all the parts are clean, the cylinder stop or trigger must be adjusted or replaced if broken. The hand spring and hand pin get stuck sometimes, usually due to a lack of lubrication and the need for cleaning. (To avoid repeating myself, let's just accept the fact that every part we're going to discuss from here on is negatively affected by dirt, trash, oil, etc.) After excessive pressure has been applied to them when cylinders get stuck, the hands often need to be adjusted. Always check to make sure the star on the extractor was not damaged by excessive hand pressure when a cylinder does not release properly.

A stuck trigger can be caused by the hand's sticking against the ejector star. In this case, the ejector/hand will have to be adjusted. Another cause is a weak trigger spring, often the result of someone's cutting on it in an attempt at a smooth, soft trigger. Many such guns feel great. The problem is that they just do not work. If this spring has been cut or ground down, replace it. While it does not happen often, the transfer bar has been known to stick between the hammer and firing pin. This requires an adjustment to the firing pin or transfer bar.

To check out internal problems that cause misfiring, allow the revolver to cycle through the firing position. As the mainspring has been removed, you will have to apply the pressure to make the action work. After cycling the action through the firing mode, hold the hammer fully forward in the fire position to be sure the firing pin is coming through far enough every time for positive firing. Maintaining the hammer in its forward position, make sure the cylinder is locked into the correct firing position and that there is not an excessive gap between the cylinder and the frame. Also be sure the transfer bar is not broken and is in the correct position.

There can be several reasons why the cylinder does not lock into place at the correct time, or does not lock at all. The cylinder stop itself can be bent or broken and must be replaced. A worn cylinder-stop housing will require the changing of the cylinder. The cylinder stop might not be coming up high enough to fully engage, which will require your adjusting the cylinder stop to a higher position. The extractor star might be worn completely, or in spots that do not allow the cylinder to fully lock into place every time. Wear on the hand itself usually moves the cylinder about the same amount unless there is wear on both the ejector star and the hand. This condition can require the hand's adjustment or replacement or the

replacement of the cylinder ejector. The extractor is not sold separately from the cylinder. It is not uncommon for the cylinder-stop plunger to get stuck. It should be replaced if rusty.

Encountering hammers and/or triggers that are very hard to move, or even frozen tight, is not uncommon. Such problems usually have nothing to do with the working parts under the sideplate, so before doing anything inside the revolver, check that there is no lead or residue between the barrel and cylinder. Also make sure the face of each chamber clears the barrel and that the extractor rod and center pin are not bent. The action can also lock up if the yoke is misaligned and in need of centering or replacement. A firing pin that sticks forward into a fired cartridge will lock the firing mechanism down. This can be overlooked once the fired cartridge is removed, so be sure the firing pin is returning to its spot in the frame. If it is slow, replace the firing pin spring, firing pin, or both. Only now do we look at the hammer block and internal parts to find any internal cause of this problem.

When you reach this point and have taken care of the problems we covered earlier but the cylinder remains hard to rotate, you have a misaligned yoke, a bent or loose extractor rod, a bent center pin, or an extractor spring problem. With the cylinder out of the frame in the load position, spin it while looking at the forward end. You'll be able to see if the extractor rod is bent. If you cannot straighten it completely, it must be replaced. Almost straight will not do.

Extraction problems can sometimes be solved by removing the cylinder assembly and honing the chamber that is giving the problem. While it is wise to mark the offending chamber or chambers while firing, they are usually easy to see. Using an inside micrometer on each chamber will show you how much variation there is. If you do not have equipment to smooth up the inside of a cylinder, you can polish with some fine emery cloth strips wrapped around a rod that will fit the chambers. It is amazing how much difference can be made by just polishing each chamber to a bright finish. While you have the cylinder out of the frame, put fired brass into each chamber to see that the extractor is getting a good hold on each rim to extract them properly.

Taurus handles defective cylinders and extractors under its limited lifetime warranty so unless someone has made modifications or damaged the assembly by shooting improper reloads, you may be just as well off returning the gun to Miami. If you do the work yourself, note that Taurus sells only complete cylinder assemblies, including the extractor. Since it is important that any new cylinder be timed to the individual revolver, it is a good idea to acquire a new hand at the same time you get the cylinder assembly.

Installing Melded Rear Sights

When installing an adjustable rear sight, "melding" it will make it look like it is part of the slide. It will also help accuracy.

By Dennis A. Wood

DON'T BOTHER GETTING your dictionary out to look up the word "melded." The closest definition you'd find has to do with card playing. The only thing I can figure is that this word combines the words melt and blended. The idea of melding, as it applies here, is to install an adjustable rear sight on the rear of the slide so that it looks like part of the slide.

If the rear sight sits high, the front sight should be at a commensurate height. However, high-sitting front sights can often catch on things at inappropriate moments and also have a tendency to drag on the inside of a holster. It's better if the rear sight is melded into the slide. Installing the rear sight in this way places the sight blade almost 0.750-inch further to the rear of the slide, creating a longer sight radius that contributes to more accurate sight-to-target alignment.

Adjustable sights are preferable unless you are shooting across a poker table, where sights are not always necessary. Fixed sights do not allow adjustments for differing bullet weights or powder charges. Most fixed sights are just what the name implies—fixed in position and targeted at the factory for a certain bullet weight. If lighter or heavier weight bullets are to be used, sight alignment has to be adjusted if you want to hit where you're aiming.

The two brands of sights preferred by my customers are made by Bo-Mar and Pachmayr. The dimensions on the drawing were taken from both brands of sights using a computer measuring machine. These are nominal figures and allowable tolerances would be a few thousandths of an inch either up or down. Both of these sights are sturdy and have accurate adjustments. The Bo-Mar has one screw that goes through the base and pushes the bottom of the sight base up against the inside faces of the dovetail in the slide, thus locking it in place. The Pachmayr has two lock-down screws. On the Bo-Mar sight, one small spring inside another spring controls elevation pressure. The Pachmayr has two springs, one at each side of the dovetail, for anchoring.

These aspects should be pointed out to the gun owner, and may factor into which sight will be chosen for installation. Both are similar in the installation process in that they need the same number of milling cuts. Placement of the milled cuts differs, but the tooling used is the same.

Most pistol slides are harder than Hades and are not very kind to normal high speed steel cutters. Investing in carbide cutters will go a long way toward getting you through the milling cuts should a few jobs of this sort come your way. At one time, I was a nonbeliever and tried to get through the job with high speed steel cutters to do the four required cuts. I eventually finished the job, but not

The milling machine setup for cutting the dovetail is for a M1911-style slide but the procedures can be used on any pistol or revolver with at least 0.250-inch of material above the firing pin hole.

Left—You can see the difference between an original slide (left) and one with all cuts needed for a melded sight (right). Carbide cutters make the job go easier.

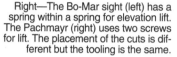

Right—The Bo-Mar sight (left) has a spring within a spring for elevation lift. The Pachmayr (right) uses two screws for lift. The placement of the cuts is different but the tooling is the same.

before dulling the tools severely and experiencing more snaps, crackles and pops than any breakfast cereal could make. Bite the bullet and get carbide cutters; they last longer and cut more freely on the harder steels you are likely to encounter when installing sights on pistol slides.

Carbide end mills are available from Enco Manufacturing, 5000 W. Bloomingdale, Chicago, IL 60639. The four cutters used for this job are a $1/2$-inch four-flute carbide end mill, a $5/16$-inch four-flute carbide end mill, a $3/16$-inch carbide ball end mill, and a 60-degree by .359-inch carbide dovetail cutter available from Brownells. If your budget is tight, the $5/16$-inch endmill will work in lieu of the $1/2$-inch end mill. The carbide dovetail cutter runs around $43, but it will most likely last until you retire and settle on an island surrounded by hula girls.

The procedures demonstrated here are for a M1911-type auto slide, but can be employed on any pistol or revolver with at least .250-inch of material above the firing pin hole.

Take the slide off the frame and remove all the internal parts from the slide. The rear sight will also need to be removed. I use a block of steel made up to fit snugly on the inside of the frame rails so that the slide is not collapsed from the pressure of the jaws when using the mill's vise. There are several slide-holding fixtures made just for the M1911 slide and its clones. If you have one, it will work for this job. If you use a milling vise to hold the slide, tape the sides of the slide with heavy-duty duct tape to prevent scratching the sides. With the slide in the vise, use a small machinist's level to level the top of the slide. Using your dial Vernier, measure from the breech face of the slide back 1 inch, and scribe a line. Collet the $1/2$-inch carbide end mill in your mill. From this scribed line, go rearward toward the back face of the slide and remove the metal until the depth of the original dovetail for the rear sight is reached. This amounts to a depth of about .115-inch. I mount the slide in the vise with the bore parallel with the axis of the table, the bore end pointing to the left, and use the cross slide for feeding the cutter. Even though carbide cutters are being used, keeping a lot of oil on the cutter will flow the chips out of the way and reduce friction, extending the cutter's sharpness and life.

Once this first milling step has been completed, remove the $1/2$-inch cutter and insert an edge finder in the quill. Run the edge finder up against the ledge that was created at the 1-inch scribed line. With the edge finder turning so that the bottom end runs true with the shank, we now have a starting or zero point. To guarantee that the milling table is moved the right distance, I set up a dial indica-

tor, with 1 inch of travel and the tip of the indicator against the left side of my vise, and zero it out. Move the table to the left until you reach the "F" dimension minus half the diameter of the edge finder as recorded by the dial indicator. For example, if installing the Bo-Mar sight and using a $1/2$-inch diameter edge finder, the "F" distance is 0.465-inch less half the 0.500-inch diameter (0.250) of the edge finder for a targeted table movement of 0.215 on the indicator. Lock the table in place and remove the edge finder from the collet. Insert the $5/16$-inch four-flute carbide end mill. This cutter is used to relieve the load of material removal for the dovetail cutter. Move the cross slide back and forth until the "A" depth dimension is reached. For the Bo-Mar sight, this depth is 0.103-inch. Once the clearance cut is made, remove the $5/16$-inch cutter and insert the 60-degree by 0.359-inch dovetail cutter.

Touch the bottom of one cutting edge on the dovetail cutter to the bottom of the slot you just cut, and lock the quill at this depth. I run the carbide dovetail cutter at 300 rpm and feed it directly into the $5/16$-inch clearance cut, moving slowly while using a small pump oiler to flood lots of cutting oil onto the cutter. Carbide is tough material, but it will crumble if heavy-handed pressure is exerted while cutting, so feed slowly. This cutter will eventually get through and out the other end of the sight slot. Here again, the flooding oil will help the cutter's rotation move the chips out of the way and prevent the cutter from binding and breaking this $43 investment.

There should now be a dovetail cut into the slide with a bottom width of 0.359-inch. It needs to be cut to the "C" dimension for the particular sight you are installing. Subtract the .359-inch dimension from the "C" dimension and divide the result in half. This is the amount that will need to be removed from each end of the dovetail. Zero out the dial indicator touching the left side of the milling vise, move it the appropriate amount to the left, and pass the dovetail cutter through the slot once again. Once this pass has been made, move the table to the zero point and then to the right the same amount. Pass the cutter through the slot once again. The idea is to make the bottom of the dovetail cut in the slide the same width as that of the bottom of the dovetail on the sight base. Raise the quill, remove the carbide dovetail cutter, and place it in the vault along with your wife's diamonds. Set the mill table to the zero point, which would be the middle of the dovetail cut in the slide.

Insert the $3/16$-inch carbide ball end mill in the quill and move the table to the left by, depending on which sight is being installed, the "G" dimension plus half the diameter of the ball end mill which

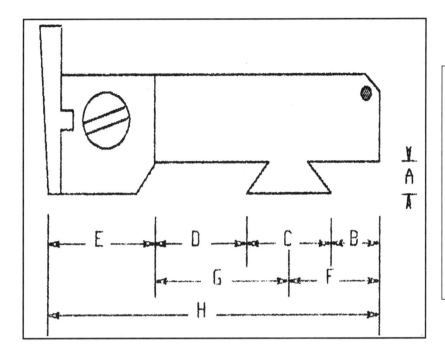

BASIC SIGHT DIMENSIONS

	BO-MAR	PACHMAYR
A	.103	.100
B	.283	.432
C	.364	.371
D	.352	.220
E	.409	.3875
F	.465	.618
G	.534	.406
H	1.407	1.411

These are nominal dimensions and may vary 0.005 either way.

is .094-inch. Feed the cutter down until it just touches the area to be milled. I usually run this cutter at 400 to 500 rpm and feed it slowly across the slide. Yes, I use lots of cutting oil. Mill down until you reach a depth of 0.140-inch. I only feed down about 0.015-inch at each pass, as this cutter is somewhat small and may flex or break if it is overburdened. Once the $^3/_{16}$-inch round-bottomed groove has been cut, clean it out with an oil-displacing solvent. Dye up the groove with layout blue. Remove the $^3/_{16}$-inch ball end mill and replace it with the $^5/_{16}$ four-flute carbide end mill. Touch this cutter to the top of the slide so the 0.140-inch depth of cut needed blends in with the depth of cut made with the $^3/_{16}$-inch ball end mill. Mill the material left to the rear of the $^3/_{16}$ groove from the middle of the groove back to the 0.140-inch depth. The blue layout dye lets you see when you get to the required depth. Hopefully, the bottom of the dovetail in the slide and the bottom of the dovetail on the sight base are the same. If they are, the sight will not fit into the slide dovetail. This is by design, and means you did it right. Using a 60-degree sight base file with two safe sides that do not cut, file the slot in the slide a bit at both ends until the sight base needs a deliberate tap with a nylon faced hammer to get it in place. The fit should be snug, not overly tight, and certainly not loose. The $^3/_{16}$-inch radius at the front end of the sight elevator clearance cut into the slide may need a few swipes with a round needle file so that the sight is allowed to travel to its full depth at this point. Once the sight looks centered, measure from each side of the slide to each side of the sight base with your dial Vernier until it is sitting dead center.

Now that the sight is centered in the rear of the slide, the elevation screw hole will need to be drilled in place. Use a #22 drill to go through the sight and the base, creating a starting spot by twirling the drill with your fingers. Drift out the sight and drill the #31 diameter hole and tap for #6-48 thread. Use a new, sharp drill and tap for this step along with, yes, lots of cutting oil.

Although the sight is perfectly acceptable, and will work as intended when installed in this fashion, it seems to bother some folks that the dovetail is visible at each side of the slide. This cosmetic flaw can be corrected by milling the slide along the sides of the sight base, using a $^1/_4$-inch carbide ball end mill to blend the radius into the bottom of the dovetail. Drift out the hinge pin at the front of the sight and leave the dovetail base in place in the slide. Tighten both of the hold-down screws, or the single screw, that go through the sight base and bear against the bottom of the dovetail cut in the slide. Place masking tape on both sides of the sight base. Using the cross slide, feed the $^1/_4$-inch carbide ball end mill toward the side of the base until it just starts to scratch the tape. Set your table travel stop so that the leading edge of the $^1/_4$-inch ball end mill stops halfway past the front edge of the sight base. This end mill should be run at 400 to 500 rpm and downfeed should be kept at 0.010- to 0.015-inch on each pass until you get to the bottom of the dovetail cut into the slide. Once one side has been cut, the same procedures are used for the other side. A round or half-round needle file is then used to clean up rollover burrs created by the milling process. Deburring can be done without cutting oil.

Working Charco/Charter Arms Revolvers

Even though a revolver's design is simple, there is no guarantee that working on it will be, as some of the Charter Arms wheelguns prove.

By Butch Thomson

LIGHT WEIGHT AND comparatively low prices combine to make Charter Arms' Charco revolvers one of the top-selling budget handgun lines on the market today. I've sold a lot of these guns over the years, and it seems like I've worked on just as many.

These Charter revolvers are made to be as light as engineering will allow. To keep the weight down, the alloy grip frame and trigger guard fit inside the steel frame. Every part seems to be made with weight in mind. That makes carrying the gun easy but, when combined with heavy recoil, it also can create other problems. The barrel sleeve often comes loose when heavy loads are fired. An older model Bulldog 357 I'm working on has a setscrew under the cylinder latch housing that keeps the barrel from loosening. Later models do not have this feature, and many of their shrouds work their way off.

Before we start taking a Charter apart, let's talk about what we can do about loose barrel shrouds. Silver soldering the shroud back on will discolor and warp the sleeve unless it is done with the utmost care and control. It is best to lightly rough up the barrel and inside of the sleeve, then epoxy it back in place. A coarse sandpaper can be used for this job, but I recommend doing it with a small grinding wheel on your Moto-Tool. You want the surfaces to be rough enough so the epoxy will have something to stick to other than a smooth surface. The cylinder and crane should be completely out of the revolver before you start your work. The crane screw holds the cylinder in the revolver. When this screw is removed, take out the crane screw washer and put it back on the crane screw. Swing the cylinder out of the revolver and pull the crane away from the firearm.

The cylinder and crane assembly are the source of many of the Charter guns' problems. When the ejector rod head starts coming loose all by itself, several problems can occur. The most common is the failure of the cylinder to open. Even more difficulties can arise if the cylinder becomes hard to open. When the shooter forces the cylinder open, the lightweight crane often bends. If you try overpowering the thumb piece (cylinder latch) to make the cylinder open, you could damage the cylinder latch, cylinder release screw, latch washer, latch plunger, plunger spring, latch cover plate or the latch retaining screw. Any one of the parts may need to be replaced or repaired after the stuck cylinder occurs. Attempting to force the stuck cylinder to open can damage the cylinder latch hole in the frame, the ejector rod tip, the ejector, the ejector rod head, the ejector rod collar and the threads under the collar on the ejector rod.

Always examine the cylinder latch and the cylinder for excessive looseness and damage caused by forcing stuck cylinders, even if it is not one of your complaints. When all these parts are tightened and seem to be okay, see if the ejector rod head comes loose easily. If so, you can expect it to loosen under recoil. A little tightener on the threads will help hold it all together, but if you use too much, you won't be able to get it apart again.

The ejector itself is held to the ejector rod by a pin driven through a hole $1/4$-inch behind the face of the ejector star. Ejectors are restricted to factory-only installation and aren't for sale, so be careful as you work on and around them. Before removing the ejector, slowly spin the cylinder while your thumbnail rubs the end of the ejector rod protruding through the star of the ejector face. After

CHARTER ARMS UNDERCOVER REVOLVER

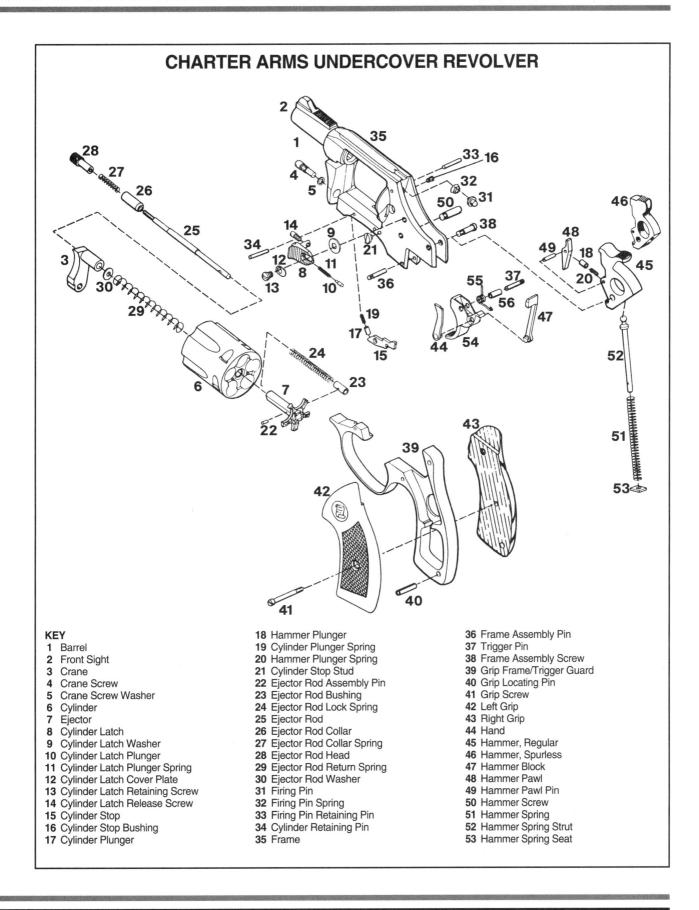

KEY

1 Barrel
2 Front Sight
3 Crane
4 Crane Screw
5 Crane Screw Washer
6 Cylinder
7 Ejector
8 Cylinder Latch
9 Cylinder Latch Washer
10 Cylinder Latch Plunger
11 Cylinder Latch Plunger Spring
12 Cylinder Latch Cover Plate
13 Cylinder Latch Retaining Screw
14 Cylinder Latch Release Screw
15 Cylinder Stop
16 Cylinder Stop Bushing
17 Cylinder Plunger

18 Hammer Plunger
19 Cylinder Plunger Spring
20 Hammer Plunger Spring
21 Cylinder Stop Stud
22 Ejector Rod Assembly Pin
23 Ejector Rod Bushing
24 Ejector Rod Lock Spring
25 Ejector Rod
26 Ejector Rod Collar
27 Ejector Rod Collar Spring
28 Ejector Rod Head
29 Ejector Rod Return Spring
30 Ejector Rod Washer
31 Firing Pin
32 Firing Pin Spring
33 Firing Pin Retaining Pin
34 Cylinder Retaining Pin
35 Frame

36 Frame Assembly Pin
37 Trigger Pin
38 Frame Assembly Screw
39 Grip Frame/Trigger Guard
40 Grip Locating Pin
41 Grip Screw
42 Left Grip
43 Right Grip
44 Hand
45 Hammer, Regular
46 Hammer, Spurless
47 Hammer Block
48 Hammer Pawl
49 Hammer Pawl Pin
50 Hammer Screw
51 Hammer Spring
52 Hammer Spring Strut
53 Hammer Spring Seat

making sure that the cylinder isn't wobbling around, see if the ejector rod's tip is uneven or wobbly. It often will be if someone has pounded on the cylinder trying to get it open. When you drive out the pin holding the ejector to the rod, nine parts—counting the ejector rod assembly as only one—will be released at once. Remove them slowly and in order, keeping the ejector rod bushing in the exact same position as it came out of the rod. Reversing ends, or even putting it in upside down, can make it impossible to reassemble the gun. If it can be put together differently, it might be excessively loose or excessively tight. There is always a chance that it might go in either way without any problem, but it won't most of the time. You'll avoid unnecessary work by just putting it back the way it came out.

Take the ejector rod out of the crane/cylinder assembly and unscrew the head. Pull the head, spring and collar off the ejector rod, then roll the rod on a flat surface to be sure it is not warped. Check the tip of the ejector rod that locks into the frame for bends, file marks, or other damage. I can't explain why, but on several of the guns that have come into my shop, the end of the head that locks into the frame has been ground down. I suspect someone decided that grinding some metal off the tip of the ejector rod is the way to repair a bent rod or sticking cylinder. It does make it fit more loosely, but a loose rod is the last thing you want. Recoil will make a loose rod bounce around in the revolver's frame and open up the cylinder latch hole. It will also loosen the rest of the firearm and wear the revolver out in short order. The condition can also be dangerous. You can straighten or replace a bent rod but if someone has been grinding on the rod, replacement is the only option.

Remember my advice about using excessive pressure when trying to open the cylinder latch if you get a revolver with a stuck cylinder. Insert a screwdriver behind the ejector rod head and push it forward toward the muzzle. If it moves enough, you will be able to press on the back side of the cylinder and pop it out. If it won't go forward, screw the head back onto the ejector rod with a small pair of needle-nose pliers. Turn it just enough to allow the rod to go far enough to release.

Another cause of stuck cylinders can be a broken or bent cylinder release. If that is the case, opening the cylinder as described above requires no help from the cylinder release. When the cylinder opens easily, see if the cylinder latch works when the cylinder is swung open, or is out of the revolver. The cylinder latch release screw should come through the frame to be almost, but not quite, flush with the recoil plate. If it ends beyond flush and into the cylinder well, it will bind the cylinder by sticking into the ejector rod's hole. Check this if the cylinder is stuck but everything else seems to be working. Push the cylinder latch forward, then try to open the cylinder at several different points along the way. When the latch release screw is broken or missing, the revolver can only be opened from the front as described. We will get to the cylinder latch when we get inside the frame.

The small cranes on the Charter revolvers are looser than others, but they should only have slight movement in the open position and none in the closed position. When you can wiggle a Charco's cylinder, the revolver is no longer safe. I am not talking about a small amount of cylinder play; I am talking about lockup. Many of the small 38 Specials have had +P ammunition fired through them and are loose as a goose. Unless you can tighten the gun with new parts, it should be discarded as dangerous.

After you have removed the revolver's grips, cock the hammer and insert a pin through the hole in the bottom of the mainspring guide bar. Now release the hammer and remove the mainspring assembly. Charter revolvers must have a very stout hammer spring or they will misfire. If misfires are one of the gun's problems, a mainspring that is too soft or has been cut is a likely cause. If a Charter spring has been cut—and it is easy to tell—you need to replace it. If the spring seems to be only a little light, you can take it off the mainspring guide, stretch it out about $1/4$-inch longer than it was, then see if it functions correctly. If you stretch it too much, the spring will never work correctly. Misfires can also be caused by the hammer block, which you can check when you remove the trigger assembly.

Remove the hammer screw, and slide the hammer out the top of the frame. Check the sear and the hammer pawl for damage. The hammer takedown screw comes out the left side, while the two takedown pins should be driven out from left to right. Some of these pins are directional and should be in correctly, but you never know how the last person might have installed them. After the pins are out, the grip/trigger guard can be pulled out the bottom of the frame. The five-piece trigger assembly is held in the frame by the same type of takedown pin. Before removing the trigger, take a good look at how it is installed in the frame. Take special note of how the spring set fits, because this one is not easy to get back in right. The three-piece cylinder stop is also "fun" to put back into the frame as it is being reassembled. Just make sure it is going back the way it came out, because it is easy to break. If the cylinder stop sticks or breaks in the locked position, you'll know because it will not allow the cylinder to open or the action to work. When it is broken, or stuck in the down position, the cylinder will spin freely, causing the gun to either not fire at all or fire out of alignment with the barrel.

If someone has been grinding on the trigger sear to get a softer trigger, you may be able to sharpen the sear edge without removing any more metal. If too much metal was taken, a new trigger will have to be installed for the revolver to be safe. The same is true of the hammer sear but you have a little more leeway as long as you make sure the angle is sharp. When someone has worked on a sear before you, always mount it on a jig to correctly refinish the sear angles. If you don't have a jig to work a Charter, try this: outline the frame on a wooden block with the hammer and trigger retainers in their exact location. Drill your holes to the correct size and use the right roll pins so that the hammer and trigger can be placed in exact relation to the frame's locations. Measure them with a micrometer to see that they are correct and how the sear surfaces line up. If one side of the sear tries to release before the other, it must be replaced or repaired.

Examine the hammer pawl if the double action sometimes fails to work or won't work at all. The pawl might be sticking and failing to reach its fully open position. These seldom need to be replaced but often require a good cleaning and, occasionally, a new pawl spring.

The cylinder latch assembly on the Charter is often problematic, mostly because of abuse, misuse, untrained gunsmithing, etc. The latch is a simple assembly, but different from any other. It only works one way. Many of these Charter cylinder latches have been taken apart and put back together incorrectly or with parts missing. The cylinder latch plunger and plunger spring are located inside the cylinder latch, which is held in place by the cylinder latch screw. When the cylinder-latch screw is removed, these two parts come flying out along with the cylinder-latch cover plate, a small piece of metal with a hole located on one end. The hole end faces the front of the revolver and if it is installed backwards, it will not work. The cylinder-latch release screw is screwed into the latch through the recoil plate in the revolver frame. As we mentioned earlier, it is important that this release screw be turned in all the way. If it is too short, it will not release the cylinder. If it is too long, or not screwed in all the way, it will come through too far and lock the cylinder. It must be straight or it will bind the action and possibly strip the threads out of the cylinder latch.

The hammer block, or transfer bar, sometimes tends to hang up on the rear of the firing pin. Grinding a little greater angle onto the top of the bar, when necessary, will help it slip up and over the firing pin. However, two things must be noted before you do anything. If you remove too much metal, the bar will be too low to transfer the full blow of the hammer to the firing pin and you will start getting misfires.

Also consider that the firing pin, not the bar, might be the problem. This only occurs when the firing pin has been worked on or installed wrong. Check it out before removing any metal from the transfer bar/hammer block.

The firing pin and firing-pin spring are also held by a retaining pin. Excessive dry firing is the main cause of damage to firing pins. They are easily replaced and should be when there is evidence of flattening that could keep them from sliding through the frame with ease. If a new pin is unavailable, you can file off the flattened metal edges on the original pin. Remember, however, that the pin was beaten flat and is therefore shorter. It should be replaced at the first opportunity.

Charter 22 revolvers have a special problem when they have been dry fired. The firing pin is long enough that it goes through and pounds on the edge of the rimfire cylinder. This dents the edges of the chambers, making loading difficult and extraction even harder. The metal that is dented over into the chambers can be very carefully filed away to prevent further harm, but it does not change the fact that the cylinder has been damaged. If these dents are too deep, the revolver will start misfiring because the firing pin is only pushing the rim into the preformed dent instead of crushing it to make it fire.

Failures to eject are not restricted to the rimfire versions; this also happens on other calibers. Along with a damaged extractor, a damaged cylinder might be the cause. With the assembled cylinder outside the revolver, load the cylinder and see if the extractor lifts the cartridges up at least $1/2$-inch as you push up the ejector rod. If the cartridges slip off the extractor past this point, don't worry. This happens with many Charter revolvers, but it doesn't put them out of business. If the cartridges fall off before that half-inch point, you have a problem with the extractor, or with the cylinder itself. See how loosely the cartridges fit into each chamber; there should be very little slack. Some 38 Special cylinders show signs of swelling after +P ammunition has been fired. Swollen chambers can be dangerous, as the metal has been weakened to the degree that it is beginning to give. At what point it will let go is anyone's guess, but the risk isn't worth taking. A new cylinder is the only answer to this problem. Chambers that are merely dirty, scratched or "ringed" can be polished out without weakening the metal.

Certain Charter revolvers have adjustable rear sight arrangements, but they are not all the same. If you order a sight, be sure to include the gun's serial number. On some of the early models, the sight was adjustable for elevation only, while later models had corrections for both elevation and windage. Even the later ones came in several different sizes. Some used one screw and a retaining pin and others two screws. Just order by serial number and save time and money.

Don't get impatient when you are putting a Charter handgun back together, because getting all the parts in just right can be hard on the nerves. Remember, the parts are delicate and break easier than those on many other firearms. So go slowly and do not force anything.

Fitting M1911 Extractors

When the M1911's extractor isn't doing what it was designed to do, make these modifications.

By Chick Blood

Tools needed to rework an extractor hook are, from top to bottom, a Swiss-pattern flat file, a square needle file, a triangular needle file, a square stone, and a small hard buffing wheel in either Foredom or Dremel flexible shaft. All are available from Brownells.

STOVEPIPES. FAILURES TO FEED. Dented case necks or cases that fly up into low mount scopes, over a shooter's head or into his face. Every one of these problems can be traced to an extractor that has either gone wrong or been ill-fitted in a Model 1911 or any of its clones, no matter the caliber.

The extractor, if functioning as it should when the slide is released, accepts a round from the magazine, sets it up for chambering and locks onto the case rim. As soon as the bullet leaves the barrel, pressure begins to drop and recoil starts moving the slide to the rear. In the process, the extractor hook pulls the spent case clear of the chamber, presents the left rear of the case to the ejector and becomes the pivot point around which the case is thrown through the ejection port.

It's pretty simple and, since 1905, has worked very well on who knows how many pistols, unless the extractor was too tight, too loose, too long or broken. If it is broken, the obvious remedy is to replace it, but all extractors are not created equal. Even factory-made replacements will have lengths differing in critical thousandths of an inch. They will also have varying degrees of bend in them from their midpoints, referred to here as a "hump," and their hook. The greater the bend, the more hook pressure is exerted. The less bend, the less hook pressure is exerted.

Some practitioners of extractor fitting say hook tension for hardball rounds should be somewhere between $3^1/2$ to $4^1/2$ pounds and

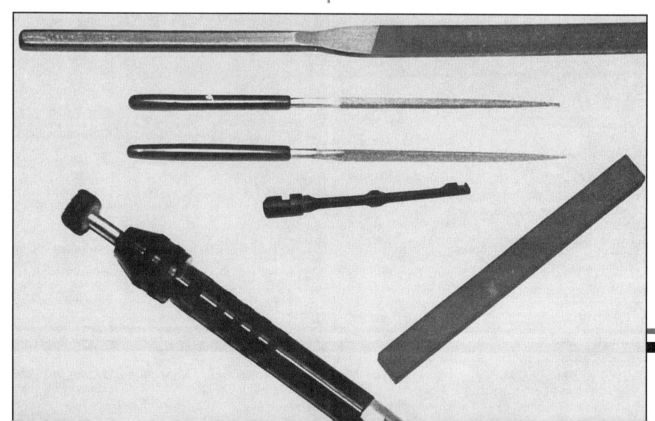

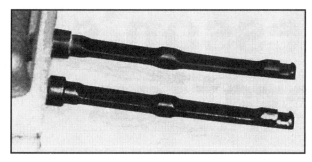

This reworked extractor hook (bottom) had the base of its slot beveled and a notch cut into the slot's lower front. The lower front edge of the hook was slightly relieved. Compare this to the unaltered extractor on the top.

$3^1/_2$ to 4 pounds for target loads. The parameters for these specific recommendations are governed by two truths. If there's not enough hook pressure on the case rim, the hook won't "grab," and extraction becomes unreliable. If there's too much pressure, the case rim won't cam into position from the magazine without getting hung up, and feeding becomes unreliable.

The guideline I follow for adjusting hook pressure is governed by whatever works as a result of bending the extractor in or out. Before you do any bending, though, take a closer look at the slotted, or hook, end of the extractor. More often than not, the lower edge of the slot—the portion that parallels the frame—will be sharp and well-defined. To make it easier for a case to slip into the slot, the edge must be beveled to about a 45-degree angle. Working with a small, square, diamond needle file quickly turns that edge into a bevel. Following that, break any sharp edges on the bevel to create a smooth radius and slightly round off the front, bottom corner of the extractor's hook.

Next, use a triangular needle file to make a small relief cut that angles toward the front of the extractor from the lower, forward corner of the slot. The cut doesn't have to be over $^1/_{16}$-inch long or deep. Combined with the alterations made previously, the cut makes it even easier for case rims to enter the extractor slot. It also provides extra clearance during the extraction process.

To check the fit between the tip of the extractor and the case rim, take an empty case in one hand, the extractor in the other, and link them together with the front of the hook over the rim. Hold both up to a light. The tip, or front, of the hook, should not contact the bevel of the case. If it does, the extractor is too long and its tip will try to climb the bevel, causing excessive tension. If your examination shows that to be a probability, the top edge of the extractor tip must be lowered until it clears the cartridge bevel. Use a stone instead of a file and work carefully, checking your progress often. When you're finished, polish everything you've done to the extractor's business end.

Moving rearward of the hook, you'll note the extractor has a hump in its middle. The outer side of this hump presses against the slide. Quite often, merely filing down the slide side of the hump will relieve excess pressure on the hook. To really fine tune a standard extractor, file it down regardless of the pressure.

That brings us to bending, which can be accomplished in several ways. All the are trial and error methods, so take your pick. You can lock the extractor in a padded vise at its midpoint and tap it with a small, brass hammer. You can insert the rear of the extractor into the back of the slide and use smooth-jaw pliers to bend the extractor between the halfway point and hook end. A third way of bending is to use two pair of smooth-jaw pliers, one at the halfway point, the other between that spot and the hook end.

Whichever method you employ, don't work an extractor back and forth too often. You'll weaken it. Weakened too much, it's going to break. It might not happen on the first round fired or maybe not for 500, but the extractor is going to break. Tap or bend it once or twice in the direction you want it to go and install it in the slide.

Insert a dummy round in a magazine, release the slide forward, then pull it back slowly. On extraction from the chamber, the dummy round should droop down a little before it contacts the ejector. It should not fall out of, or be held inflexibly, by the extractor's hook. Falling out indicates too little pressure is being applied while a rigid hold suggests excessive pressure.

Now let's add a final touch that involves no further adjustments to the extractor. Field-strip the pistol, hold the frame in one hand and a fine, flat file in the other. The ejector is located on the top left hand side of the frame. Use your file to put a 30-degree bevel on its front right edge and polish the bevel. Along with a properly fitted extractor, there's no better way to eliminate empty shells flying up into your face or over your head. This assures they'll eject to the side like they're supposed to.

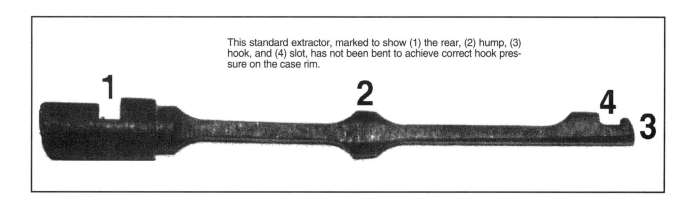

This standard extractor, marked to show (1) the rear, (2) hump, (3) hook, and (4) slot, has not been bent to achieve correct hook pressure on the case rim.

Smith & Wesson's Third Generation Pistols

You may not see a Third Generation pistol all that often, but these tips, plus thinking defensively, can help you improve them when you do.

By Chick Blood

THE THIRD GENERATION of Smith & Wesson autoloaders was a long time coming, but when it did arrive, things got busy in a hurry. For a while, just about everyone called the line's evolvement "The Gun of the Month Program." To me, it seemed more like "The Gun of the Week."

Targeted primarily for law enforcement, the first S&W autoloader, the Model 39, came out in 1954. It was designed solely for 115-grain FMJ 9mm ammo, which caused problems for many agencies, particularly the Illinois State Police, which preferred soft-point or hollow-point rounds and demanded the gun accept them. In response, Smith & Wesson made an extractor change in the Model 39, and it became the Model 39-2. There was also a Model 39-1, chambered for the 38 AMV cartridge and sold as the Model 52A, but very, very few of these were made. The 39-2 continued until 1971, when S&W adapted 14-round prototypes produced for the Navy's Seals and offered them for sale as the Model 59.

Through the 1970s, the 59 and 39-2 had inertial firing pins. The factory wish list for both weapons included a strong desire to make them both as safe as the S&W revolver. To achieve this, a cross-bolt safety to lock the firing pin was added in 1980 and, to positively distinguish the new from the old design, a three-digit numbering system was used. The Second Generation was born as the 439, 459, 539, 559, 639 and 659. The digit 4 identified an aluminum-alloy frame; 5 denoted carbon steel, and 6 represented stainless steel.

Up to about 1987, S&W constantly reviewed evaluations of the Second Generation from police departments, noting that reports of too-heavy double-action trigger pulls and too many sharp corners were the most frequent, but by no means the only, complaints. In response, the factory smoothed up the double-action mode, rounded off the corners, added new sight systems and fixed barrel bushings, made greater use of carbon and stainless steel, re-designed the sear spring, and added an ambidextrous safety, new grips and a new firing pin. There wasn't much left of the Second Generation by the time all the changes were made, and thus was created the Third Generation.

Along with the creation came four-digit model numbers to positively, absolutely, definitely distinguish this blessed event from any that had gone before. The first two digits identify the basic model: 39, 59 and 69 are 9mm; 10 is 10mm; 40 is 40 S&W; and 45 is 45 ACP.

The third digit designates the type of model, as noted below:

Number	Model
0	Standard
1	Compact
2	Standard with decocking lever
3	Compact with decocking lever
4	Standard, DA only
5	Compact, DA only
6	Non-standard barrel length
7	Non-standard barrel length with decocking lever
8	Non-standard barrel length, DA only

The fourth digit represents the material from which the model is made: 3 means the pistol has an aluminum-alloy frame with stain-

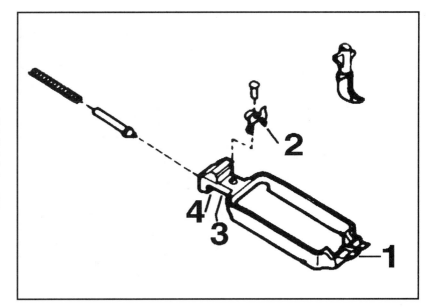

The main elements of Third Generation drawbar are the tail (1), the trigger play spring (2), the neck (3), and the surfaces where the trigger makes contact (4). The trigger straddles the neck of the drawbar, and the mating surfaces must be smooth and free of binding. The tail of the disconnector seats between the two tabs on the drawbar's tail, and may be polished to reduce friction. The slot in the frame for the drawbar should also be deburred, and this may require a special reamer (see text).

less-steel slide; 4 represents aluminum-alloy frames with carbon-steel slides; 5 denotes that the gun has a carbon-steel frame and slide; 6 means the gun has a stainless-steel frame and slide; 7 is a stainless steel frame with carbon steel slide. Got it?

Unless you happen to be an Authorized Service Center, you may not see too many Smith & Wesson Third Generation models—or any other current production S&W—coming your way for repairs. The company, probably in answer to Taurus' lifetime warranty, has adopted one of its own. However, let's assume one of these pistols has been brought to you with the request to work out some perceived roughness and lighten up the trigger pull a bit.

Field-strip the pistol by removing the magazine, cocking the hammer and pulling back the slide to align the slide latch with the notch on the slide's lower left. Push out the slide latch right to left and remove it. Move the slide and barrel assembly forward (the hammer will fall), control the recoil spring as you remove the recoil spring guide from the barrel underlugs, and remove the barrel. For the moment, set this group aside and detail strip the frame.

Turn the frame upside down and locate the U-shaped hole in the bottom of the grip insert. The hammer spring and plunger seat against this hole. Use a small punch to depress them. This frees the cross pin retaining the grip insert, hammer spring and plunger. Remove the grips to the rear and downward after flexing them outward to clear the frame. Lift the hammer strut clear of the frame to remove the spring and plunger. About two-thirds up the frame is a small pin that retains the sear spring. Be extremely careful in removing and replacing it (during reassembly) to avoid raising burrs on the frame or bending the pin itself. Go from right to left in disassembly. Go left to right in reassembly and make certain the pin is precisely aligned with its hole in the frame before driving it home. After removing the sear spring, push out the hammer pivot right to left. The hammer pivot is attached to a side plate that also carries the sear pivot.

Remove the sear, hammer and hammer strut. Unless the hammer strut is damaged, there's no need to drive out the pin joining it to the hammer.

The ejector, sear trip lever and firing-pin safety-blocking lever can now be lifted out. The ejector spring and firing pin safety springs follow. They're small. Don't drop, mutilate or lose them.

Use a small jeweler's screwdriver to turn the disconnector in either direction to clear the trigger bar. Remove the disconnector downward. The magazine catch/release button is on the pistol's left side and has a small plunger beside it. Depress the plunger while unscrewing the catch button. Remove the button, spring and plunger to the left; move the catch to the right and drift out the trigger pin. The trigger-bar assembly is then removed to the rear. The spring at its forend is the trigger play spring. It is riveted in place and is not normally removed. The trigger spring and plunger, located forward in the trigger well, and trigger come out next. Leave the trigger pin plunger and plunger-spring retaining pin in place unless there are signs of damage. Detailed stripping of the frame is now complete.

Cleaning up the internal workings of a Third Generation gun requires several pieces of specialized tooling. There are broaches and reamers made for every hole and recess in the frame. Some of this tooling can be substituted with mini-drill bits twirled between thumb and forefinger, but at least one is a multiple-stage tool for which there is no substitute.

Rather than grope around trying to get by, make the investment in proper tooling. It will make your life easier.

Trigger, Drawbar Assembly

What follows is not a step-by-step procedure, but more like a list of all things to be considered when working on a Third Generation pistol.

Assemble the drawbar spring and plunger and insert it into the

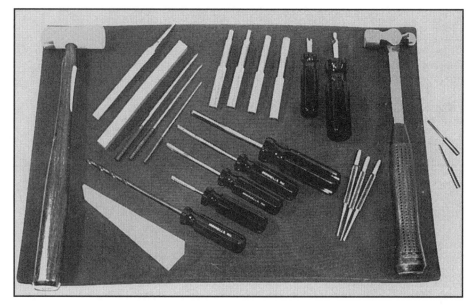

A duplicate of the tooling used at S&W Armorer's School, this set contains 20 pieces including 6 specialized reamers and 4 broaches. Available from Brownells for $160, retail, the tooling can also be used for First and Second Generation pistols.

hole forward of the trigger guard. Insert the trigger and trigger pin. After seating the plunger nipple into the trigger, push the trigger forward and hold it there. Slide the drawbar into the frame until you see the trigger points, pull the trigger to the rear and simultaneously push the drawbar forward to achieve engagement with the trigger. Keep a slight pressure on the rear of the drawbar and cycle the trigger.

If you feel drag, it could be due to burrs or roughness in the spring and plunger hole. Use a drawbar plug hole reamer to smooth up the recess, and retest.

The drawbar could also be dragging against the frame. If so, polish the drawbar's sides with crocus cloth and clean up its rails inside the frame by wrapping the cloth around a small, flat file. Next, check for any drag between the trigger and the neck of the drawbar. If present, carefully work each side of the neck with a smooth mill file. If that doesn't free things up enough, use a wooden or plastic wedge to widen the trigger between its points. Go easy with this. The trigger and drawbar are hardened. It wouldn't do to get ham-handed and crack either one. Finally, check the trigger-pin hole and trigger pin for any roughness.

Excess Trigger Play

The trigger-play spring is riveted to the neck of the drawbar and is intended to retain the trigger without a lot of slop. If there is excessive movement between the trigger points and their engagement surface at the front of the drawbar, it can be corrected with a perfectly square, $1/2$- by $1/2$-inch stone. Place the stone on top of the drawbar just behind the trigger-play spring and twist the stone against the spring to force its twin tangs forward, then re-check for excess play.

Your goal isn't a tight fit, which would really bind things up, but one that minimizes slop and still assures an easy release. You can enhance the release further by lightly polishing all drawbar/trigger engagement surfaces.

De-burring the Frame

You've already reamed the drawbar spring and plunger hole, or should have, in the steps previously described.

Another reamer is used to remove burrs or roughness in the disconnector hole at the frame's upper rear and the magazine catch hole. A third is used to remove any imperfections in the slide stop lever's hole, a fourth reamer is used to smooth up the hole for the hammer/trigger insert pin, and a fifth to true the sear pin and magazine catch plunger/spring holes.

As I said, and excepting the highly specialized drawbar spring/plunger hole reamer, you might be able to substitute for these reamers. Again, I recommend you don't. They have been carefully designed to reduce drag-inducing friction within the pistol while maintaining the tolerances necessary for safe, reliable function.

Disconnector/Sear Drag

The Third Generation series disconnector has a head, wings, a body, a tail and is supposed to move without binding when fitted between the sear tangs. If it doesn't, lightly draw-file, then polish, both sides of the disconnector that extend up from its tail. It wouldn't hurt to polish the inside surfaces of the sear tangs, either.

Barrel/Slide Drag

After reassembling the pistol, work the slide slowly, muzzle down. If the barrel is moving freely with the slide, you'll feel no drag. If there is a glitch, remove the barrel and examine the locking ring, located forward of the breech. If you don't see any rub marks, coat the locking ring with indicator fluid or a black magic marker, re-marry the slide/barrel group to the frame and cycle the slide slowly a few more times. Remember to keep the muzzle down.

Check the locking ring again. Any barrel contact with the slide will show up as rub marks or scrapes in the coating you just

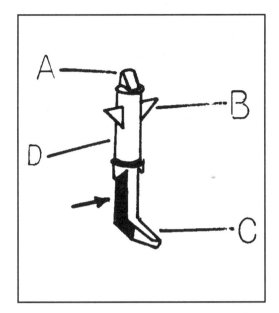

The elements of the disconnector are the head, wings, tail, and body. The small arrow indicates the area on one of two sides which should be polished to eliminate sear/disconnector drag.

Smith & Wesson Model 4006 Third Generation semi-auto.

applied. Use a strip of mild emery cloth to polish the locking ring free of coating, check the operation and repeat the coating and polishing as necessary until no barrel-to-frame contact is indicated.

Sear/Hammer/Springs

Third Generation sear- and hammer-engagement angles are exactly like engagement angles on any other pistol, revolver, rifle or shotgun. They should not be altered, merely refined.

Such refinements are a case of being damned if you do and damned if you don't. Don't go far enough and you get damned for half-baked trigger work. Go too far and somebody's lawyer damns you. Up to now, I've been able to avoid both with my universal sear stoning fixture designed by Ron Power.

It's called "Universal" because its adapters allow it to be used for many different kinds of sears, as many different kinds of hammers, and it cuts both sear face and sear relief angles. I say cut, but in this case I mean polish.

The fixture can also be used to lower the hammer hooks and decrease sear/hammer engagement. Here again, my emphasis is on polishing. The hooks on these handguns are factory undercut 12 degrees in reference to dead center of the hammer pivot-pin hole. Cutting the hooks too deep can create major safety problems and changing the angle of the undercut to avoid them is not part of this discussion. We're talking lessening friction between, not altering engagement surfaces of, interactive gun parts.

One other thing to consider is the hammer spring. The trigger pull of Third Generation pistols can be eased by replacing the fac-

tory spring with a reduced-power spring designed to function safely in a specific model. Wolff Precision Gun Springs is an excellent source for them, but be certain to order according to model number. For example, the 4006 factory hammer spring is rated at 20 pounds. Wolff's are 16, 17 and 18 pounds.

Whether or not you opt to include a new hammer spring in your re-work, polish the hammer strut before finally assembling the pistol and fully check out all functions on the range prior to returning it to service. Remember, Baby Jane triggers and full loads just don't add up to total reliability in a duty weapon.

Reassembly Tip

When reinstalling the ejector, sear release and firing-pin safety levers, use a drift punch. Insert it from the right and install the firing pin safety lever. Install the sear release by canting it forward into its slide slot, then roll it back with your thumb to align it with the drift. Push the drift through the sear-release lever, align the ejector lever and continue pushing the drift until it projects out the left side of the frame. Line up the hammer and sear with their pivot pin holes, then use the side plate to push out the drift, left to right, securing hammer, sear and levers in place. Make certain all three levers can be fully depressed to clear the slide when its joined to the frame.

Contacts: Brownells Inc., 200 West Front St., Montezuma, Iowa 50171; Wolff Precision Gun Springs, P.O. Box 1, Newtown Square, Pa. 19073.

Troubleshooting Ruger P-Series Pistols

Reliability in functioning isn't a problem with these guns. Trigger pull and accuracy can stand some work. Here's what to do.

By Butch Thomson

RUGER'S P-SERIES centerfire autoloaders have been controversial handguns from the first day the first 9mm pistols hit the market nearly two years after being announced. The gun has been modified a number of times through the years, but the basic design has remained the same: an inexpensive, stainless-steel double-action pistol.

The P-series pistols are generally popular and good sellers. You'll get many shooters who say their Ruger works perfectly. You'll get lots of others who will come to you less than happy with the gun, hoping you can solve the problems they're having with it.

From my point of view, it seems Ruger took a page from the group of old military manufacturers who felt mass-produced, loose-fitting parts could be interchanged on the battlefield. And, like those older military guns, since you can't change the design of the handgun, you must work out the individual problems of each pistol.

To illustrate how to do that, we chose two P model Rugers to work on, the P89DC in 9mm and the P91DC in 40 S&W that Ruger calls a 40 AUTO to underscore the competition between itself and Smith & Wesson. (We've shown a diagram of the P90, which is the same as the P91 except for caliber.)

These pistols' main assets are their low price and reliability. With factory ammunition this pistol will nearly always feed and eject. If yours is failing to feed or eject, try a different magazine before attempting to correct the problem in ways we will cover later in this article. Later Ruger magazines seem to give fewer problems than the first ones, so a replacement should be the first option you consider, especially if you are working on an older Ruger.

Check the empty pistol (while it is fully assembled and the slide closed) for play between the slide and frame. See if the hammer is dragging on either side of the hammer slot in the rear of the slide. The barrel should be very tight in the closed slide, without movement at the muzzle end or breech. Find out if the pistol is having an accuracy problem. You need to know where it is shooting and what kind of group it will give. All P-model magazines fit loosely, but see how much wobble yours has and how much vertical movement there is while it's locked in place.

If you don't follow Ruger's disassembly directions to the letter, you will not get a P pistol apart. Open the slide and let the slide stop lock the action open. Remove the magazine. Reach inside the breech, pushing the ejector forward toward the muzzle and down into the magazine well. Release the slide stop while holding the slide, letting it slowly move forward. When the slide-stop latch aligns with the notch cut for it, it can be removed. This notch aligns slightly before the slide is fully into battery, about 2 millimeters on the 40 caliber and 4 to 5 millimeters on the 9mm. I would not be surprised to find other readings on some of the different series. The slide stop does not just pop out. It is held in place by a spring that fits into a deep groove cut into the slide-stop pin. When you are sure the slide stop is properly aligned, a sharp tap with the plastic handle of a screwdriver will release it. It does not come all the way out because a second groove is machined into the other end of the slide-stop pin keeping it from coming out. When the slide stop spring locks into this second notch, you can remove the slide assembly.

With the slide upside down, it is easy to push the recoil spring and spring guide toward the muzzle so they can be lifted up and out of the slide. The recoil spring is directional and must not be put on backwards. The smaller end goes onto the rod first with the larger diameter fitting into the muzzle end of the slide. If this has been

RUGER P89DC AUTO

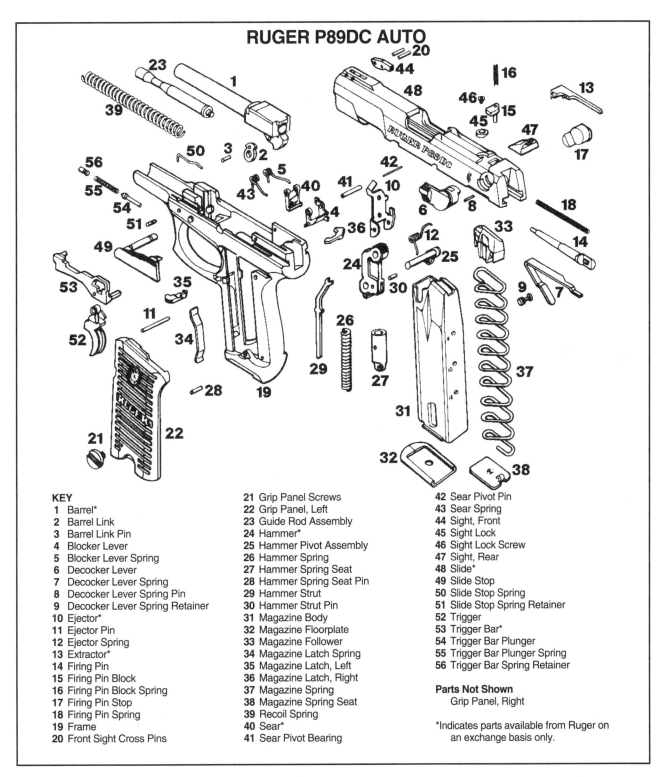

KEY
1 Barrel*
2 Barrel Link
3 Barrel Link Pin
4 Blocker Lever
5 Blocker Lever Spring
6 Decocker Lever
7 Decocker Lever Spring
8 Decocker Lever Spring Pin
9 Decocker Lever Spring Retainer
10 Ejector*
11 Ejector Pin
12 Ejector Spring
13 Extractor*
14 Firing Pin
15 Firing Pin Block
16 Firing Pin Block Spring
17 Firing Pin Stop
18 Firing Pin Spring
19 Frame
20 Front Sight Cross Pins

21 Grip Panel Screws
22 Grip Panel, Left
23 Guide Rod Assembly
24 Hammer*
25 Hammer Pivot Assembly
26 Hammer Spring
27 Hammer Spring Seat
28 Hammer Spring Seat Pin
29 Hammer Strut
30 Hammer Strut Pin
31 Magazine Body
32 Magazine Floorplate
33 Magazine Follower
34 Magazine Latch Spring
35 Magazine Latch, Left
36 Magazine Latch, Right
37 Magazine Spring
38 Magazine Spring Seat
39 Recoil Spring
40 Sear*
41 Sear Pivot Bearing

42 Sear Pivot Pin
43 Sear Spring
44 Sight, Front
45 Sight Lock
46 Sight Lock Screw
47 Sight, Rear
48 Slide*
49 Slide Stop
50 Slide Stop Spring
51 Slide Stop Spring Retainer
52 Trigger
53 Trigger Bar*
54 Trigger Bar Plunger
55 Trigger Bar Plunger Spring
56 Trigger Bar Spring Retainer

Parts Not Shown
   Grip Panel, Right

*Indicates parts available from Ruger on
   an exchange basis only.

reassembled incorrectly, you may have found your feeding problem.
   Slipping the barrel forward and up out of the slide, you may find, as I did, that Ruger barrel lugs fit like a five-year-old's feet fit his daddy's shoes. Ruger considers them part of the barrel assembly

and says they fit and work the way they do by design.
   Given all the years I've spent fitting barrel lugs to improve accuracy, I could not resist making one from 41-40 steel that fit tightly, both in side play and in hole size. It took me three tries to get one

right, but after I did, the P-89's group size went from 5 inches plus to 3 inches.

On some P-series pistols, you can wiggle the muzzle end when the gun is fully assembled. If you find this on your gun, you may as well abandon thoughts of improving accuracy without doing some major work. These guns are investment castings and vary a great deal in their degree of hardness, making modification a problem. The stainless-steel slide can be cautiously worked on, but the cast alloy frame is easily damaged.

Polishing inside the slide only makes loose parts even looser, although the extractor and extractor slot in the slide are exceptions. To get the extractor out of the slide, use a 2-millimeter punch to reach across the top of the left side of the slide port. Insert the point of the punch between the extractor lip and slide with care because this extractor is a restricted part and is easily damaged or broken. Now push the extractor out of the slide about 3 millimeters and pry it forward until it comes out of the slide. The right decocker lever will come out after the extractor is removed. Polish only the top and bottom of the extractor, making sure you don't remove any metal from the claw. It is small enough that it cannot afford to lose any metal. Since the rear of the extractor is fitted into the slide to lock the right decocking lever in place, removing metal here could cause this lever to be loose or fall out while firing. It will hurt the appearance of the pistol if you scratch the polished side of the slide when you are polishing the roughness in the extractor slot. A piece of emery cloth over the tip of a screwdriver will clean the rough edges of this slot without any damage to the finish.

It is now time to remove the rear sight, a job that isn't always as easy it should be. Some of these fit so tightly in the slides they can barely be driven out, but others will fall out after you have loosened the rear-sight lock screw. If your sight fits so tightly that it was very hard to drive out, use a belt sander to remove a little metal from the bottom of the sight. Belt sanders make it easier to uniformly remove the metal without cutting away one edge more than the other. Make sure you take the sight screw out before doing this, because if the vibration makes the screw come out and fall on the fast moving belt, you may never see it again. When the rear sight is too loose, you can tighten it by tapping down the slot's front or back edges with a small brass hammer. The front sight is held in place by two small roll pins.

Be careful to keep the firing-pin block and firing-pin block spring from coming out as you remove the sight. After those parts are removed, you can go ahead and take out the decocker spring retainer. This little part can be a real problem to displace. Using a punch or screwdriver, you must push the decocker spring down into the slide and completely away from the spring retainer. As you hold the spring out of the way, you must use a screwdriver tip to push the tight-fitting retainer out of its hole in the left-hand side of the slide. You will probably decide this is impossible, after trying many times. But it does work. By dragging the tip of a small, sharp screwdriver in a racking action, I can loosen it enough to get hold of the retainer's outside edge to pull it out. Once the decocking spring is removed, the left decocker lever will come out, followed by the firing-pin assembly.

I repeat what I said about polishing most of the slide parts at this point. The only thing you'll want to do with these parts is remove the burrs and sharp, rough edges. I do recommend rounding the sharp edges on the base of the firing-pin block that goes through the slide, and I suggest polishing out the rough edges on the rear of the firing pin. This unique firing pin has nine machine cuts on its base, and most are rough. Just remove the roughness; do not round off any of these edges.

Getting to the insides of the gun requires removing the grips, and they are tightly fitted. In fact, some Ruger grips have been broken by people trying to pry them off after removing the grip screws. These grips are secured by the screws on the bottom and lips on the top that fit inside the frame. By reaching inside the magazine well and pushing one grip panel out away from the frame, you can avoid damaging the grip. If you do pry them, make sure you only do it at the bottom of the grip panel.

Inside The P-Series

Before we do anything to the inner workings of a P-series Ruger, I will tell you that the gun doesn't lend itself easily to modification. For example, if you cut off a couple of coils to lighten the trigger pull, you'll also have to remove a small amount of the firing-pin return spring, or you will have misfires. But when you lighten the firing-pin return spring, sometimes the firing pin will not return fully and also cause a misfire. At this point, you don't know which problem is causing your misfires. Too much or too little of which spring? Aftermarket kits are balanced and work better in every case.

Use a punch to drive out the hammer-spring-seat pin located close to the base of the grip under the bottom of the panels. As you remove the punch, the hammer-spring seat, hammer spring and the hammer pivot assembly will come out the bottom of the frame. The hammer pivot assembly can then be pulled out from the right side of the frame, and the hammer will fall out.

Ruger did little in the way of polishing or otherwise finishing out these hammers, but the rough casting marks can be removed on your polishing wheels. A piece of tape over the sear edge will help you remember to protect this small, sharp area that is so easily damaged. It is also wise to use a file to remove the rough casting marks before using your buffing wheels. If the P model you are working on has had much use, it probably has drag marks on one side of the hammer where it drags against the slide. When this is the case, use your belt sander to remove a little metal from this side of the hammer. Make sure you only do this to the top half. This hammer is already very loose in the frame, and removing any metal from the bottom half would cause a major problem. Finishing the exposed part of the hammer will make the pistol look better.

Disassembling from this point on is much easier, you'll find, than putting the gun back together.

Pushing out the ejector pin with your punch will release both the ejector and ejector spring. Pushing out the front sear pin will release the sear and the sear spring, while pressing out the back sear pin will release the blocker lever. The sear and blocker lever both have sharp, rough edges but care must be used in smoothing them. Use a fine stone just enough to make the sear edge itself smooth. Check the blocker lever for burrs and rough edges, but do not try to round off its sharp edges.

The sear is one of seven parts, besides the frame, that Ruger will not restrict to factory installation. A number of other parts are

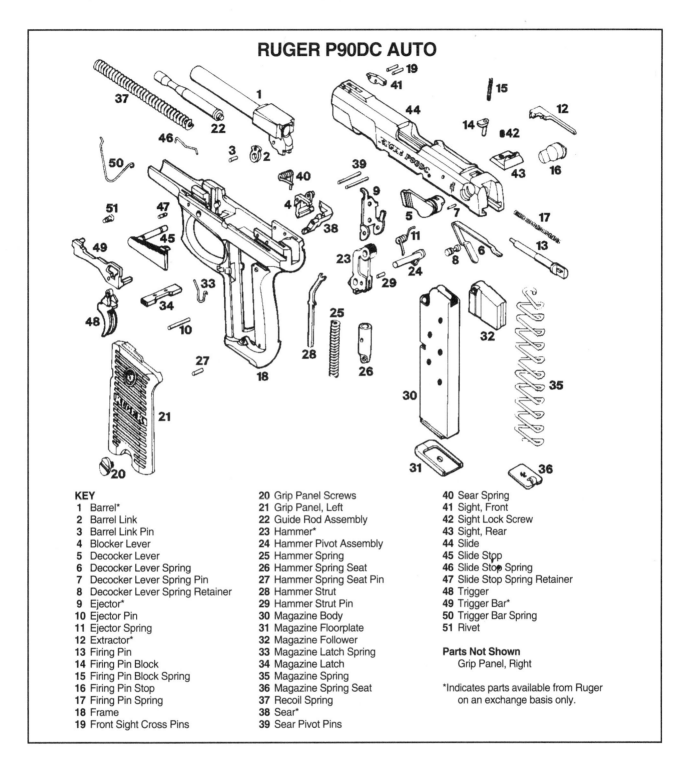

RUGER P90DC AUTO

KEY

1	Barrel*	20	Grip Panel Screws	40	Sear Spring
2	Barrel Link	21	Grip Panel, Left	41	Sight, Front
3	Barrel Link Pin	22	Guide Rod Assembly	42	Sight Lock Screw
4	Blocker Lever	23	Hammer*	43	Sight, Rear
5	Decocker Lever	24	Hammer Pivot Assembly	44	Slide
6	Decocker Lever Spring	25	Hammer Spring	45	Slide Stop
7	Decocker Lever Spring Pin	26	Hammer Spring Seat	46	Slide Stop Spring
8	Decocker Lever Spring Retainer	27	Hammer Spring Seat Pin	47	Slide Stop Spring Retainer
9	Ejector*	28	Hammer Strut	48	Trigger
10	Ejector Pin	29	Hammer Strut Pin	49	Trigger Bar*
11	Ejector Spring	30	Magazine Body	50	Trigger Bar Spring
12	Extractor*	31	Magazine Floorplate	51	Rivet
13	Firing Pin	32	Magazine Follower		
14	Firing Pin Block	33	Magazine Latch Spring		**Parts Not Shown**
15	Firing Pin Block Spring	34	Magazine Latch		Grip Panel, Right
16	Firing Pin Stop	35	Magazine Spring		
17	Firing Pin Spring	36	Magazine Spring Seat		*Indicates parts available from Ruger
18	Frame	37	Recoil Spring		on an exchange basis only.
19	Front Sight Cross Pins	38	Sear*		
		39	Sear Pivot Pins		

replaced on an exchange basis only, and the old parts are not returned, according to Ruger guidelines. (These are marked with an asterisk on the parts lists.)

Pick up the frame of the P model and work the trigger back and forth. Even though most of the working parts have been removed from the frame, you will still notice a rough and gritty feel as the trigger and trigger bar move inside the frame. This trigger is not held in a rigid position by a pin or anything; it just sits in the frame. The trigger bar provides a little rigidity as it holds the top of the trigger.

The trigger itself is already very loose, so push it to one side and then the other as you work it back and forth to find just where the rough spots are. Most of the drag is in the trigger bar, another of Ruger's restricted parts, so pay special attention to it. You will need to know just where to polish so you can avoid removing metal from a part that already fits sloppily in the frame. I would like to tell you where to polish, but none of the P-series pistols I have worked has ever been the same.

The pin portion of the slide-stop spring assembly holds the slide-stop spring down inside the frame. The slide-stop spring-retainer pin is a small pin with a deep groove cut around it that makes it a weak part. The slide-stop spring snaps up into this groove when the pin is installed and holds the pin in place. This pin also has a taper-cut point on one end to guide it into place while being driven into the frame.

It is necessary to hold the slide-stop spring down while pushing the retaining pin into the inside of the frame. The slide stop spring is very strong, so it takes a lot of pressure to do this. Without knowing this, you may think something under the spring is keeping it from moving. After you have pushed this pin in 2 millimeters, release the spring because you will need to move your other hand to the front of the hole above the front of the trigger guard. As you push the spring retainer pin inside the frame, the trigger-bar spring, plunger and retainer will be released and your hand must be there to restrain them. The spring retainer pin will be inside the barrel seat portion of the frame at the same time, so do not let it get away. Driving this slide-stop spring retainer pin into the frame without holding the spring down can bend or break the pin and can damage the spring or frame.

Now, all of these parts can be removed and the trigger and trigger bar can be lifted out of the frame. The frame is rough and oversized where the trigger fits, but since that's the way Ruger designed it, there is not a lot you can do with this part of the pistol. Polishing the left side of the trigger bar will help it work more smoothly, but removing much metal will make a sloppy fit even worse. The same thing is true of the inside of the frame where the trigger bar rides. This cast frame is easily damaged and hard to polish, so I recommend doing the inside by hand with fine emery and light oil.

One of the common ways trigger pulls are "improved" on the P model pistols is by cutting two or three coils off the trigger-bar spring. It does make the trigger easier to pull, but it has a bad side effect. Sometimes the trigger bar will not return to its fully seated position, and the trigger will not re-engage. For a police officer, this could be a death sentence. For the average shooter, he will think that his gunsmith does not know his business. This strong spring helps hold the trigger bar solidly in place, and the trigger bar is the only thing holding the top of the trigger with any rigidity.

Putting It Together

As we said earlier, reassembly is a little harder than disassembly.

To put the P-series back together, reassemble your trigger and trigger bar and re-install them inside the frame. Put the slide stop into the frame all the way into its operational position. Now put the trigger-bar plunger, spring and retainer back, returning the slide-stop spring into its slot as you push the trigger-bar spring retainer into its normal position.

Make sure the front end of the slide-stop spring is locked firmly into the trigger-bar spring retainer before releasing either. Again, use your punch to press the slide-stop spring down far enough that the little retainer can be slipped into place. Looking down into the top of the frame, make sure the slide-stop spring has fit into the groove cut in its retainer pin. Put the hammer in place, fitting the lug of the trigger bar into its slot in the hammer. While holding these in line, slide the hammer pivot assembly into place. At this point, slip the blocker lever into place and return its pin, making sure that the pin does not go through so far as to hinder the upward movement of the trigger bar while the trigger is being pulled. Now pull the trigger and make sure the blocker lever is moving up and down, and the hammer is moving back and forth with the pulling of the trigger.

The bent end of the sear spring fits in the slot cut into the sear face, while the straight end goes into the slot cut in the top of the blocker lever. A slave pin will help hold the sear and sear pin together while reinstalling. If you do not want to use a slave pin, it will help if you use both the sear retainer pin and a punch the same size as the pin. Slide the punch into the left side of the frame and into the sear just until it starts to come through where the sear spring goes. Do the same thing with the sear pin on the other side. Put the spring in with both ends into their respective slots and press down on the coil body of the spring until it is in its working position. Sliding the punch into the body of the spring will hold it in place. By lifting up on the punch, you can bring the other end of the spring into alignment with the sear-retaining pin. The pin can now be pushed through the sear spring. Push the punch out the other side. Again, make sure the pin does not come through too far because it will block the movement of the slide. Pull the trigger, and the hammer should cock. You need to use a slave pin that is .90 x $\frac{1}{2}$-inch to hold the ejector spring in place while you reinstall the ejector.

The firing pin goes back in with the notch to the top. Make sure the firing-pin return spring is fully to its rear position before putting it back in the slide. Both the right and left decocking levers are put into the slide at this time. Sometimes it is difficult to reinstall the extractor. You must be sure the right decocking lever is in its proper position so the back end of the extractor will fit into the groove cut into the decocking lever. Drive the extractor rearward while holding the claw end out 2 millimeters from its normal position. Ruger cut this extractor's locking lug at an angle to make it easier to re-install. The decocking lever spring is very strong and must be held down fully into its working position for the decocking spring retainer to be replaced. Use your punch to reach through the retainer hole in the slide to make sure the decocker spring is in its correct position. Push the spring all the way down and put the spring retainer back in, making sure it goes all the way in. If you can still see the inside rim of the retainer pin, it is not far enough in. Replace the firing-pin block assembly and the rear sight.

Adjustable sights, such as those made by Millett, can help if the P model is shooting a reasonable group that the windage-only adjustment will not center. Some gunsmiths have made barrel bushings to improve the accuracy, but the expense is prohibitive on this low-cost gun. Since Ruger will not sell you the barrel, ejector, extractor, hammer, sear, slide or trigger bar, it is difficult to do any modification or custom work on the P model guns.

Section 3
Long Guns

Working Chinese SKS Rifles 168

Troubleshooting the Remington
    1100 Shotgun 172

Working the Winchester 94 177

Gunstock Repairs 181

Performing the Ruger 10/22 Team
    Challenge Conversion 185

Mounting Rifle Scopes 188

Working the Browning Auto-5 192

Sporterizing Mauser 98 Rifles 196

Correcting a Bad Muzzle Crown 201

Installing Recoil Pads 204

Troubleshooting Remington
    Model 700 Rifles 210

Gunsmithing the Winchester 1300
    Shotgun 213

Maintaining Ruger Mini-14
    Rifles 217

Repairing and Maintaining the
    Mossberg 500 220

Glass-Bedding for Bolt-Action
    Rifles 224

How to Lengthen Chambers and
    Forcing Cones 228

Reworking Ruger 77/22
    Triggers 232

Installing Screw-In Chokes
    Without a Lathe 234

Installing Steel Butt Plates and
    Grip Caps 239

Removing Shotgun Barrel Dents 243

Bead Sight Basics 248

Benchworking Winchester
    Model 70 Rifles 249

Working the Savage Model 110 253

Working Chinese SKS Rifles

These popular rifles will separate the real gunsmith from the parts swapper, because you never know if the parts will fit—if they're available at all.

By Butch Thomson

THERE IS SOMETHING about being able to buy a rifle for less than $100 that turns a consumer's head every time. But when that rifle comes into your shop with problems that could easily cost more than that to fix, it's the consumer's stomach that turns.

Chinese-made SKS rifles fit both those statements. In the last couple of years, we've seen a proliferation of the low-cost guns coming into the country. I've seen some that are in excellent condition. Others have been questionable, if not downright dangerous.

The exception to this is the new, higher-dollar Sporter model with a thumbhole stock. These are special-order items, and U.S. buyers are paying a lot more for them. The Chinese are, thus far, building them very well, and I suspect they will continue to do so until the buyers start demanding cheaper prices. The rifles we're going to discuss repairing here are the cheaper ones.

To appreciate what you'll be up against when you start working with an SKS, it helps to understand that every SKS is bought from the Chinese Communist government. It is true that American buyers deal with companies that are set up to do business with the West, but these are little more than fronts. If doing business the "Western way" will get hard currency into China, then that's the way it will be.

It also helps to understand how the guns are made. There are seven manufacturing facilities in China that "make" SKS rifles, but in reality, they are little more than assembly points. Most of their parts come from hundreds of small shops all over China, and almost all have to be fitted at the point of assembly. Good parts are mixed with bad. Some rifles will have good barrels but bad receivers, or it may be the other way around. This is true of all the parts in the rifles.

There is also a lack of uniformity on chrome-lined barrels, ranging from the merely inconsistent to a point that the linings have come out of the rifles. We have even been told of a threaded barrel

The three basic types of Chinese-made SKS rifles are, from the top, pinned barrel, screwed-in barrel, and the more expensive, but quality, Sporter.

Virtually all the SKS gas tubes are hand-fitted to the individual rifles, and have different lugs. You can see where they've been ground on and filed down to make them fit.

that was driven into a non-threaded receiver and pinned in place.

The SKS rifles are not only inconsistent in the way they are assembled, the metal used for the parts varies widely, too. Cheap Chinese steel is made the way we did it 100 years ago. China also makes a top-quality steel, but it obviously will not be used in rifles they sell us for $37. To illustrate this point further, we took seven Rockwell hardness tests up and down the same barrel and got seven different readings. I've had the same experience with receivers. As we go along, we'll go a little deeper into the metallurgy of the different parts and how it affects what you'll be doing to the rifles.

Soft metal is to blame for a majority of problems you will encounter with the SKSs—most commonly, broken extractors followed closely by feeding and ejection failures. Your biggest problem won't be mechanical—it will be justifying the high cost of professional repairs when you didn't pay much for the gun.

Your major problem will be getting parts. I have found—and other gunsmiths confirm this—that the ones you will get actually fit less than 20 percent of the time. They can be made to fit only about 70 percent of the time. For this reason, the SKS will show who is a gunsmith and who is a parts exchanger.

Before you start working on the SKS, you should make a visual check of the barrel and bore, making special note of the chrome lining's condition. If it is coming loose—and I've seen several that were—you're on the way to a blown-up barrel. Sadly, many shoot-

ers see this happening, but discount the seriousness of the situation and just keep on shooting. If this condition exists and you decline to have it repaired, I suggest you sign a liability waiver indicating that you are aware of the problem but didn't want anyone to fix it. If your cousin sells insurance, buy a policy naming me as beneficiary after you sign the waiver.

Field Strip Reveals...

Field stripping the SKS allows you to determine just what you're working with in terms of manufacturing quality, and it will quickly reveal any problems the gun has.

To accomplish this, swing the takedown lever up and over, pulling it out as far as it will come from the receiver. The takedown lever does not come all the way out of the rifle. Now the rear receiver cover can be removed, and you may extract the recoil spring and spring guide from the bolt assembly. Take out the bolt assembly by pulling the bolt handle to the rear of the receiver and lifting it out. Now you can reach into the receiver and lift the bolt out.

We'll remove the gas piston tube and forearm piece next. Lift the butt end of the tube assembly lever up until it reaches the top of the groove, cut into the receiver, in which it travels. It is sometimes difficult to remove these tubes. This gives the impression that it has not released, leading you to force it past the groove. The real problem is that they are so poorly fitted, usually a bit too long, that they have been driven into position. But if you force the tube assembly lever out past its groove, you can damage the tip of the gas piston port.

The takedown bar holding the trigger guard in place is very often so stiff that it makes takedown difficult. You can drive this piece out of the receiver from the top with a good punch and make its spring lighter by grinding the back side to thin it slightly. Don't overdo it because these bars come loose during firing if they are not tightly fitted.

To remove the trigger assembly, turn the safety up into the stock and use a punch to push the takedown lug forward into the rear of the trigger guard. This takedown lug is a solid steel bar that is driven into a hole in the rear of the receiver. Some of these are so stiff they require as much as 50 pounds of pressure before releasing, while others fall out with virtually no effort.

To correct one of the stiff lugs, you must drive it out from the top of the receiver. Grinding no more than 1 millimeter of metal off

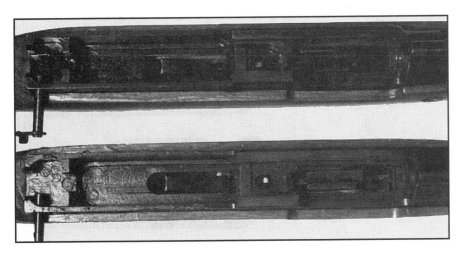

The condition of the metal on an SKS dictates the type of problems you'll have. The top receiver is of better quality, marked by smoother machining. The bottom one shows the roughness that usually results from working with very soft metal.

No two SKS rifles are the same. The receiver on the right has a screwed-in barrel and is more closely fitted than the pinned barrel that belongs to the left receiver.

will correct the problem. But if you do this, it must be done uniformly from end to end. If any one part of the piece is shaved more thinly than another, the lug can bend or break at the weakest point. A lug that is too soft can be placed in a vise and bent slightly to the rear. Again, you must do it carefully to avoid breaking the part.

As I said, broken extractors are quite common. These were designed to last forever, even under the worst battlefield conditions, but poor metal defeats the original plan. If we replace them with a high-grade steel part, the bolt can be damaged because it likely is made from the same metal that the extractor was. Where the originals were heat treated to make them hard enough to take a beating, the newer SKS extractors are brittle and break from the shock of just a few hundred rounds or as many as several thousand. The point is, you never know.

Each broken SKS extractor I have seen did have a common trait—its metal was porous, sandy and very brittle. A simple file test on the bolt and extractor will quickly show you how hard they are. Then examine their machine-finished surfaces. These should be smooth; if yours looks grainy, order replacements because they are on the way out.

Remove the extractor by driving the holding pin out from left to right, taking care not to lose the spring when it pops out as you remove the pin and plate. The extractor's removal also releases the firing pin. Some of these are hardened excessively, to the point of being brittle, but will continue to work well unless the rifle is rapid-fired. This allows the breech bolt to get hot enough to expand the metal, binding and ultimately breaking the firing pin.

If you make your own firing pin from a better steel, it is imperative you make it according to ATF specifications. They watch this area closely, and nobody wants to be in trouble for illegally modifying a gun.

If you removed the gas tube and noticed that it didn't fit well, you can improve it by grinding or filing off a small amount of metal from the tube's butt end. Make sure to remove the gas piston rod before starting. As it was with the takedown lug, the job must be done evenly and flat to ensure that more metal is not taken from one side than another. If the tube base is too wide to fit into the slot in the receiver, removing a little metal off each side of the tube's butt end will make it fit without having to drive it in.

The rear forearm cap is held in place by a rivet that has been ground down. If you need to remove the wood, this rivet will have to be driven or drilled out. In most cases, you will have to remove the wood in conjunction with the grinding operation on the metal parts. The rivets are almost always damaged on removal, so I recommend you replace them with tightly fitting roll pins. In most cases, the problem is solved by the work you do on the rear. It is unusual to have to remove metal on the front end (muzzle end) of the gas tube, so be dead certain it is required before you do. The front is critical to the gas system and must fit snugly with no side-to-side play.

From my experiences with this gun, the tubes and pistons are made of higher grade metal and have been properly heat treated, making any other modification unnecessary. One word of caution: Don't routinely buff the gas piston to remove carbon fouling like you would on other similarly operated rifles. On the SKS, buffing will remove metal along with the carbon. Use a toothbrush and solvent to clean this one.

Correcting any problems with the extractor and the gas system

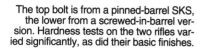

The top bolt is from a pinned-barrel SKS, the lower from a screwed-in-barrel version. Hardness tests on the two rifles varied significantly, as did their basic finishes.

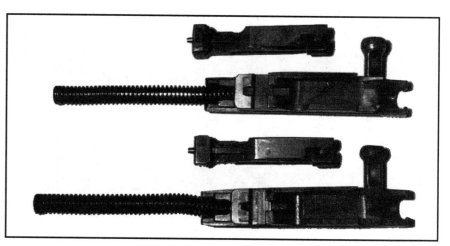

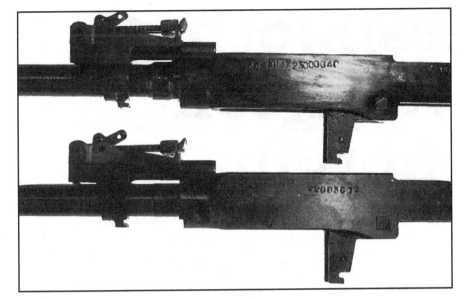

The top receiver uses a screwed-in barrel, the bottom a pinned version. Since each type uses a different locking lug, their magazines aren't interchangeable. That affects how you'll approach the job.

will solve 99 percent of the shooter's complaints about feeding and ejection. The problems that can't be solved can usually be traced to an aftermarket magazine that may not fit properly.

The SKS trigger assembly seldom needs work, and changing the sear for a lighter pull is very dangerous. Only the surface of the three-part sear mechanism is hardened. Filing or buffing will remove the hard surface and effectively destroy these parts.

Making one is impractical because you will invest more time than the rifle is worth. The closest you will come to repairs in this group is occasionally having to work the hammer fork. It sometimes wears out, allowing the hammer to wobble around. Drilling the hammer and installing a new, oversize pin corrects the problem.

Aftermarket Magazines

You will occasionally have to replace the magazine latch, especially if aftermarket magazines are going to be added to the rifle in place of the fixed ten-shot originals.

When you have to fit one of the fixed magazines to an SKS, make sure it is very tight, or it will cause feeding problems. Getting the latch to fit tightly isn't always a standard project.

In some cases, you will have to remove a modicum of metal from the front of the assembly; other times you'll have to weld on additional metal to support it. If shaving metal is your option, be certain not to take it from the rear.

This would put excessive pressure on the small pin that holds the latch in the trigger housing and allow it to wear excessively fast. Don't try to fit an SKS magazine in any location but to the latch located on the bottom of the rear sight. Attempting to fit a magazine on the front hook by grinding metal will make the cartridge feed too low, causing jams and other dissatisfaction.

Other Changes

If someone wants you to install the detachable AK-47-type magazine adapter to an SKS, note that you must have a federal firearms manufacturer's license. You must then file all the paperwork with

the government and get its approval before "manufacturing a different class of rifle." ATF is vague on the issue of an individual legally installing those on his own rifle if the parts were purchased prior to all of the rule changes. (The last were effective January 1, 1993.)

When it comes to other questionable modifications to an SKS, be aware that you may never get a firm decision from the government.

In fact, answers to your questions will vary depending on which agent you talk to at any given time. Free folding stocks are strictly forbidden, although similar arrangements that have been permanently pinned in place are okay in the eyes of the government.

Replacing the SKS original stocks with one of the synthetic aftermarket stocks is not as easy as many suppliers would have us believe. The wooden top forearm piece must be removed in the same manner we explained earlier, which itself is not a problem. The difficulty is in getting the synthetic pieces to fit, and I have seldom seen one that doesn't require a lot of fine tuning. Since very few SKS parts interchange between rifles, it is unreasonable to expect an aftermarket piece to do any better.

The same theory applies to the scope mounts that several companies make for SKS rifles. Don't even bother with an inexpensive mount that requires drilling and tapping into the top of the existing receiver cover. All the Loctite in the world won't keep these in place because the soft metal on the rifle just will not support the screws for any extended period of time.

You may have a little bit better luck getting replacement receiver covers to fit some SKS rifles, but the rifles vary so much from one to another that you stand just as much chance of having problems. Some aftermarket manufacturers recognize this possibility and have added extra metal to allow theirs to be cut to fit. This is good, but it also greatly increases the amount of time it takes to fit one to a rifle.

The bottom line is that properly fitting, aftermarket parts for an SKS rifle are practically non-existent. Granted, some will fit, but you can't really blame the parts supplier if it doesn't.

Troubleshooting the Remington 1100 Shotgun

The Remington 1100 Shotgun has 95 moving parts, gas operation, a design that has been changed several times over the years, and it often inspires home repairs.

By Butch Thomson

SINCE MOST OF THE Remington 1100's 95 parts are moving, it isn't uncommon for some of them to break from time to time. That sounds simple enough, but sometimes it isn't.

The gas-operated, semi-automatic shotgun has undergone a number of internal changes over the years, with a resulting variation in parts. Most of the parts will interchange with varying degrees of success. But gunsmiths must be aware of the changes that have been made, in order to be on the lookout for problems caused by improper parts that might have been used to "fix" this shotgun before it gets to your bench. This combination of factors can sometimes make it very hard to determine just what is causing a particular problem with an 1100.

To understand what we are facing, let's begin by looking at this shotgun's gas operation. It is important that a gas-operated firearm feed the gas cylinder/piston the right amount of gas pressure. Excessive gas will create unnecessary pressure in the piston assembly and lead to excessive wear and damage. This will affect the overall performance and operation of any gas-operated firearm, and can be bad enough to be dangerous. Remington has changed the size of the orifices, the angle they are drilled, where they are drilled, the facing angles, and so forth, in its barrels so many times that the manufacturer's shop manuals carry over a full page—single-spaced and small print—of these changes, and when they were made. With such a wide variety of ammunition on the market, Remington kept trying to get the best gas-release combination to handle all. A 200-page manual would not be sufficient to handle all the possible combinations. Remington engineers also decided it was impossible to make the 1100 shoot both $2^3/_4$- and 3-inch shells satisfactorily, so they started making two different guns, magnum and standard. Most of these parts can be physically interchanged, but many will not work properly between the two versions.

Excessive recoil from an 1100 can be a sign of improper mating between the barrel and the rest of the gas system. Ironically, the problem can be caused by either too much gas pressure or too little. Excessive pressure will open the breech too quickly while there is too much pressure still in the barrel, allowing the breech to blow back so hard that it gives excessive kick. Insufficient gas pressure allows the breech to remain locked too long, giving the shooter the same recoil of a pump or other locked-breech shotgun. Swelling of the fired shell is a sign of the breech's opening early and showing excessive gas flow. (Also check for an oversized chamber.) Low pressure often leads to a short stroke of the action. This will show up as improper or soft ejection and other feeding problems. Cleaning the gas ports will sometimes take care of this. Remington downplays the importance of the gas-port variations, but will tell you they can create problems when changing barrels between different Model 1100s.

Over 90 percent of repairs on the 1100s will be feeding, extraction, and ejection problems. As these guns get older, more and more parts become interchangeable, so look for a balance that will make the 1100 work right. As we take it apart, we will point out items that will help in your repairs of this shotgun.

As you unscrew the magazine cap, always be prepared for the magazine-spring retainer to be missing from the shotgun you are working on. If it is, the magazine spring can shoot the cap more than 20 feet and damage whatever it hits. Even if the retainer is in place, the spring has been known to come out on its own after the cap is removed. With the breech half open, the barrel and forearm can be removed from the receiver, but these will not slip right out unless this is a well-worn shotgun. By wiggling and pulling the barrel and receiver apart, it is usually not hard to separate them. Some will stick, but they can be loosened by opening the breechbolt all the way back, pressing the release, and letting the bolt slam forward into the barrel. Doing this several times will drive the barrel forward out of the receiver. This procedure, unlike prying, will not damage anything.

The gas-piston assembly will sometimes come off the magazine tube and stick in the barrel lug, and sometimes it will stay on the magazine tube where it belongs. Always check the barrel seal to be sure the piston and piston seal are on right. I have had hundreds brought into my shop that were assembled wrong. The piston seal goes on first, with the flat base fitting snug against the front face of the action-bar assembly and the angle cut facing the muzzle. The gas piston goes on next, with its angle cut facing into the matching angle of its seal. The rubber barrel seal then goes on, and should fit the magazine tube very tightly. When slipped down to the notch in the magazine tube, it will still be tight. These seals need to be replaced if they are frayed, flattened, or stretched until they are loose. Many gun owners will stretch these onto the front flat edge of the piston, or put them on in the wrong assembly order.

Remove the trigger assembly from the receiver by driving out the two trigger-plate pins and wiggling the trigger guard while pulling down on the trigger assembly. Look inside the receiver to see if the feed-latch bar is solidly staked into the receiver. Many of these will be loose and even fall out when you remove the trigger assembly. This is of little importance, because when the shotgun is properly reassembled, the front trigger-plate pin keeps it from moving around, while the trigger assembly holds it in its groove by putting proper tension on this spring. Staking the part back into place makes this shotgun easier to reassemble, but leaving it loose makes it easier to clean.

Pulling the operating handle straight out from the receiver will remove it from the breechbolt. If the gas piston assembly is still on the magazine tube, slip it off, but avoid stretching the rubber gas seal. Grip the action-bar, pulling it off the front of the magazine tube, to remove the action-bar assembly, the action-bar sleeve, and the breech assembly in one stroke. Before doing anything else, reach inside the receiver and push the link forward through the same path from which the action-bar slipped.

It is usually unnecessary to remove the interceptor latch from the receiver. The interceptor-latch retainer was designed to be installed and removed with a special tool. This interceptor should fit tightly, with no wobble at all. Movement up and down should be smooth, and its spring must fit into the groove cut into the rear arm of the interceptor. This spring sometimes gets out of its slot and gets in behind the interceptor. This will keep the shotgun from feeding correctly, and can show up in nearly all forms of feeding problems, depending upon in which position it is holding the interceptor. Fir-

ing a shotgun with this problem can cause major damage to the 1100. The interceptor-latch spring is also staked into the receiver; it cannot be removed and replaced without metal damage to the receiver. Most 1100s have a forend support assembly that clips over the action bar, but earlier models did not have this part. Do not try to install one if it does not need it.

The action-bar assembly also varies from year to year. The two most common complaints from owners are that the operating handle comes out too easily and gets lost, or that it sometimes is too hard to get out. It is the operating-handle plunger that holds it, and this is part of the action bar. Some of these have a removable retainer and some are solid.

Before tightening this operating handle, ask yourself what exactly you want. I tightened one for a man a few years ago, and he brought it back a few days later. His exact words were, "I want it tight while I am hunting, but I want it to come out easy when I get home to clean it." He was not kidding, and could not see why a gunsmith could not make it that way. If it needs to be tightened, and your action-bar assembly has a removable operating-handle plunger retainer, remove the retainer. Put it on your drill press with a bit $1^{1}/_{2}$ times larger than the hole, and very carefully open up the cone-shaped hole, with the retainer upside down. A little goes a long way, so make sure it is just a small amount. When reassembled, this will make the operating handle fit tighter.

The solid bars have a small hole on their undersides that goes through to the bottom of the operating-handle plunger. You can take a small punch that goes through the hole and drive this ball (plunger) a little further out the top. Again, a little bit does it. If you drive it too hard, it will break through the top of the action bar, and then you really have problems. Before you do anything, make sure the plunger and its spring are clean and working freely. Also check the cup-shaped hole on the bottom of the operating handle. Some 1100s have a slot cut into the rear of the operating handle, and the plunger is in the rear of the action bar assembly rather than on the bottom. They still work the same way, just from a different location. Make sure the operating handle is cut or slotted to fit the bar; it may have been changed as we discussed earlier. Next, check the slots or cup-shaped hole in the bottom of the operating handle to make sure they are clear and clean. Slip the handle into the action bar and see how much play it has. If it is too loose, tightening up the plunger will not make it work. In this case, replace it with one that is thicker. If it is tight, but still comes out too easily, the operating-handle plunger is not holding it tightly enough. Using a drill bit the same size of the cup-shaped hole, clean the hole. Just polish it with the drill tip; do not try to cut it deeper. If you cut this hole deep, the plunger will pop up into it, and the operating handle cannot be removed. That is the end of a good shotgun, because it cannot be disassembled again. Always try it before reassembling it inside the shotgun.

The breechbolt itself is easy to work on, and you should check the travel of the firing pin before taking it apart. With the locking block pushed up, the firing pin should move easily into firing position. With it down, this locking block should block the firing pin from reaching a primer. Remington has boxes full of homemade and incorrect firing pins that have been taken out of 1100s returned for factory repair. We have seen several that have had their front collars ground down by people with the mistaken idea this will stop the shotgun from misfiring. They believe this will allow the firing pin to go through the locking block easier. What this will do is allow the shotgun to fire without the breech being properly locked, creating one blown-up shotgun and one hospitalized shooter. This collar was designed to prevent firing unless the breech is properly locked.

The firing-pin retainer pin is driven out from the top to the bottom. This releases the breechbolt buffer as well as the firing pin and firing-pin spring. As soon as these come out, the locking-block assembly will fall out the bottom of the breech body. The only other parts in the breechbolt are the extractor, extractor spring, and extractor plunger. We have discussed dogleg extractors elsewhere, so we will not go into detail here. To remove the extractor, the plunger must be pushed toward the rear of the breechbolt and held there while the extractor is pulled straight out. Make sure the extractor plunger moves back and forth smoothly and forcefully, or it will not hold the extractor solidly enough to extract the fired shell. If you remove the extractor, always pull the plunger out of the bolt face. A small screwdriver or punch can be used to pull the plunger spring out. Make sure these are free of rust and are clean. Rust in the extractor-plunger hole can create ejection problems and ultimately cause the destruction of the breechbolt.

The action spring is hidden away in the 1100's stock, and is often forgotten in the search for feeding/ejection problems and cures. The action spring and tube collect trash and moisture, as the link forces the action-spring follower down the action tube so fast that it creates a vacuum. This vacuum, along with the residue thrown off the bolt as it slams against the rear of the receiver, will suck trash, dirt and water inside. The stock must be removed before the tube can be reached. It is necessary to put both the lock nut and washer back on this tube before reinstalling the tube nut. By pushing the action-spring plug up into the action tube about 3 millimeters, it is easy to slide the action-tube spring plug out the side of the tube. This permits the spring and follower to come out the rear of the spring tube. Always brush the tube out and check for rust, then lubricate it with a light oil. Heavy oil and grease will create a hydraulic effect that will slow the action and stop the gun from ejecting or feeding correctly. The magazine tube is also a place that collects dirt and water because shooters often load it with dirty or wet shells. If dirt or rust slows down the magazine follower, it may not push a shell out of the tube fast enough to feed properly.

We have saved the trigger assembly until last. Mixed or improperly fitted parts can really give problems. Remington trigger assemblies are coded to match specific receivers and are not to be interchanged. Start your trigger disassembly by using a small screwdriver to remove the sear spring. Slip the end of the screwdriver into the coils right behind the sear and pull it back. This will release the spring from the sear and allow its removal. The trigger-plate pin bushing can be gripped from the same end that the trigger-plate pin detent spring is attached, then pulled out of the trigger housing. You must drive the trigger pin out from right to left because it is directional. I have found some that have been installed backwards. If it does not come out with moderate force, it may be in backwards. These pins are made directional by three slots driven into one end to spread the metal and make

them tight when they are driven into the trigger housing.

To remove the trigger assembly, take a small screwdriver and carefully pry up the front arm of the left connector just enough to lift it up and over the connector-guide lug made into the trigger-guard body. When this is lifted over the top of the lug, the trigger assembly can be lifted out the top of the trigger housing

One of the most common repairs on the 1100 is fixing a stuck or broken safety. After the trigger is removed from the trigger housing, the safety can be worked on. The safety-spring retaining pin is above the safety and can be pushed out either way. Push it out with a punch, and hold your thumb over the spring hole while you pull the punch back out. You may have to use a small punch to pull the safety spring out of its hole. The safety-detent ball should fall out of the spring hole with the trigger housing held upside down. However, dirt and oil often hold it in so tightly that it will not come out by tapping and any other type of coaxing. When this happens, try working the safety back and forth until you can get the ball to move up enough into the spring hole to remove the safety. After the safety is removed, you can use a punch to push the detent ball out the bottom of the spring hole. After cleaning, a medium-weight oil is best to use on the ball as it is reinstalled. The medium-weight oil will create a better seal to keep the dirt out. If you need to make it a left-hand safety, just reverse the safety button when you reinstall it.

The trigger assembly should be checked to make sure that both the right and left connectors are moving together with just a very small amount of play between the two. Both connectors should move up and down without restriction, and should not be filed or cut on in any way. Modifying the connectors is not the correct way to do a "trigger job" on the 1100. As these are stamped parts and sometimes have sharp edges, it is all right to use a buffer to remove these sharp edges. Sometimes the signs of buffing will make you think they have been ground on, but a careful inspection will show the difference between grinding of metal and buffing off sharp edges.

Removing the carrier from the trigger housing requires removing either the right or left trigger-plate pin bushings. Push the trigger-plate pin out the side with a punch that will go through the hole and keep the carrier in place. There are three powerful springs that now come into play in removing the carrier. The carrier-dog follower spring is released as the carrier is removed, while the hammer spring is contained by the disconnector arm. The third spring is the carrier-latch spring. It must be released slowly to allow the carrier latch to fold over the front of the trigger housing without a forward snap that might break it. If the sear locks solidly onto the hammer, you can push the hammer back into the cocked position and remove this spring from the operation. As the sear spring has already been removed, you do not want to do this unless the sear grabs the hammer solidly so it will not "fire" halfway through your carrier-removal operation. It is easier to put the trigger in a vise and use a screwdriver to hold the carrier-dog follower down while pulling out the punch that is holding the carrier in place. Let the carrier slip forward and up slowly; it will come free, and you can slowly release the pressure on the carrier-dog follower. If you cocked the hammer, be sure to release it at this time.

A small punch is used to drive out the carrier-latch pin. Remember, this is a tough little spring, so hold the carrier latch firmly when it is released. Use the same punch to drive out the carrier-release

REMINGTON MODEL 1100 AUTOLOADING SHOTGUN

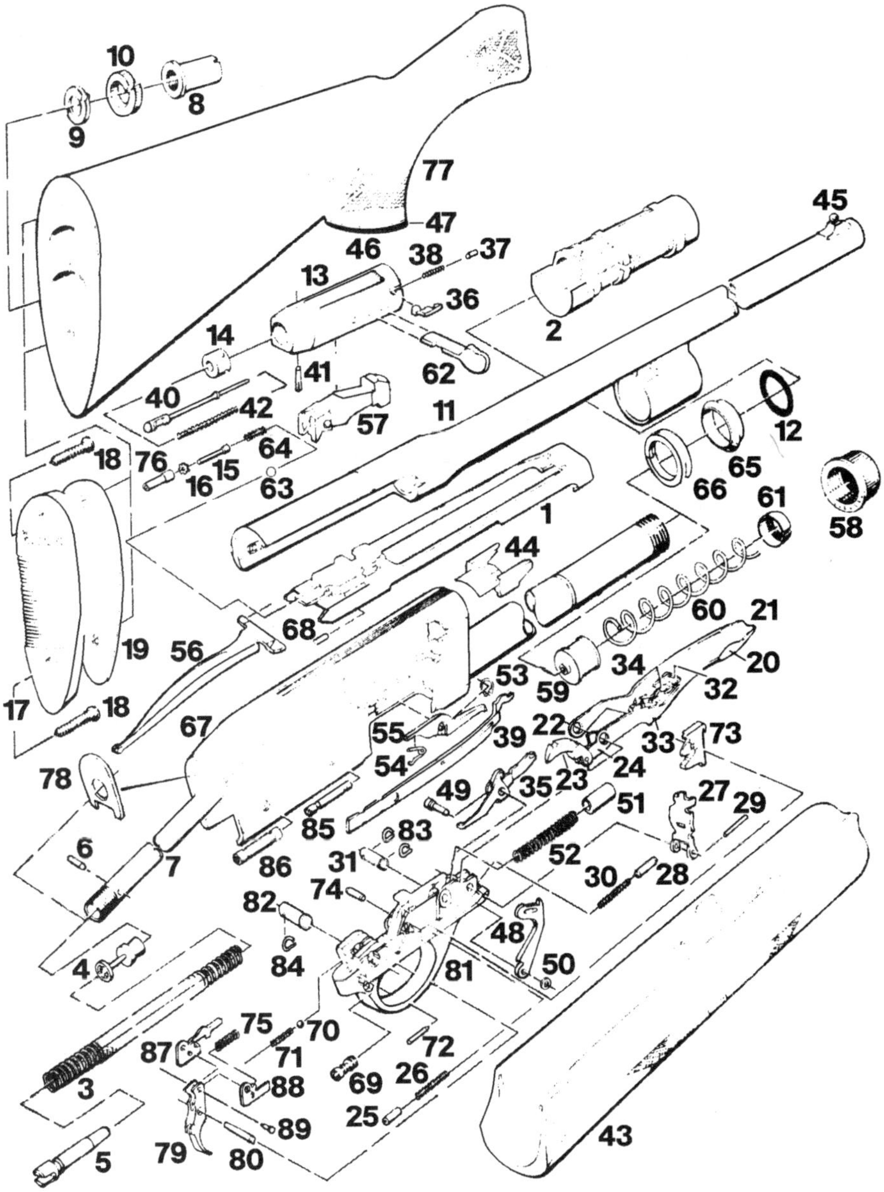

KEY

1 Action Bar Assembly
2 Action Bar Sleeve
3 Action Spring
4 Action Spring Follower
5 Action Spring Plug
6 Action Spring Plug Pin
7 Action Spring Tube
8 Action Spring Tube Nut
9 Action Spring Tube Nut Washer
10 Action Spring Tube Nut Lock Washer
11 Barrel Assembly
12 Barrel Seal
13 Breechbolt
14 Breechbolt Buffer
15 Breechbolt Return Plunger
16 Breechbolt Return Plunger Retaining Ring
17 Buttplate
18 Buttplate Screws
19 Buttplate Spacer
20 Carrier
21 Carrier Assembly
22 Carrier Dog
23 Carrier Dog Pin
24 Carrier Dog Washer
25 Carrier Dog Follower
26 Carrier Dog Follower Spring
27 Carrier Latch
28 Carrier Latch Follower
29 Carrier Latch Pin
30 Carrier Latch Spring
31 Carrier Pivot Tube
32 Carrier Release
33 Carrier Release Pin
34 Carrier Release Spring
35 Disconnector
36 Extractor
37 Extractor Plunger
38 Extractor Spring
39 Feed Latch
40 Firing Pin
41 Firing Pin Retaining Pin
42 Firing Pin Retractor Spring
43 Forend Assembly
44 Forend Support
45 Front Sight
46 Grip Cap
47 Grip Cap Spacer
48 Hammer
49 Hammer Pin
50 Hammer Pin Washer
51 Hammer Plunger
52 Hammer Spring
53 Interceptor Latch Retainer
54 Interceptor Latch Spring
55 Interceptor Latch
56 Link
57 Locking Block Assembly
58 Magazine Cap
59 Magazine Follower

60 Magazine Spring
61 Magazine Spring Retainer
62 Operating Handle
63 Operating Handle Detent Ball
64 Operating Handle Detent Spring
65 Piston
66 Piston Seal
67 Receiver Assembly
68 Return Plunger Retaining Pin

69 Safety Switch
70 Safety Switch Detent Ball
71 Safety Switch Spring
72 Safety Switch Spring Retaining Pin
73 Sear
74 Sear Pin
75 Sear Spring
76 Slide Block Buffer
77 Stock Assembly
78 Stock Bearing Plate
79 Trigger Assembly

80 Trigger Pin
81 Trigger Plate Safety
82 Trigger Plate Pin Bushing
83 Trigger Plate Pin Detent Spring, Front
84 Trigger Plate Pin Detent Spring, Rear
85 Trigger Plate Pin, Front
86 Trigger Plate Pin, Rear
87 Connector, Left
88 Connector, Right
89 Connector Pin

pin. Each of these parts should be checked for damage or modification. If any are to be replaced, check the new part against the old one for size and detail, remembering what we said about all the changes Remington has made in this shotgun.

Some of the more common problems are stuck carrier-dog followers, which will lead to failures to feed. A bent carrier latch will not lift a second shell to the chamber when the shotgun is fired, even though it may work fine while working it by hand. When the carrier dog is worn or loose on the base of the carrier, it will get the shotgun out of proper cycle and jam the action.

If the front edge of the carrier is worn excessively or bent, it will keep the trigger from engaging as it supposed to, and will create jams. These front edges are hand fitted in the Model 1100, and will vary greatly from shotgun to shotgun. If you need to fit one, leave a little extra metal on the front edge, taking off a little at a time until it is working correctly. It is very easy to go too far with this, thinking you have removed hardly any metal at all. There is a lip or tongue that sticks up, about an inch back from the front tip of this carrier. The size, shape, and height of this lip is also very critical, but, unfortunately, it is one thing that often gets bent or filed by someone who does not know what he is doing. Here's what usually happens: This lip lines up with the action bar. If everything is not in proper alignment, the lip will keep the carrier from moving far enough to load the shotgun easily. Someone looks in and sees that by bending this lip the carrier will let the shells feed in easily. The problem created is that they now feed in when the shotgun is not properly closed and locked. Some people grind the lip down to just get it out of the way, which is akin to cutting your head off so you do not have to shave or get a haircut. When this has been done, the shotgun will not work correctly until a new carrier is fitted. To make it more complicated, there are more than 20 different carriers, each of which must be ordered by serial number. I would never suggest that a parts supplier could make a mistake, but comparing the new part to the old one before installing it might save you a lot of time later on.

The 1100s have good triggers for automatic shotguns. Light triggers will cause the shotgun to fail to cock on occasion, or worse, to double fire. A fully automatic 12-gauge shotgun is a shock to the shooter who is not expecting it. A light stoning of the sear notch on the hammer and the same on the sear will smooth any roughness that needs to be taken care of. Removing the sear from the trigger housing can only be done after removing the carrier-dog assembly

from the trigger housing. The sear-pin hole does not go all the way through the trigger housing. It only goes through into the inside of the carrier-dog follower hole. You can reach into the carrier-dog follower hole at a 45-degree angle with your punch, and push the sear pin back enough to be able to grip it on the other side to pull it out.

Removing the hammer is a different story, because most 1100s rivet the right end of the hammer pin so it will not come loose when the shotgun is fired. Be very careful if you try to drive this pin back through with enough force to fold in the riveted end through the trigger housing. This trigger housing is a cast-aluminum body and will break easily. The trigger housing is also very expensive to replace, and must carry the same code as the one that was broken. Remington does not like to pass out restricted parts, and prefers to fit these themselves. Drilling these out is also tough because their riveted ends are always thinner on one side. This makes your drill go to the side and off into the soft aluminum unless you are very careful. If you do get the old one out, do not try to reuse it, if it is weaker than it was before it was removed. This pin receives a lot of shock and vibration, and will work its way loose unless it is strong and well locked in. If one end of this pin is loose when the shotgun is fired, it will break the trigger housing, and you will have an expensive repair on your hands.

The 1100 generally has the same types of external features as other shotguns, and its ribs, beads, stocks, forearms and the like need the same maintenance and care. Broken forearms are common on this shotgun, because the wood, even though it is reinforced by fiberglass, is so thin that it cannot take much abuse. Stocks are often replaced on these shotguns without the stock-bearing plate being properly reinstalled between the receiver and the stock. This creates chipped or broken stocks that must be repaired or replaced. Leaving off the action-tube spring-nut washer or lock washer prevents the stock from properly fitting.

All too often, you will encounter a stock that has been cut too short, and the tube nut sticks out past the cut stock. If it is only a small amount, you have some options. You can drill out a space in the recoil pad, taking care to not to go too deeply, or you will feel the tube nut when firing the shotgun. The tube nut itself can be cut into, since it is longer than it needs to be. Notch the edges and you can still screw it onto the action-spring tube. Do not shorten the tube, as some have done, because the 1100 will not work without the full travel of the action-spring set. The 1100 just cannot have too short a stock; its design will not permit it.

Working the Winchester 94

The Model 94 is easily worked on, but presents a challenge in finding or making parts. Here are some key things to watch for when you tackle it.

By Butch Thomson

BEFORE WE BEGAN talking about maintenance and repair on the Winchester Model 94, it's important to realize that this firearm has been in manufacture for nearly 100 years. Many modifications have occurred during this time, but, unfortunately, many were made not so much to improve the rifle but to improve the bottom line by reducing costs. One of the glaring examples is when this rifle was made with a stamped carrier. This stamped carrier bent very easily, disabling the rifle in the process.

There are over sixty variations of the Model 94, so always remember to order and use only parts that match the serial number of the rifle you are going to work. Older Model 94 parts are not available from U.S. Repeating Arms Corp., the present manufacturer, which has only had the license for a few years. I am sorry to say it is a fact that most parts suppliers do not take the time to log the different models of this rifle, something which makes working the older 94s problematic.

Total disassembly of the 94 is rarely necessary, unless it needs to be thoroughly cleaned. The most common problem with the 94 is failure to feed and eject properly. When this is your problem, be sure to check the spring cover first, making sure the spring-cover screw is tight. If the spring cover has any looseness at all, it can block the carrier and jam the rifle. But when this problem exists, don't just tighten the screw and assume that's all it was.

If the spring cover jams the carrier and the shooter tries to force the action to work anyway, internal parts will be damaged. Many carriers have been bent and broken by shooters who won't take no for an answer from their gun. The action needs to be disassembled to make sure there's no internal damage. It's better for you to spend a little more time and make sure everything is all right, rather than have to take it apart next week because you didn't fix it right the first time.

I never take any part of a 94 action apart unless I take the stock off. Removing the upper tang screw releases the stock, allowing it to be pulled straight away from the receiver. You will find many of the older 94s have this screw so wallowed out that it is hard to remove. A cutting wheel on a Moto-Tool or your gunsmith file can bring these back into shape without much effort. After all, you want to be proud of your work when it leaves the shop. If you do not dress up these damaged screws, you may find that no one will believe you did the good work inside the gun.

The head of the hammer screw is on the opposite side of the loading port. With the removal of this screw, the hammer/trigger assembly slips out of the receiver. Hammer springs/mainsprings vary in different year models. Some have leaf springs and others have coil springs with hammer-spring guide rods. Don't drive the hammer-spring guide rod out the side of this trigger assembly as you do with a Marlin 336. Instead, cock the hammer and push the trigger stop up flush with the bottom of the lower tang. (The trigger stop is located about an inch behind the trigger.) While holding the hammer with your thumb, pull the trigger and let the hammer slowly go all the way forward until the spring and guide come out. The pins that hold the trigger stop and trigger-stop spring also vary as some are roll pins and others are solid. They can be driven out from either side, as can the hammer bushing. If the hammer bushing is dented or damaged in any way, it will affect the smooth operation of the hammer. Never try to soften the hammer fall on a 94; it will sometimes misfire if you do. The firing-pin system of this rifle requires full force from the hammer.

It's easy to lighten the trigger of a 94. In fact, it's too easy; these rifles can fire as the top side of the lever pushes the trigger stop out of the way. This happens when the sear area of either the sear or hammer has been filed excessively. As this sear is so easily removed and the sear lip is totally exposed, it gives the false impression that cutting away a little of the sharp lip will make a softer trigger pull. Wrong. This will make it go off all by itself. To work on this trigger, the sear area must be kept flat and sharp. You can change the angle as long as you don't take off too much. With this trigger a little goes a long way. The hammer has a safety lip on the left side above the sear notch. Do not remove or change it, as it prevents accidental discharge.

Some folks suggest that you should remove the trigger stop because they do not like this "extra safety." If you want to create a real questionable situation, this is a good way to accomplish it. In fact, our shop will not work on a 94 if the trigger stop has been removed or modified—unless we are permitted to reinstall or repair it.

In the older Winchesters with the leaf hammer spring, it's very important that the hammer is rolled over off the spring as described above before the spring screw is removed or reinstalled. If there is pressure on the spring while the screw is removed, it will destroy the last couple of threads as it pulls out under pressure. Trying to reinstall it under pressure will cross-thread and destroy it. The gun you're working may already be crossthreaded.

The lever-pin stop screw on the left side of the action is the first one to remove for taking down the action. On the right side, $1/2$-inch above the front of the loading port, is a small hole. With the breech closed tight, insert a small punch into this hole and push the lever pin out. The lever-pin stop screw must hold this pin in place and cannot be too long or it will bind the bolt. When it is too short, the pin can work over into the receiver just above the cartridge guide and lock the whole action down. The original screw, when put in tightly, will always work correctly. However, many side-mount scope bases use this screw hole and they come with their own screws. These usually work, but need to be checked for length. If they start getting mixed up with other screws, problems can occur.

The lever-link screw head is also on the opposite side of the loading port, and is the second one to remove for taking down the action. Pre-'64 models did not use a screw, but used a pin that was grooved in the middle. The link had a tapped hole in the front end so a setscrew could fit down into the groove to keep it from coming out. When this screw is removed, the lever, link, and locking bolt can be pulled down out of the receiver. Take a good look at the locking bolt so you will remember how it goes back in, and then you can lift it out of its groove.

The friction stud is a very important part in the 94. While its spring is strong, you should be able to push it in without any problem. Push with your finger and it should snap right back out. If it sticks or drags, you will need to drive its retaining pin out with a small punch. Winchester calls this a friction stud stop pin. It is common for this hole to become rusty; it must be cleaned and the spring replaced if this happens. The firing-pin striker, pinned into the locking bolt, is also a regular source of rust and accumulated dirt that can cause misfires.

At this point, because there is no longer anything to hold it in place, the breechbolt will slide right out of the rear of the receiver. The firing pin will also fall out. The firing pin has a slot on the bottom, close to the front, and is also tapered forward on the bottom of the back. For some reason, many people try to put this in upside down. When they do, they will damage the firearm when they try to drive the lever pin back in. When you need to replace the firing pin, make sure the one going back in is the same as the one coming out. I doubt anyone knows how many different firing pins Winchester has made, some of which will interchange, while many will not. It gets really exciting when the wrong pin is installed and the rifle fires when the bolt is closed—even though the hammer stays back. If you install a tapered lightweight firing pin in a 94 that came with a full-weight pin, you may get an occasional misfire that no one can figure out.

At this point, we are discussing top-eject 94s, where the ejector is on the bottom and the extractor is on top of the breechbolt. Again, we hit the same problem as with the firing pins; too many different ones have been used over the many years of production. You'll need a sharp eye to carefully compare the old part with any replacement part, and you'll have to check the springs for similar length and tension.

The extractor on the 94 normally lasts forever, but is not difficult to change if the need arises. The two extractor pins can be driven out from either side, and seldom cause problems even though replacement extractors often require fitting. Make sure the cartridge rim fits under the extractor lip with no excess pressure and without a gap, and that the bolt still closes onto the barrel with the proper headspace.

The ejector spring is surprisingly strong, as it must be to properly eject a cartridge or case. The ejectors are a little easier to replace, since many will interchange, even though they are made with slight differences. Make sure they fit into the ejector slot on the bottom of the breechbolt. The ejector face must not extend more than 3 millimeters beyond the bolt face, and it must work smoothly.

The carrier screw is located on the left side of the receiver and is threaded on the head end. Most carriers are machined, but if you get one of the promotional models with the stamped-out carrier, you may have trouble getting the proper replacement. The carrier-spring screw is located on the right side of the receiver. This spring comes out easier than it goes back in.

The two cartridge guides, right and left, slip in and out easily. Take a good look at the slots cut in each of these so you can make sure they are replaced the same way they came out.

If you want to side-mount a scope on one of these top-ejectors, there are now several "no gunsmith" mounts on the market. Again, if they are to fit properly, you must go by the serial number or year of manufacture. The sight-plug screws on the top of the left side at the back of the receiver are two different sizes, depending on the year of manufacture. There are three different front lever-pin stop screws, sized in the same manner. If you have the right sideplate, these work well. I don't use it very often anymore, but you can buy a side-mount drill jig from any gunsmith-supply company. These receivers can be difficult to drill and tap, so a jig is necessary. All internal parts must be removed from the receiver before the jig is mounted and drilling begins. After you have finished tapping the receiver, make sure to remove any burrs and rough edges from each hole.

It's difficult to get all the metal chips off the inside of this receiver because of the problem of reaching the many machine cuts and grooves. Make sure you get this perfectly clean, since the smallest metal parts will work loose and create problems later on. I have never known a side-mounted scope baseplate that has been mount-

WINCHESTER NEW MODEL 94 LEVER-ACTION CARBINE

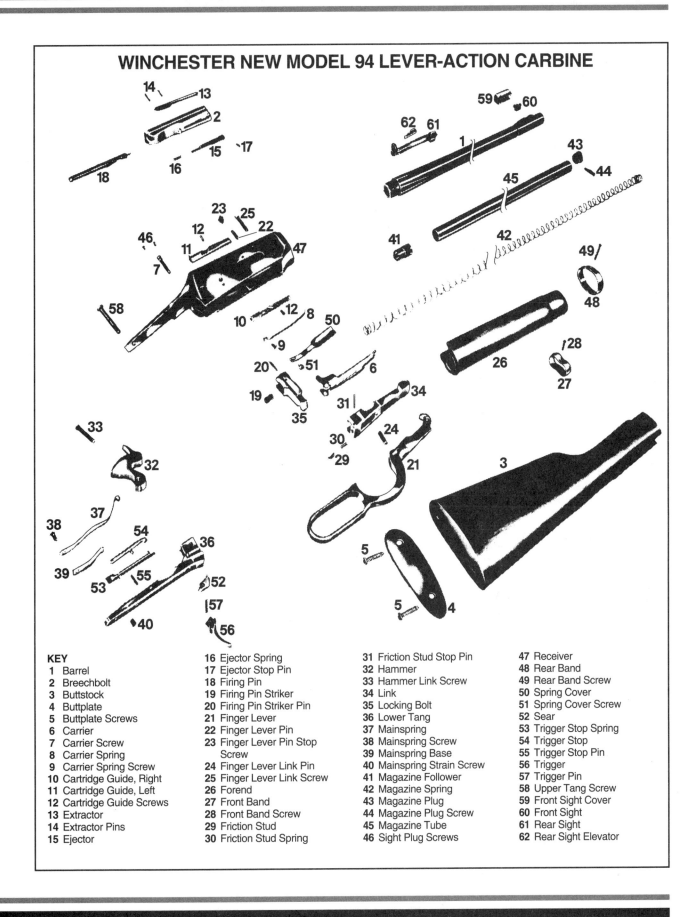

KEY
1 Barrel
2 Breechbolt
3 Buttstock
4 Buttplate
5 Buttplate Screws
6 Carrier
7 Carrier Screw
8 Carrier Spring
9 Carrier Spring Screw
10 Cartridge Guide, Right
11 Cartridge Guide, Left
12 Cartridge Guide Screws
13 Extractor
14 Extractor Pins
15 Ejector

16 Ejector Spring
17 Ejector Stop Pin
18 Firing Pin
19 Firing Pin Striker
20 Firing Pin Striker Pin
21 Finger Lever
22 Finger Lever Pin
23 Finger Lever Pin Stop
　　Screw
24 Finger Lever Link Pin
25 Finger Lever Link Screw
26 Forend
27 Front Band
28 Front Band Screw
29 Friction Stud
30 Friction Stud Spring

31 Friction Stud Stop Pin
32 Hammer
33 Hammer Link Screw
34 Link
35 Locking Bolt
36 Lower Tang
37 Mainspring
38 Mainspring Screw
39 Mainspring Base
40 Mainspring Strain Screw
41 Magazine Follower
42 Magazine Spring
43 Magazine Plug
44 Magazine Plug Screw
45 Magazine Tube
46 Sight Plug Screws

47 Receiver
48 Rear Band
49 Rear Band Screw
50 Spring Cover
51 Spring Cover Screw
52 Sear
53 Trigger Stop Spring
54 Trigger Stop
55 Trigger Stop Pin
56 Trigger
57 Trigger Pin
58 Upper Tang Screw
59 Front Sight Cover
60 Front Sight
61 Rear Sight
62 Rear Sight Elevator

ed by drilling and tapping to come loose, but I have seen many of the others give problems. (The open sights on the 94 do not need any comment because they are easily replaced with Winchester's or any other aftermarket sights.)

The only other thing we need to look at on the top-eject 94 is the magazine tube. Because this is a brush rifle, it often gets treated a little rougher than other rifles. The magazine tube is often dented, and usually has rust and dirt inside. The magazine plug is secured with one screw. Be sure you hold the plug in place as you remove this screw, because the magazine spring can launch the plug into the darkest corner of your shop. The magazine spring itself should be clean and rust-free. Turn the rifle butt up to see if the magazine follower will slide out smoothly. If it doesn't, always take the magazine tube off the rifle before cleaning it out. Dirt will collect in the groove where the tube fits into the receiver. Remove the tube by removing both barrel-band screws and slip the tube out. Slip the band off the wood forearm and remove the forearm to clean under it, always making sure to get the tube seat cut into the receiver clean. If there are dents in the tube, clean it out and slide the magazine follower through it. If it sticks, the tube needs to be replaced or repaired.

Years ago, we used ball bearings and drove them through the tube to take out the dents, although this occasionally warped the tube. We've been able to save badly damaged tubes with the dent remover we made in our shop. We have five different sizes, but the one that gets used the most is for the 30/30 Winchester or Marlin.

If you don't have a dent remover, you can make one out of a piece of metal the size of the tube and at least 6 inches long. You must use a metal that will polish very slick. Round off the front end and taper it back about 1 inch, then round off the sharp edge on the back leaving a flat surface to be able to drive the piece through the tube. Make sure it is highly polished and the tube is clean inside before inserting the dent remover. Using a light oil, drive the dent remover through the tube. It should slide through under its own weight until it hits the dent. A dent remover that is not slow-tapered (at least 1 inch) or that is too short will warp the tube.

Last of all, let's look at a few of the aforementioned things that the competition shooters are getting into with the new "Old West" competition matches.

They are becoming very popular, and no one knows just how far and fast they will go. Unfortunately, what is desired most for these matches is the removal of safety devices and a hair trigger for speed shooting. Just mention either of these and watch your insurance agent pass out on the spot.

There are some things you can do to make a better competition gun without sacrificing your safety or integrity, including doing the trigger work we described earlier. Polishing and rounding the sharp edges of the bearing surfaces of the ejector will help speed the ejection process. The internal machining of the receiver on new 94s can also be smoothed up. The breechbolts come a little rough from the factory, so the smoothing and deburring of these parts will enhance the smooth operation of the rifle.

One thing being done to rifles that I do not recommend is the trimming of the friction stud spring and the rounding off of the face of the stud. The most common thing is the removal of the trigger stop and, as I have already said, this is a no-no. Many people hate the excessive play and long travel in the trigger of the 94. This is part of its lever design, and even though some gunsmiths are filling in part of the space between the trigger and the front of the trigger slot in the tang, be careful not to overdo it. It must have enough movement to stay safe and allow all the parts to move freely.

Sight changes on these rifles for competition shooters will vary according to the shooter. After all, sights are a matter of personal preference more than anything else. Even though your idea may be better, if it doesn't work properly, you lose. The new generation of USRA side-eject 94s need a special look, but I'll only mention the differences to avoid repeating myself.

These rifles are drilled and tapped, with scope mounting done like all other modern rifles with their special bases. They come with hammer spurs in the box from the factory that only have to be screwed into the holes that are already drilled and tapped in the hammer. They also have a crossbolt safety that blocks the hammer from reaching the firing pin. This should slow down a few lawsuits from accidental discharges—a good reason for putting it in.

Side ejection on the new 94s is accomplished by moving the extractor from the top to the right side of the breech bolt. This is done by bending the end of the ejector as far to the left as the inside of the receiver will allow. This allows the cartridge to go out at a 45-degree angle rather than straight up. By cutting off the top right side of the receiver to allow extra space for the cartridge to eject, this side-eject works well without any major parts changes inside the rifle. Parts are easy to get from the manufacturer.

Most Winchester 94s have 65 parts, but if you're going to work on an older model don't be surprised to find that it has mixed parts from several series. If it doesn't, I would be amazed. This is a rifle that is easy to work on, but will challenge your gunsmithing abilities to get or make parts.

Gunstock Repairs

Gunstocks frequently become cracked, chipped, or broken. A replacement might be best, but read what we have to say first.

DENTS AND BRUISES on hunting guns are probably the most common ills that you will encounter. Since neither seriously affects the normal functioning of the weapon, few shooters bother to have them removed. It is only when a serious problem occurs—such as a split pistol grip or a break across the tang—that most shooters will consider having their stocks repaired. Others, however, take a sense of pride in their shootin' irons and want even the tiniest flaw corrected immediately.

The only tools required to raise dents in wood are a soldering iron, an old towel, and a cup of water. A dent in wood is merely a compression of wood fibers and the application of steam to the area will cause the fibers to swell and again rise to the surface of the wood.

To remove a dent from a gunstock, lay the stock on a padded surface so as not to further damage the stock's finish. Then plug in your soldering iron or soldering gun and dampen a corner of your towel. Place the damp towel over the dented area of the stock, covering only the dented area and not the wood surrounding the dent. Now place the soldering gun lightly on the damp towel right over the dent and steam will emanate from the towel almost immediately, shooting it into the dented area. You want to make certain that you don't hold the hot soldering iron on the towel long enough to scorch the wood underneath, just long enough to convert the water to steam and that's it. As long as you can see steam pouring out from the towel, there should be no problem.

After the first application, dampen the towel again, place the hot iron on the towel over the dented area, and allow more steam to flow into the dented surface. Repeat this procedure until the dent is raised to the surface of the stock. This may take as few as three applications or up to 20 or more, depending on the depth of the dent, type of wood, remaining finish on the stock, and other factors. That's all there is to it!

The above method will handle 90 percent of the dents found in gunstocks—not gouges where wood has been *removed*; the steam method will not replace wood, only swell the fibers and make them rise to the surface. There are, however, some dents that just won't yield to the method described above. In cases like these, apply a steady stream of steam directly to the center of the dent for a minute or two, which usually does the trick.

Making an apparatus for delivering a steady stream of steam is quite simple. All you need is a tin can with a screw-on lid, a short piece of copper tubing with an inside diameter of approximately $1/8$-inch, and about an 18-inch length of rubber hose of a diameter to fit snugly over the copper tubing. Punch a hole in the lid of the can so a 2-inch length of copper tubing will fit snugly into the hole; solder this in place. Then attach the rubber hose onto this piece of copper tubing. Also insert about a 4-inch piece of copper tubing in the opposite end of the rubber hose. Fill the can about half full of water, screw the lid on tightly, and place it on a source of heat. In minutes the water will start to boil and shortly thereafter you will have a steady stream of steam coming out of the copper tubing attached to the rubber hose. If more pressure is required, you can crimp the end of the tubing slightly, which will act much like the nozzle on your garden hose.

If the dent should occur in checkered areas of the stock, after raising the dent with steam, chances are the checkering itself will require touching up a bit. Usually, the entire checkering pattern will not have to be recut; only the area that came into contact with the steam. Use a conventional checkering tool or a three-square bent-needle file to recut the damaged area. Then take a toothbrush con-

A damp cloth and soldering iron or gun may be used to raise many dents in gunstocks.

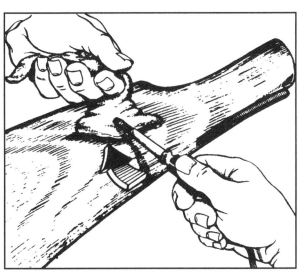

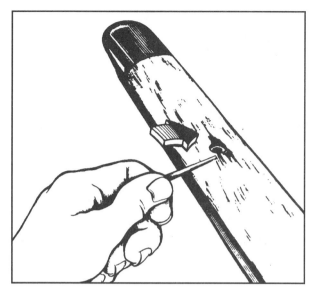

To repair a gouge like this in a gunstock, either use filler or splice in a piece of wood. This gouge would be an ideal candidate for a diamond inlay.

taining a dab of Dem-Bart stock finish and go over the entire pattern. This method will normally blend in the newly cut lines with the old. If it does not match, you will have to recut the entire pattern.

Repairing Gouges

Gouges or deep gashes in gunstocks that cannot be removed with steam have to be filled—either by splicing in an inlay or with a wood filler such as shellac sticks of the proper color to match the wood, walnut wood-dust and glue, etc. The only trouble with the various fillers is getting an exact match to the wood being repaired. It takes a keen eye...plus a lot of luck. If the gash isn't too large, the raw wood can be stained to match the finished wood and then transparent shellac can be applied to form an even surface. Like most repair techniques, you should acquire a reasonable amount of experience before attempting to use this on your favorite pride and joy.

Deep gouges or places where the wood in the stock has been splintered away require splicing or plugging to repair the flaw. It takes careful matching of the color and grain of the wood but—if done properly—such a splice is hardly detectable. Of course, strength of the repair is another consideration. The repaired area must be as strong as the original wood, but this should be no problem in this day and age with the many fine glues and epoxy kits available to the stocker.

To repair a small gouge in the wood, a plug is normally used. A round hole of sufficient depth is first cut out true with a Forstner bit and then the plug is turned (or obtained) to the exact size of the hole previously drilled with the bit. This plug should fit snugly, but without so much pressure that it might possibly split the wood. Walnut dowels are available, but are difficult to find all the time. Furthermore, most of these will have the end grain exposed, which makes the repair more conspicuous. A better plug is one with the side grain exposed so as to more closely match the sur-

rounding area of the stock where the repair is to be made.

An end-grain plug may be turned on the lathe by first gluing a 1-inch thick piece of walnut to some scrap stock that may be attached to the faceplate of the lathe. Set the tool rest across the bed so that it is parallel to the faceplate's surface, then turn the plug from the end—the same as when turning a disk. When turned to the correct diameter for the hole in the stock, cut the plug off to the required length. A $1/4$-inch plug is usually plenty for most repairs, but on some curved surfaces, a $1/2$-inch plug may be necessary. As the plug is inserted into the cutout, align the grain in the plug to match that of the existing stock around the repair. Then, when stained and finished, the repair will be almost unnoticeable.

Sometimes it is almost impossible to repair a gouge without it being highly noticeable. In cases like this, it may be best to inlay an attractive piece of contrasting wood to cover the gouge much like the inlays used on Weatherby custom rifles. Another technique is to carve a design in the area to camouflage the gouge, adjusting the carving to blend in with the gouge.

Split Buttstocks

One of the most common stock repairs will be repairing a split heel or toe of the buttstock. It doesn't take too much of a jolt to split off a piece of wood when the firearm is dropped or allowed to slam to the ground. The repair entails finding a piece of matching wood—with the same grain running in the same direction as the original—and splicing it into the area of the missing wood.

First remove the old finish down to the bare wood, so as to clearly see the original grain and color of the wood. Now the split must be prepared to accept a new piece of wood. This is accomplished by cutting the ragged break smooth and even. Depending on the type and size of the split, you might want to first use a fine-tooth saw to cut out a square notch in the stock and then use a wood rasp and file to smooth the cut up a bit. Or, if the break is not too ragged, perhaps a rasp or plane will suffice without any sawing. To check the accuracy of the cut, lay a flat-edged ruler or other straightedge on the smoothed surface and hold it up to eye level against a strong light. Any dips or waves in the cut should be detected instantly. Additional cuts with a file will get the surface smooth and level. You now want to make certain the cut is absolutely clean—free from oil, sawdust, and the like—because a good solid joint cannot be made if dirt is present.

With the surface prepared, find a piece of wood that closely matches the original in both grain and color. This might be a difficult problem, especially if the stock being repaired is rather old. This is why it is a good idea to save every piece of suitable stock wood that you might come across. Often you will encounter a rifle or shotgun that needs a complete replacement of the wood. The old stock is removed and placed in the "junk" bin with the others that have accumulated over the years. Old broken stocks usually have plenty of good solid wood left on them that can be used to repair other stocks, and the age of these old broken stocks will more closely match a used stock than if new walnut or other wood is used.

Once a suitable piece of wood is found, closely examine it to see what section will be the best to use for the repair. When one is chosen use a fine-tooth saw (such as a hacksaw) to cut off a block of wood to fit into the notch in the stock being repaired. In doing so, however, be sure to allow enough wood for working the repair down to the exact shape of the original stock. During this examination, you will notice that the bottom line on most stocks (in the case of a broken toe) travels straight from the pistol grip down to the toe of the stock. On some designs, however (especially some guns made in Europe), the stock may curve somewhat as it approaches the buttplate. Determine which of these stock designs you are working with, and proceed accordingly.

The surface of the replacement wood must be as flat and smooth as the notch cut out from the original stock. Allow about $1/4$-inch excess wood all around to allow for final shaping. Any excess wood can be rasped or planed off until the patch blends into the lines of the stock.

Before doing so, however, the replacement wood must be tightly secured to the original stock. Mix up a batch of epoxy glue and, using a piece of clean wood as an applicator (such as a toothpick), smear a small amount of the epoxy onto the bearing surfaces of the replacement wood and also onto the existing wood where the replacement wood will make contact. These two surfaces must be completely covered with a very thin coat of epoxy for maximum strength. To ensure good coverage, press the replacement wood into the notch in the existing stock and then slide the replacement wood back and forth a few times for added insurance. Then align the replacement piece correctly, press the two pieces together firmly, and wipe away any excess epoxy that is squeezed out from the joint.

A tight fit can be obtained with this type of joint only if the pieces are held tightly together during the drying process. Conventional wood clamps can be used, but due to the angle at this point in the stock, heavy rubber bands are better. These, however, must be supplemented with either wire or tape to ensure maximum tightness. Let the joint dry overnight before continuing.

Methods of final shaping vary from shop to shop, but one preferred method is to use a sanding disk to cut away the excess wood. Merely hold the stock with the glued-on replacement against the sanding disk, "eyeballing" the shape as the work progresses. As the shaping nears completion, switch to various grades of sandpaper to obtain a smooth final finish. Some stockers prefer to use wood rasps for this shaping, ending up with sandpaper and sanding blocks. Either method will work fine; use the technique that suits you best.

When the repair has been sanded to completely and accurately match the existing stock, it is ready for finishing. Wet this portion of the stock and then dry it quickly over a heat source. Be careful not to burn the wood; hold it over the heat only long enough to evaporate the moisture. Keeping the stock moving at all times will help eliminate burning. This process will bring the whiskers in the wood to the surface, where they can be cut off with steel wool. The wood is then ready for refinishing. In doing so, match the original finish as closely as possible. If this is impractical, it is best to refinish the entire stock to ensure a better match.

In a few rare cases, it is almost impossible to match a replacement piece of wood with the original. When these instances occur, remove the finish from the stock and dye the entire wood surface, adding a little here and there until a perfect shade is produced overall. The stock is then refinished by one of the methods that closely matches the original.

When restoring collector guns with a split heel or toe in the buttstock, many gunsmiths do not like to remove any of the original wood. Rather, they inlet the replacement piece with inletting black similar to stock inletting. To do so, first obtain a piece of matching wood of approximately the correct size, with a little to spare. The original stock is thoroughly cleaned in the area of the break, and then inletting black is applied to the irregular wood on the original stock. The new replacement wood is then placed onto the stock and firmly pressed into place before removing. A chisel or Moto-Tool with a cutting burr is used to take off the black marks left by the inletting black. The process is repeated until the new replacement piece of wood looks like it grew to the original stock. This method is time consuming, but if done correctly, will give the best fit possible to the split buttstock. This technique is also useful for splits around the tangs—another area where splits are prevalent.

Many side-by-side double shotguns are in use in this country and abroad and most of them manufactured before World War II had short chambers. When firing modern high-powered $2^3/4$-inch shotshells in these chambers, the chamber pressure increases considerably and also causes heavier recoil. After many rounds are run through these shotguns, chances are the stocks can't take the pounding and eventually give way—usually around the grip area where the standing breech joins the stock. When such a break occurs, it is usually best to replace the entire buttstock, but if the split is only minor, a repair may be in order.

In making a repair to the forward end of a buttstock, the same technique is used as described for repairing a split in the toe—that is, the wood surface is first cleaned around the area of the repair, the surfaces are squared and planed smooth, a new replacement piece is cut and secured in place with epoxy, and finally the replacement piece of wood is shaped to match the original. A professional refinishing job can make the repair almost unnoticeable. On some repairs of this nature, however, it may be best not to cut away any of the existing wood, especially on high-quality stocks. In cases like these, it may be best to inlet a replacement piece of wood to the existing stock. The method employed is very similar to that used to

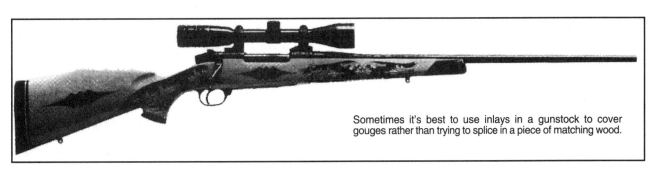

Sometimes it's best to use inlays in a gunstock to cover gouges rather than trying to splice in a piece of matching wood.

inlet barrels and receivers into stock blanks.

A replacement piece of wood that closely matches the grain and color of the original wood is obtained and cut to the approximate shape. Inletting black is then applied to the rough edges of the original stock, after which the replacement wood is firmly pressed against this area in the original wood. When lifted up, the black marks on the underside of the replacement wood indicate where wood has to be cut away. Cuts are made with a rotary rasp and again placed in position onto the original stock, lifted up again, and more wood cut away where indicated by the black marks caused by the high spots on the existing stock. This procedure is repeated several times (sometimes as many as 50 or more tries) until the replacement piece fits perfectly. A splice in the stock as just described will fit so perfectly and snugly that the stock could be turned upside down without the replacement part falling out. Of course, once such a fit has been obtained, you'll still want to glue the part in place.

Cracks and repairs along the sides of stocks (not around edges) are best made with small inlays. To get the shape required, coat the stock around the defect with inletting black, press a piece of white paper over it, and trace the impression on the piece from which the inlay is to be made. Shape up the inlay carefully with a rasp and file, trying often for fit. The edges should also be tapered slightly to ensure a tighter fit. Coat the inside of the recess with epoxy and then coat the replacement inlay. Press the inlay in place and wipe away any excess glue that is squeezed from the edges. Clamp the inlay in place and let it dry overnight. Sand down to the surface of the existing wood and finish.

Breaks At Grip

When a rifle or shotgun stock is cracked at the grip or broken completely in two, it is best to replace the entire stock. However, a temporary repair can be made by forcing the crack open as far as possible with a thin metal object (such as a hacksaw blade or chisel) and then squeezing in some epoxy. A syringe or hypodermic needle loaded with epoxy is good for this purpose. Clamp the joints together and let dry overnight, then drill through the stock from side to side and insert a $1/8$-inch brass wood screw. Countersink the screw head, then fill this countersink with a wood plug. Sand down and refinish.

After repairing the break in the grip, try to determine why the stock broke in the first place. First, disassemble the metal parts from the stock and clean them thoroughly. Coat the receiver with inletting black and fit it back into the stock; remove again. Notice where the inletting black left marks inside the bedding area of the stock and use a chisel to remove these high spots, relieving all pressure at sides, rear of receiver, etc. If the smudges indicate the recoil lug does not have a good bearing against the shoulder in the stock, use fiberglass bedding.

Many broken gunstocks can be repaired by using epoxy in combination with dowels or pins. Even broken stocks that look hopeless can often be repaired and refinished to look as good as new.

The weakest part of any gunstock is usually the pistol grip, although a lot of stocks are cracked around the toe or heel. The pistol-grip area should be repaired with epoxy as well as a dowel or pin. A birch dowel is usually considered to be best, Brownells, Inc., offers a wide assortment of metal stock-repairing pins that serve the

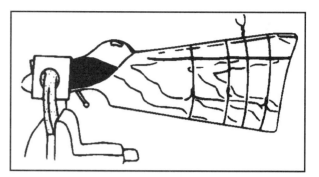

The repair to the toe on this stock is held in place with iron wire while the epoxy dries.

same purpose as dowels; they are also stronger.

To repair a typical break in the pistol grip of a gunstock, select a dowel of a size that the stock will logically accept, then drill straight through the cap of the pistol grip and on through the broken surface into the other side of the break for a perfect fit. You will probably have to do some reshaping and sanding in the grip area after the dowel has been press-fitted. Then the opposing surfaces are liberally coated with epoxy and everything is brought together.

Now comes the problem of clamping the two pieces together. The curved surfaces always seem to resist C-clamps. A better clamping method is to use long pipe clamps that bear against the forend and butt of the stock, holding the pieces in horizontal alignment. C-clamps can be used to hold the broken pieces in vertical alignment until the epoxy has cured, but supplement these with heavy rubber bands.

An epoxy joint is strong and will probably last for years without any other reinforcement, but additional work will ensure a much better job. Drill a $3/8$" hole in the upper tang recess, down through the pistol grip, and into the buttstock itself. Coat a dowel with epoxy and tap it into the hole. The excess wood is removed with a chisel and the tang mortise is cleaned up. If necessary, glass bed this tang area.

Once the repair has been made, remove any beads or runs of epoxy with a sharp chisel, then smooth down the epoxy until it blends into the stock contours. Any recesses or holes can be filled with dabs of epoxy, then smoothed with a damp rag after it thickens. Avoid getting glue into the checkering or marring the checkering with tools and sandpaper.

At this point, depending on how bad the area looks, a certain degree of refinishing (and perhaps recutting of the checkering) is in order.

Stocks having small lengthwise splits can sometimes be repaired by breaking them entirely apart at the splits, and then gluing them with epoxy. When the break is made, be careful not to bruise the edge and don't lose any of the splinters; all should be kept in position, leaving one end of any splinter attached if possible. The surfaces are then coated with epoxy and carefully worked into place before the parts are clamped in position. Care taken to acquire a perfect fit between the two sections will go a long way to ensure a tight-fitting joint that will be stronger than the original. Then, with a little care in matching dyes, stains and finishes, a job can be finished that is hardly detectable by any but the experienced eye.

Performing the Ruger 10/22 Team Challenge Conversion

As more and more shooters demand these guns, the need to make drop-in parts that actually drop in and to solve other difficulties associated with this upgrade become important.

By Dennis Wood

BECAUSE OF THE inherent accuracy and reliability of the Ruger 10/22 autoloading rifle, it has become the overriding favorite of gunsmiths who are building guns for Sportsman Team Challenge competitions, events which include two rifle legs. In fact, the competition has spawned a healthy aftermarket industry for all sorts of 10/22 modifications that can make the 10/22 even more accurate and reliable.

One of the most common changes made to 10/22s is adding an aftermarket barrel. There are about five or six styles of aftermarket barrels available for this rifle, and all claim to be a drop-in fit. The aftermarket barrels I have examined, most of which had match-grade chambers cut into them, were well made, and they usually price out at around $275 to $300 retail.

The positive effects of adding a match-grade barrel and shooting match-grade 22 ammunition in a 10/22 can be astounding, as a recent conversion I performed showed.

First Step

A shooter who owned a stock 10/22 rifle wanted a conversion done, and he wanted to use a Volquartsen heavy stainless steel bar-

This is a Team Challenge 10/22 containing many of the modifications noted in the text, including a compensated barrel, trigger job, composite thumbhole stock, and a heavy target barrel and special chamber. The rifle shown also has a special set of blocks to get the shooter's eye in line with a totally erect head position on the stock.

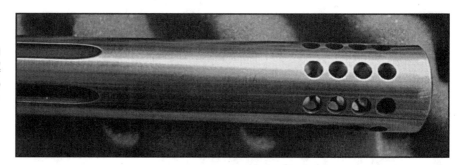

Some Volquartsen heavy stainless steel barrels come with integral muzzle compensators, which have eight rows of four $^{17}/_{64}$-inch diameter holes to vent powder gases.

rel with integral muzzle compensator. The compensator has eight rows of four $^{17}/_{64}$-inch-diameter holes to vent powder gases. This barrel measures $20^3/_{16}$ inches in length including the muzzlebrake, and has an advertised diameter of 0.926-inch from muzzle to chamber end without any taper. The Volquartsen barrel I received for this rifle miked 0.928-inch at the rear and 0.927-inch at the front diameter of the compensator, very close to the advertised dimensions.

To install one of these drop-ins, remove the two screws on the barrel block and take off the factory barrel. Measure the length of the factory barrel shank that goes into the receiver from the rear face to the shoulder. This should be about 0.750-inch, plus or minus 0.005-inch. Measure the length of the barrel shank on the new barrel to see that it is within this tolerance range. The shank diameter of the factory barrel runs around $^{11}/_{16}$-inch or 0.6875. The new barrel should be as near this dimension as possible, unless the original barrel was sloppily fit. The barrel shank hole in the receiver should be inspected for burrs and any high spots that will appear shiny. Try the new barrel in the receiver receptacle for fit.

The shoulder at the front of the receiver acts as a barrel support shelf and may need to be relieved somewhat so that the new barrel will clear. Almost all of these barrels are made so that the fit will be tight, almost a press fit. There is also one manufacturer who actually threads the receiver hole after line boring and also threads the barrel shank for fitting. In the event that the barrel shank will not enter the receiver, there are several options for fitting. If you have access to a lathe, the barrel can be set up in it and the tenon diameter either turned to fit or polished with emery cloth as it turns, to achieve a tight fit. Running an 11/16-inch reamer into the receiver hole by hand or at a very slow drill press speed will true up the receptacle if it appears to be misshapen. The idea here is to not remove any more material than necessary to have a tight fit.

The replacement barrel I used weighed in at 3 pounds, twice the weight of the factory barrel with a diameter of 0.927-inch. To fit the barrel in the factory stock, you will need to relieve the barrel channel to accept the new barrel. Also, Volquartsen recommends that two 1-inch-wide epoxy barrel support pads be glassed into the barrel channel to help support this heavy barrel. Install one pad in front of the action screw and the other pad at the forend tip. (However, because I used a Volquartsen black composite thumbhole replacement stock, these pads were already built into the forearm. Once the new barrel was mounted on the receiver, the barreled action actually did drop in and fit properly, something you don't always encounter with so-called drop-in-fit items.

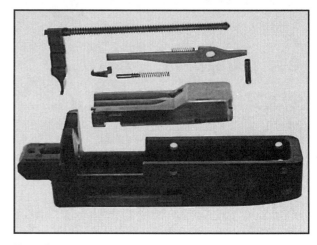

The 10/22's receiver and bolt parts fit together in this order.

The customer liked the idea of having the receiver match the color of the stainless-steel barrel, so the receiver, trigger guard, and all other parts previously blued or anodized were bead blasted with fine aluminum-oxide grit beads. The blasted parts were then coated with a clear-matte bake-on lacquer finish and then baked at 350 degrees for 30 minutes.

Scope Base Installation

This job also called for the use of a cantilever scope base manufactured by Weigand Combat Handguns, Inc. This cantilever base requires that three holes be drilled and tapped into the barrel for placement so that the rear of the base extends back over the receiver. This base was designed to be used on heavy bull barrels of the style and diameter used for this conversion. Although this mount was said to fit barrels up to 0.960-inch in diameter, the radius cut into the bottom of this mount did not fit the barrel contour very well at all. To fix it, I set up a $^{15}/_{16}$-inch ball end mill in my mill and milled the radius of the base to a contour which matched the barrel radius more closely, which also resulted in reducing the gap between the rear of the base and the receiver, in this case 0.014-inch. This was exactly the gap between the upper inside face of the scope mount and the top of the receiver.

I then drilled two clearance holes into the rear of the mount so they would line up with the two front holes used for base mounting

The Weigand cantilever scope base mounts onto three holes tapped into the barrel. The two rear holes need to be drilled.

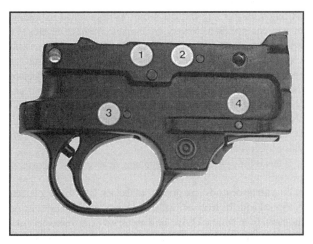

The trigger group includes the following items: 1) hammer pin, 2) ejector pin, 3) trigger pivot pin, and 4) magazine-release pivot pin.

in the receiver. The cantilever mount would now act as a bridge connecting the barrel and receiver.

The major complaint I had with this mount is the lack of critical instructions concerning screw-thread diameter. There are three base mount screws included with this mount, but nothing to designate what the screw size is. If I hadn't routinely checked the screw threads, I might have assumed they were #6-48 threads, common to most scope-base mounting holes, and drilled and tapped the holes in the barrel for that thread.

As it turned out, the mounting screws are #6-40 threads with an 82-degree tapered head, which requires the use of a hex wrench. Instead of using the supplied #6-40 screws, I chose to go with #6-48 screws for mounting the cantilever base to the barrel. My reason: The two front base holes in the receiver are #6-48 threads, and these two holes attach the rear of the base to the receiver. If had used both the #6-40 and #6-48 threaded screws, it would be confusing to the owner or another gunsmith who may happen to work on this firearm in the future, especially if the screws were mixed up on a workbench.

To attach the base, drill three holes in the barrel at the proper spacing using a sight drilling jig. Then tap these three holes to #6-48 and cut three stainless steel screws to length and fit them in place. Set up the barreled action in a drill-press vise and level the top of the base. Chuck up a No. 11 bell-type center drill in place and then remove the base, leaving the center drill lined up over one of the rear scope base holes. Double-check to make sure the alignment is correct, then put the cantilever base back on the barrel and screw it into place without moving the setup. Use the center drill to spot drill the base for one of the through-holes. Remove the base and center the center drill over the other rear receiver hole. Attach the base once again using the same procedure.

Then, remove the base from the receiver and drill two $^9/_{64}$-inch through-holes in the base. Use a step drill to cut the screw head clearance down to the proper depth in the base. (A center drill should be used to spot drill these two holes because it is a stiff short drill that doesn't walk off location. This may seem like a lot of fooling around to get this base centered over the tapped holes now in the receiver, but I found out a long time ago that if you take the time when you first do a job, you won't have to spend a lot more time trying to fix a catastrophe.)

Wrapping Up

This mount was designed to be used with Weaver-style scope rings, so I had my pick of rings. I chose Burris Z-rings in Safari grade to hold the Burris 6- to 18-power variable scope over the bore of this conversion. These are steel scope rings that have two V-notches cut into the bottom sides of the rings so that they will fit on Weaver-style bases. As purchased, they would not fit on the Weigand base, so I set up each ring in my milling vise, leveled it, and removed 0.050-inch from the bottom side of each V-notch so that the rings would slip onto the base.

Once everything was together, it was time to compare the trigger pull after I had worked on the gun to what I had begun with. Before I had begun work on the gun, I noted its trigger pull was $5^1/_2$ pounds before disassembly, and one of my goals was to smooth it out and reduce it to $3^1/_2$ pounds. After installing some new trigger parts and polishing others, I was able to make the trigger let off and break cleanly and safely at $2^1/_4$ pounds on average.

All the additions, including the scope and rings, made the rifle scale out at $8^1/_4$ pounds, but its performance is worth the extra weight. Group sizes have been cut in half, and it is a distinctive, attractive firearm to boot.

Mounting Rifle Scopes

The task isn't as hard as it once was because of updated technology and better materials. But here are some tips on mounting scopes that you'll need to know.

By Frank Fry

TODAY'S GUNSMITHING REPERTOIRE includes things our predecessors never thought of—glass bedding, synthetic stocks, and plastic parts, to name just a few. In short, those guys had to do lots of things that we are no longer required to do.

One of those tasks that has almost been eliminated is the tedious job of drilling and tapping each and every receiver before mounting a scope. The techniques we use today for the few jobs that do require drilling and tapping run from pretty basic and simple "eyeballing" the hole locations to using more complicated drilling jigs from Forster, B-Square or other firms.

But even as simple as things have gotten, we've all seen otherwise nicely done "custom" rifles with scope-mounting holes that are not perprndicular to the bore or with extra holes drilled in the receiver ring and bridge. These are just a couple of examples of what can happen if the job is attempted by the uninitiated amateur.

Actually, it isn't just amateurs that have difficulties. Many pro-

fessionals do, too. It seems that the use of modern scope-base drilling with jigs and fixtures seems to have lulled us into an overdependence on these very drilling jigs. We have developed a dependency on the jig or fixture for hole location. Without constant visual monitoring of hole locations in relation to the barrel, an apparently perfect job of receiver drilling with the most advanced mounting jigs available may produce an inferior or less than desirable scope position. In carrying this to its conclusion, you could also correctly note that factory-drilled holes often have similar deficiencies. There is no guarantee that factory hole positions will provide perfect positioning.

If this is the case, can scope-mounting holes ever be considered exact?

Exactitude depends on a number of factors: Is the barrel perfectly aligned with the receiver? Is the barrel bent? Is there pressure on the barrel from the stock? Are the dimensions of the receivers exact from one production run to another? These, and perhaps several other variables, can cause the mounted scope to appear badly mounted and make the scope run out of adjustment before a zero is obtained. The problem may be more apparent on one of the lower-priced scopes, some of which may have limited crosshair adjustment.

Scope mounting, then, can be considered a combination of separate problems that need to be solved before the job is started. Barrel alignment, scope adjustment, parallax, eye relief, size of lens openings and purpose of the scope must all be taken into consideration.

The Tools

Before getting into the mechanics of scope mounting, some of the more common tools that are required for scope mounting should already be in your shop, including a scribe, center punch and centering drills, screwdrivers, drill press or mill, drill bits, taps and tapping accessories, along with some that are specialized. One such specialized tool that many scope installers claim they cannot do without is the optical collimator or boresighter. It is available from several companies (Redfield, Bushnell, Tasco, Sweeney, etc.) in varying degrees of accuracy and cost. We must remember, however, that scopes were mounted long before these optical devices had been invented, and the old-fashioned method of looking through the bore and sighting in on a distant target will work just as well today as it did way back when.

The number of scope-mount manufacturers is quite large, but the systems themselves consist of only a few basic types: two-piece Weaver types, one-piece Redfield styles, and a handful of side and

The two major mounting systems are two-piece Weaver-style and one-piece Redfield types. There are several others, but you'll encounter the Weaver and Redfield makes most often.

other specialized mounts. Hole spacings have also become standardized, so factory drillings will accept either one- or two-piece bases. Not many years ago, the hole dimensions may or may not have matched up between competing scope-block manufacturers, a nightmare that fortunately seems to have been eliminated.

Today's gunsmith mounts scopes primarily on rifles and shotguns that have been factory drilled and tapped. However, looser import laws over the last few years have made the military rifle appear more often. The skills needed to drill and tap those receivers will have to be revived. (See "Tapping and Die-Cutting Threads" elsewhere in this book.)

A sure sign of professional work in any scope-mounting job is to have screwdrivers that fit the screw slots exactly. This prevents ugly raised edges along the slot, or, in the case of Allen screws, a rounded, wallowed-out look to the recessed head. Phillips heads also get worn out and ugly when the gunsmith uses rounded blades or the wrong-sized tips. A tip with clean, sharp sides must be used.

Getting Started

Is mounting the scope on a drilled and tapped receiver quick and easy? In the majority of cases it is, but problems arise when the scope and barrel do not point at the same object.

Vertical-alignment problems can easily be taken care of with shim stock available through Brownells. Metal stock can also be cut to fit by scribing the shim after a trial installation. Removing the shim and cutting to the scribe mark is the only way to get an exact fit, since the shim must curve to match the action. Brownells' shims are pre-cut to fit but will have to be manually aligned, for the cutouts for the screw holes are large and are of little use as locators.

Another method that can be used is the paper shim. Matchbook covers, for example, make excellent shims and are easily trimmed to exact size after the scope mount has been cinched down. The paper is also compressed in this process and loses its flimsiness. Soaking the fiber shim with stock finish can help prevent moisture

A center punch and a center drill are two tools you can't do without when you start mounting rifle scopes.

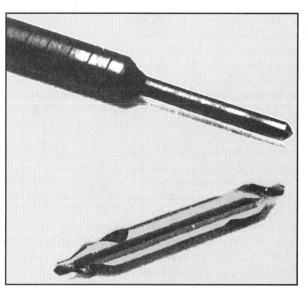

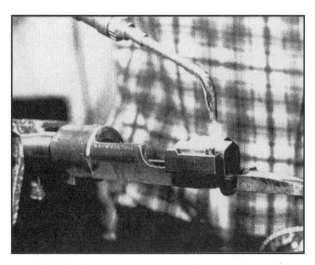
Annealing with direct heat may help you drill a receiver that is otherwise too hard to work. Be careful that you don't heat it so much that it hardens even more.

accumulations. Any shim will need to be colored to match the base. A flat-black paint seems to match up with most bases. A black felt-tip marker can be used on the paper shim, and it blends in well.

Those problems that involve horizontal alignment are more difficult, but there are several methods of curing them. The simplest is turning the blocks or mounts around, fixing the problem through minor variations in manufacturing. Unfortunately, this does not always work. Another measure involves a minor physical shift of Weaver-style bases. Tighten the base screws, then back off them off about $1/2$-to $3/4$-turn. Each block is given a crisp smack in opposite directions. Make sure the blows will shift the blocks in the direction needed. A wooden block will help protect the scope bases and receiver from any damage that might occur from a wild hammer. When the screws are re-tightened, the shifted block will remain in position. For minor horizontal alignment errors, this method can sometimes be sufficient.

If the alignment problem is so great with Weaver-style mounts that it is obvious it cannot be removed by this method, a more drastic method can be employed. Slightly loosen both the scope rings on the base and the rings' half-clamp screws. Push the scope's objective bell in whichever direction brings the target to the center of the crosshair. This will twist the scope rings slightly on the bases. Adjust eye relief and square the crosshairs to the vertical with the scope in this twisted position, then re-tighten the ring-clamp screws. The bottom of the ring will not sit perfectly flat on the bases, but for most adjustments, any twist on the mount will not be noticeable. Re-snug the ring clamp to the base and check with the boresighter. The scope can be removed and re-installed without changing the point of impact only on that rifle. This method has been used successfully on magnum-recoil rifles.

If this is not a sufficient fix, the only alternative may be to use a set of rings and bases that have horizontal adjustments built into the scope base. These are most often found on Redfield, Leupold, Conetrol and some Williams bases.

When it comes time to drill and tap a receiver, be sure to use the bore scope for positive scope alignment to barrel. It is suggested even when using drilling jigs like the adjustable Forster model. It holds the barrel in V-shaped clamps, and the receiver is supposed to align itself. But even this excellent jig fails on occasion, and the old eyeball and boresighter method is needed.

This technique can be used if you cannot afford the expense of one of those fancy contraptions, and it works very well on all drilling jobs. It is a bit more time-consuming, but you will find that it goes surprisingly quickly. Scope bases must be mounted TDC on the receiver, so the receiver must be squared before starting. The bases are then squared to the receiver.

To ensure perfect alignment, the scope should be placed in the bottom halves of the rings that are attached to the bases. The scope, ring halves and bases can be shifted slightly on top of the receiver as an assembly until the crosshair is centered on the target.

If bore alignment seems perfect, look at the relation between the scope and receiver. The scope should be parallel; if something looks out of line or wrong, it probably is.

The bases and rings can be held in place with string or strong rubber bands looped around the screws that hold the ring half together and the nut that locks the rings to the bases, a somewhat crude but effective method. The trick is how to mark the hole positions without disturbing this alignment. Here, a miracle of modern products comes to our aid. A fast-acting epoxy, applied to the bottom of the base, will allow sufficient curing time to shift the scope for alignment. After this has been done, the scope is left in position until the epoxy has set, usually 5 to 10 minutes. The scope and rings can then be removed and the bases will remain on the receiver, perfectly aligned.

Check and double-check the exact position of the receiver on the mill or press before you start drilling.

The Next Step

Locating the hole centers on a mill is a matter of mathematically determining hole spacing and half the width of the block. Dialing the numbers in the X and Y axes should locate the center. Check visually before center drilling.

If a mill is unavailable, a drill press will do the job satisfactorily. Spot the center of the screw hole with a spotting punch or two light taps on a No. 29 drill bit (for 6x48 screws), rotating the bit 90 degrees between taps. A center punch on the X made by the two marks will deepen the point enough to keep a drill bit from wandering. A wiggler can be used to center the dimple under the drill-press quill. A dimple from a small center drill gives the drill a wander-free start.

For maximum accuracy, the newly-drilled hole can be tapped before moving the receiver to the next drilled location. Changing the bit to tap and back again after each hole is drilled may seem to take more time than it is worth. Drilling all the holes, then tapping, may save time, but whatever you've gained will be lost along with your temper if a tap breaks off because it was not lined up exactly square with the hole.

The bases can either be left epoxied to the receiver or removed, as you see fit. A tap with a plastic mallet on the side of the base is often enough to break it loose. A little heat, steel wool in #0000 grade lubricated with a bore solvent, and careful scrubbing can remove the epoxy stuck to the receiver without damaging the blueing. If the base will not pop off with a mallet tap, heating the base gently with torch while tapping with the mallet should do the trick. To prevent any change from occurring in the blueing, do not heat the base above the point that water sizzles. Most epoxies will soften before the temperature of boiling water is reached.

It is amazing how many mounting jobs are ruined by bad screwdrivers. One that fits properly will support the screw by friction alone.

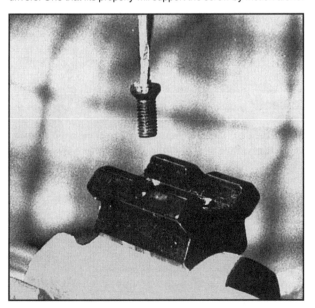

Problems To Know About

You are going to find some receivers that are harder than your landlord's heart. There are two primary reasons: The first is that the receiver is case-hardened. Many military Mausers fall into this category.

This is easily taken care of by grinding through the case-hardened skin with a small grinding stone in a high-speed hand grinder. The metal below the hardened surface will probably be soft and can be easily drilled. There is probably no need to drill completely through the receiver. Remember that the drill will have to penetrate the case-hardened surface as it exits the opposite surface. Drilling completely through that opposite case-hardened side can ruin a drill bit through friction, or worse, break it off in the hole. Tap only far enough to provide enough threads for the screw.

The second cause is a heat-treated receiver that is hard and tough all the way through. This is a more difficult problem, but spot annealing may help soften the receiver enough to drill. Heat can be applied with a very fine tip on a torch, heating the spot to be drilled to a dull gray a number of times.

The heat can also be transferred to the spot by heating a metal rod pressed against the receiver. The trick here is to anneal, not to get the metal so hot that it may harden further. This process may have to repeated a number of times as the drill sinks deeper into the metal because the annealing will be fairly shallow.

If the action just refuses to cooperate, a carbide drill and warp speed on the quill should sink the drill through. To save time, vocabulary and hair, drill and tap only deep enough for the depth of screw required. Tapping will be a long and arduous process. Tap slowly, with lots of fluid, backing off four or five times more often than normal. If the tap squeaks, immediately remove and re-sharpen it. Trying to force a tap will almost certainly result in breakage and a bigger problem.

When using an optical collimator, the crosshairs should be double-checked after mounting and set just slightly below the center of the target grid in the collimator. This will generally put the impact on the paper at 100 yards. Of course you know that final sighting in must be done by the person who is going to shoot the rifle. Too much sight variation occurs between individuals to have a universal zero. Some shooters don't realize this and will assume the scope is zeroed for all bullet weights, all ranges, all conditions and all shooters.

This gentle reminder may prevent someone from blaming you for a lousy scope-mounting job and ruining his once-in-a-lifetime hunt, claiming he couldn't hit the only two-zillion-point buck ever seen, because the scope was off. Don't laugh, it happens, and it's always your fault!

Sharpen up those drill and tap scope-mounting skills. The demand is coming back!

Working the Browning Auto-5

If you know your way around John Browning's famed autoloader, you can also handle a couple of Remington and Savage shotguns built on the same mechanism. Here's a step-by-step guide.

By Dennis A. Wood

SHORTLY AFTER 1900, John Moses Browning took his idea for an autoloading shotgun to the U.S. Patent Office after parting ways with the Winchester Gun Co. The relationship ended when Winchester president T.G. Bennett wanted nothing to do with an "automatic."

Gathering his prototypes from the drafting room, Browning left Winchester to make an appointment to see Marcellus Hartley, president of Remington Arms Co. Over the phone, he received an enthusiastic response, so a meeting was set up to show Remington his wares. Sitting in Hartley's office, Browning was told that the president of Remington Arms Co. had died of a heart attack that

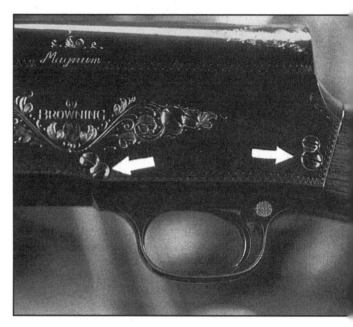

Drifting out the trigger assembly and lock screws allows removal of the entire trigger group. It usually isn't necessary to completely disassemble this group.

very morning. Lacking any potential American manufacturers with the means to produce his newly created semi-automatic shotgun, Browning began the search elsewhere.

The famous firearms manufacturer, Fabrique Nationale d'Armes de Guerre, located at Herstal, Liege, Belgium, was waiting with open arms. By the end of 1961, F.N. had produced 1,377,785 of the Model A-5 shotguns. Remington Arms produced approximately 300,000 of its Model 11, and Savage Arms produced thousands of the Model 720, with very little variance from the original design, under license from the F.N. factory. These shotguns are but three of Browning's legacies, and because of the numbers that were produced, you may run across them from time to time. If so, here's what to look for:

Disassembly, Parts

We'll be dealing primarily with the Browning Auto-5 here, but all the procedures for disassembly and parts replacement apply to the Remington Model 11 and the Savage Model 720.

When working on the Auto-5 or any other firearm, the rules of common sense and safety should always be followed. Always be sure the firearm is unloaded and the magazine tube empty. Ask the shooter about the problems he is having with the firearm. The more information you receive the better off you are.

Complete disassembly of these firearms is a prerequisite to thorough cleaning and, of course, blueing.

The first thing you'll want to do with the A-5 is pull the bolt handle all the way back so that the action locks back, bolt open.

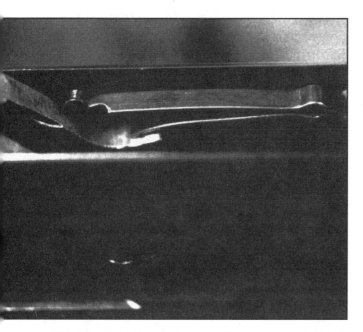

Older Browning A-5 autoloaders have lifter springs on a stud inside the receiver.

Unscrew the magazine end cap at the forend tip. If the magazine cap has been powered on, wrap an old piece of leather belt around the magazine cap and use vise-grips to loosen it. The forearm wood slides forward, coming off with the barrel, recoil spring and friction rings.

With the shotgun in a vise with protected jaws, trigger guard up, remove the lock screw for the stock screw at the rear of the bottom tang, then remove the stock screw. If the stock is a little stubborn, a few whacks with a rubber-faced dead-blow hammer at the rear face of the receiver may convince it to release. Once the stock is removed, depress the carrier latch button while holding the bolt handle with your off hand and ease the bolt forward. Try not to let the bolt go flying forward because that might damage the front of the ejection port.

Returning the gun to the vise, remove the trigger-plate lock screws, then the front and rear trigger-plate screws on the left side of the receiver. On the Remington and the Savage models, the front trigger-plate screws are actually pins, but they do have lock screws. These pins can be drifted out once the lock screws are removed.

The whole trigger group can now be removed. On the older model A-5 Brownings (before 1958), the Remington Model 11 and the Savage Model 720. the carrier spring is mounted on a stud on the receiver wall. With the newer A-5s, the carrier spring is integral to the trigger-plate assembly.

The rear end of the receiver tang holds the action-spring tube containing the action-spring plug, action spring, and the action-spring follower. To relieve tension on the spring, drift out the cross pin with a $^3/_{32}$-inch punch. Pushing the pin with one hand, hold some tension on the action-spring plug with your other hand so the plug, spring and follower don't go flying out a window. A 45-caliber bore brush dipped in solvent will scrub the crud buildup inside the action-spring tube quite nicely.

On the Savage 720, the end of the action-spring tube is threaded into the rear of the receiver tang. There are two flats on the end of this tube that can be used to turn the tube off with a crescent wrench.

The carrier assembly consists of six parts, and normally, disassembly is not necessary. The carrier assembly has a screw and lock screw on the right and left sides of the receiver. These carrier screws should be identified as to which side they came out of. If they are switched at reassembly, the lock screws will probably not line up properly. All of the older Brownings were marked on the tip of the right screw going into the receiver for replacement identification. If you are blueing and the screws are not marked, it will save some time to do so for reassembly.

Removing the bolt assembly is the next step. For this step in takedown, I suggest placing the magazine tube in the protected jaws of your vise with the right side of the receiver facing up. Close the vise with enough pressure to hold the magazine tube firmly, but don't overtighten.

Use the breechblock link to slide the bolt in the receiver so the locking-block latch pin lines up with the half hole along the bottom edge of the ejection port. While keeping the latch pin aligned with the half hole, take a $^3/_{32}$-inch punch and drive out the latch pin from the left side of the receiver. When the punch is withdrawn, the locking-block latch and spring on the bottom of the bolt will be free. Watching for it to pop up and out, remove both at this time.

While pulling rearward on the bolt handle, use the link to push the bolt forward to remove the bolt handle. The bolt assembly will now come out the front of the receiver. Unless you are blueing the metal, the magazine cut-off, along with its spring, can be left in place at the left front of the receiver. If the magazine tube is damaged and being replaced, the magazine cut-off screw will have to be backed off to remove the magazine tube.

To remove the cartridge stop, place the receiver in your padded vise with the bottom facing up. The older Brownings, the Remington Model 11 and the Savage 720 all have a slotted-head pin threaded from the top of the slot down about $^1/_8$-inch, which holds the cartridge stop in place. Newer Brownings use a roll pin. If you find a roll pin holding the cartridge stop in place, a $^3/_{32}$-inch punch will drive the pin down into the receiver for removal. There are two variations in the cartridge stops. Those made for the Remington Model 11 from 1905 until 1931 use a different style than those used after 1931, so watch for the difference if replacing one of these.

The carrier latch assembly is removed much the same as the cartridge stop. Check to see if it has a slotted-head screw or a roll pin, and disassemble in the same manner as the cartridge stop.

When removing the magazine spring retainer, the Menck corkscrew tool helps contain the spring inside the magazine tube. When released of tension, this spring seems to go on longer than one of my old Uncle Walley's jokes.

The trigger assembly can normally be cleaned and oiled without disassembly. If it must be taken down completely, place the hammer in the cocked position with the safety on. With a small-bladed screwdriver, get underneath the safety sear and depress the follower and spring so the safety sear can be pushed forward off its pin. Watch for the follower and spring to come quickly out of its hole. If you were able to contain them, remove the follower and safety spring.

Place the safety in the fire position. With your left hand, hold the hammer to keep it from coming forward and pull the trigger, at the same time easing the hammer forward with your left hand. With a $1/8$-inch punch, drive out the hammer pin and remove the hammer. The mainspring screw can now be removed at the trigger guard tang. Newer models have a small cross-pin that goes through the tang and above the trigger spring. A 0.060-inch-diameter punch will handle removal of the cross pin.

When removing the trigger spring, the safety ball can easily be lost, so watch for the little ball to try and get away from you. A middle leg on the trigger spring puts pressure on the safety ball. When the spring is removed, the safety ball is free to wander. Invert the trigger guard to drop the ball out. On the older model A-5s, two grooves on the inside of the tang capture the trigger spring, so the spring will have to be slipped out the rear by pulling on the through hole with a punch.

Drive out the trigger pin with a $3/32$-inch punch, remove the trigger and then the safety. Check the safety for burrs and re-insert it into its hole in the trigger plate, making sure it slides back and forth freely. If it sticks in either direction. look for high. shiny spots on the safety and polish these spots smooth. With the safety in its hole in the trigger plate, put the trigger and trigger pin back in place and make sure the trigger pivots smoothly on the pin.

With tweezers or small needle-nose pliers, install the safety ball into the socket for it. To install the trigger spring, depress the spring with a punch and then install the cross pin. On the older models, the trigger spring slides in the grooves in the trigger-plate tang forward until the screw hole in the rear aligns with the hole in the lower tang. Check the feel of the safety movement. If it moves too freely, the center leg on the trigger spring will need to be bent downward to increase the pressure on the safety ball. If the safety moves excessively hard, the center leg on the trigger spring will have to be bent up a bit. Replace the mainspring and the screw for it. Place the hammer and hammer pin in place in the trigger housing. Check to see that the hammer pivots freely on the hammer pin. With the hammer in the cocked position, install the safety sear, spring and plunger. Make sure the lower end of the safety sear has rotated into the proper position.

If the trigger can't be pulled after assembly, it is possible that the top part of the safety sear that strikes the inside of the link is too short or that the link may be bent. If this is the case, replace the safety sear and reshape or replace the link. With the hammer

Stock tang screw removal should let the stock come off. If not, a few whacks with a rubber mallet should do the trick.

cocked, disengage the safety sear with your thumb. Push the safety to the "ON" position. Pulling the trigger as hard as possible, the hammer should not fall.

If the hammer falls, the safety is worn or the rear of the trigger that should contact the safety is short. If either condition exists, replace the safety or the trigger.

Upon inspection of the carrier assembly, look to see that the two legs which extend to the rear have not become misaligned. Place a steel straightedge along the outside of the carrier legs to see if they are parallel with the lifting portion of the carrier. If they are out of alignment, place the front of the carrier in a vise and with a brass hammer, tap them into shape. The carrier screw holes should be in perfect alignment. To check these holes, a 0.185-inch pin or the shank end of a No. 13 drill should slide freely back and forth through both without any binding. If the holes are misaligned, one of the carrier legs will have to be bent so they are once again in line.

To disassemble the breechblock, drive out the firing-pin stop pin from left to right with a $1/8$-inch punch. The firing pin can now be removed. Check to see that the spring is straight, not broken or starting to crystallize. If it looks doubtful, replace it. Rotate the locking block and link forward and out of the breechblock. Unless the link is badly damaged, there is no need to disassemble it from the locking block. If the link is replaced, the link pin must be staked in place to prevent side movement that could jam and damage the action.

To remove the right or left extractors, drive either of the retaining pins from the bottom of the breechblock to the top with a $3/32$-inch punch. There is an old and a new style extractor. The new style can be modified into the old style, if need be, by removing material at the back of the extractor.

To inspect the extractors, take the breechblock in one hand and place the rim of a dummy round between the right and left extractors. Push the dummy round so pressure is applied to the base of the dummy, forcing the right extractor outward.

If carrier screws are switched during reassembly, the lock screws won't line up properly.

Slide the dummy shell flat on the face of the breechblock until the extractor has reached its most outward movement. Tip the dummy so it will show a gap in clearing the left extractor.

This gap should be about 0.015- to 0.030-inch. If the gap is wider than 0.030-inch, the extractor may drop the cartridge or fail with extraction. To correct this condition, tap the hook of the left extractor inward. Insert the dummy round and again tilt down, but without exerting pressure to the left extractor. If it does not release, the hook on the left extractor is too sharp or is bent too far inward and is creating excessive hook. If the hook feels too sharp, use a fine file or a hard Arkansas stone to remove the sharp edge.

If the left extractor does not move outward by pressure applied to the hook end, check the extractor spring to see if it is jammed between the extractor and the bolt body in the extractor spring hole. With coiling pliers, turn the last coil on each end of the spring in so the ends of the spring will not bind in the spring hole.

Check the firing pin for straightness and the tip for roundness and burrs. If all is well, install the firing pin and spring, the firing-pin stop pin going in from right to left. Make sure the rounded, polished end of the firing-pin stop pin is situated toward the right side of the breechblock.

Inspect the disassembled receiver for cracks, burrs and or other abnormalities. Flush the receiver out with cleaning solvent. and if you have compressed air, blow the receiver dry. If you notice an imprint in the rear of the breechblock, the action spring has become weak and should be replaced. This could also be caused by the improper setting of the recoil mechanism. If you don't have one, get a copy of the proper settings of the friction rings for the loads being used.

If the action-spring tube is cracked or broken, replace it. If it has been bent and then straightened, the tube should be reamed with a 0.413-inch (letter "Z") reamer so that the spring has no problem with drag. Check the inside top surface of the receiver for rub marks, shiny spots where the blueing has worn off. If noticeable lines exist, the link should be replaced.

The carrier latch can be checked with a straightedge along the side that faces the inside of the receiver. Make sure the carrier latch tip—the part that actually contacts the cartridge rim—has the right angle. There should be a $1/16$-inch gap at the hump on the carrier latch. The rear end of the carrier latch should always be left as it comes from the factory. In the event of extreme wear and rounding of the rear edges of the carrier latch, a very slight amount of metal can be removed to square it up.

But a word of caution here, excessive clearance between the carrier and the carrier latch will result in feed problems.

Stock and Forearm Repairs

Inspect the tang screw hole in the stock to see if it has become elliptical from recoil battering. If the hole has become excessively elongated, there is no recourse other than drilling it out with a $3/8$-inch bit, plugging with a hardwood dowel, and drilling a new tang screw hole.

You see quite a few of these shotguns with cracked forearm wood. If the crack is not excessively oil-soaked, it can be epoxied and clamped for repair. I've noticed A-5 stocks and forearms usually do not have any finish applied inside the forearm or in the cavity beneath the buttplate. This will usually cause the wood to absorb moisture, swell and crack. If this is the case, advise the owner of the potential.

Sporterizing Mauser 98 Rifles

A recent influx of Mauser 98 rifles creates several sporterizing possibilities. Here are some ideas.

By Dennis A. Wood

PETER PAUL and Wilhelm Mauser are two names that will live in history as far as firearms development and success are concerned. Peter Paul Mauser is given the bulk of the credit for his part in the development of the Mauser turnbolt rifle which was an adaptation of the Dreyse needle gun. The Mauser's main improvement was a firing mechanism that cocked itself automatically as the bolt was operated and used a firing pin instead of a firing needle for rear-ignition cartridges. Probably the most important event in Mauser history happened in April of 1898, when the German army adopted the Model 98 Mauser rifle. Within a short span of time, nations such as Turkey, China, Mexico, Serbia and several South American countries opted for the Mauser 98 rifle to equip their armies.

At the end of World War I, with the surrender of the German Army, many of these Model 98 Mausers found their way to the U.S. along with our returning soldiers. Now, more than 75 years later, we are seeing even more Model 98 Mausers coming into this country, imported by arms dealers who purchase the rifles from Third World armies that are now upgrading to more modern armament. Some of these can be real bargains and with some effort can be turned into very fine sporting rifles.

Any time you encounter one of these original Mausers, a thorough inspection should be done on the receiver, bolt and the inside of the barrel. Many of these surplus rifles I've had the chance to look over have had corrosive-primed ammunition fired through them, which ultimately results in the barrels being pitted to the point of ruin. The bolt faces on some will have a pitted ring around the firing pin hole from the steady diet of corrosive primed ammo and the lack of attention to cleaning. Original Mauser 98 rifles had all their parts identically serial numbered, but when the rifles were collected from the surrendering German army, many of the bolts were separated from the rifles. As a result, many of these surplus rifles come into the country with mismatched bolts, so always check for headspace and excessive setback of the locking lugs.

A surplus military receiver should also receive a Magnaflux magnetic particle inspection. When doing this, the receiver is placed between a north/south magnetic charging setup. A low current is sent through the receiver, aligning most of the receiver's molecules. The receiver is then bathed in a solution containing iron particles that find their way into any cracks or inclusions that may

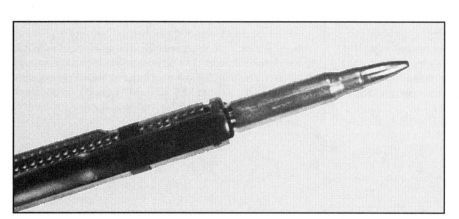

With controlled-round feeding, the extractor holds cartridges through chambering and firing.

Unaltered, the Mauser cartridge follower will not allow the bolt to go forward after the last round.

be present. Cracks or inclusions will show up as an interruption in the magnetic flow or position of the molecules and can be seen under a blacklight lamp. After the receiver has been magnetic particle inspected, it is then de-magnetized. It's better to find out if you have a bad receiver before any costly work is started rather than finding out afterward.

The barrel, if it is to be retained, should be inspected for rust, pits and throat wear. If the plan calls for rebarreling and chambering to a different caliber the barrel will most likely be discarded, but don't throw it in the junk barrel just yet. Remove the barreled action from the stock and take down the rifle until just the barreled action remains. To remove the barrel, a strong barrel vise is needed that clamps around the barrel tightly and will hold it without slippage. If there is no worry about marring the barrel, then a vise with serrated pipe jaws will surely hold the barrel tightly enough. A barrel wrench that fits around the receiver ring and recoil lug is the best choice of all the barrel wrenches available. There are in-line barrel wrenches available that fit into the rear of the action and the bolt raceways. The danger here lies in the possibility of twisting the action out of shape due to a stubborn barrel.

Most of these barrels have been on their actions for almost 60 years and may not want to part company very easily. A good soaking in penetrating oil for several days and the judicious use of heat from a propane torch will help in removing an extremely tight barrel. Use the heat from the propane torch to just warm up the action so the penetrating oil can permeate into the threads; we don't want to anneal the receiver ring. With the barrel clamped tightly in your barrel vise, slide the barrel wrench onto the receiver ring and recoil lug. A 3-foot section of black gas pipe added to the handle of the receiver wrench will help persuade even the most stubborn barrel to part company with the action. Hopefully, after a few days soaking in penetrating oil, the heat from the propane torch and the added muscle from the gas pipe on the barrel wrench handle, the barrel will separate from the action. If you ever run into an extremely

stubborn barrel, it can be sawed off about $1/4$-inch from the front of the receiver. Face off the barrel stub in your lathe to about $1/8$-inch from the front of the receiver and then bore out the barrel stub until you can pick the remaining barrel threads from the action threads. I've only had to do this once as a last resort for barrel removal.

There are mandrels available that will fit into the action and tighten up in the receiver threads. These mandrels have centers in each end for lathe or mill work once the barrel has been removed. With the mandrel in place and centered in the lathe, the front of the receiver can be faced off square to the centerline of the action. Using the mandrel in an indexing fixture and tailstock center in the mill, the outside of the action can be trued up and the ears of the cartridge charging guide on the receiver bridge removed.

Consider yourself fortunate if you've been lucky enough to find a 98 Mauser that has matching numbers on the receiver and the bolt. When these rifles were confiscated from the surrendering German infantry most all of the bolts were separated from the rifles and tossed into a pile. If you are rebarreling the action, a mismatched bolt will be no problem, as headspace will be set with the installation of the new barrel. Any rifle found to have a mismatched bolt but an original barrel should always be checked for headspace before any attempt to fire it. Before rebarreling, the locking lugs should be lapped in for 80- to 100-percent contact with the mating surfaces—100 percent is best. This is a must with a mismatched bolt prior to rebarreling. There are commercially available lapping tools for this job or one can be fashioned from the discarded barrel that was taken off, if it survived removal. The discarded barrel is cut off 3 inches from the thread shoulder. A brass plug is lathe-turned as closely as possible to the dimensions of a cartridge case for which the new barrel will be chambered. The brass plug need not have the neck of the case replicated; just make the plug like the case from the shoulder to the head, only 0.050-inch longer.

To disassemble the Mauser 98 bolt, place the safety in the halfway or straight up position, which will retain the striker in the

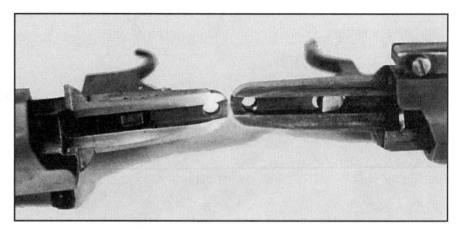

The action on the left has an altered bridge, tang and cutout for a new lower bolt handle. The action on the right has not been changed.

rearward position. Rotate the bolt shroud counterclockwise until it unthreads from the bolt body. Bolt extractor pliers are available for a tad more than $10 that makes extractor removal and reassembly a piece of cake on the Mauser bolt. The large claw extractor is a big part of the controlled-round feeding aspect of the Mauser 98 so popular with some hunters. This system was eventually copied on the pre-'64 Winchester, the latest version of the Model 70, the Ruger Model 77 and the new Savage Model 116 Safari Grade available in 458 Winchester Magnum. As a round is pushed forward from the magazine by the advancing bolt, the rim of the cartridge slips up and between the bolt face and the extractor hook, and is held there until it is chambered. After firing, it is then pulled backward and ejected when the left edge of the cartridge head hits the ejector. Controlled-round feeding is an important feature when other men are shooting back at you in a war, or you are hunting critters with big, long teeth.

The only disadvantage with the Model 98 as issued is, you cannot just drop a round on top of the follower and close the bolt. The big extractor hook will not snap around the case rim and into the case's extractor groove. It's too thick and protrudes too far to the left. This could mean trouble if your magazine is out of ammo and a large set of teeth is coming your way, but then again, they did issue bayonets with these rifles. Be careful not to bend the extractor collar out too far when removing it from the bolt. We don't want to distort the collar too badly or, worse yet, break it. We should now have just a bolt body that should be cleaned in a good parts cleaning solvent.

Since there is no barrel to put any pressure on the front of the bolt, we'll need a jig and the brass spud to create some. Turn the barrel stub, with the brass spud in the chamber, into the receiver until it puts pressure on the bolt face, creating some resistance when lifting the bolt handle. Remove the bolt and paint the inside faces of the locking lugs with a layout blue or a permanent black ink felt tip marker. Replace the bolt and work it as though you were chambering a round. Remove the bolt and check those inside lug faces for the amount of dye removal. The chances for completely even dye removal are about as good as winning your state lottery. Most likely there will be removal of the dye more on one lug than the other. Place a dab of 320 grit carborundum paste on the inside face of each lug and re-insert the bolt into the action. Work the bolt up and down

several times and once again check the inside faces for bearing amount. Continue this procedure until the desired 80 to 100 percent contact is achieved, all the while maintaining pressure on the bolt face from the brass plug. This lug lapping procedure should never be done on a barreled action. It will increase headspace to a potentially dangerous condition, allowing a cartridge to possibly separate at the head and damage the rifle or the shooter. Once you reach the desired amount of locking lug contact, clean out the bolt body and the inside of the action with a good parts-cleaning solvent to remove all of the lapping grit. Any lapping compound left inside will continue to work on the internal parts, and we don't need that.

Once the bolt shroud has been turned free of the bolt body, it's a simple matter to disassemble the cocking piece and firing pin from the bolt shroud. There is a slight shoulder at the point where the firing pin flares just in front of the firing-pin spring. With this shoulder resting on top of your protected-jaws-equipped vise, push down on the bolt shroud until the cocking piece can be rotated and then removed. Slowly relax the tension from the firing-pin spring on the bolt shroud, letting it come up. Slip the bolt shroud off of the firing pin and remove the spring. Check the firing pin for straightness and any deformities and replace it if necessary. Wolff Precision Springs has extra-strength firing-pin springs available that will increase the firing-pin speed and increase lock time, if so desired.

Bolt handles on Mausers protrude straight out to the right or are bent down, depending on the version you have. Whichever the case, neither bolt handle will clear a low-mounted scope if the plan calls for optical sights. The bolt handle lift angle will need to be lowered to keep the bolt handle from bumping into the scope's eyepiece. All styles of replacement bolt handles are available, from simple $7 pieces to $100 engraved or checkered types.

The old bolt handle can be easily cut off with a 1-inch abrasive wheel mounted on a shaft in your Moto-Tool. Make sure safety glasses are employed when using these little cutoff wheels. There are also jigs available that will hold the bolt body at any desired angle for welding the replacement handle in place. Set up the bolt-holding welding jig so that the locking lugs are at a 35-degree angle from the bottom of the jig. If you are using an oxyacetylene welding outfit to bond the new bolt handle in place, use a gizmo called a "heat sink" that fits inside the rear of the bolt to draw heat from the torch out the back of the bolt. This deters the heat from travel-

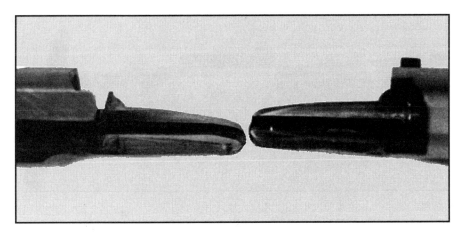

Altering the tang eliminates having to put a groove in the wrist of your replacement stock. The receiver bridge has also had the charging guide ears removed.

ing up toward the locking lugs and also helps to prevent carbonizing on the inside of the bolt body. A heat-stopping paste, liberally applied to the locking lugs and at least 2 inches rearward from the locking lugs, will also help protect them from annealing. A filler rod of 4130, 4140 or 4150 composition will blend well with the new bolt handle and should match in color when blueing. If you have access to one, a MIG or TIG outfit is a better option when welding. Heat from these welding systems is more concentrated around the weld and does not travel like an oxy setup will. The MIG and TIG welding outfits can also be used with a shielding gas like argon that helps contain the heat and makes for a much smoother filling weld.

When the replacement bolt handle has cooled, it can be ground or milled to shape. The bolt can also be set up in the lathe and its sides turned to the final width. The bolt handle area should then be inspected for any voids the weld did not fill. Set up the bolt body in your mill with the locking lugs at a 35-degree angle and mill a flat on the inside bottom of the bolt handle that will rest against the action. A milling cut in the receiver, 0.470-inch wide from the back face of the receiver bridge, 0.315-inch deep at a 55-degree angle to the bottom face of the receiver, will provide the new resting place for the bolt handle and give plenty of clearance for even the lowest mounted scope.

The cartridge follower on original, unaltered Mauser military rifles will not let the bolt continue forward once the magazine has been emptied. Done by design to let the soldier know that he was out of ammo in the heat of battle, this is easily overcome when sporterizing by grinding a bevel on the left rear of the cartridge follower at a 30-degree angle and polishing to the desired finish. This will allow the bolt to ride over the rear of the follower and push it down for bolt closure.

Let's assume by now you have had a new barrel in your choice of caliber installed and properly headspaced, the new bolt handle has been attached and fitted, and that you've beveled the rear of the follower so the bolt will close when the magazine is emptied. If you want to stick with the original two-stage trigger issued on the Mauser and adapt it, I would suggest you read *Gunsmithing* by Roy Dunlap, or *Modern Gunsmithing* by Stan Baker. These two gents describe all the pitfalls involved with trying to turn this sow's ear into a silk purse.

Fully-adjustable aftermarket triggers available from Timney, M. H. Canjar, Dayton-Traister and Ted Blackburn are miracles in steel, and better options than messing with the original. Replacing the original is an opportunity to add another utilitarian touch that also adds to the cosmetic appearance of the Model 98-turned-sporter. The top of the bolt stop/release is filed, milled or ground flat, removing the tiny nub and smoothing the top surface. A replacement, such as an oval piece of cold rolled steel stock, is fashioned, then silver soldered onto the top of the bolt stop/release. Before silver soldering, disassemble the bolt release completely. We do not want to remove the temper in the spring that makes the bolt release operate. The top of the replacement piece of steel can then be serrated or checkered for a better purchase.

In its original state, the rear tang of the Model 98 action has quite a deep groove milled into it for the cocking piece on the bolt to ride in. If left in this condition, a replacement stock will need to have the groove continued into the top of the wrist for bolt removal. The top of the tang can be tapered down with a file until the top of the tang is blended with the upper rear edge of the cocking piece groove. With this added touch there is no need to continue the groove into the top of the wrist, which looks ugly anyway. Tang dress-up can be carried one step further by turning the rear action-screw hole into a blind hole. This can be done with a $^3/_8$-diameter cold rolled steel plug that has been welded in place. You'll need a tool bit that has had the left-facing cutting edge ground to a 45-degree angle. Place a $^3/_8$-inch diameter rod in your lathe chuck with about $^3/_4$-inch protruding from the jaws, and face that end off square. Turn the protruding diameter down to about 0.214-inch in diameter with a length of 0.150-inch. The 0.214-diameter may vary up or down a few thousandths of an inch. What you want to end up with is a slip fit into the rear action through threads that are in there now. The 0.150-inch length may also vary a little. This end of the plug fits into the through hole also but should be short by at least one of the threads from the bottom of the cocking piece groove. Once you have achieved the slip fit of the plug into the rear action-screw hole, remove the plug from the chuck and hacksaw the length to $^3/_4$-inch overall. Place the plug into the chuck once again with the rough sawn face out. Face this end of the plug off until you have an overall length of $^5/_8$-inch. Place a drill chuck in your tailstock and centerdrill the end of the plug.

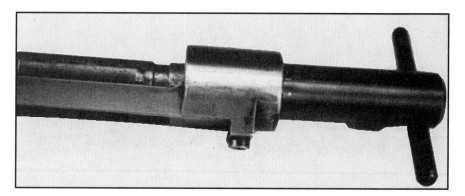

Before rebarreling, the locking lugs should be lapped to achieve 80 to 100 percent contact. Do not use a lug lapping tool (shown here) on a barreled action.

Replace the center drill with a number 5 drill bit and drill to a depth of $^1/_2$-inch. Replace the number 5 drill bit with a $^1/_4$ X 22 plug tap and thoroughly coat it with a good cutting oil. Loosen the hold-down nut on your tailstock and push the tailstock toward the hole drilled into the end of the plug. Turn the lathe chuck manually while feeding the tap into the hole. Once the tap starts to cut, continue turning the chuck by hand until you have cut five or six threads. Loosen the drill chuck in the tailstock from the tap and back it off. Loosen the lathe chuck and remove the plug with the tap still in it. Place the plug in your vise and, with a tap handle on the tap, back it out. Replace the plug tap with a bottom tap and finish cutting the threads to full depth, using plenty of cutting oil. Clean off the tang area top and bottom with a bluing and rust remover. Blueing is an oxidation and will not allow the weld to get a good hold, so it needs to be removed.

Clamp the plug in place, making sure it is straight, up and down and sideways. Tack weld the seam at the 45-degree chamfer at the bottom of the tang, and remove the clamp. Fill in the hole on the top of the tang with filler rod, using enough to ensure a good fill. Once again, use 4130, 4140 or 4150 filler rod. Fill in around the seam at the 45-degree angle on the plug and the bottom of the tang hole. Once the welded area has cooled down, the cocking-piece groove can be opened up once again in the milling machine or with hand files, and the weld around the plug seam at the bottom of the tang smoothed with files. Besides looking kind of nifty, this blind action screw hole has almost twice the thread as the old hole, affording more holding strength. The now blind top of the tang will prevent moisture from rain or snow rusting the screw in place, and acts as an extra assist for the recoil lug. This treatment works not only for the 98 Mauser but 700 series Remington rifles as well. The differences are in the tapped hole size and number of threads per inch, and a slight variation in the length of the plug going into the rear action hole.

There are replacement stocks available for the Mauser Model 98 in just about every style, shape and wood type this planet has to offer. Composite stocks are also available for the 98. Be careful if you think you can get a true drop-in stock, however. As sure as you shoot, if it will just drop in, the fit will be poor with too much surrounding play. Be prepared to do a glassing job of the barreled action to the composite stock. I've hunted in northern Wisconsin with a composite stock in temperatures down in the single digits and lower. A composite stock will remain stable and will probably never warp, but it just does not have the insulating qualities against the cold like wood does. It won't keep the cold from the barrel and action from transmitting through to your hands.

The installation of sling swivels and recoil pads have been covered elsewhere in this volume, so there's nothing that can be added here. The bottom metal (trigger guard and floorplate) on the issue Mauser Model 98 leaves much to be desired in terms of easy access when unloading a full magazine of ammo. Most likely, the inventors' intentions were to keep the floorplate from inadvertently dropping open and spilling rounds in the field. In battle conditions, these rifles were no doubt kept loaded anyway. When sporterized, an easily accessible dropping floorplate is much handier for unloading. There are replacement computer-numerical-control-machined one-piece trigger guards with magazine boxes and straddle floorplates made of steel that will do quite nicely on the sporter. The cost of these setups will set you back almost a week's pay, but add to the looks and value of the finished rifle.

Whichever blueing choice is made, after the new finish has been applied, the bolt raceways should be polished with 600-grit wet-or-dry paper. The blueing will wear off in these areas anyway, so just keep a thin coat of light oil here and the bolt will operate smoothly. There are commercially available polishing mandrels for this procedure, but a piece of hardwood, like maple, will get you through this step just as well. Polishing the cartridge-feed ramp with fine grit Cratex bullet-shaped rubber polishing points in your Moto-Tool will help a soft-nose bullet find its way into the chamber without deformation.

Any and all of these procedures can be done by a budget-minded owner in stages as funds allow.

Correcting a Bad Muzzle Crown

If you are having accuracy problems, a bad muzzle crown might be the cause. Fixing it is no big mystery.

By Dennis A. Wood

"WHAT'S WRONG WITH my rifle?" Have you ever had somebody ask you this immediately after you've answered the phone?

It's often hard to resist suggesting that the nut at the back of the stock might be a part of the problem, but I try not to do it. The more logical reply, and one more inclined to foster good public relations, is usually an attempt to analyze the problem over the phone. That's a feat normally restricted to those who can walk on water, so I end the conversation by suggesting the gun owner bring the offending firearm in to let me see what could be wrong.

Determining why a rifle that shot 1-inch groups the last time it was used to punch in paper won't hit a barn from the inside now, requires the step-by-step elimination of potential problems. A talk with the owner may help find out what happened after the accuracy and before the disaster. Were different handloads used this time around? Was the gun caught in rain or snow the last time out? When was the last time the barrel was completely cleaned of bullet jacket or lead fouling? Are the scope or sight mounting systems secured tightly to the action? Has the firearm been dropped onto a surface that might affect any of the above? In other words, find out whatever the owner can recollect to help you get the problem solved. If they just don't know or can't remember, then you'll need to individually go through the following investigative procedures. We'll assume there was no drastic change in the ammunition like different bullet weights or handloads, so this was not the cause of erratic grouping. The use of different lot numbers of factory ammunition, powder, primers or bullets may produce different groups, but nothing like we found in this instance.

The sighting system should be checked for tightness. Scope base screws can be a hair-pulling problem if found to be loose, as can open-sight base screws. If this condition exists, the mounting screws should be cleaned with a good oil-displacing solvent. A drop of thread sealer applied to each screw will help keep the adverse effects of vibration down to a minimum. Once the base screws have been turned down as far as they will go, keep the screwdriver in the slot and lightly tap its end with a small hammer. This will seat the threads of the base screws a tad deeper. As you tap on the end of the screwdriver, continue to turn the handle. You may get another $1/16$-turn of seating depth.

The action and barrel bedding, along with the proper torque of the action screws, should not be overlooked as part of this inspection. Even though the action may be glass bedded, the action screws can cause compression of the underlying wood fibers if they have been overly tightened. This compression will cause the barrel to bend slightly upward, playing hell with accuracy as the barrel heats up and expands slightly. This is a good case for using aluminum or nylon sleeves around the action screws, sometimes referred to as pillar bedding. These pillars or sleeves will not allow the wood fibers to become compressed, therefore preserving the bedding.

The forend barrel channel should also be looked over for any offending bearing points that may change bullet impact as the barrel heats up and expands. The absence of finish inside the barrel channel will most assuredly allow the wood there to warp a little bit as humidity levels rise and fall. It's certainly an invitation to trouble after the gun has been exposed to wet conditions during a hunting outing. This could cause pressure to be exerted against the barrel on either side of the channel if the forend warps after drying, something not conducive to the best accuracy. If you find a warped forend, the only thing you can do is scrape the barrel channel until the offending pressure spot is removed. I've also encountered forend wood that had a propensity to warp no matter what was tried. In those instances, about the only thing that worked was creating several channels—usually four—running the length of the forend. These channels, made with a V-gouge, were cut to a depth of $1/4$- to $3/8$-inch and filled with epoxy. That cured forend warping.

Thoroughly inspecting the bore's lands and grooves will reveal any buildup of bullet jacket material or lead. This neglect of cleanliness will eventually contribute to poor accuracy.

In the situation we're addressing here, the gun owner thorough-

Setup for a barrel in the adjustable-jaw chuck. The ¼-inch radius tool will form a standard factory crown. With a different tool bit and the tool post turned, a recessed or target-style crown can be applied.

ly soaked the bore with Shooter's Choice solvent and hung the rifle from a basement ceiling rafter to let the solvent drain onto old newspaper spread out on the cement floor. That wouldn't ordinarily be a problem but he wrapped a string around the wrist of the stock and tied it to the rafter, and it broke. The rifle fell straight down and landed full weight on the muzzle.

The owner didn't notice a burr at the very edge of the rifling on the muzzle that was caused by the fall, but he certainly noticed a marked loss of accuracy. The burr tore a groove in each bullet that passed over it, upsetting the bullet's gyroscopic stability once it left the bore. A more severe burr may even cause a bullet to yaw or tumble enough to keyhole on target impact.

I realize that we've taken a somewhat circuitous route getting to the subject, but that's sometimes what it takes when analyzing accuracy problems. The obvious answer doesn't always reach out and grab you.

Of several ways to crown a muzzle, the most obvious is to remove the barrel and set it up in a lathe chuck to true up the muzzle once again. This necessitates the use of a chuck with individually adjustable jaws. When chucking on the outside diameter of the barrel, allow only as much of the barrel to protrude beyond the jaws as you can safely reach with your cutting tools. A dial indicator

with the indicator point on top of the lands in the bottom of the barrel will give you a reading of the amount of muzzle run-out. The outside of a rifle barrel seldom if ever runs true to the bore. In the polishing process prior to blueing, the metal on the outside of the barrel is moved around and some removed to the point that there will be run-out. Rotate the lathe chuck, turning it by hand, and watch the dial indicator. This is where the adjustable jaw chuck justifies its purchase price. Adjust the jaws so the indicator shows the least amount of movement possible. If you end up with zero movement, so much the better. Try for no more than 0.0005-inch (five ten-thousandths). Once you have removed as much run-out as you can, face off the end of the barrel until the burr or dent is completely gone. Removing just ten thousandths of an inch of metal on each move, you'll be rid of even the nastiest of burrs in three passes. The rifling is susceptible to getting beat up again if the muzzle is left flat, so some means of recessing the rifling is the next step.

The most commonly seen form of crown is the radiused style, which is standard on most factory sporter-weight barrels. High speed steel or carbide tool bits are available with radii ground specifically for this chore. Prices for the high speed steel tool bits start at about $10. Carbide bits cost quite a bit more but will last a long time if you don't drop them. (They shatter quite easily.) If you are so inclined, it is simple to make up your own bit using whatever size tool blank fits your need. Dress a shafted stone to the desired diameter—a .250-inch radius is most common—in your Moto-Tool. Grind this radius into the chosen-size bit, keeping in mind that you do not want to get this tool too hot and anneal it. Quench it in cold water every now and again to avoid the heat buildup.

The flat recessed style of crown is most commonly found on target rifle barrels and on many manufacturers' varmint-weight barrels. After the muzzle is faced off flat, the outside edge of the barrel is chamfered and metal is faced off from the bore out toward the chamfer on the outside edge, stopping about $1/16$-inch short of the chamfer.

Lately, we've seen some crowns with a conical shape of 10 to 11 degrees that progresses from the outside edge of the barrel inward to the bore, much like a countersink tool would cut. When all is said and done, as long as the crown works, it doesn't really matter what style is used. The purpose is only to protect the rifling at the bore from damage, so pick the style that looks best to you and go with it.

If a metal lathe is not at your disposal, the job can still be accomplished with some specialty tools produced just for this task. Brownells offers handle-turned piloted cutters that will crown a muzzle and achieve the intended purpose. Hardened steel pilots are available for all common bore diameters. These pilots fit inside four fluted cutters that will face off the muzzle at 90 degrees to the bore line until whatever burr that might be present is removed. An aluminum T-handle that threads onto the stud at the back end of the cutter helps maintain pressure and control. Eight fluted recessing cutters at 11 or 45 degrees will get you through this stage of crown-

ing. Liberally dousing the pilot and cutter with a good coating of cutting oil throughout the process will extend the cutter's life by reducing abrasive friction and heat. When using one of these hand-turned cutters, keep it turning in a clockwise direction, backing it out to remove chips and oiling often until the desired depth of recess is achieved. Avoid running it backwards.

Hand-turned crowning tools will save you time in those instances where a lathe setup would prove impractical. You may not have a barrel-removal wrench or vise jaws for a particular barrel contour or you may just plain need to get the job done quickly. This is where the hand-turned tool will shine, and it certainly will do a reputable enough job. Getting the outside chamfer on the barrel is the only drawback I've encountered with the hand-turned crowning tools. This can be accomplished with a smooth-cut file if you have a steady hand. Wrap a strip of masking tape around the barrel about $1/16$-inch back from the edge of the front so the ends of the tape overlap. Carefully file up to the edge of the tape, striving to maintain a 45-degree angle.

Shotgun muzzles occasionally get dinged up to the point that the end of the barrel is no longer square to the bore line, which may be cause for cutting the barrel shorter than its original length. There are hand cutting tools available for this task as well, along with bore pilots for the gauges involved. All the lubrication and clockwise cutting instructions that apply to rifle or handgun muzzles are equally important here.

Barrel crowning is no big mystery. When done properly, many rifles will actually shoot better than they did before the job was performed because you have sharp, crisp rifling at the last point the bullet contacts before free flight.

If you don't have a lathe, piloted hand cutting tools can be used to repair a damaged muzzle. When using these, make sure you keep them turning in a clockwise direction.

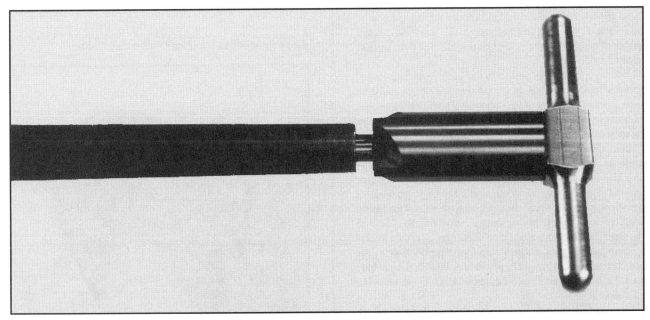

Installing Recoil Pads

A recoil pad is almost a necessity on today's long guns. Done right, it can also add to the gun's aesthetics. Done wrong, you will regret it.

By Chip Todd

NOWHERE IN THE shooting world will you find a more popular or universally used accessory than the recoil pad. It is used for both altering the pull of the stock and for helping to reduce recoil. These applications make rifles and shotguns more pleasant to shoot, especially for long shooting sessions. Do you think the large number of people who prefer long guns would like them quite so much without a pad?

I find the installation of pads to be one of the most frequent and profitable jobs in my shop. As a result, I advise any aspiring gunsmith to learn the basics of the project. It's a service the average gun store cannot do in-house, so you will encounter lots of guns that need recoil pads.

Understanding that it takes a predictable amount of energy to accelerate a given mass at a given rate, and accepting that Newton's laws are absolute, nothing can reduce the rearward energy from the gun. A pad can, however, store that energy and release it over a longer period of time, thereby giving the shooter the feeling of less recoil. This is like having someone strike your shoulder with a hammer (instantaneous application of energy), compared to having them push on your shoulder for a longer period of time. The same amount of energy might be absorbed by your shoulder in both cases, but it doesn't take much thought to decide which would be less desirable.

The term "recoil pad" used to refer to ventilated pads which were very soft, while "buttpad" referred to solid pads used mostly on rifles of lesser recoil. Now there are some space-age materials that are solid, but still capable of absorbing recoil and releasing it in a sinusoidal fashion. You cannot eliminate the rearward thrust of a firearm; just distribute it over a greater area and/or apply it over a broader period of time. By sinusoidal motion, I refer to applying the total force in a thrust starting from zero and accelerating to a peak, and then reducing in a decelerating fashion.

Despite the widespread usage of pads, it is often hard to find a shop that does a truly professional job of fitting a firearm to the shooter and installing a recoil pad. The fit, shape, and cosmetic considerations (or lack thereof) of most installations results in a poor function and a lack of aesthetics. This needn't be the case, as a few basic instructions are all most gunsmiths need to properly do a pad installation.

The shape of the pad's rear face is important, as it determines whether the buttpad gets hung up under the shooter's armpit or drags on his clothing. There are rear-face shapes ranging from straight up and down to ones that have a large vertical radius. I usually go by the categories supplied with the manufacturer's literature. Some of the more popular shapes are known as rifle, Skeet, trap, magnum, benchrest, and slip-on, the latter being a sock-like unit which is stretched over the butt end of the stock.

The slip-ons require no gunsmithing and are handy for guns that might be used by several shooters with arms of different lengths. These are produced with a sort of "catch-all" taper meant to fit most stocks. I don't see many of these now, but at one time they were very popular. That was back in a more utilitarian era of shooting.

A screw opening cut without detergent lubrication still hides from sight when released, but lubing it makes the job easier.

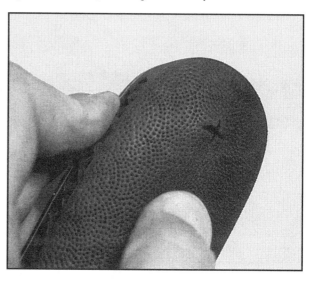

A recoil pad must be chosen based on style, face size, and thickness. The thickness depends upon how well the stock fits the shooter—pull being the consideration. The pull of a stock is the distance from the butt of the stock to the location of the trigger. The pull for most people is generally measured by holding the firearm with the shooting hand around the grip and with the trigger finger in position to fire the gun. The buttstock is then placed along the forearm with the butt end against the bicep muscle when the upper-arm is down and 90 degrees from the forearm. The gun should feel comfortable to the shooting hand and be lightly touching the lower bicep. This measurement determines whether or not the stock will feel natural to the shooter. Such a feel is essential to the accuracy of the shooter/firearm combination, and is frequently overlooked because of not being fully understood.

Too long a pull will cause the shooter to extend his trigger hand forward enough to cause a strain on the shoulder and upper arm muscles. If it is too short, the shooter will feel cramped, as it puts the upper arm too far backward for comfort and pulls on the tricep and deltoid muscles. From the standpoint of function, a pull too long for the shooter will often cause the butt to get caught under the armpit when rapidly raising the firearm for a shot. If it is too short, it may result in placing the butt too high on the shoulder when the gun is raised. Either condition gives the shooter a feeling of limited control of his gun.

With this in mind, choosing the proper pad for the situation involves deciding if the length or thickness of the pad is a consideration. If the stock is deemed too short, then thickness will be the first consideration. You may have to cut some off of a stock which is too short in order to install a recoil pad with enough thickness to properly reshape the energy curve of the recoil. Pads are easily found in fractional-inch increments, from the thin rifle sizes of $1/2$-inch to magnum dimensions of $1^1/_2$ inches.

Materials used for pads range from the super energy-absorbent materials, such as Sorbothane, to neoprene or red rubber. Several manufacturers use catchy names to describe their version of modern materials, Pachmayr's "Decelerator" pad being one of those. These new materials last longer than the natural rubber variations,

since they do not oxidize, crumble, or crack. Neoprene has proven itself over the years, and is the main material used in recoil pad production. One decided advantage of neoprene is its ability to be produced in many colors and in just about any degree of hardness, although the overall softness of the pad is controlled mainly by the structure of the webbing and reliefs in the sidewalls.

Construction of the pad is instrumental in its looks and performance, because webbing, or the lack of it, plays an important role in how the pad is perceived by the customer or shooter. Webbing can also determine how the pad functions, as the percentage of open space and the angle of the webs act like using a softer material in some cases and can duplicate compound-durometer construction in others.

The most popular webbing is a cross or "X" configuration. This is much more aesthetically pleasing than the application of a purely scientific design. Some of the newer elastomers are paired up to give a complex force curve. Harder shapes are molded within a softer exterior shape to achieve a progressive nature to the recoil resistance. This is an involved method of obtaining what could more easily be duplicated with good webbing design.

Those who prefer a pad with smooth, solid sides should try the ones which depend more heavily upon the material and less on the design. There's a lot to be said for a design which won't pick up dirt or dust in its crevices. Included in this category are rifle pads which are used solely for their beauty and traction surface. These are usually made of neoprene and are shaped to present a slightly rounded profile with nice smooth radii to enhance comfort.

There are pads, like the 990 Magnum pads from Pachmayr, that are so soft and retain memory so well that they require a pin be installed in the gun cabinet lest they take a set where they have been resting. The accompanying photo shows the Pachmayr 990 Magnum pad with its rest pin. This is a bit of a nuisance, but definitely worth the extra trouble on large-caliber guns.

Rear surfaces are as varied as the styles of pads. The selections include screen, leather grain, pebbled, ribbed, basketweave, stippled, line checkered, smooth, grooved, and boldest of all, the pigeon. The basketweave and the pigeon patterns are the most

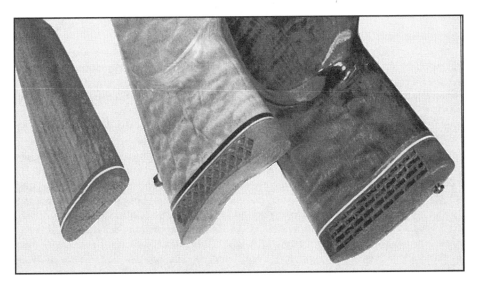

The type of rifle will often determine the type pad you want. From the left: a carbine stock with rifle-type pad, a standard recoil pad on a light rifle, and a Pachmayr 990 Magnum pad with pin. The pin keeps the pad from adopting a shape other than your shoulder's.

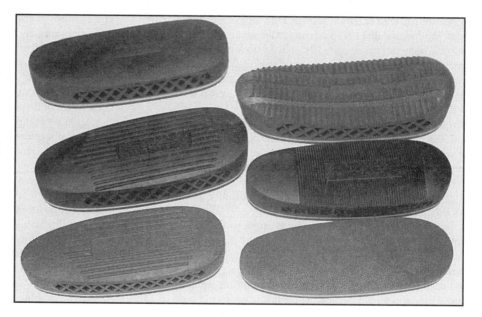

The surface style you want depends on the shooting you'll be doing. Among the more popular are pigeon, lined, checkered, spacer, ribbed, and stippled.

effective against slippage, but in some cases there can be too much drag to allow a good performance. The direction of the "file tooth" pattern, which distinguishes the pigeon from the others, is such that the grip of the pad is much greater against a downward force than it is against the upward drag. This aids in getting the gun up to the shoulder faster while reducing downward slippage. The basketweave is very busy, yet must have a good following as it is offered year after year.

While pads can be colored at will, most styles are offered in black, red, and brown. Opinions vary on which color goes best with which wood and are no less subjective than the choice of what color shirt one should wear. The gunsmith, or shooter, must also choose whether or not to use a pad with white and black laminations between the pad and the stock. This white outline motif lends a professional quality to the pad and shouldn't be overlooked when selecting a pad. Of course, this is only an opinion. More utilitarian, the Jenkins pad comes in green, presumably for camouflage reasons.

Choosing the correct pad with which to start is more important than you may think. If it is too large, you may have to grind down to the metal stiffener inside, which will ruin the pad. If it is not long enough to allow the continuation of the stock's bottom line, the job will look amateurish without anyone really being able to say why. When you are making a new stock, you have some flexibility that isn't there when installing a pad on a finished firearm. Unfortunately, most of your jobs will be on finished stocks unless you specialize in stockmaking. The length seems to be more of a problem than the width, as the width isn't dealing with a skewed angle.

I choose pad shape and thickness first, the degree of energy absorption second, and the color and surface texture last. Before choosing the color and texture, one should decide which is more important, function or aesthetics. If the answer is function, then the choice is a little easier. The pad needs to address how quickly the firearm might be moved up and how firmly it needs to grip the

shoulder. Texture and shape would be the most important considerations in this case.

If the shooter leans toward aesthetics, you should determine whether he wants the pad to draw the eye or remain subtly in the background. A basketweave texture will certainly grab your eye, but would detract from an otherwise eye-catching piece of wood. I prefer to put my money into interesting wood, so I usually take a low-key approach to my recoil pads.

The proper angle for the buttface is the single most important decision you, as the gunsmith, will have to make. You need to question the owner to see if he has noticed an excess of recoil, especially a blow to the cheek. This upward blow to the cheek is caused by the face of the butt being angled in at the bottom. The way to predict how the stock will act is to stand the butt on end with the barrel pointing upward. If the barrel leans toward the trigger guard, you can be sure that it will kick up into the cheek. This is often not discerned as a cheek blow, but just an extra hard kick. In most cases, you will want to have the barrel pointing straight upward when the butt face is flat on the ground.

If the barrel doesn't point straight up in this test, you may need to cut the butt face perpendicular to the bore. To mark the butt, position the gun with the barrel pointing straight up and mark the stock parallel to the ground. I mark both sides, but that isn't necessary if you are going to use a table saw or band saw.

Positioning the stock in a horizontal attitude during the cutting process will not be all that is needed to get the butt square. You'll also need to check the holding setup to see that the barrel is perpendicular to the saw blade's line of cut. A large square will be helpful but not essential, as the cut can be within several degrees either way and not be noticeably off. You just need to be close and have the stock firmly held during the cutting. This can be done with clamps and blocks of wood, firm sandbags, or a table vise, depending upon what kind of saw you have available. I use a table saw, although I would prefer a radial-arm saw for this purpose. With

The type of recoil also helps determine the pad used. If the barrel is vertical, it indicates a zero buttface angle, if it cants at an angle, your shooter will get a nice cheek blow on recoil.

limited space, I opted for a table saw and have made an adjustable cradle with which to hold stocks for cutting. The cradle has slides that fit into the miter grooves in the table, allowing me to make cut after cut in a controlled manner. It isn't worth this if you are only doing an occasional stock job. I feel the same way about the stock grinding jigs, and have never bought one. I don't find it very difficult to grind off the excess pad material in a freehand manner, but a lot depends on your hand/eye coordination.

I also recommend using a saw blade with as many teeth as possible and with some set to the teeth. A blade without set can give a smooth cut, but it can also very easily burn the wood and will pick up oil and sap, causing drag. I would stay away from blade dressings such as silicone-based products as they quite often cause world-class painting headaches. Sherwin-Williams "Sur-WilClean" or an oven cleaner will take burned-on sap off blades—oven cleaner being the last resort.

If band sawing the butt end, use a good guide as band sawing is an inexact science at best. A clamp with an edge that can be guided by a fence or straightedge, along with a slow feed rate, will help smooth out the jiggling of the blade. Use a skip-tooth blade if you have one, as they run cooler.

The screws that come with Pachmayr pads are certainly adequate for the job, but I prefer type AB threads over theirs. ABs hold better without as much damage to the wood or as much splitting force. Some pads come with countersunk-type heads. They should

not be used, in my opinion. The pads usually have flat surfaces inside, and even if they have countersunk seats for the screws, the wedging force of the head will distort the mating surface and cause an unsightly gap. I prefer Phillips-head screws for this application, only because the shanks of Phillips screwdrivers are almost always round. A square shank, or a shank which is not clean and smooth, will do irreparable damage to the pad. A good-fitting blade is also a necessity, as damaging the Phillips recess will probably cause you to destroy the pad to get the screw out. I haven't had this happen yet, but have come close to having to do this on some guns brought in to me.

One of the first questions asked by owners bringing pads to be installed, is, "How do you get the screws in?" Good pads have no entrance holes for the screws; it is better for the installer to cut his own holes and be responsible for the neatness. The pad will have a hollow space for the screw head molded into it above the screw hole found on the back face. To get nice, hidden holes in the pad's outside face, you need to locate where to cut the openings. This is done by inserting a pin punch or pointed awl into the screw hole and pushing lightly until you can see a bump in the outer face of the pad. An X-Acto knife blade is then pushed straight down on top of the bump and into the pad until you can feel it strike the sides of the screw hole. It is advisable to lubricate the blade with a dishwashing detergent in order to get the cleanest cut possible. Don't use oil, grease, or other petroleum derivatives, as they can cause damage to some pads and will stain clothes.

Removing the blade, spread the pad's surface and reinsert the blade 180 degrees, pushing in until you strike the other side of the screw hole. Re-soap the blade and repeat the procedure to get an "X" cut. When the blade is removed and the pad rinsed, the cuts will close up and be virtually invisible. The photo shows a pad which was cut without lube, and even this will be invisible when relaxed. Never put anything into this "X" hole without lubricating it first with a liquid detergent. It only takes once to make the hole look bad.

Another way to make a screw entrance hole is to use a core punch to cut a round hole. While this can be done neatly, it will show and won't be as professional in appearance as the "X" cut method.

When locating the pad on the butt, it is essential that you have it low enough for the line of the butt's bottom to continue along straight to the pad's tip. (A broken, non-continuous line is the best way to advertise "Amateur Gunsmith.") Notice the bottom line of a good stock/pad installation and you will see this continuation.

A good method for transferring the locations of the holes in the pad to the butt is to use a transfer punch. This tool is made of a rod with a small point in the middle of one end that just fits through the holes in the pad. The transfer punch should be lubed with detergent and inserted through the "X" cut and almost through the hole in the pad. The pad should be held in the correct position on the butt and the punch struck sharply with a hammer. Then drill a suitable pilot hole in the location marked with the punch for the first screw. It's very important to be sure that the holes are drilled perpendicular to the butt face. If the butt face is concave, keep the drill in a radial attitude to the curvature. You will want the screw head to seat flatly onto the pad's inner surface, even though it won't show. Other-

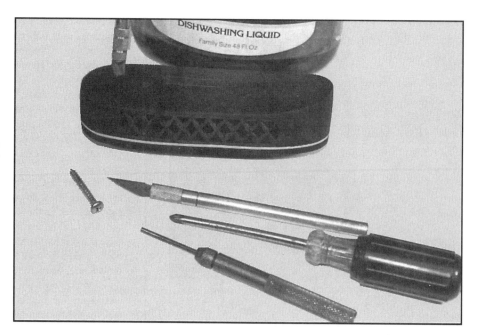

To "X" cut a pad, you'll need a Phillips-head screwdriver, Number 11 X-Acto blade, transfer pin punch, and a pad screw.

wise it will create a gap between the pad and the butt surface.

Lube the screw with detergent and insert it into the pad completely. Also lube and insert the smooth-shanked Phillips screwdriver, and drive the pad's screw into the stock. Align the pad and tighten the screw until the pad is held in place firmly. Use the transfer punch again to mark the other hole's location and loosen the first screw. Rotate the pad out of the way and drill the second pilot hole before adding the other screw.

Locating the pilot holes can be done with a ruler and pencil, but it is easier to make a miscalculation and have to redrill and dowel up a misplaced hole. I have done it both ways, depending upon my mood at the time. Either way, always be sure that the shank of the screwdriver is round and lubed or you will defeat the purpose of the "X" cut.

In the case of a stock like that of the Mini-14, which has an oddly shaped buttplate, the odd inset area can be filled with a thin piece of wood which has been wet and curved to fit. You may be lucky enough to need to cut that portion of stock off for the pad, but don't count on it. The Mini-14 comes with quite a short stock. As an alternative, you could cut the metal piece, leaving it to cover up the odd place in the wood, or cut a piece of black plastic (which would go well with the black and white laminations of the pad) and use that to fill the top of the butt end.

After the pad has been tightened down, mark around its underside with a sharp scribe or a razor-thin piece of white chalk. If you use a scribe, wipe some chalk into the scratch to make it more visible. Then remove the pad, which is now ready for some roughing-out.

If you have a disk grinder stand with a table, this will be the easiest way to rough-cut the perimeter of the pad close to the scribed line. A belt sander runs a close second. I cut pads with a car-body grinder for many years before I was lucky enough to find a large disk grinder stand. Grind, but leave about $1/16$-inch outside the scribed mark so there will be enough for the final grinding operation on the stock.

With this rough grinding done, reinstall, using all the basic precautions, and align the pad as you secure it. How the final grinding and fitting is done depends on whether the stock is finished or unfinished wood. The finished stock will be much harder to do than the raw stock, so I'll concentrate on that.

Using $3/4$-inch masking tape, carefully tape around the pad, covering up the finish on the stock and making sure the tape is right up against the pad's undersurface. Stretch the tape tightly, making certain all wrinkles are out. A wider tape may be substituted, but it will be harder to get it to lay smoothly all the way around.

I would suggest some type of hand-held device for the finish grinding, but it can be done on a disk or belt sander. I use a 9-inch body grinder with a 36-grit disk. This may sound pretty coarse, but the grit depends on your experience with body grinders. Grits finer than 80 or 100 work you too much and tend to pull the pad's edges out of shape, although I like the finer grits for the last little bit of smoothing up.

When grinding the pad with a disk, make sure the disk's surface is rotating toward the pad and away from the paint or wood side, or is grinding parallel to the pad's butt edge. If the grinder is touching the pad near the shoulder's surface, the grit will roll the rubber (or neoprene) over, giving a flared look to the pad and leaving some thin flash-like material.

From the operator's view, grinders turn the disk in a clockwise direction, so if the barrel is pointing away from you, the far edge of the disk should be moving the grit to the right. You should be grinding on the buttpad with the rubber dust going off to the right. Angle the gun with the barrel about 45 degrees to your left so the front edge of the grinding disk is attacking the pad at a like angle from the stock/pad interface. Keeping the disk as parallel to the stock surface as you can, watch the masking tape and not the stock.

This will allow you to see the instant the tape is starting to get ground and give you a moment to lighten up.

It will take some concentration to grind down to the level of the masking tape without grinding through it. With practice, you will develop the touch and be able to grind halfway through the tape and leave just the adhesive on the wood. We'll discuss later what to do if you should sneeze while grinding and happen to break through the finish. It would be prudent to wear a dust mask if you are prone to nasal tickles, as you will only be able to fix grind-throughs of a minor nature. There is the possibility of having to refinish a stock if you damage it seriously.

If you happen to grind away a little of the finish, try to keep from touching the bare wood any more than necessary. It is vulnerable and you don't want any dirt or body oil to get into the grain. Then, finish up your pad-fitting operation and remove the tape to determine how badly you have hurt the gun's looks.

This is the time to bump the edge of the recoil pad sharply against the floor to jolt out the ground-up pad dust. It will amaze you how much will come out of the crosswebbing. The only bigger surprise is how much can get into your finishing if you have some of that left to do. I blow the pad off with compressed air and wipe the pad with trichloroethane 1,1,1.

Look at any spots on the stock ground bare and notice if the wood has been stained. A sharp change in color or grain prominence will let you know if the wood had been stained before finishing, a matter which has the potential of ruining your day. If the finish appears clear and over bare wood, you may be safer using a varnish like Birchwood Casey's Tru-Oil to restore the finish. I look for a darker appearance in the pores of the wood. If it is much darker than the bare wood, it likely has had some dark brown (walnut) filler rubbed into the pores to accentuate the grain. Do the same thing with Birchwood Casey's Walnut Filler and let it dry overnight.

After letting the filler dry, rub as much as you can off with a clean rag, and then refinish with the Tru-Oil. I paint the bare spot with liquid Tru-Oil and wipe the varnish off the original finish around the spot. Several coats should fill the grain and make a continuous surface. Wait about 24 hours and, using a fine compound, rub the varnish carefully to blend the new finish in with the old.

If the bare stock was new, you would do well to file the fix-up instructions in your memory, because everybody goes through a finish sooner or later. On the bare stock, you are free to grind the shape you want and have the luxury of using an orbital sander with 320-grit paper. This will give the stock a smooth feel and should look as if it were done by someone who knew what he was doing. To leave obvious grinding disk marks is another way to tell the world that you were in a hurry or just inexperienced. Suffering from impatience myself, I've had to go back and redo some jobs in the past.

Now it's time to take off the pad and reinstall it with glue. I prefer to use a carpenter's glue like the yellow glue from Borden. It seems to grip better than white glue, but that might just be my imagination. Nevertheless, the glue has enough shear strength that it keeps the pad from getting out of line. This glue lacks strength in the tensile direction so that the pad can be removed without much trouble.

Spread the glue around on both surfaces and reinstall the pad. The excess glue, when still wet, can be easily cleaned up with a damp rag. It's always a real problem when you get a pad to replace that has been glued on with epoxy or contact cement. Don't do it.

I certainly hope that you have good results with your first pad, but if not, it will be easier the second time.

Troubleshooting Remington Model 700 Rifles

This series of rifles seldom causes problems, but here are some quick-and-easy solutions to common complaints.

By Rich Hopkins

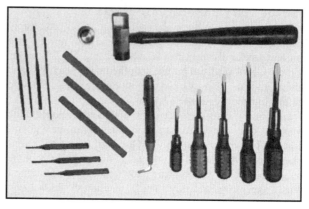

Most repairs to the Remington can be made using basic hand tools. Always use hollow-ground screwdrivers when working on firearms.

Left—For best accuracy, the muzzle of a Model 700 should be crowned. Any damage to the muzzle will adversely affect accuracy. Right—The barrel only rests on a small portion of the stock near the hole in the forend. Between this point and the action, the barrel is free-floating.

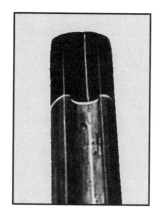

THE REMINGTON MODEL 700 is arguably one of the finest bolt-action rifles made today. It's a high-power repeater, available in a variety of centerfire calibers. Two grades are available, the standard ADL and the BDL version, which has a floorplate built into the trigger guard.

The Model 700 is generally accurate and, other than those caused by dirt, few problems will be encountered. However, as we all know, nothing is perfect. At times, even the best rifles can suffer from problems. Some of the more common problems we've seen with the Remington 700s include loss of accuracy, bolt binding, failures to extract, misfiring, and failures to eject. Here are some solutions to these difficulties:

Loss of Accuracy

The Model 700 is known for its accuracy, so when an owner brings one to you and says it shoots all over the paper, there is a good chance there's a problem with the rifle. A quick check of the muzzle will show if the crowning or the rifling at the muzzle is damaged. Open the bolt and check to be sure that the rifle is unloaded. Shine a bore light into the receiver and inspect the rifling and the eccentricity of the crown. If there is any problem, place the barrel in a lathe, and turn back the barrel and recrown.

If the rifle still has the standard wood stock, the stock should be

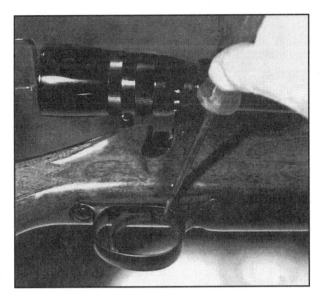

The bolt-stop is located inside the trigger guard, just in front of the trigger as shown by the pointer. The magazine floorplate is opened by pressing on the release button directly to the right of the pointer.

inspected next. If the stock is warped, the barrel could be forced out of alignment. To check the alignment of the barrel in the barrel channel, you will have to remove the barrel and action from the stock. Open the bolt and check to be sure that the rifle is unloaded. With the safety in the forward or fire position, press upward on the bolt-stop release located in front of the trigger. Pull the bolt to the rear and remove it from the rifle. Unscrew and remove the trigger-guard screws from the stock, and then remove the barrel and action.

Inspect the barrel channel of the stock. Like most bolt-action rifles, the barrel of the Model 700 rests only on a small area (about $1/2$-inch) at the forend tip of the stock. Any glazed spots in the barrel channel indicate barrel contact with the wood. Pay particular attention to the area around the point where the barrel joins the receiver.

Coat the barrel with inletting black or Prussian blue (available from Brownells, Inc.) applied in a thin, even coat. Apply the black to the lower half of the barrel. Reinstall the barrel and receiver in the stock, and then reinstall the trigger screws, and tighten. This will seat the barrel in the stock.

Remove the trigger-guard screws and the barreled action from the stock, and check the barrel channel again. Any high spot or warpage in the channel will be easily spotted. Using conventional inletting tools, any interference can be scraped away. Only a slight amount of scraping should be required to remove the unwanted contact points from the channel. If these areas are large and require a lot of scraping, I suggest replacing the stock. After the high spots have been removed, reseal the barrel channel with linseed oil or a similar sealer to prevent additional warping.

Metal fouling is not very common in the larger centerfire calibers. In smaller high-velocity cartridges, however, it is very common and can seriously affect accuracy. To eliminate this fouling, clean the bore using Outers Foul Out. This device electronically removes lead, rust, copper, and dirt from the bore. With a retail price of around $360, it's expensive, but it works. Every shooter can buy a solvent such as Hoppes Copper Solvent, Accubore, or J-B Bore Cleaner. Unfortunately, these solvents may still leave some fouling.

After removing the fouling, bore-sight the rifle and check the accuracy with ammunition from different lots.

Bolt Binding

Over half the problems that I've encountered with firearms are caused by dirt. I'm always amazed that so many shooters don't clean their guns. And if they do, they often do a poor job. The Model 700 bolt is jeweled for smoothness. When the bolt does not operate smoothly, dirt is often the only problem. Remove and check the bolt and mating surfaces on the action for powder residue and dirt. Clean as necessary using powder solvent and a toothbrush. Dry the parts using a clean patch wrapped around a flat piece of brass or wood. Don't use a screwdriver, as it could scratch and burr the metal of the receiver. When dry, oil lightly.

If the action is clean, check the mating surfaces for burrs. Also check for burrs on the ejector hole on the bolt, and check for sharp corners on the bolt lugs. If burrs or sharp corners are found, a small amount of filing, followed by honing and polishing with crocus cloth will remove them (Figure 1).

The extractor ring may be high, causing the bolt to be tight, or the extractor rivet may be loose. To correct this, remove the extractor ring and eliminate any high spots in the ring channel. Refit the ring and tighten the rivet, checking for smoothness. If this doesn't solve the problem, replace the ring, using a new rivet.

Figure 1 (Left): To remove the ejector, drive out the retaining pin shown here. The ejector hole in the bolt must be free of all burrs. Figure 2 (Right): To replace the firing pin, drive out the retaining pin. Hold the bolt plug against the tension of the mainspring while removing the pin.

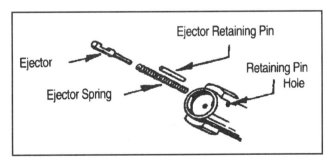

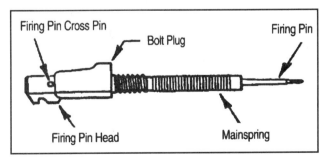

To disassemble the bolt, force the firing-pin head rearward until a coin or washer can be inserted in the slot of the firing-pin head.

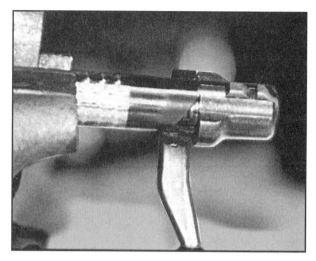

To insert the bolt in the rifle, the bolt must be cocked. When cocked, the firing-pin head will rest in the higher notch.

Failures to Extract

Assuming the rifle is clean, check for a tight or rough chamber, using an unloaded, sized case. This should slide in and out of the chamber with little resistance. If the chamber is tight or rough, ream and repolish. If there is no problem in the chamber, fit a new extractor to the bolt.

Misfires

There are three causes of misfires—faulty ammunition, a broken firing pin, and dirt. Correcting an ammunition problem is very easy, and I don't need to go into detail about it. To correct the other two problems, you will need to remove the firing pin from the bolt.

Start by removing the bolt assembly from the rifle as described earlier. With the bolt secured in a vise with padded jaws, use a wooden dowel to force the firing-pin head rearward until a coin or washer can be inserted in the slot near the back edge of the firing pin head. Unscrew the bolt plug and remove the firing-pin assembly from the bolt. Check the end of the firing pin. It should be smooth and rounded. If not, it will need to be replaced. If the pin is not broken, clean all of the parts with a degreaser, and dry using compressed air. Lubricate the firing pin and mainspring using a good gun grease.

The entire firing-pin assembly can be replaced as a unit, with no adjustment required, or you can replace only the firing pin. To replace the pin, you will need to disassemble this unit. Be careful: The mainspring is compressed (Figure 2). A suitable holding device is required to prevent the firing pin and/or the firing-pin head from flying across the shop or into your eyes when the cross pin is removed.

With the firing pin held securely, compress the mainspring by drawing the bolt plug toward the end of the firing pin. When the cross pin is exposed, hold the firing pin and firing-pin head securely and drive out the cross pin. Slowly release the tension on the mainspring and disassemble the parts.

To install a new firing pin, you will have to drill a hole in its

shank for the cross pin. Make sure that the recess in the firing-pin head is clean, and assemble the firing-pin head to the new firing pin. Seat the shank of the new firing pin firmly into the firing-pin head. Using a No. 42 drill (0.093-inch), drill through the cross-pin hole in the firing-pin head and through the new firing pin. Reassemble the parts. Compress the mainspring as before, and drive the cross pin through the firing-pin head and the shank of the new firing pin. Release the tension on the bolt plug. Clean and lubricate the firing pin and reassemble the bolt, again using a coin or washer to hold the firing-pin head.

The bolt must be cocked so that it can be installed. If it is uncocked, the firing-pin head will be recessed well into the bolt. To cock the bolt, place the bolt plug in a padded vise to prevent movement. Turn the bolt handle so the firing-pin head engages the cocking (higher) notch on the bolt.

Failures to Eject

This condition can be caused by dirt, burrs at the ejector hole of the bolt, a loose extractor rivet, or by the extractor dropping the shell. To correct the first two problems, you will need to remove the ejector from the bolt.

With the bolt removed from the rifle, drive out the ejector-retaining pin. The ejector will pop out of the bolt when the punch is removed. Pull the ejector spring from the hole in the bolt. Clean the ejector and the ejector hole using an aerosol cleaner. Check the hole and ejector for smoothness, and deburr the hole or replace the ejector as necessary. Dry the hole in the bolt using compressed air.

To reassemble the ejector parts, put the spring and the ejector in the bolt. Push the ejector in and hold it against the tension of the spring. Align the slot in the ejector with the pin hole and drive in the retaining pin.

When the problem has been corrected, be sure to thoroughly clean and oil the rifle before calling the job done. This little extra step will greatly be appreciated by the gun owner.

Gunsmithing the Winchester 1300 Shotgun

Model variations, a tendency to be abused by their owners, and unique parts combine to make the Winchester 1300 a gunsmith's challenge

By Butch Thomson

IF YOU STAY around this business for very long, you will eventually see a gun owner who treats his $2000 over/under shotgun with kid gloves but literally beats his cheaper shotgun to death. He comes back to your shop and says something to the effect of, "I never had a problem with my over/under. I just don't understand why they don't build these better."

Then you have the fellow who tells you, "I want a cheap shotgun I can toss in my truck, and if it gets beat up, I don't have to worry about it." That guy will get the gun filthy, abuse it plenty and come back saying, "This shotgun is a piece of garbage. It worked for a while, but not when I needed it."

I know such incidents happen because, in these two cases, it was my customers talking, and in both instances the shotgun involved was the Winchester Model 1300. It is a commonly seen shotgun because it is inexpensive; and because it is inexpensive, it often receives abuse that no shotgun should have to endure. It should come as no surprise, then, that the 1300 often needs repairing.

Here's a quick look at some of the problems you're likely to encounter on the Model 1300:

History

Winchester's Model 120, 1200 and 1300 shotguns are of the same design, but each varies internally, the changes connected more to the date of manufacture than to model number. For example, parts for Model 1200s with serial numbers above 382,500 are different from the lower numbers. Changes are scattered throughout the production of these shotguns, so always include the serial number along with the model number when ordering parts.

The parts may vary, but repair and maintenance on all these shotguns is similar, so we will cover the variations along with common repairs as we take one apart and reassemble it.

Most of the working parts of this shotgun are in its trigger assembly, so plan on finding a lot of the needed repairs there. Remove the trigger-guard pin by pushing it out either side. On some of the shotguns, this part is plastic and should be pushed out, not driven. Others have metal pins that can be hard to remove. They may have to be driven out, but try pushing them first to avoid deforming or breaking the plastic ones. The trigger assembly will come out the bottom of the receiver by pulling down the butt end first. The front end hooks into the receiver and must be pulled to the rear.

The slide supports are on each side of the trigger assembly. They contain both the right and left cut-off bars, which are responsible for most of this firearm's feeding problems. The dirt and trash you often find between the cut-off bars and the receiver will keep the bars from working properly. Thoroughly clean these and the inside of the receiver before looking elsewhere for feeding problems.

There are times, though, that cleaning is not enough. When these bars have been forced to work with a lot of buildup behind them, they will often warp. This will require resetting or replacing the bars. A dirt buildup behind the bars will, over a period of time, bend them into the action. Continued use of the shotgun will work the cutoff tip out and away from the cartridge rims and, after you've removed the trash, make the tips be too far away from the shotshell rims. When two shells try to feed at the same time, the right-hand cutoff needs to be realigned to catch the shell rim with the working of the action. People often bend the tip enough to make it catch the rims, but the shotgun will not be repaired correctly. Remember what caused the bend in the first place and return the bar to its original condition and shape. The bottom edge was straight all the way to the tip's curve. These good, high-quality springs can be reformed without any damage. They're so good, in fact, that they are very hard to bend back. After trying several times without success, it's tempting to use excessive pressure and bend the spring too far. No matter how strong they might be, these springs cannot be bent back and forth to get them right without being destroyed, so go slow and be careful to do it right the first time.

If the shell does not release at all, either of the stops may be at fault. Looking inside the bottom loading gate while pumping the action with a dummy shell in the magazine tube will show you if it is the left or right cutoff that is not working right. If it is the right, then the opposite of the above repair is needed because the tip is too far into the center of the receiver and isn't properly releasing the shell. Repair the right cutoff just like the left, according to whether it is staying in too far or not going in enough. If it stays out too far, it will drop a round on the ground as you pump the action, and will fail to feed or jam. Adjusting the right-hand bar will correct these problems.

Replacing the side supports requires the exact part because different sets used different springs and settings. These bars are taken out of the trigger assembly by removing one or more screws from the plates. New models have only one; some of the older models had two. The bar extending from the right-hand slide support through the trigger assembly is the pivot pin for the carrier assembly. Remove it slowly, holding the carrier while you are removing it. When the carrier comes off, it also releases the carrier plunger and the plunger spring.

Push the safety off and, while holding the hammer down, pull the trigger and slowly let the hammer up into the fired position. Trigger modification these days opens the door to legal nightmares, and for that reason I don't advise it on these shotguns. If you are going to do it, any work must be done only on the hammer part of the sear, not on the trigger sear itself. If you insist on softening the trigger pull on your own personal firearm, then the high part of the sear can be cut down just a small amount. This will make your trigger pull shorter, but removing more than a little can make it go off as you close the breech. The best way to smooth the trigger without danger is to stone the hammer-sear notch and remove just a little metal from the top edge. A little goes a long way here.

One of the Winchester's most common problems is a stuck or broken safety. To get to it, you must disassemble the trigger housing. The disconnector assembly is removed by pulling it out of the trigger housing to the left. The disconnector spring is a stout one and will get away from you if you aren't careful as you pull it out of its position in the trigger housing. The hammer spring is not bad at all, as you push the hammer retaining pin out from the hammer and trigger housing. The hammer pin is flat on one side and notched for the disconnector bar. It must be replaced exactly as it came out of not only the two hammer-spring supports, but the hammer as well. The trigger retaining pin is easily pushed out with a punch, which then lets the trigger come out the top of its housing. The safety

spring is the base leg of the hammer spring. The safety button can now be slipped out the side of the trigger housing for cleaning, repair or replacement. Remember, all parts of the hammer must be replaced just as they came out, including the leg of the hammer spring into the side cut in the safety button.

The only other problem unique to this Winchester pump shotgun series is related to the two plastic magazine throats, located at the bottom and the top. These parts will last forever unless they are broken, through improper use or repair. When a throat is broken, it is nearly always the bottom one that someone has been prying on. It is best to replace both top and bottom if you have to replace one.

To get at the throats to replace them, it is necessary to remove the magazine tube. The tube is screwed in with clockwise threads, but is hard to remove even on a new shotgun. If the magazine tube gets bent or warped in the effort, do not try to reuse it, just replace it. If you have a dented tube and need a fast repair, use your barrel dent remover. This same tool can be useful in checking the tubes. Just screw it out until it is touching, but not dragging hard, and slide it up and down the tube while you turn it around inside. This will identify any damage the tube may have had that wasn't noticed.

Unnoticed damage to the magazine tube is one of the major causes of feeding problems in these shotguns. A bent magazine tube, or one with dirt or rust inside, will keep the follower from moving with the speed it needs to function properly. There is always the possibility that the magazine spring is bad, but the only times I've ever found this, someone had been working on it or it was badly rusted itself. Dents are easy to see, but something like stepping on the gun in hunting camp can "egg shape" the tube just enough to not work right, yet still be unnoticeable. A bad bend will prevent the tube's working at all; a little one will just cause poor feeding. After taking the barrel off, check these by removing the spring retainer and spring. A properly working magazine follower slides up and down in the magazine tube without any problem. Tubes are easily cleaned with an oversize shotgun brush.

The breech assembly cannot be removed until the barrel is taken off. The magazine spring retainers are sometimes missing or loose on these shotguns, something to bear in mind when you remove the magazine cap so it won't unexpectedly pop apart on you. With the breech open and the magazine cap removed, the barrel will come off with a little wiggle and pull.

With the trigger assembly out of the receiver, you are now ready to remove the breech assembly. All but the latest models have a slide arm bridge retaining screw that fits through the slide arm bridge into the breechbolt slide, holding the two together. These screws often break and must be drilled out. When the screw is broken, the action arms will come out the front of the receiver with the slide arm bridge.

Always take the slide arm bridge off the bottom of the breechbolt slide and check the inside. Actions that do not lock and unlock smoothly are sometimes caused by residue collecting inside the breechbolt slide and not allowing the breechbolt to easily rotate into its locked position. This same problem is also caused by a barrel that is not fully seated into the receiver. Always check between the receiver face and the butt of the barrel and make sure they are tight. If they do not tighten up without excessive tightening of the magazine cap, take them apart and check for foreign residue somewhere

WINCHESTER MODEL 1300 XTR SLIDE-ACTION SHOTGUN

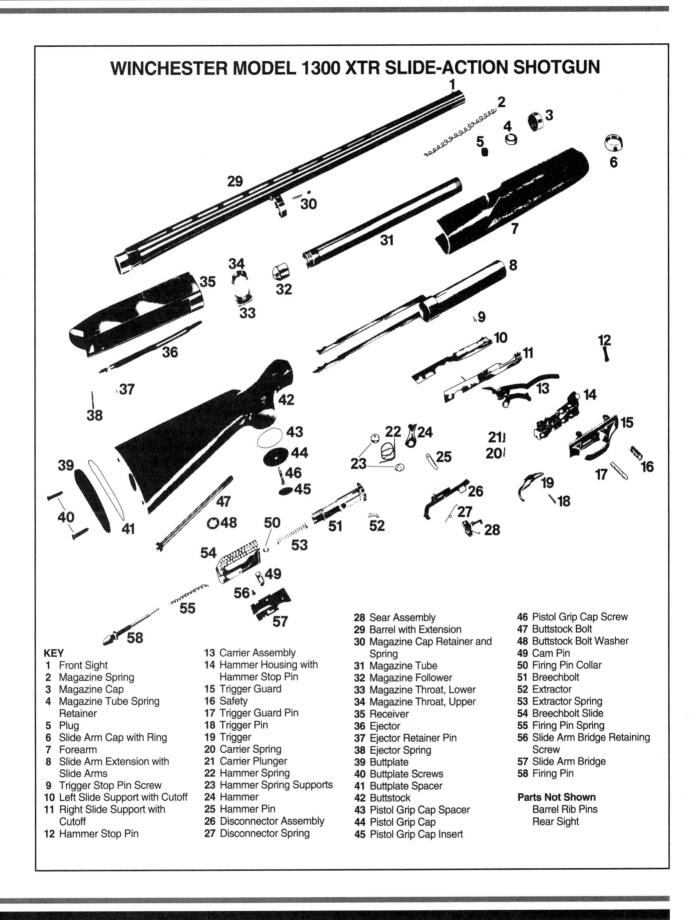

KEY

1 Front Sight
2 Magazine Spring
3 Magazine Cap
4 Magazine Tube Spring Retainer
5 Plug
6 Slide Arm Cap with Ring
7 Forearm
8 Slide Arm Extension with Slide Arms
9 Trigger Stop Pin Screw
10 Left Slide Support with Cutoff
11 Right Slide Support with Cutoff
12 Hammer Stop Pin
13 Carrier Assembly
14 Hammer Housing with Hammer Stop Pin
15 Trigger Guard
16 Safety
17 Trigger Guard Pin
18 Trigger Pin
19 Trigger
20 Carrier Spring
21 Carrier Plunger
22 Hammer Spring
23 Hammer Spring Supports
24 Hammer
25 Hammer Pin
26 Disconnector Assembly
27 Disconnector Spring
28 Sear Assembly
29 Barrel with Extension
30 Magazine Cap Retainer and Spring
31 Magazine Tube
32 Magazine Follower
33 Magazine Throat, Lower
34 Magazine Throat, Upper
35 Receiver
36 Ejector
37 Ejector Retainer Pin
38 Ejector Spring
39 Buttplate
40 Buttplate Screws
41 Buttplate Spacer
42 Buttstock
43 Pistol Grip Cap Spacer
44 Pistol Grip Cap
45 Pistol Grip Cap Insert
46 Pistol Grip Cap Screw
47 Buttstock Bolt
48 Buttstock Bolt Washer
49 Cam Pin
50 Firing Pin Collar
51 Breechbolt
52 Extractor
53 Extractor Spring
54 Breechbolt Slide
55 Firing Pin Spring
56 Slide Arm Bridge Retaining Screw
57 Slide Arm Bridge
58 Firing Pin

Parts Not Shown
Barrel Rib Pins
Rear Sight

between the barrel and receiver. The Winchester breechbolt assembly requires oil to work as it should, and I find many of these that have not been oiled inside the breech assembly since they were at the factory.

Part-time gunsmiths complain the loudest about the broken slide-arm bridge retaining screw because they sometimes have real problems removing the broken screw. They occasionally stick very hard and are so small that they break easily. The complaints about how difficult they are to remove are well founded.

These unique three-stage screws have small threads while having a larger body to fit the slide-arm bridge. The small threaded end often has to be drilled out of the breech slide body, but if done improperly, you can mess up the slide body—not an inexpensive mistake. If your hands are steady, you can take a reversible Moto-Tool with a small dentistry burr and drill into the center of the broken screw in a counter-clockwise direction. The screw usually will come loose before you've gone much more than 2 millimeters deep. If not, you still have the hole in the center to use your smallest easy-out to remove the screw.

Their rounded heads are made so they won't hang on moving parts, yet they must be large enough to keep the breech assembly from coming out the front of the receiver when the barrel is removed. Through the years, I have seen many modified repairs to this part of the Winchester—oversized holes tapped into the breech slide or even extra holes and screws—because someone thought one small screw was not enough to take the punishment. When the shotgun is in good working order and kept clean, this small screw is all that is needed.

Later models do not have this screw, so the slide bars must be used to push the breechbolt assembly to the rear of the receiver. The action bars can then be pried away from the sides of the receiver and raised enough to be lifted out of the carrier slots cut into the slide-arm bridge. When these are loose, the slide arm can be eased off the front of the magazine tube. Some of the early models had removable slide arms for easy replacement. On older, well-used Winchester shotguns, the working ends of the slide arms should be carefully inspected for wear. Fit the slide-arm bridge into the notches of the slide arms to check for wear. They should fit snugly without excessive rounding of the edges.

With the breech assembly out of the shotgun, slip the action arm back onto the magazine tube and slide it back into the receiver. The arms should be in the exact same position without being attached to the slide-arm bridge as they are when attached. They should move from the open to closed positions with no drag on the sides of the receiver. The bars are commonly warped or bent, but they must be straight to work without problems.

Press the ejector bar flat against the inside of the receiver and remove the breechbolt assembly. On later-model receivers, this ejector is held in place at the front by a small Phillips-head screw and in the rear by a slot cut into the receiver. Older models' ejectors were free, secured only by a pin extending through a slot in the front of the ejector and the slot in the rear of the receiver. This allowed them to move about as the action was worked, creating a self-cleaning action that would usually work out any trash and dirt behind them. The new ones do not move back and forth, so they must be removed to clean behind them. Their design naturally collects considerable grime.

Although they're small, Winchester extractors are very strong and seldom break unless mistreated. Unfortunately, this happens all too often with firearms. Mistreated dog-leg extractors break in the curve about 3 to 4 millimeters from the front tip. This is often caused by someone using excess pressure when trying to pry out a stuck hull. Always check out the extractor's front claw to be sure it is sharp, not rounded off. These claws are hard and seldom wear out, but some of these guns have fired untold thousands of rounds and need to have their extractors replaced. The extractors are not expensive and are easily replaced, snapping into place and staying there under their own extractor spring's tension.

Also, this is the time to replace broken firing pins, always making sure the new one matches the old. Winchester has made several different ones, and they do not interchange even though they look like they would.

Remember, in this group of Winchesters, parts will vary from shotgun to shotgun. Always order with part numbers and serial numbers. Even then, don't believe the supplier hasn't made a mistake: Check the new part against the old one to make sure they are the same before you start work.

Maintaining Ruger Mini-14 Rifles

The ever-popular Mini-14's most common maintenance problem is heavy carbon deposits in its gas system. Here's how one gunsmith goes about working it.

By Dennis A. Wood

THERE WILL NO DOUBT never be another John Moses Browning as far as firearms design is concerned. If accolades for time are in order, old John would rate at the top of the heap. Some of the designs contrived by this late firearms designer are still going strong some 70 years after his death.

As long as awards for firearms design are being passed out, another name that should appear at the top of the list should be William Bannerman Ruger. He's been producing innovative firearms since 1946, an achievement that is not likely to be duplicated. Given today's political and economic climate, there is little incentive for anyone to develop a new firearm design, especially in the semi-auto style.

That may be overstating it a bit, but it is unlikely that many companies or individuals will come up with something like the Ruger Mini-14 and Mini-Thirty rifles. Both were born of the failed effort to develop the Ruger XGI, which was intended to be a civilian version of the M-14, only in a less cumbersome size. The original

intent was to chamber the gas operated semi-auto in 308 Winchester, but the action proved unable to handle the pressures from the cartridge. As far as I know, there were no 308 Winchester caliber Ruger XGI rifles produced for public sale.

At about the same time Ruger was experimenting with the XGI, large numbers of SKS and AK-47 semi-automatic rifles chambered for the 7.62X39 Russian cartridge began coming into the country, along with trainloads of low-cost ammunition for them. The 223 Winchester (5.56mm) had been adopted by our military for well over 20 years and was used in the AR-15 civilian version of the M-16. The ready availability of military surplus ammunition and the resulting low-cost shooting fun did not go unnoticed. Ruger capitalized on this knowledge and chambered both the Mini-14 and Mini-Thirty for both the readily available military cartridges. Sooner or later, one of these Minis will make its way into your shop, probably in need of a good cleaning. As happens to most gas-operated rifles, the gas system eventually will "carbon up" to the point that it has to be cleaned. Takedown is pretty much the same for both rifles, so, although we are dealing with the Mini-14 here, these instructions also apply to the Mini-Thirty.

As always, open the action and check the chamber and bore to prove to yourself that the rifle is indeed empty and safe to deal with. The Mini-14 has a bolt hold-open device that automatically engages to hold the bolt and slide back in the rearward position. This device only functions with an empty magazine in the rifle. The magazine follower has a lip that is captured by the hold-open device upon firing the last round of the magazine. The bolt hold-open latch, at the left side top of the receiver, is a little cylinder-shaped button. Once the empty magazine is removed, the bolt handle can be pulled back and the button will pop up and the bolt can be released forward. To activate the bolt hold-open device without a magazine in place, pull back on the bolt handle until it is all the way back. Depress the bolt hold-open latch button and then ease the bolt forward until the bolt is stopped by the latch. Magazines can be inserted into the rifle with the bolt held open or with the bolt in the bolt forward position.

Three basic sub-assemblies, the barreled action, trigger group and bolt assembly, are involved here. For the sake of simple cleaning, the rifle need only be taken down to these groups. If other problems exist, you'll need to go well beyond the instruction pamphlet provided with the firearm.

To disassemble the Mini-14, the first thing that you must do is remove the magazine and set the hammer in the cocked condition. Pull the bolt handle all the way back, cocking the hammer, then release the bolt forward. Push the safety back to place it in the on position. Place the rifle in your padded-jaw vise with the trigger guard pointing up. It works best for me if I hold the barrel in the leather-faced jaws of my vise.

The trigger guard is also a latch that pivots forward with a little persuasion from an easily-made hook tool. I use an old screwdriver with the blade ground off that has been heated up and bent at the tip. A short length of shrink tube over the tip keeps the tool from marring any metal surfaces. Hook the tip into the cutout in the rear of the trigger guard and pull up. This disengages the rear of the guard, which will pivot forward and rise up and out, coming free of the rifle. For the moment, just set the trigger group aside.

Lift the rear of the stock up and pull backward on it to remove the stock from the barreled action. Set the stock aside and rotate the barreled action so the right side of the action faces up toward you and the bottom of the receiver is away from you. This way, the recoil spring and guide rod are less likely to pop into your face when they are removed. Pull forward on the recoil spring guide and then, while holding it tightly, release the spring's tension rearward and remove it. The bolt handle and operating slide are no longer under tension and will slide fore and aft quite easily.

At the right rear of the receiver, you will see a half-oblong shaped cutout. Pull the bolt handle back until you can feel it fall into this cutout. Pull the bolt handle up and the operating slide should come off the barreled action. You may have to rotate the handguard around slightly for the operating slide to clear for removal.

Pull the bolt forward until it will rotate at the front and it will come out of the ejection port of the receiver. Observe carefully how the bolt rotated to come out. When you replace the bolt into the receiver make sure that the fin at the rear of the bolt body gets into the raceway in the left side of the receiver. You will also notice a small cutout in the reinforcing web in the receiver. Once you get the bolt in place, it will be helpful during reassembly to pull the tail at the end of the firing pin through this cutout as you set the bolt in place.

The handguard is held in place at the rear by a thin spring steel pinch clamp. At the front, the handguard is secured by four hex-head machine screws that are tapped into the gas block. A $9/64$-inch hex wrench will remove all four of these screws. Once the gas block has been separated, be careful that the little gas port bushing doesn't get away from you. This is a tiny little tube that transfers the gas escaping through the gas hole in the barrel into the gas block and through the gas piston to work the action.

You will immediately see that there is a black carbon build-up in and around these parts. A scrubbing with a good solvent should remove all of this carbon, but if you get some that is stubborn, #0000 steel wool soaked in your solvent will dislodge it without hurting the finish, if the gun is blued. Some of these parts are not easily accessible for the steel wool and will have to be scrubbed with a steel bristle brush. A thorough overnight soaking in a solvent like Shooter's Choice will loosen most of this crud. Whenever possible, I use an evaporating solvent in cleaning semi-auto gas systems so the carbon cannot combine with whatever lubricant was used and gum up the gas system with a shellac-type material. When putting these parts back together, make sure the gas piston hole points up toward the little gas tube. If it doesn't, you will have a single shot instead of a semi-auto.

Pulling up on the rear of the trigger guard and pivoting it forward will allow the removal of the trigger group.

At the left side of the receiver, there is a plate or cover for the bolt hold-back latch system. Pushing up on the thumb cut will reveal the internal parts and give access for cleaning and lubrication. A dab of your favorite gun grease will keep things working smoothly in this area. Observation will show you how these parts relate to one another.

We've gone a bit beyond what Ruger calls normal takedown for cleaning. Their recommendation is to break the rifle into the three sub-assemblies and swish the parts around in a cleaning solution, then give each part a serious blasting with compressed air. For most purposes, this should be enough to keep this rifle operating until your grandchildren are old enough to use it. If a firing pin breaks, or for some reason the extractor doesn't extract, the bolt group will need to be disassembled. The bolt design of this rifle is ingenious, in that everything is held together with a single pin. This pin is actually an extension, or leg pin, that is a part of the extractor. When this pin end of the extractor is drifted out, all hell breaks loose if you are not prepared for parts coming out under spring tension. The pin holds the ejector and its respective pin in place, along with the extractor plunger and its spring. Although it isn't under tension, the firing pin is also held captive by this pin. Reassembling all these parts and getting them lined up properly will have you babbling to yourself in short order. If there is no major cause for disassembling the bolt, don't do it.

The trigger assembly is extremely strong and is something that Ruger is very sensitive about. The manufacturer recommends that this unit not be disassembled. Triggers and hammers will not be

The gas system should be cleaned in a good solvent, preferably an evaporative type. Take care not to lose the gas port tube.

sold to anyone and any needed replacements are made only at the factory. As this is a semi-auto-operated firearm, the sear engagement should not be altered or tampered with to avoid a dangerous situation.

There are several aftermarket extended magazine release latches available that can be easily installed in just a matter of minutes. A cross pin holds the magazine release and its operating spring in place. A hole in the rear end of the hammer strut will accept a straightened-out paper clip to hold the spring back while the hammer is in the cocked position. If you need to disassemble the trigger group, place a paper clip in this hole and then release the hammer forward. A 0.187-inch cross pin holds the hammer and trigger guard in place. Once this pin is drifted out, these two parts will come free of the trigger group. At the rear of the trigger group is a 0.125-inch pin that contains the trigger and secondary sear. Drifting out this pin permits these parts to be removed. The pin in between these two on the left side of the trigger group is staked in place and operates as the pivot pin for the safety. No attempt should be made to remove this pin. Observe how all these parts fit into the picture along with the trigger return spring and the safety detent spring. Assembly is in reverse order. On all pivoting and moving parts, a dab of a good lubricant will help keep parts wear to a minimum.

There are all sorts of aftermarket fiberglass and folding stocks available for these rifles. Choate makes a recoil pad that will extend the length of pull about an inch. This should help those who feel the factory stock is a little short for them. B-Square makes what they call a no-gunsmithing scope mount for either of these rifles—if it is not the Ranch version, which is provided with rings for the integral bases provided.

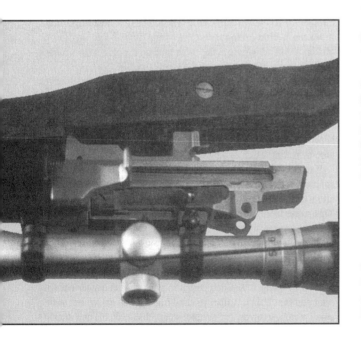

Lifting up on the stock removes it from the barreled action, giving you access to the action spring.

Repairing and Maintaining the Mossberg 500

With as many Moss-berg shotguns as there are in the field, some are bound to need fixing at any given time. Here are some common problems and simple solutions.

By Butch Thomson

THE MOSSBERG 500 is one of the most common and popular shotguns on the market today. A steady flow of them comes through the repair department, not because they constantly need service, but due simply to their sheer numbers. There are so many in use that we always have one or two on the rack.

As we disassemble one of these Mossbergs, let's keep in mind that this is an inexpensive shotgun, and we probably should not put much money into a repair bill. Fortunately, the Mossberg's problems are usually simple, most commonly involving a broken plastic safety button or a failure to feed.

The starting spot for repairs on the Mossberg 500 is the removal of the barrel by unscrewing the barrel nut—or takedown screw, as Mossberg prefers to call it. One must open the breech to its full-

back position and wiggle the barrel back and forth to remove it from its tight-fitting aluminum-alloy receiver. The barrel should not fit loosely in the receiver; at best, this is bad news and at worst could even be dangerous. If it can be wobbled around with the breech closed and locked, the receiver or barrel must be repaired. Barrel repairs are seldom needed, but when they are, it is usually easier and less expensive to replace them rather than make any time-consuming major repair, since these are among the least expensive barrels on the market. However, repair and modification of shotgun barrels is a whole different subject, so we will not dwell on it now.

On the other hand, you might have to replace a broken front sight bead. Mossberg has its own unique sight beads, and it's a good idea to keep a few on hand.

Work on any part of the magazine-tube assembly will require the removal of the tube from the receiver by unscrewing the tube. This is a standard right-hand thread, but care must be taken since the tube will crush or bend easily. Grip only the solid muzzle end of the tube with a barrel wrench or similar tool. To unscrew it, turn it upside down and shake it until the small wooden rod comes through the takedown screw hole. The rod has a rubber ring around it to keep it from falling out at the wrong time and getting lost or broken. Pull and wiggle at the same time on the plug so this rubber ring can make its way through the screw threads.

The magazine-tube shell follower is plastic. If it has rough edges or is cracked, it should be replaced, because this can make the follower stick, and create a failure to feed. Rust or dirt inside this tube can also creates feeding problems. Inspect the tube to make sure it is perfectly round before reinstalling. You can check for a warped tube by rolling it across a hard, flat surface.

If the disconnector is failing to operate, cleaning it might be the solution. It can be removed by pushing the trigger pin in enough to allow the disconnector to be removed without pulling the trigger. This same technique works for the action-lock lever, except its spring is on the same pin. The sear notch on the hammer should never be filed to make a lighter trigger pull. Also note that removing a coil from the mainspring will lead to misfires.

Removing the trigger assembly from the receiver is accomplished by using a $3/16$-inch punch to push out the trigger-housing retaining pin. This is a fiber pin and must not be driven out with a small punch, screwdriver, or other sharp object, as this will damage the pin. Holding the shotgun upside down, lift the rear of the trigger housing assembly slowly, and pull back toward the butt as soon as it clears the receiver. The front of the Mossberg trigger has two plastic lugs that are easily damaged. If they are worn or broken, the only proper repair is to install a new trigger housing—an expensive repair for a inexpensive gun.

Total disassembly of the trigger assembly is not recommended and is seldom needed. When it is required, remove only the parts necessary for the repair. Even though I know some gunsmiths will disagree on this point, I recommend cleaning this assembly with a good cleaning tank and an air gun—without disassembly. The plastic trigger housing is easily damaged, and if it is necessary to start removing parts, the retaining pins should be pushed out with a proper size punch, not sharp objects. When reassembling, take care when driving these pins back, because chunks of the plastic can be broken out of the trigger housing.

When the trigger assembly is removed, the cartridge interrupter (on the ejection port side) and the cartridge stop (on the opposite side) can be lifted out. If one of these sticks and does not loosen by tapping on the side of the receiver, a small screwdriver will pop it out with very little pressure. Both should always come out without problem. If for any reason either does not come out easily, look for the reason rather than applying a lot of pressure. These parts can be bent, and they will not operate properly when bent incorrectly. They fall out so easily that occasionally someone is prompted to epoxy the shell stop into the receiver. This should never be done, but as we all know, things like this happen.

Problems with these two parts are a major cause for improper feeding in the Mossberg pump shotgun. If there is a feeding problem, here are some possible solutions:

Problem 1. The shotgun does not feed a shell from the magazine tube onto the elevator. First, check to make sure the shells are not sticking in the magazine tube. By fully loading it, make sure each shell comes past the tip of the cartridge stop without hanging up. If one does hang up in the tube, remove it in the manner described earlier. If the shells move freely, then the cartridge stop or interrupter might be the problem. This can be solved by adjusting these two parts. However, it is absolutely necessary to properly diagnose which part is giving the problem and how much adjustment is needed.

If the shell is coming back against the cartridge stop but will not feed onto the elevator with a full cycle of the pump, then the stop needs adjustment at the face surface. The face surface is where the shell stops against it or the pressure surface that rubs against the action bar. To determine which, see if the face surface is moving at all when the action bar moves its last $1/2$-inch as the pump is pulled fully to the rear. If it doesn't move, remove the cartridge stop bar and check the pressure-surface angle cut to make sure its sharp front edge is not bent in or rounded off. If it is still in good condition, see if it is bent so far into the shell's path that the action bar is failing to grab it. When this is the case, the cartridge stop bar must be bent outward right behind the pressure surface—just enough to allow the action bar to grab the pressure surface. This will allow the cartridge stop to move and release the shell as it is designed to do.

To bend this part, place the back 4 inches firmly in your vise. Using a point guide on the front, bend it enough so it will come back just 1 millimeter from where it was. Sometimes the pressure surface will be just right but the face surface is too far out or in, requiring the part to be placed in the vise where the part starts curving into the face surface. Such a small part is difficult to bend, but you must still be careful not to overdo it.

Problem 2. Sometimes, the interrupter will let more than one shell at a time out of the magazine tube, or it won't release any at all. The front tip, or shutoff, should move up to stop a second shell from coming out of the magazine tube just as the first shell is fed to the elevator. As the breech closes, the cartridge interrupter is pushed down to allow the next shell back to the cartridge stop. If it is not stopping the shells, it needs to be bent inward slightly to grab the shell. If it is not releasing the shell, it requires bending outward slightly to allow the release. This part should be locked in the vise with only about an inch protruding. Again, 1 millimeter of adjustment in or out is all that should be done at one time.

One note of caution: I know gunsmiths who are so experienced and have worked on so many Mossbergs with feeding problems that they will put these two parts on a padded workbench and use a brass hammer to hit them just right so they will "mike out" every time. I do not recommend you try this.

Problem 3. A second shell sometimes drops out the bottom as a shell is being fed into the barrel. This is a problem with the cartridge stop, and is solved by bending the pressure surface inward 1 millimeter. This gets a better grip on the shells coming from the magazine tube as the cartridge interrupter releases them.

The safety should be in the On position when reassembling the bolt assembly. Check it to be sure before starting to remove the bolt. If you are not already familiar with the inside of this shotgun, it is wise to look very closely at how the parts fit together before removing them. Remember, parts must be installed exactly the same upon reassembly. Move the forearm/action slide so that the bolt assembly is three-quarters toward the rear of the receiver. At this point, the bolt slide will be in alignment with cuts in the side of the receiver. The bolt slide can now be lifted up and out of the receiver, and then slipped out the front. Then remove the elevator by lifting the front end straight up and out of the upside-down receiver. Now apply pressure on the sides of the elevator until the two spring arms move together enough that the two lugs on the back of their arms are released from the two holes in the sides of the receiver. Finally, when the lugs are free, the elevator can be lifted out of the receiver.

To inspect the bolt assembly, start by looking at both the right and left extractors, making sure the spurs are still sharp and not rounded off. Extractors must move in and out freely to easily grip the rim of the fired hull. Their springs must be strong enough to hold the swollen hulls that sometimes don't want to come out.

The Mossberg's bolt assembly has 13 parts, three retaining pins and three springs. Make sure you do not mix up the firing-pin retaining pin with the left-hand extractor retaining pin. Taking these three pins out of the bolt allows all the bolt components to be dis-

MOSSBERG MODEL 500 SLIDE-ACTION SHOTGUN

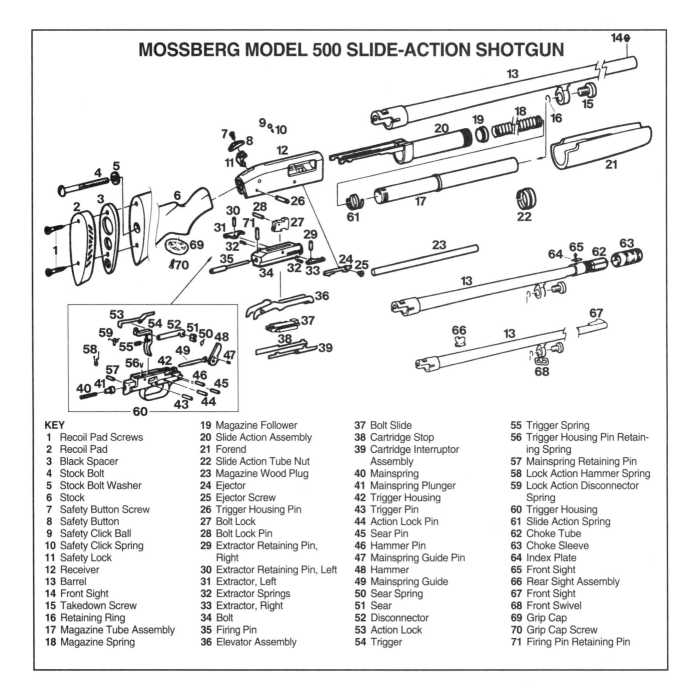

KEY

1 Recoil Pad Screws	**19** Magazine Follower	**37** Bolt Slide	**55** Trigger Spring
2 Recoil Pad	**20** Slide Action Assembly	**38** Cartridge Stop	**56** Trigger Housing Pin Retaining Spring
3 Black Spacer	**21** Forend	**39** Cartridge Interruptor Assembly	**57** Mainspring Retaining Pin
4 Stock Bolt	**22** Slide Action Tube Nut	**40** Mainspring	**58** Lock Action Hammer Spring
5 Stock Bolt Washer	**23** Magazine Wood Plug	**41** Mainspring Plunger	**59** Lock Action Disconnector Spring
6 Stock	**24** Ejector	**42** Trigger Housing	**60** Trigger Housing
7 Safety Button Screw	**25** Ejector Screw	**43** Trigger Pin	**61** Slide Action Spring
8 Safety Button	**26** Trigger Housing Pin	**44** Action Lock Pin	**62** Choke Tube
9 Safety Click Ball	**27** Bolt Lock	**45** Sear Pin	**63** Choke Sleeve
10 Safety Click Spring	**28** Bolt Lock Pin	**46** Hammer Pin	**64** Index Plate
11 Safety Lock	**29** Extractor Retaining Pin, Right	**47** Mainspring Guide Pin	**65** Front Sight
12 Receiver	**30** Extractor Retaining Pin, Left	**48** Hammer	**66** Rear Sight Assembly
13 Barrel	**31** Extractor, Left	**49** Mainspring Guide	**67** Front Sight
14 Front Sight	**32** Extractor Springs	**50** Sear Spring	**68** Front Swivel
15 Takedown Screw	**33** Extractor, Right	**51** Sear	**69** Grip Cap
16 Retaining Ring	**34** Bolt	**52** Disconnector	**70** Grip Cap Screw
17 Magazine Tube Assembly	**35** Firing Pin	**53** Action Lock	**71** Firing Pin Retaining Pin
18 Magazine Spring	**36** Elevator Assembly	**54** Trigger	

assembled. If it is necessary to replace an extractor, always compare the new one to the old one. Sometimes you will find that it is not the same, and fitting will be required. Even if the old extractor is broken, it is a lot easier to make the new one match the old if you still have the old one for a pattern.

If there is rust inside the extractor spring holes, make sure you get it all out, and make sure the sides of the holes are smooth. Rough spring holes will cause an occasional binding of the extractor spring, leading to an occasional failure to extract. This, in turn, will have the owner standing in your shop with a perplexed look on his face as

he says, "Sometimes it works, and sometimes it doesn't."

Before you begin working on a gun with an extraction problem, check out the chamber of the barrel. It is common to find chambers that are in such bad shape from rust pitting that the best of extractors won't work reliably. If you install new extractors and extractor springs on a gun with a bad chamber, it may work better for a while, but you have not solved the problem.

Replacing the firing pin is easy. Remove the retaining pin and the firing pin; its spring and washer will pop out. This firing-pin washer is important. It keeps the correct spring tension on the firing pin, and it guides the firing pin on its strike course. In spite of this, we find many Mossbergs that have been reassembled without the washer being reinstalled.

I said at the beginning of this article that the most common job was replacing a broken safety button. This is easy to do—except for having to hold five of the six parts in exact alignment while you tighten the safety-button screw. Make sure the safety-detent spring is moving properly and the safety-detent ball is on top of it. Once you add the safety-detent plate with the ball in the second hole (closest to the screw hole) it helps keep things together. The safety block must be turned forward as though it were a trigger, and held in place on the inside of the receiver. All this is done with the safety in the On position. Now, with the screw already inside the safety button, all holes can be aligned and the screw tightened. Be sure it is snug, but do not overtighten it and break the safety button again.

The ejector can be removed from the field-stripped receiver by removing the ejector screw and dropping the ejector out. Inspect the ejector spur to make sure it has its original shape and is not rounded off or broken. I always remove the ejector when cleaning the Mossberg, because it often collects dirt and trash around and behind it.

There are three types of choke tubes manufactured by Mossberg for their shotguns. The original Accu-choke tubes have a knurled ring that protrudes outside the barrel for installation and removal. The Accu-choke II tubes are mounted flush and screw all the way into the end of the barrel. Either style is designed for lead shot only. The Accu-steel tubes are the only ones which will handle steel shot. Many owners will buy these tubes separately, so be sure to inform them that there will be a small gap between the end of the barrel and the tube when it is fully tightened. (Some barrels will have more gap than others, and some will show little or none.) All Mossberg shotgun owners should be told that if steel shot is used, they need to get steel tubes, if their shotguns are tube-equipped. The tube should be tightened until it is snug but not overly tight. If it is tightened too much, the barrel, tube, or both will be damaged.

Some Mossberg riot guns come with a heat shield for the barrel. Care must be exercised when installing or removing this shield, since it may scratch the finish on the barrel. The six-shot model has two metal rollers that the screws go through, while the eight-shot model has a plastic spacer. The problem is that the two screws are not long enough to go through the rollers and start into the nuts on the other side, unless you clamp the heat-shield lugs together to get the screws started. Of course, if the screws were any longer they would, when tightened up, come through the nuts and have sharp edges protruding from the side of the heat shield. So go ahead and clamp the heat-shield lugs to start the screws, but make sure the shield is in the right place, as any forced movement after tightening will mar the finish.

Reassembly is usually considered merely the opposite of disassembly, but with the Mossberg shotgun, it is necessary to mention some parts of the reassembling process. Here are 11 things you should be aware of:

1: The safety must be in the On position, and the ejector must be in place.

2: The action bar with forend must be slipped into place by starting the slide bars through the bar cuts in the receiver.

3: The elevator arms are squeezed together enough to allow their lugs to fit into the receiver and enter the $1/4$-inch holes that house them. Don't apply more pressure to the elevator arms in removal or reassembly than is necessary to allow them to go into place or be removed. With its lugs in place, the elevator should be lowered until the front is level with the outside edge of the receiver.

4: The bolt is slipped into the barrel end of the receiver while depressing the ejector enough to allow the bolt to slide into place. Make sure the ejector is fitting into the ejector slot in the side of the bolt.

5: Push the elevator down onto the top of the bolt.

6: Move the bolt until the rear of the bolt is even with the rear of the cuts in the side of the receiver.

7: Pull the action bars back to the place they were located (when I warned you to look at them and remember their position while disassembling the shotgun).

8: Install the bolt slide by holding it at about a 45-degree angle, front down onto the bolt. The hook on the bolt slide will fit into the corresponding notch on the bottom of the bolt. Lower the back of the slide slowly into position while moving the forend/action bar forward. This will allow the bolt slide to drop into place with ease. Do not force any of these parts. If they are not moving with ease, they are not in proper alignment. If they are not free-sliding, you must disassemble and start over.

9: Slip the cartridge stop and cartridge interrupter into their respective slots, with the forend forward.

10: Make sure the hammer is in the cocked position. Hold the trigger assembly in at about a 45-degree angle, front edge down, and insert the front lugs into their slots in the receiver. Push forward and lower the back of the trigger at the same time until it snaps into place. This will work without force if it is being done right. If the trigger housing has been worked on and a takedown pin or some part is not in proper position, this will prevent the trigger housing from going back into the receiver.

11: Make sure the trigger-pin hole is aligned with its hole in the trigger housing before inserting the trigger-housing pin. Do not drive this pin in as it will disintegrate easily. Push or tap it in softly.

The shotgun is now assembled and ready to be checked for proper functioning. But first, make sure the breechlock and safety are working—even if you didn't work on them directly.

With a little practice, the Mossberg is easy to work on. This makes repairs fast and easy.

Glass-Bedding for Bolt-Action Rifles

Accuracy is still the object, but you'll find that glass-bedding a bolt-action rifle is considerably different from bedding the M1 or M1A.

By Thomas J. Stuntebeck

The Mauser M-98 stock as it appeared before glassing, showing degreasing and some evidence of shrinkage away from the action.

ALONG WITH ERODED BARRELS, sorry triggers, and poor sighting arrangements, nothing seems to affect a rifle's accuracy more than a poorly bedded action.

Much of the accuracy inherent in older military bolt-action rifles was due in no small measure to the close inletting the stock-making machines of the day were capable of producing. With today's computer-operated equipment, one would think stocks would wrap around a barreled receiver like another skin, but such is not the case. The industry seems to have opted for a more general fitting of both wood and polymer stocks, with only a few expensive exceptions. I admit that many modern rifles with this general fitting will still produce fine accuracy, but I think it's due mainly to the ballistics and quality of the ammunition. The question that remains is: How long will they remain accurate?

I have seen rifles that would produce 2-inch groups at 100 yards out of the box, but opened up later to where a hat would barely cover a group. Wood fiber compresses under recoil and the softening

effects of oils and solvents. Action screws eventually will reach the limits of tightening down. At that point, the barrel and action begin to "walk," and shots disperse themselves in ever-widening groups.

In a new rifle, a well-sealed stock interior can delay this action for a time. I heartily recommend sealing all stocks, new or old, if glassing is not in the immediate future. When the time comes to glass-bed, very little oil or solvent softening will be present, and a better job will result. In the meantime, the stock will not absorb moisture and warp, or rust the metal parts below the stock line.

A point of debate from the beginning has been "to free-float or full-length-bed" a rifle. Rules of thumb will make a liar out of you every time, but I believe that all but the heaviest of the benchrest and varmint barrels can benefit from free-floating. By definition,

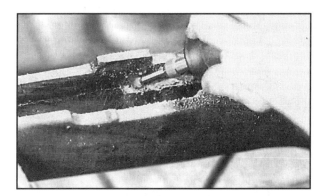

Routing the stock can be done with curved chisels or a high-speed hand grinder with a ball-shaped burr about $1/8$-inch in diameter.

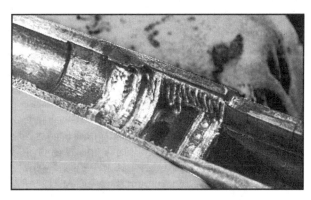

Routing to the approximate depth of the burr creates a shallow cavity all around the inside of the stock in areas you want glass to settle. Don't be afraid to leave it rough.

free-floating means a barrel that is free of touching the forearm, from the receiver to the end of the stock. I would amend that only with the inclusion of a 1-inch glass pad out in front of the receiver, under the barrel.

There are those rifles which will, for unknown reasons, do better if bedded completely from the rear tang screw to the forend tip. They appear to be in the minority, but should be considered if a free-floating glass job does not appreciably improve the accuracy. If added strength is needed in a very thin forearm, this is also the way to go, and we'll discuss that procedure here as well.

In the trade, there are those who maintain that a rifle is not properly glassed unless the action and magazine cavities are laid up as a completely glassed area. Under certain conditions, I agree with that, but not in all cases. If the rear of the barrel, receiver ring, and recoil lug are adequately supported along with the rear of the receiver from the trigger area to the rear tang, and the areas around the action screws on the bottom of the stock are adequately reinforced, much more is a waste of effort and glassing compound. This is called two- or three-point bedding, depending on whether or not you consider the pad under the barrel a third point of suspension.

Remington rifles will readily take to full-action glassing because of their rounded shape, as will many rimfire actions of the same shape. Winchesters, Springfields, Mausers, and similarly configured receivers require a more specialized preparation and treatment for the same job. I will do a full-action glass treatment on request, but left to make my own decision, I feel the two/three-point system accomplishes the same thing with fewer complications before, during, and after. A Mauser M98 and a Winchester 670 will be addressed specifically in this article.

When I first started glassing rifles in the early 1960s, I'm not sure Brownells had glass kits on the market. I was using Versamid, Epon Resin, catalyst, powdered dye, and glass flock in some very exacting portions. Needless to say, Acraglas Gel opened a few new doors for me in this field. I don't always cheer progress, but I make a large exception in this case. The 50-50 portions of gel and hardener can be as small as $1/8$-teaspoon of each, or a tablespoon or more—just be sure the portions are equal. It's a great system.

Routing the stock is done with curved wood chisels or a high-speed hand grinder with a ball-shaped burr, ideally about $1/8$-inch in

diameter. The idea here is to create a shallow cavity all around the inside of the stock in those areas where you want the glass to settle. Any finish that has been put on the inside of the stock is also removed, and the raw wood exposed. Don't be too careful about making these cuts nice and smooth; the glass will adhere better if the surfaces are rough. Creating a few pits throughout these areas doesn't hurt either.

Since reinforcement is another of the desired effects, I go at least the depth of the router burr into all square corners, and undercut the areas behind the receiver tang and the rear action screw in the trigger guard area. Clean out most of the wood in these areas but leave a small "island" of the original wood in any noncritical area that will establish the proper depth when everything is put together. I try to leave a $1/2$-inch-square patch on the flat area just behind the front recoil lug. The rest of the space gets routed or roughened up, even into the lug recess. If a "pad" of glass is desired under the barrel in front of the receiver ring, rout the barrel channel out as far as you want the glass to go. If that happens to be the full length of the forearm, changing to a larger burr may make the work go a little faster and easier. Be sure you have relieved enough wood along the channel to free up the barrel to shape the glass for full-length bedding, reinforcement, or free-floating. Otherwise, pressure from the forearm may create the same conditions you're trying to cure.

To free-float the barrel with this technique, lay two or three thicknesses of wide masking tape along the length of the bottom of the barrel. Be sure it is smooth, or every wrinkle will imprint on the glass. Cut off as much from the rear of the barrel as you want for a suspension pad, and coat the entire barrel with release agent.

Unless it is desirable for the glass to flow above the stock line, care should be taken during routing to stay about $1/8$-inch below the top of the stock. This is especially true of rifles that start off with good wood-to-metal fit. A small amount of resin will push up as things are tied together, but can be wiped off with a wet rag or paper towel.

I use the release agent that comes in the kit for coating action screws and painting the parts of stocks where I don't want glass to stick. These areas include magazine wells, trigger recesses, barrel channels beyond the 1-inch point in front of the receiver, the outside edges of the receiver and trigger guard cavities, and the top

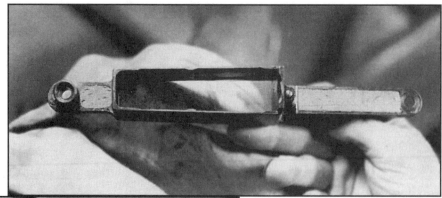

Any areas on the receiver that might get hung up in the glass—like the upper portion of the trigger guard and the magazine assembly—should be packed with children's modeling clay.

Painting release agent on parts of the stock you don't want glass to stick to will make cleanup easier.

edge of the barrel channel. Laying masking tape across the bottom of the barrel channel in front of the suspension-pad area and coating it with release agent makes a neater job, if you are not doing a full-length glass suspension. The excess glass comes out much easier, and you have a ready-made cutoff point to look at.

On the receiver, pack all the areas that might get hung in the glass with modeling clay. That includes pin holes and any screw holes that aren't needed to hold things together for glassing. I include all recesses that may allow glass to flow away from where it was intended. Pack clay into the recess in the stock where the trigger mechanism rides, and on through to the bottom of the stock as well. This will keep a great deal of glass from moving away from the routed areas and which might create gaps or, as Brownells puts it, "voids." I also pack clay into the striker channel on top of the receiver where the sear comes through, and level it off at the sear hole on the bottom. This helps keep the glass where it is placed.

Fill in all the recesses in the inside of the trigger guard with the modeling clay. On a Mauser, I fill in the floorplate-plunger retaining-pin recesses on the back of the magazine well, as well as the floorplate-lock recess on the bottom of the trigger guard. I have seen the cavity behind the front action screw used as an additional "recoil lug" on military actions, but I have my doubts about its value, so I block it off with clay. The Winchester Model 670, being a blind magazine, has just a trigger guard, so I fill it inside with clay, and level it off top and bottom. After this, I spray all the metal pieces with some of Brownells' aerosol release agent. I want to be sure to cover all surfaces, and I feel the spray will do a better job

than painting on the release agent that comes with the kit. The spray is worth the investment, so get it along with the regular glass kit.

Preparation is everything when working with glassing compound. Neglect it, and you may have to destroy a nice piece of wood. The least you can hope for is a major patching job, a wasted batch of glass, or another complete routing job. Check everything at least twice before you begin mixing, because you won't have time to do it later.

The Winchester, like many other rifles, is semi-free-floating in that the barrel is clear of its channel—all but the last inch or two at the front. I don't remove this material until after the glass has hardened. A rattail rasp and 100-grit sandpaper around a dowel cleans it out nicely for a full-length free-float. The Mauser barrel free-floated in its military stock even though the handguard-spring recess was left open. The stock had undergone extensive degreasing and apparently had shrunk away from the action enough to produce some uncharacteristic inaccuracy. In looking at the finished glasswork, it was easy to see how much shrinkage had taken place. The entire action cavity was smaller.

In rifles that have essentially good bedding and barrels that may already be free-floating, support the barrel in the channel at the forend tip with a folded 30-caliber bore patch or a piece of cardboard about $1/16$-inch thick. Then draw the action screws down snug, but not completely tight. This will ensure the barrel stays free-floating without the need to clear it out again.

There are different schools of thought on lay-up technique. One says do the whole thing at one time, another says do the trigger guard first and clean it up before doing the receiver. Still a third will specify the opposite sequence. If time isn't critical, doing the two parts in separate operations may produce a better job, although I have done it all three ways and haven't been able to see a significant difference in accuracy.

To apply glassing compound to a stock, I use a cake-decorating spatula that I cut down like an artist's palette knife. I start with the trigger-guard area, packing slightly more into the routed cavities than I know will be needed. I do this area first so I can push the action screws on through without getting them coated with glass. Then I tape them in place so they won't fall out while I pack glass compound into the action area.

I start from the rear tang area of the action recess, and work toward the front. I want to get the smallest cavities filled while the compound is in its most liquid state. It is setting up all the time it's being used, and is easier to work into the larger openings as it thickens. Apply the glass from the bottom of the action recess to the top. This allows you to see if any pockets exist where glass should be going. Don't be too sparing with the compound, because it's better to have a little too much than not enough. Avoid getting compound on the action-screw threads, if possible; a glassed-in thread is like the kiss of death. Lower the barreled action until it just touches the top of the action screws. Pull the tape off the front screw and start it in a turn or two, then go to the rear screw. Go from one screw to the other until the action is seated properly and the screws are merely snug, not hogged down.

On a stock with a good finish, it is best to lay masking tape along the top edge of the stock and around the magazine area. Press it down firmly, and trim it to the contours of the cavities with a sharp knife. I extend the tape coverage to the sides of the stock and out on the forearm as far as I can foresee glass being forced up and out of the stock. I then paint the taped areas with release agent. Obviously, none of this is necessary on a stock still in the building stages, but it can't hurt, and will make clean up a bit quicker and easier.

After the glass has set to the point where it will "dent" with a thumbnail and is no longer sticking to the fingers, remove the material that has pushed up out of the stock. Use a dull knife, as the kit instructions indicate, or a plastic scraper like those used on windshields. I made mine out of thick plexiglass and haven't scarred a barrel or receiver that I can recall. At this time, pull out the action screws and clean off any glass that is stuck to them, especially the threads. Coat them with release agent and reinstall them to a snug fit. Removing and reinstalling the action screws, in spite of the fact that you have coated them with release agent, is a good idea. They might break loose after the glass is set, but I want to be sure they do. Let everything set up for 6 to 8 hours—overnight works well for me.

Trimming out the excess glassing compound can be done with the high-speed hand grinder, fine-toothed wood rasps, rattail rasps and/or flat metal rasps, and a narrow wood chisel. Basically, whatever works for you and produces a clean finish is fine. Take care in removing any glass above the stock line. If release agent has been properly applied, most unwanted glass material should chip off with a thumbnail or dull-edged scraper. Dig out all the modeling clay and save it; it will last for several more jobs. The clay will come off the metal parts with a scrubbing in the solvent tank, and will wipe off or can be scrubbed of the stock with a stiff toothbrush.

Above—Use a dull knife or something like a cake-decorating spatula to apply the glassing compound to the stock. Do small cavities like those shown here while the glass is in its most liquid state.

Below—The same tool you used to rout the stock can be useful in trimming out excess glass compound from the trigger-assembly recess and other areas.

Seal any places on the wood where raw material may have been exposed in the trimming process. I apply tung oil with my fingers where it is needed. Do not get it on the new glass, if possible.

After the stock and metal parts have been cleaned up, reassemble the rifle. If the barrel was free-floated, check to be sure there is a "spring-back" action when the barrel is squeezed into the forearm. Check the clearance with a piece of paper about the thickness of a business card—some say a dollar bill is fine. Insure that it moves freely under the barrel from the forend tip to the receiver or the suspension pad in front of it.

Conclusion

The Mauser M-98 used in this article was a 30-06 that, before glassing, produced shotgun patterns at 25 yards and only periodic, widely dispersed hits at 100 yards. After glassing, still in its military configuration, it produced 1.25-inch groups at 25 yards and 7-inch groups at 100 yards. It was discovered that the accuracy was no better than that because of a severely washed-out barrel, so bad in fact that only the throat area marked the lead bullet that was forced through the barrel.

The improvement that it did make, such as it was, speaks well for the value of glass-bedding.

How to Lengthen Chambers and Forcing Cones

There are many reasons for the modern hobyist or shotgun gunsmith to equip himself to measure and lengthen both of these shotgun dimensions. Here's how.

By Michael R. Orlen

If the opened shotshell extends into the chamber forcing cone (left), the result will be a partial blockage of the shot column. This will cause extremely high chamber pressure and excessive recoil. Many older shotguns cannot take this abuse. A lengthened cone (right) keeps the shot from being excessively compressed before it enters the barrel.

IN THE EARLY 20th century, when many classic double, pump, and semi-auto shotguns were built and sold, there was no consensus among gun makers about the "correct" length of shotgun ammunition. For instance, 10-gauge shotguns were chambered for either $2^7/_8$-inch or $3^1/_2$-inch ammunition, and 12- and 20-gauge shotguns were commonly chambered for ammunition ranging from 2 inches to 3 inches in length. Shotguns of 16 gauge were chambered for $2^9/_{16}$-inch or $2^3/_4$-inch shotshells. The .410 was common in 2-, $2^1/_2$-, and 3-inch shotshell lengths, and the European gun makers added a metric dimension to all this confusion, making the chamber-length possibilities seemingly infinite. It's not hard to see why gunsmiths can benefit by being able to change shotgun chamber and chamber forcing cone lengths to allow older, still serviceable shotguns to fire modern ammunition.

In addition to having chambers of various lengths (often too short to accommodate a modern shotshell), these early shotgun chambers had very short forcing cones that were designed to work with shotshells now obsolete. These older shotgun shells were made without a protective shot cup. Because of this shotshell design, a relatively quick seal of shot column to bore was necessary. The short forcing cone of our older shotguns was important to ensure that very little gas passed by the shot column as the shot went from shell to bore. This gas would certainly have been disruptive to the shot column, and any disruption would have a detrimental effect on the shotgun's pattern.

Modern shotgun ammunition has its shot column completely protected, usually in a one-piece wad and shotcup. Since the shot column is now protected from the expanding gas propelling the shot charge, the abrupt forcing cone is no longer necessary; in fact, even better patterns can now be had by lengthening the chamber forcing cone so the shot column receives less damage as it is forced from shell to bore.

The longer forcing cone has the additional benefit of acting as less of an obstruction to the shot column. This allows chamber pressures to build a bit more gradually, spreading the recoil sensa-

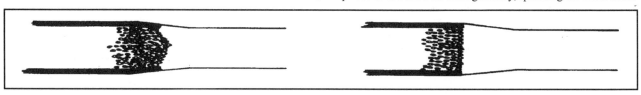

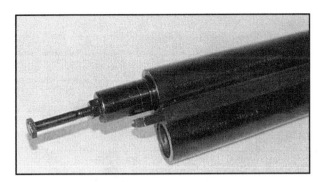

As this simple chamber gauge shows, the chamber on this double gun is short by today's standards. If a 2³/₄-inch shell is fired in this chamber, the shell will open into the forcing cone causing extremely high pressure and damage to the shot column. The result will be excessive recoil and poor patterns.

tion over a longer period of time, resulting in lower felt recoil.

The long chamber forcing cone is a feature that the public has been thoroughly sold on in recent years. Shotgun manufacturers are now offering the long forcing cone in many target grade guns, and gun writers in every magazine covering shotgun sports have at one time or another endorsed the long forcing cone. I mention this only to point out that many gun owners are already sold on this simple chamber alteration, so when you suggest doing such work, they'll be receptive.

Here is how the modifications are done.

Hand Lengthening

Lengthening a chamber and lengthening a forcing cone are the same operation when both are done with a long forcing cone chamber reamer. If it's a short chamber that you are lengthening, you will first have to determine its length by carefully measuring it with a chamber gauge. This is a very simple procedure, since you are only concerned that the gauge goes in all the way or does not. It is helpful to first clean the chamber to ensure that dirt and rust do not impede the gauge.

To lengthen a chamber and/or a chamber forcing cone by hand, you will first need to secure the barrel in a bench vise. I like to use a couple of pieces of 2-by-4-inch lumber and an old shot bag to pad the vise. Make sure the barrel is held very tightly in your vise because there is a great amount of torque exerted during this operation.

With a well oiled and sharp, long forcing cone reamer, begin cutting your new chamber by turning the tool clockwise. You will be amazed at how quickly a sharpened tool begins to remove material. After cutting no more than ³/₈-inch, remove your reamer, brush off

the chips, push a patch through the bore, re-oil, and resume cutting. Always rotate the reamer in a clockwise direction—even when removing it from the bore.

Continue these steps until your chamber gauge shows that your chamber is the desired length. Now take note of how much of your forcing-cone reamer is outside of the shell recess while it is cutting. Since a shotgun's headspace is not determined by the length of the chamber or the forcing cone, this dimension can be used to tell you when your chamber has reached its desired length.

At this point I like to make one more cut, using very little pressure on the tool. This will give you a very fine finish on the new forcing cone and very little polishing will be needed to finish it off.

Lathe Lengthening

If you do a lot of shotgun barrel work, you will find that lengthening forcing cones and chambers is made easier on a lathe.

To set up your lathe to handle this task, you will need a milling vise mounted on your tool post. A very good one is made by Palmgren and is available in the Brownells catalog. Attach the vise to your tool post with the vise jaws parallel to the lathe ways, clamping it down with an inverted tool holder. You will also need some sort of floating adapter to attach your reamer to the lathe spindle. This will allow the tool to follow the bore as it cuts its new forcing cone. The adapter can be held in a collet or in a three-jaw chuck.

To align a barrel with your lathe spindle, insert a tapered chamber mandrel into the clean chamber of your shotgun barrel (shotgun chamber mandrels in 12 and 20 gauge are also available from Brownells). With the barrel and mandrel securely held in the lathe headstock, raise the lower jaw of your milling vise to meet the barrel. Pad the vise jaws with a section of canvas shot bag.

If your vise has a V-groove milled in its lower jaw, align this groove with the center of the barrel. It is helpful to turn the shotgun barrel counter-clockwise (as you face the headstock) until the shotgun's vent rib contacts the lower vise jaw. There will be considerable torque exerted on the shotgun barrel during machining, and this will keep the barrel from rotating in your vise. Close the vise around your barrel and mandrel.

Next, loosen and then re-tighten the bolt that controls the tilt of your milling vise. This will ensure there is no tension. Loosen your three-jaw chuck or collet and move your lathe apron to the right, observing the mandrel's alignment with the collet or chuck. Remove the mandrel and attach your tool holder to the lathe spindle. With your chamber well oiled, insert your long forcing cone reamer and attach the reamer to the floating adapter. Set your spindle speed to 55 to 65 rpm and begin milling the barrel by moving it toward the tool using the apron hand wheel.

You will have to stop, remove chips and re-oil your tool a few

The ball-type brake cylinder hone is a great tool for finishing a long chamber forcing cone. These are readily available at any auto parts store. Be sure to use one that fits tightly in your newly-machined forcing cone.

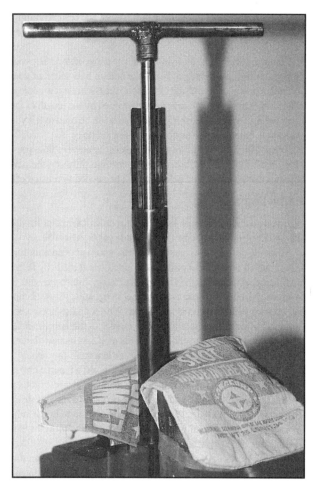

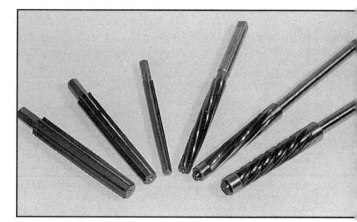

This is an assortment of long forcing-cone chamber reamers. The three on the left are the straight fluted reamers available from Brownells. The next item is a 28-gauge spiral fluted tool made by Clymer Manufacturing. On the right are two spiral fluted solid carbide reamers made by J.G.S. The solid-carbide tools are harder than chrome, and they allow you to lengthen chambers without having to remove chrome after the job is done.

Here is a shotgun barrel set up vertically in a bench vise. Be sure to keep the vise very tight. A great deal of torque will be exerted while lengthening the chamber and forcing cone.

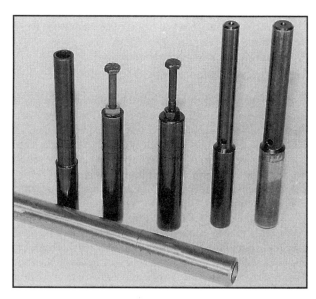

Chamber mandrels are helpful in setting up a barrel for chamber lengthening in the lathe.

This milling vise is made by Palmgren and is available in the Brownells catalog. An old shot bag can be used to pad the vise and protect the barrel's blueing.

Above and below—This shows how to set up the lathe to lengthen a chamber forcing cone. The top photo shows the floating drive adapter that allows the reamer to follow the bore. The canvas shot bag that normally pads the vise and protects the barrel's blueing has been omitted for clarity.

times during the milling process. When you reach the desired chamber length, make a final cut at very low feed rate. I like to use the auto feed set at its lowest position (on my Southbend lathe that is 0.0015-inch per revolution). This will give you a chamber and forcing cone surface that will need very little polishing to complete.

Polishing

Polishing a finished forcing cone can be done in a number of ways. A brake cylinder hone can be used on an electric drill. I find that the "ball type" brake cylinder hones work best.

Try to find one that will fit snugly in your forcing cone. Start polishing with a dry hone, and when you have honed the forcing cone to a reasonably smooth finish, oil the hone and run it for another minute. Be sure to oil the new chamber and forcing cone before returning the barrel to the owner. You will find that freshly machined and polished forcing cones rust very quickly if you skip this step. Once the barrel has been used a bit, the surface of the forcing cone will be burnished and less likely to rust.

I prefer to polish forcing cones on the lathe, using a piece of hardwood dowel that has been slit about 3 inches along its axis with a hacksaw. I insert a length of medium-grit emery cloth in the slit and wrap the remaining emery cloth clockwise around the dowel. Spin this very rapidly in the lathe using the three-jaw chuck to attach it. A little experimentation will show you the correct length of emery cloth needed to polish the chamber and forcing cone. It should fit very tightly in the forcing cone, and it should be used dry.

A very hard application of this device will quickly polish the cone and both burn and load up the emery cloth. Continued polishing will give your forcing cone a polished and burnished surface. This will give you a very smooth forcing cone finish that will stand up to the scrutiny of even the most demanding shotgun shooter.

> ## A Safety Concern:
> *Never lengthen the chambers of a Damascus or laminated steel shotgun barrel!*

Here is a very simple method for polishing a chamber and forcing cone. Make sure the emery cloth fits very tightly in the new forcing cone. As it loads up, it will burnish the surface of your new chamber and forcing cone.

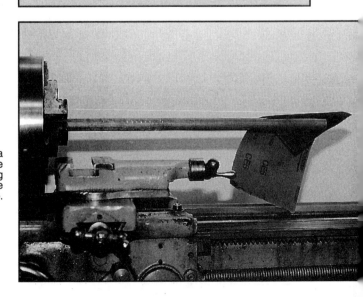

Reworking Ruger 77/22 Triggers

For just $9, you can make Ruger's good little sporter and its variations better.

By Chick Blood

IN 1919, a brand-new 22 caliber rifle showed up on the firing line of the National Rifle Matches, then held at Camp Caldwell, New Jersey.

It was the Winchester Model 52 and it was to undergo a number of changes in configuration before it was discontinued in 1980 as the Model 52D. One of those changes, occurring 20 years after its debut as a target rifle, resulted in the trimmer, lighter-barreled Model 52 Sporter, the loss of which has been

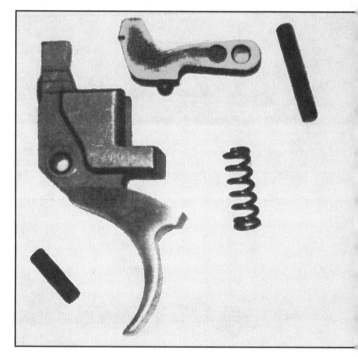

The total number of parts to be reworked or replaced in performing a 77/22 trigger job are shown above. No further disassembly of the rifle is required.

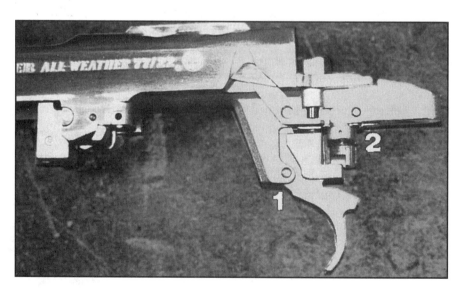

The trigger/sear assembly of a 77/22 is taken down by pushing out two pivot pins—the trigger pivot pin (1) and the sear pivot pin (2)—with a proper size drift punch.

The sporter version of the Ruger 77/22 preceded the target model by many years. With the Winchester Model 52, it was the other way around.

lamented since the gun went out of production in 1958.

Twenty-five years after that, Sturm, Ruger and Co. introduced a small bore sporter of its own at the 1983 SHOT Show in Dallas, the 77/22. It was a nice little gun then and a nice little gun now. It was also reasonably priced and more than accurate enough for small game, plinking or some success in silhouette matches.

Now, Ruger is showing a heavy barrel, target/varmint model of their sporter, the K77/22VBZ, chambered for 22 Magnum. Maybe one day, they'll decide to make a pure, 22 target rifle of it, complete with an adjustable stock and bring the evolution of the 77/22 full turn.

Since all models of this rifle share the same design, you can rework their triggers in the same way and, in my opinion, the triggers do need some work. They come out of the box with a $4^1/_2$-pound pull. That's not considered heavy on a centerfire rifle and would be a pleasant surprise on most pistols. But why on a bolt-action 22? Liability lawsuits and utterly crazed court-awarded settlements. With understandable justification, Ruger isn't alone in practicing extreme caution.

Excluding a fairly pricey Anschutz, I have yet to shoulder any currently manufactured 22 bolt-action sporter with a pull of less than $4^1/_2$ pounds. In most cases, these can be taken down to a crisp $2^1/_2$ or 3 pounds at no increased risk of liability and without entering the aftermarket for already modified, non-factory parts. With the exception of using a Wolff reduced power sear spring, the 77/22 is a good example, but remember that alterations you make to any factory trigger are likely to void the warranty.

After removing the rotary magazine, check to see that the chamber is empty. Depress the bolt stop on the left side of the receiver, raise the bolt handle and remove the bolt. Backing out the front and rear mounting screws frees the barreled action from the stock.

To remove the trigger, hold it in place while you push out the trigger pivot pin. The trigger is under tension from the sear spring, and you remove both downward from the trigger assembly. Next, push out the sear pivot pin and turn the receiver upside down. Sliding the sear forward will allow it to drop out of the receiver. There is no need for further disassembly.

Use a strip of crocus cloth "shoe shine" style to polish the trigger and sear pivot pins. Reducing pin diameters is to be avoided, so don't use anything coarser than crocus cloth and take it easy. Next, place the trigger and sear on a flat surface and get familiar with how they relate to one another. The trigger has a flat on its upper rear that interfaces with the upper front portion of the sear. Wrap your crocus cloth around a flat needle file, steer clear of the trigger notch and polish that upper flat. Next, polish the face of the trigger that extends rearward below the notch. The sear has a flat immediately above its notch that interfaces with the upper flat of the trigger. Pol-

ish it, then do the same to the radiused surface that extends downward from the sear notch. Do not alter any engagement angles or round off any edges. The only purpose of the polishing is to reduce or eliminate any friction that exists. Finally, polish both sides of the sear by rubbing it back and forth on a fresh piece of crocus cloth held down on a flat surface.

When reassembling, replace the factory sear spring with a Wolff #30171 reduced power sear spring (around $3 from Wolff). This will further improve let-off without having a negative effect on the safe operation of the 77/22 and is much preferred to chopping coils off the original spring.

The trigger pull resulting from this should be $2^1/_2$ to 3 pounds, depending on how well you polished the parts involved, and have little or no creep.

Though the 77/22 has a three position safety, I wouldn't advise you to take the trigger pull down below $2^1/_2$ pounds on it or any other bolt action 22. I recently repaired one that had to have its pull increased. It had been worked down so much that the safety and firing pin released when the bolt was pushed home. I never did find out who messed it up as badly as it was, but I suspect it wasn't the Butler.

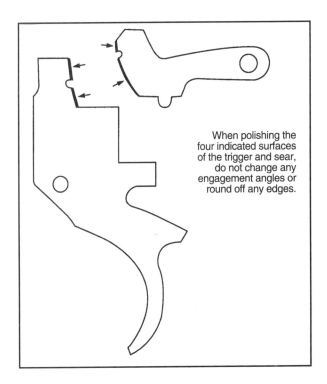

When polishing the four indicated surfaces of the trigger and sear, do not change any engagement angles or round off any edges.

Installing Screw-In Chokes Without a Lathe

A lathe is preferable for choke work, but hand tools are an option. Here are some tips.

By Chick Blood

MAYBE IT'S THE economy, or simply the urge to upgrade a favorite scattergun, but I've been getting many more requests recently to install choke-tube systems in shotguns that were purchased before choke tubes existed.

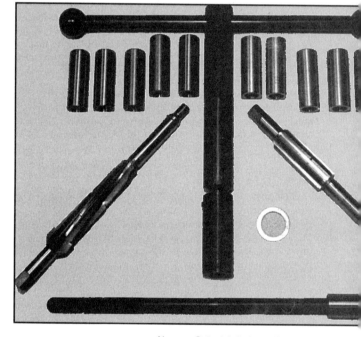

Above—Colonial choke-tooling kits include five steel pilots, five bronze bushings, reamer, tap and barrel spacer. A floating tap wrench, maximum bore gauge and additional pilots and bushings are available separately.

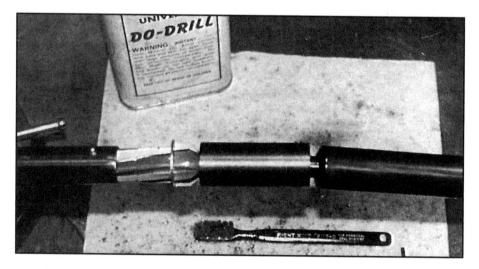

Left—When reaming the barrel, the tool should always be turned clockwise during cutting and removal operations to avoid damaging the reamer. Plenty of elbow grease, frequent chip clean-off and lubrication are required. Note the barrel spacer's position on reamer.

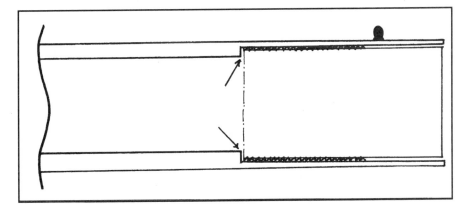

In a correctly accomplished choke tube installation, a small space or "ring" will be present between the end of the choke tube and the bore. If it isn't, tube damage or barrel blow-out can result.

In cases where the gun under consideration belonged to Grandpa, was passed on to Dad, I rarely undertake the modification. Today's shotguns use 1040 steel in their receivers. Many older shotguns used a milder steel, such as 1020, which isn't as strong and may present a danger under the pressures developed by modern loads. This isn't to say an old gun will go to pieces the instant a high-brass shell is ignited in its chamber. It may not happen for another 1,000 rounds. It may never happen. But if it does, the injured party's lawyer will file a liability suit at the nearest county seat. I don't want my name on it. And, I personally can't stand the thought of ruining the value of a fine old Parker or Purdey by installing screw-in chokes and refuse the job on principle.

Until a few years ago, choke work required you to have a lathe with a bed long enough to accommodate a shotgun barrel. If you weren't so equipped, the only way to accomplish the job was to send the gun to someone who was, perhaps another gunsmith or aftermarket suppliers like Hastings, or Colonial Arms. The latter two offer choke installation services with trade discounts.

Though the lathe remains the favored method among those doing a great deal of choke work, it is no longer the only way. Simple hand tools, devised by Colonial Arms and Clymer Manufacturing of Rochester Hills, MI, have made choke system installation possible without a lathe.

This tooling is not cheap, and you must purchase it by gauge and type of choke tube system being installed. I suggest you do a bit of research and purchase only the tooling that best fills your market's demands after discussing your needs with the sources listed here. That way, given retail prices that range from $140 to $200 per installation, you'll only have to rework three or four guns to get on the fat side of your investment.

Since I have some of Colonial's 12-gauge tooling, here's how to use it. The basic procedures are similar with any tooling you choose to buy.

Taking the Measurements

After making sure the gun is unloaded, remove the barrel, thoroughly clean the bore, and keep in mind during your measuring process that some manufacturers expand the end of their barrels. The order in which you take your measurements doesn't matter, but take them all.

For choke tube installations, the bore diameter of a shotgun is measured internally from the end of the barrel's forcing cone to the point where the choke begins at the barrel's end. If no choke exists, the bore diameter is measured from the end of the forcing cone to the end of the barrel. The standard bore diameters for U.S.-manufactured shotguns are as follows:

> 12 Gauge 0.729-inch
> 16 Gauge 0.667-inch
> 20 Gauge 0.617-inch
> 28 Gauge 0.550-inch
> .410 . . . . .0.410-inch

All of the above are +0.020-inch, meaning, for example, that the bore diameter of a 20 gauge could measure out to 0.637-inch and still be considered standard. These bore diameter differences that exist between manufacturers make no difference, however, when determining the amount of choke that exists in a fixed-choked shotgun.

Regardless of gauge, when a shotgun's business end has been constricted, or choked, the amount of that constriction is deducted from the bore diameter to provide the amount of choke. Constriction of the various chokes are as follows:

> Full. 0.040-inch
> Improved Modified. . . 0.030-inch
> Modified 0.020-inch
> Improved Cylinder . . . 0.010-inch
> Cylinder. 0.003-inch
> Skeet #1 & #2   to   0.010-inch

The actual choke diameter of a shotgun is the bore diameter, which can vary, plus the amount of constriction, which doesn't vary. This should help explain why a full fixed-choke 12-gauge barrel with a bore diameter of 0.745-inch may not pattern as tightly as the same choke in a barrel with an 0.735-inch bore diameter.

Before You Start

There are a couple of simple ways to find out whether the internal bore diameter of the shotgun will allow choke installation. The first is to select the steel pilot included with the tooling kit that represents the maximum size for the gauge. Insert the pilot from the

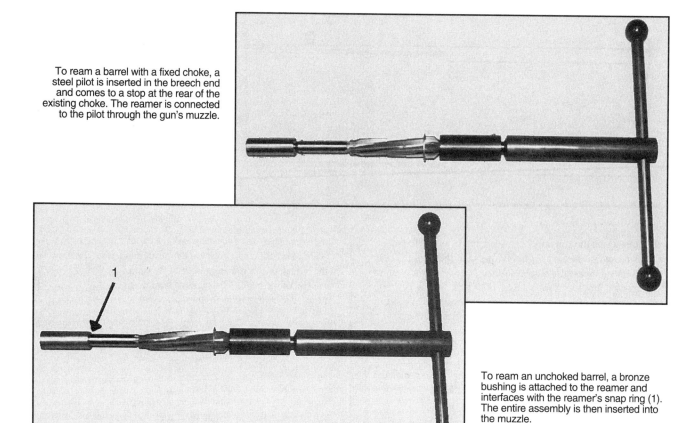

To ream a barrel with a fixed choke, a steel pilot is inserted in the breech end and comes to a stop at the rear of the existing choke. The reamer is connected to the pilot through the gun's muzzle.

To ream an unchoked barrel, a bronze bushing is attached to the reamer and interfaces with the reamer's snap ring (1). The entire assembly is then inserted into the muzzle.

breech end of the barrel. If it drops easily into the bore, the bore is too big to be fitted with choke tubes.

Simpler still is to use a Colonial maximum bore gauge. These tools, available according to gauge, are inserted into the chamber and past the forcing cone. If the gauge continues into the bore, the barrel cannot be fitted with choke tubes. As a rule, you cannot install tubes in barrels with an internal diameter (ID) that exceeds 0.781-inch for 10 gauge; 0.736-inch for 12 gauge; 0.730-inch for 12-gauge thinwall; 0.668-inch for 16 gauge; 0.626-inch for 20 gauge; 0.560-inch for 28 gauge; and 0.416-inch for the .410 shotgun. Forging ahead regardless will definitely cause choke damage and the distinct possibility of barrel blow-out.

Before installing choke tubes you must also determine whether the wall thickness of the barrel after reaming will be sufficient to assure safe operation. Do this by measuring the outside diameter (OD) of the barrel at the place where the choke tube(s) will be installed with a reliable set of dial calipers. Next, measure the OD of the tap you're using. Subtract the OD of the tap from the OD of the barrel and divide that number by two to establish the barrel's remaining wall thickness. If the resulting figure indicates the wall thickness will be less than 0.010-inch,

do not attempt installation under any circumstance.

Another element that must be included in your calculations is the concentricity of the barrel's outside diameter with its inside diameter. If not concentric, the barrel will be thinner in some spots than in others and the problem of insufficient wall thickness could rear its ugly head. It will definitely come up if anemic areas are present immediately behind an existing, fixed choke or where the installation is to be performed on an unchoked gun. You may or may not be able to make allowances. For example, the minimum OD for a 12 gauge, 0.795-inch-by-44 (thread size) Colonial choke tube installation is 0.825-inch. Say the OD of the barrel on your bench measures 0.834-inch and the wall is thicker by 0.004-inch on one side than the other. Dividing that variance by two equals –0.002-inch and the adjusted OD becomes 0.0832-inch, which is larger than the minimum required OD of 0.0825-inch.

How do you measure OD and ID accurately and simultaneously? A Clymer-made barrel-wall thickness gauge allows direct measurement in 10- through 20-gauge shotguns and is equipped with a dial indicator. The barrel to be checked out is slipped over the gauge's contact ball and the indicator's plunger lowered to contact the barrel. Both hands are used to move the barrel up and down between

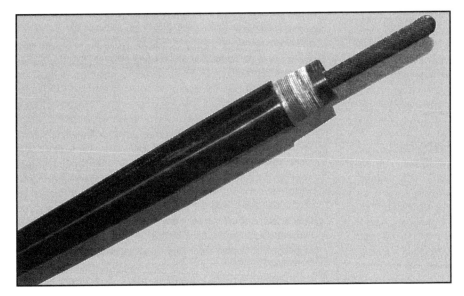

Insert Colonial's maximum-bore diameter gauge past the forcing cone. If it continues into the bore, as above, the bore is too large and the barrel cannot be fitted with choke tubes.

the plunger and the ball to give a direct reading of thickness at the point of contact. Barrels up to 32 inches long can be gauged by measuring one half, turning the barrel around and measuring the other half. When using this tool, you never put too much pressure on the arm of the fork with the contact ball on its end. This can cause the arm to flex slightly and give a thinner than actual read-out. As accurate as it is, you still have to be cautious in using this gauge, or whatever means you may use, when measuring Belgium Browning over and unders. There may not be enough metal between the barrels for choke tube installation even though your calculations tell you they're perfect.

Reaming and Tapping

Slide the barrel seating spacer over the reamer until it stops on the reamer's largest dimension. The spacer is a small, but very important, part of choke work because it will stop the reamer before the final choke seat is cut. As you'll soon discover, forgetting to put it on can really louse things up.

Next, check to see if the barrel to be fitted with chokes is chrome lined. If it is, you must remove all chrome from its muzzle end before

going any further. If we were employing a lathe, the chrome could be removed by facing the barrel. Since we're not, wrap a piece of 220-240 grit emery cloth around a flat piece of steel or a broad, flat file and sand off the chrome. Check your progress with cold blue, which colors the bare steel but not chrome. When you're finished, thoroughly clean off the emery grit to avoid damaging the reamer.

If the barrel has an existing, fixed choke and hasn't been cut off to eliminate the choked area—which can be accomplished with a hack saw or chop saw—use one of the five steel pilots that come with the tooling. They're graduated in 0.002-inch increments. The one you select should fit snugly into the bore with no wobble yet still turn freely. Choosing a pilot that's too small will allow the reamer to wander out of line with the bore during cutting operations and cause changes in the gun's point of impact. Double check your choice and bear in mind that the next biggest pilot to the one you select, if there is one, shouldn't fit into the bore at all. The chosen pilot is inserted from the chamber end of the barrel, its threaded end toward the barrel, and pushed gently down the bore. It will come to a stop when it reaches the existing choke; don't try forcing it further. Now screw the end of the reamer into the pilot through the choke.

Choke-tube tooling is available for all popular shotguns as well as for shotguns made long before choke tubes existed. Since it is fairly expensive, contact the sources mentioned for suggestions in determining which kit, or kits, might deliver the quickest return on your original investment.

If the barrel has no existing choke or has been cut off, use a bronze bushing that fits the bore without wobbling but still turns freely. Like the steel pilots, five are included with the kit. They're also graduated in increments of 0.002-inch so all the guidelines mentioned for selecting a pilot apply equally to bushing selection. However, you don't drop or push the bushing down the bore in this situation. Instead, place it on the end of the reamer, insert it into the muzzle and make sure the reamer's snap ring is in place. It acts as a stop for the bushing.

You never use a bushing in combination with a pilot and you never use a pilot in combination with a bushing. Those in the kit will do most jobs but others are available and can be ordered from either Colonial or Brownells.

When it comes to the actual cutting, you have some options. You can use a special adapter to link the reamer to an adjustable speed hand drill run at no more than 50-60 rpm. You can use a different adapter to connect the reamer—or tap—to a hand brace. You can also use a hand-held tap wrench. Like the adapters, it is hinged at one end and allows the reamer or tap to find its own center and prevent misalignment. It's called a floating tap wrench and is recommended here because, in my opinion, it will give you a better "feel" for reaming and tapping barrels the first few times you do it. Now it's time to remove some material.

Lock the barrel in a padded vise to prevent slippage, then brush or squirt a little cutting oil on the reamer and into the bore. Securing the barrel toward its muzzle will help it stay put and it won't flex as much as it would if you locked it up at its chamber end. If you're using a steel pilot, you're ready to start reaming. If you're using a bronze bushing, you obviously have to insert the tooling assembly into the muzzle. Use plenty of pressure and torque at all times.

Turn the reamer clockwise about $1/8$-inch into the bore. Remove it, still turning it clockwise. Clean all the chips off both the reamer and the barrel, relubricate both and make another $1/8$-inch cut. Never, and I stress *never,* turn the reamer counter-clockwise during any phase of the cutting operation. There's almost no better way to permanently damage an expensive piece of equipment. Continue cutting, removing, cleaning and lubricating until the reamer stops because the barrel is rubbing on the seating spacer. After removing the reamer assembly, give the barrel another thorough cleaning to clear it of chips before you tap it.

Internal threading on the barrel must be done by hand after you remove the spacer and install the tap on the same pilot or bushing used for the reaming. If it's a bushing, the snap ring must be in place. Lube the tap with a good quality cutting oil and start it slowly into the bore. Though it will cut fairly easily until it bottoms out on the choke seating surface—about 17 full turns—never force the tap beyond its stopping point. It is capable of removing the seating surface under excessive pressure and no seating surface means a poor installation or no installation. When threading is complete, be careful in removing the tap from the barrel to avoid damage to the threads and clean the bore again.

Cutting the choke seat is next. Leaving the barrel spacer off, switch back to the reamer and insert the tooling assembly into the bore. Clean and lube the reamer and turn it clockwise until it faces off the end of the barrel. Remove the reamer clockwise, clean out any chips and use a bore light or flashlight to check your work. The threads you cut in previously should end above the seat you've just finished cutting and a small gap should be visible between them. Giving in to the temptation of threading this unthreaded portion in a misguided attempt to make the choke tubes "fit deeper and tighter" will damage the seat.

Finishing Up

Remove the barrel from the vise and give it a thorough cleaning with a bronze bore brush and quality solvent. Put a little choke lube on an Improved Cylinder tube and install it in the barrel. It should screw in smoothly and fit flush with or a little below the muzzle when it has seated. Now put a light up the barrel, checking to be certain the seating edge of the tube is resting squarely against the bore, which is smaller in size. It will look like a ring. If it doesn't, a dangerous situation has been created . You can, and should, make a simple tool to double check this visual inspection. Take a 6- to 7-inch piece of welding rod or a piece of coat hanger and sharpen one end to a point. Put a 90-degree bend about $1/4$-inch long in the sharp end and use the tool as a feeler to confirm the presence of the tube seat. The feeler should catch in the seat on the way in and pass over the tube on the way out.

Remember, improperly seated choke tubes can catch shot, wad, or both, and be torn out of the gun. Be sure that the "ring" is at the interface between tube and bore with every choke tube you install. I mean every tube, not just the IC, and testfire the gun. If you have doubts—and you may have some the first few times—mount the shotgun in a rifle vise, clamp the vise to the bench and tie a long enough string on the trigger to keep you well back from the firing line. If you've messed up, it will cost you a new barrel. If you mess up and leave the testing to your customer, it will cost you a whole lot more.

A few, related, afterthoughts about sights seem appropriate about now. If the barrel you've choked is ribbed, there's little to be concerned about during reaming and threading as long as you don't crunch the rib in the vise. If you're working on a plain barrel with just a single bead, you don't have to remove it because it will probably fall out on its own during the cutting operations. There might be enough thread left on the bead for you to re-attach it with epoxy laced with powdered steel. Sometimes it stays on, sometimes it doesn't. You can also replace a bead sight by soldering on a ramp drilled and tapped to accept a new bead. If you plan to do so, however, you must do your soldering before reaming and tapping. The heat from a torch can warp a previously machined barrel and its threads in the process. Whether the barrel will require reblueing depends on how good and careful you are when it comes to sweating on ramps. A practical alternative may be to replace any lost sight by mounting a Polychoke rib.

Before tackling your first choke installation job, though, I seriously recommend a few practice runs. Scrounge around for an old barrel, cut about 10 inches off and use both ends of the piece to develop your skills. Finally, always use choke tube lube. It contains metal particles which support the threads. Also remember to periodically check your unloaded gun to make sure the choke tube is fully seated.

Installing Steel Buttplates and Gripcaps

Here's how to get the classic look of curved steel buttplates with modern materials.

By Dennis A. Wood

THE TRANSITION FROM where we were, to where we are now, as far as firearms accouterments, has been a somewhat slow process.

Traditions die hard when it comes to gun stock design and the normal functional furniture that has a place on a hunting gunstock. Accepted additions that play a functional role are normally sling swivels studs in one form or another, a gripcap to protect the wood in this area and of course a recoil pad or buttplate. Any other additions can only be considered fluff and serve no functional purpose.

We've all seen the old flintlocks with their curved steel or brass buttplates. Those things have mean-looking points at the heel and toe that look like they would hurt the shoulder under recoil. They probably do. This style of buttplate was carried on when the Winchester Models 1866 and 1873 centerfire rifles came upon the scene with their crescent shape.

The evolution of the curved steel buttplate has brought us a more relaxed version with less pronounced curve but still maintaining a traditional classic styling.

Curved steel buttplates are available commercially from several custom metalsmiths as well as the folks in Montezuma, Iowa, who stock the old tried and true A.O. Neidner style. Prices will range from $15 for a basic plate to just under $70 for a skeleton type with an open center that allows the wood grain to show through or the added touch of fine-line checkering. Buttplates can be had with checkered faces or smooth ones that can be embellished with engraving. There are even some that come with little trap doors to hide "mad money" from the little woman. This is an area where you can get as elaborate as your budget will allow.

The steel composition used in the manufacture of these buttplates is mild enough so they will take readily to any type of blueing or color case-hardening.

If your preference when working with a wooden stock is a semi-inletted and finished blank, some of the merchants handling these will rough in the end of the stock for the curved steel buttplate. If the stock wood suppliers you deal with do not offer this service, the job is not all that difficult. Patience and perseverance are the two necessary components.

The actual tools needed for the installation of curved steel buttplates are pretty basic and should be a part of your armament of tools, especially if you have already worked on a wood stock or two. An electric hand drill, a wood rasp with one side half round and the other side flat, a straight edge chisel (razor sharp), an inletting scraper and, if you have one, a bandsaw. You could probably get by with a coping saw if you are extremely careful.

To establish an outline of the buttstock, place the butt down on top of a piece of light colored cardboard. (I generally use manila filing folders.) Trace around the outside edge of the buttstock with a pencil, then cut the tracing in half with a scissors. The tracing should be a close fit to the rough buttstock. With the curved buttplate against the back of the tracing, you will be able to trace the contour of the curved buttplate directly onto the stock with a pencil. This traced line should correspond to the length of pull that is needed. For example, if your customer needs a length of pull of $13^1/_2$ inches, use a steel tape to measure from the center of the trigger to the middle of the buttstock.

At the $13^1/_2$-inch point, mark a pencil reference line. When you trace the outline of the buttplate, draw this line a little farther to the rear of the stock, about $^1/_{16}$-inch or so. The important thing to remember is to leave enough wood to work down to the desired length of pull. Once you take wood off, you're stuck with that length.

Roughing in the curve is best done with a bandsaw but, as I said earlier, if you are careful, you can probably get by with a coping saw. I usually tape the off side of the stock cut-off line with cellophane tape. This prevents the wood from chipping too badly when the teeth come through from the bandsaw blade. Keep the cut perpendicular to the center line of the gunstock. The curve should be at a 90-degree angle to the side of the stock wood.

With the saw cut completed, check the buttplate against the face end of the buttstock to see that it is a pretty close fit. The point at the top of the curved steel buttplate will need to be cut in next. This is where a razor sharp chisel will save you much sweat and anguish. A dull chisel will tear the wood rather than slice through it cleanly. The need for sharpness will be understood when cutting across the grain of the wood. Lay the top tip of the buttplate on top of the stock heel and trace it with a pencil. With your chisel, cut inside the traced line to a depth of about $1/8$-inch. Now would be the time to start coating the steel buttplate's inside face with inletting black. This will give you an impression of the high spots on the end of the stock when the buttplate is placed against the wood and tapped with a rawhide mallet.

I use Jerrow inletting black, but not as it is purchased. This brand is sort of thick and can occasionally give a false impression when used as is. I picked up a couple of small clay dishes from one of the places that sells flower pots. These are used in the raw state before they have been fired and hardened. Place about a teaspoon of the inletting black in the clay dish and thin it with a light oil. The clay dish will eventually absorb the oil out of the inletting black but a few drops of light oil will easily re-activate it. I happen to use 3-in-1 brand oil but any light machine oil will do.

An artist's brush about $3/8$- to $1/2$-inch wide works best for me when coating inletting black on everything up to barreled actions. If anyone out there has figured out how to keep inletting black from getting all over your hands and sometimes on your face, please drop me a note and let me in on the secret. I seem to get this stuff all over myself.

After coating the buttplate's inside face completely with the inletting black, set it in place and whack it with a rawhide or plastic-faced mallet. Remove the buttplate and you will see the contact areas highlighted by the black. The high spots are likely going to be quite far apart, which means you'll need to rasp them down until they meet. If you are extremely lucky, they will be closer together and a lot nearer to final finishing. This spotting-in process will need to be repeated until the inside face of the buttplate comes in full

Place the buttplate against the tracing of the buttstock and transfer the curve onto the stock.

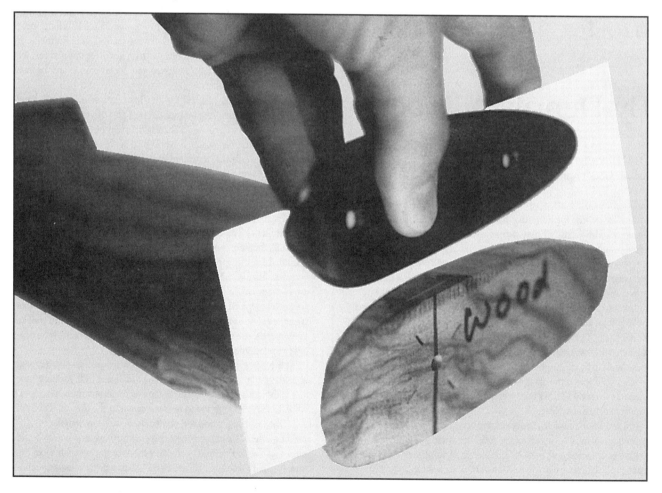

It looks much more professional to have the screws running north and south on the finished buttplate.

contact with the butt of the stock. When you get down to where contact is almost complete, an inletting scraper can be employed to scrape or shave those last few thousandths of an inch.

If you want to cheat a little bit once the outside edges of the buttplate and the point at its top have reached full contact with the stock, you could glass in the void in the middle of the buttplate. Just remember to coat the inside of the buttplate with enough release agent so it will come off once the glass has set.

In most cases, there are two securing screws that attach the buttplate to the back of the stock. I think they look best when the slots of these screws run north and south. If the buttplate came with a Phillips-style screw, it probably doesn't matter, but they should be positioned the same way. Check around the outside edge of the buttplate where it meets the stock with an 0.005-inch feeler gauge blade for any gaps that may be present. If you don't find any, proceed with shaping the outside of the wood sides down to the edges of the buttplate. A steel straight edge, 12 inches long, will help keep the sides of the stock straight while blending the wood into the buttplate edges.

Gripcap Installation

This is also an area where you can get as fancy as you would like. There are myriad styles and types of gripcaps available. For reference, the gripcap used here is made by Dave Talley of Glenrock, Wyoming. Considering that the gripcap's purpose is to protect the area from getting beaten up and chipped during use, I chose a steel oval one. You will see gripcaps made of plastic or aluminum while others are made from contrasting colored woods like ebony and rosewood.

The ways these caps attach are equally varied. The most common styles of steel gripcaps are attached with either one or two screws. The contrasting wooden caps are usually glued or epoxied in place and are normally accompanied by a forearm tip made out of the same type or species of wood. Dakota, Grisel and Talley gripcaps like the one we bought from Brownells attach to the stock with two straight thread screws (size #8-24). Custom gunmaker Jerry Fisher makes a nice one that uses a single screw placed in the center of the gripcap.

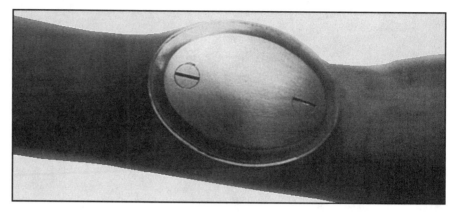

Once you have the two screws on the same plane as the bore line, dress the tops down flush with the gripcap.

The area to which the gripcap will be attached needs to be rasped or scraped flat and smooth. Once the area is as smooth as you think you can possibly get it, it's time for the spotting in process. As with the buttplate, coat the inside face of the gripcap with your imaging agent. Place the cap on the area where it will eventually be affixed and tap with a soft-faced hammer. Removing the gripcap will show an impression of the high spots. Scrape or shave these areas until the inletting agent shows complete, even coverage.

To help you maintain exactness to the centerline of the stock, place a length of masking tape over the center of both action screw holes extending back along the centerline to where the gripcap will go. Draw a pencil line along this center of the gripcap area. The gripcap can be shifted around until you get it placed exactly where you want it.

Once you have the gripcap positioned where you want it to remain forever, place one of the attachment screws in either of the gripcap's holes and tap the head of the screw lightly. This will leave a punch mark in the wood much the same as a center punch would produce. Drill a $^1/_8$-inch hole into the center punch detent. It is extremely important that this hole go in straight, exactly 90 degrees to the face of the gripcap area. If the hole is crooked, you will have a miserable time trying to get these screws aligned properly. The heads of both these screws fit with very little clearance in the recesses provided for them. You don't want them to bind on the outside diameter of the screw holes. Once you get the first hole in straight, stick a $^1/_8$-inch diameter by 1-inch long dowel into it. This will keep the gripcap from inadvertently turning on you and losing its fore and aft hole alignment. Dimple a mark for the other screw through the gripcap and drill it, being careful to keep this hole straight as well.

It is possible to purchase extra screws for these gripcaps. Whenever I can, I like to work with French or English walnut stocks. This wood is usually quite dense and therefore cuts very cleanly. The density also makes it difficult to turn a screw into a drilled hole unless it has been pre-threaded. I made up an extra screw to resemble a tap for cutting the threads into the wood when attaching gripcaps. It is a simple matter to grind two flats 180 degrees apart on one of these extra screws with a Moto-Tool and shafted stone. Sil-

versolder or weld a T-handle to the screw head for turning the tap screw, thus pre-threading the holes.

The #180-1 Magna-tip bit fits these screw slots as though they were made for each other. Screw the attachment screws down until they bottom out in the gripcap holes. While the purpose of the screws is to hold the gripcap in place, cosmetics does play somewhat of a role here. To me, it just doesn't look right when the screw slots are not aligned to the bore. It looks chaotic, as if the stocker was in a hurry to get the job done. The slotted heads of both screws provided are high enough that they will be above the gripcap once installed properly. This extra height will allow you to blend the screw head tops in with the top surface of the gripcap by filing and then finishing with aluminum oxide paper.

To align the screw slots with the bore line, envision the slots' current position as being the same as that of a clock face. These are #8-24 screws so for every complete revolution of the head, the screw will go 0.042-inch deeper into the stock. If we divide the possible positions of the slot into the 12 increments of a clock face, we would need to remove about 0.0035-inch of material in the gripcap screw hole recess for each advancement deeper. For example, when the screw hole is bottomed out with the slot pointing at 3 and 9 on our imaginary clock we would need to make the hole in the gripcap 0.010-inch deeper for alignment. The screw heads of these screws are 0.187-inch diameter. A $^3/_{16}$ end mill will cut the required amount of depth in your drill press or milling machine; just make sure you have an adequate means to measure the cutting depth.

Once you have one screw aligned, the same process is repeated for the other. The tops of the screw heads are then dressed down with a smooth cut file and finished with at least 320 grit wet or dry aluminum oxide paper. The idea is to bring them flush with the top of the gripcap.

Most of these gripcaps come "in the white," meaning they have not been blued. To ensure that the screws go back into their fitted place once they have been blued, mark one for identification. The ends of these screws usually come with a tapered tip on the thread end so I find it convenient and workable to grind one screw tip flat. Then you'll know which screw goes where when they come out of the blueing tank.

Removing Shotgun Barrel Dents

Buy an expensive hydraulic dent remover if you want. But a tool you can make on your own will do for most jobs. Here's how.

By Chip Todd

IF YOU ARE observant, you will find dents in about one out of every five shotguns. As is often the case, the owner may not even be aware of the dent, and you will have to show it to him to convince him it's there.

For this reason, I examine every shotgun barrel when it is first brought into my shop so that I can be certain he is aware of any dents or scratches already on the gun. This, of course, has to be done diplomatically. But this phenomenon isn't unique to shooters; people who take their instruments to guitar repair centers and their vehicles to automobile shops just don't notice these blemishes until their object has been in someone else's hands for a while.

The dents are usually the result of the shotgun being leaned up against something and its falling over onto something else. Of the several types of dents possible, most of the dents in shotgun barrels are smooth, spoon-shaped dents. These smooth-edged dents can usually be removed with relatively little risk to the bore. It is important to determine if there are any sharp edges to the dent if you are going to be able to remove it with predictable results.

Removing spoon-shaped dents requires an expensive hydraulic dent remover, like the one sold by Brownells, or some other mechanical method of forcing the dent out and then honing and polishing the barrel's bore until the reflections are straight.

If the object that hits or stops the fall of a barrel is hard and also sharp edged, the result is a deep, sharp ding, which is the worst news. The interior bulge can be removed, but the exterior blemish is there for good. In the case of a ding, there is nothing you can do except weld the ding, file the weld smooth, and reblue the barrel. This is beyond the scope of most gunsmiths and should be attempted only by certified welders with good TIG experience. Usually, I tell shooters who get these dents to either learn to live with them or buy a new barrel. I don't need the grief that modern juries hand out to gun companies and gunsmiths who would repair rather than replace a damaged part of a gun.

Besides cosmetic reasons for removing dents, there is at least one performance consideration for taking out dings. A dent will force the shot cup to mash the shot as the cup passes by the dent, resulting in a very poor pattern. This puts the shot into motion before it gets out of the barrel and then releases the side of the cup to once again upset the shot's location in the cup. In short, the pattern will often have a oblong pattern, or worse. I leave it up to the shooter to decide how much the dent will bother him balanced against the effort of repairing it.

If you choose to do something about the dent, the next thing that has to be decided is whether or not the barrel should be repaired or replaced. On some shotguns, the cost of a replacement barrel is less than the cost of removing any dent.

Two Methods

Some of the cost of removing dents is the amortization of the expensive dent remover. Let's look at the two commonly used methods of removing dents before looking at a new tool I designed.

Brownells, the largest gunsmith-supply house, sells an English Hydraulic Dent Remover for $145. It works well, but is a little expensive for my taste. There is, however, no denying its good results and the ease of using the tool. If you plan on doing lots of dent removing, then this might be just the ticket for you. It is certainly effective and fairly easy to use.

To use the hydraulic dent remover, run it into the barrel, position it beneath the dented area, and pump it up until the dent is removed. Additionally, the inside of the barrel has to have the dent area re-leveled to restore the straight-line reflections characteristic of new barrels, and you'll need to use customary barrel-bore polishing methods before the job can be considered finished. However-

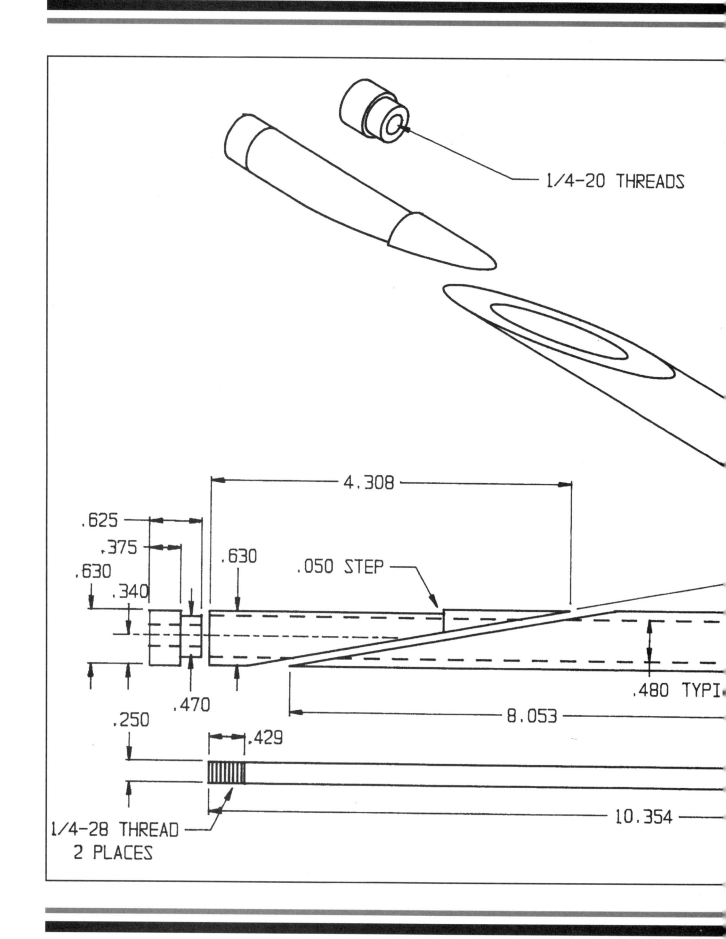

1/4-20 THREADS

4.308

.625

.375

.630

.340

.630

.050 STEP

.470

.480 TYPI

.250

8.053

.429

1/4-28 THREAD
2 PLACES

10.354

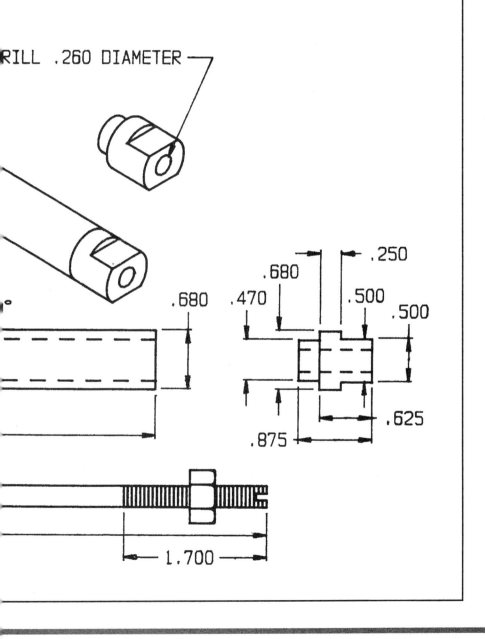

DRILL .260 DIAMETER

.680

.250

.680

.470

.500

.500

.500

.625

.875

1.700

er, there are some other ways to do the same job with a little more effort but a much lower investment.

A Cheaper Dent Remover

I have made hard mandrels to remove dents for the last 15 years because I haven't wanted to part with the money for the hydraulic dent removers before I got the next dent job. And when the next dent job turns up, there is never time to wait for the English Dent Remover to be delivered, so I use the mandrel method again.

This method involves some hardened steel pieces of increasing size, called mandrels, to force the dented metal outward until the dent is gone. These mandrels must not only be hard, but must be polished to a mirror finish or they will leave scratches that cannot be removed. The front ends of the forcing mandrels are chamfered at a shallow angle to ease them through and to decrease the force needed to overcome the friction between the dented area and the mandrel. It is usually necessary to use several mandrels before the dent is swaged back into place, but, if the chamfer angle and the surface is sufficiently hard and slick, one mandrel can do the entire job. It is imperative to use a very high-pressure-application grease, as the pressure between the barrel and the mandrel is extreme. This pressure is necessary because not only does the mandrel have to move the dent back into place, but the metal has to be compressed back into its original shape before the dent was formed.

The hard-mandrel method is good for someone who has a lathe, because the mandrels must turned and polished on a lathe to graduated sizes for a particular barrel. While the metal is still in the lathe, the surface is strip-sanded until it is ready for the ScotchBrite wheel and buffing. The lathe can save you much of the work of polishing if you use the turning motion to your advantage.

One of the nice things about hardened mandrels is that they can be used and then stored to be used on another job. I have been making and saving mandrels for shotguns for years and use them often. In spite of collecting them, I find it necessary to make other sizes from time to time. It costs you only the material expenses, which are negligible, and the labor is free if you do it yourself.

The material used should be large-diameter drill rod, tool steel, or other material that can be hardened to at least 60 Rockwell. This can usually be accomplished by heating the metal to bright red and quenching it in water. Most drill rod and tool steel comes in an annealed condition so that it can be more easily machined. In the event you can't find some tool steel around your shop, use mild steel and harden the surface with Kasenit case-hardening compound.

Kasenit requires the metal be heated to a cherry red, dipped into the compound to get the compound to stick to the piece, and dunked into water to quench it at a hard stage. The mandrel will need some polishing before use.

Using the lathe, turn a mandrel about 3 inches long and with a diameter matching the inside diameter of the barrel in the area of the dent. The ends should be chamfered to ease the mandrel into the dent area. A very sharp angle of this chamfer will make removing the dent very difficult, so the chamfer should be such that it is long and about a 10-degree angle or less. The mandrel should be blended with either sandpaper or a ScotchBrite wheel until there is

no discernible transition from the cylindrical body of the mandrel to the slight-angled chamfer.

To use the mandrel, liberally grease it, slip it into the chamber-end of the barrel, and drop it down the barrel until it is stopped by the dent. I have found that STP has given me the best lubrication. It really sticks to the surface of the tool, and I would suggest that the whole mandrel be coated with the lube. Once the mandrel is in place, put a brass rod or a good, wooden dowel on the mandrel and use a mallet—judiciously—to drive the mandrel through. As the mandrel is driven past the dent, the exterior barrel metal should be raised to the level of the rest of the barrel. Since the barrel will most likely be tapered by the choke portion, it may be necessary to make some mandrels to be used when the dent occurs in that area. I have found the size for the normal or open choke portions of the different gauges to be as follows: 10 gauge, 0.775-inch; 12 gauge, 0.729-inch; 16 gauge, 0.662-inch; 20 gauge, 0.615-inch; and for .410s, 0.410-inch.

Use these dimensions only as starting points, since the locations and dent types might dictate different diameters. Always check out dimensions of particular firearms and situations before investing time in cutting metal.

Because I am very patient and don't force the mandrels, I haven't scored any bores with them. So I have never regretted using mandrels. But with the cost of the hydraulic dent remover being so high, and the risk of scratching the bore always being present, it struck me that there must be some way to make a mechanical tool do the same job as the hydraulic dent remover. I thought of a half-dozen ways and will present one of them here.

Another Dent Remover

Somehow the use of mandrels is less than satisfying for me, so I have tried to duplicate the results of the hydraulic dent remover in a mechanical manner. Making the mechanical tool to directly press the dents out turned out to be so easy that the hydraulic method seems to be overkill.

The device uses the same principle as that of the bicycle handlebar stem, which has two main pieces: the active end with threads at one end and an angle on the other, and another with an angle on one end and a clearance hole on the other. The two angled surfaces must be quite hard and smooth if the tool is to last any length of time.

The hardening can be done by several methods, depending upon the type of steel used. In a fit of stinginess, I chose to use the case-hardening method, which accounts for the bulk of this tool's expenses.

Choose a piece of round stock for your tool and turn a portion that is about 5 inches long to the diameter that will go through the choked bore of the particular gauge you need. I find that the tool dimensions given above will go through the different bores, according to information from the *American Rifleman* magazine and my empirical measurements. However, since you will have to measure the portion of the barrel where the dent is, the figures given above are only for reference.

The length of the operator's end of the tool needs to be long enough to allow the use of the tool in the middle of the barrel. I recommend the length be enough to reach the center of a 28-inch barrel from either end. This will make the tool about 18 inches long, not counting the handle. The extra, over 14 inches, is because the tool's active area is about 3 inches from the end of the tool.

If you have the machines and knowledge to make the tool, then the accompanying plans are self-explanatory. If they aren't, it might be best to have a friend or a machine shop make the tool.

The active end (the end away from the operator) should be made from a 5-inch piece of steel. I had some 4140 steel in my bin so I used it instead of a softer steel. Since my first job was on a 12-gauge barrel, I got some $5/8$-inch-diameter round bar stock and cut off a 5-inch length to make the active end of the tool. The first step was to drill a hole all the way through the workpiece the proper size to allow tapping some $1/4$-28 threads later. This would be a No. 3, or 0.213-inch, drill if you are cutting threads instead of rolling them. Rolled threads are smoother and stronger than cut threads, so it would be nice to have them formed that way. Over the years I have needed rolled threads in most of the common sizes and have accumulated some rolltaps, but that is not necessary. We will leave the tapping or rolling of the threads until we have drilled the larger hole to its depth.

After drilling the hole for the threads all the way through the workpiece, the workpiece should be drilled from the other end. Rifle boring ensures that the hole will be in the center, if the drill isn't forced too heavily, since the drill will take the path of least resistance.

Lay the piece aside until it comes time to make the angles in both pieces. We will do the angles at the same time to ensure they are identical. This will be most important in order to have the tool come out in a straight line. We certainly don't want the tool to end up bending the barrel to shoot around corners.

The passive end (the operator's end) should be long enough to allow the active end to reach any dent. The active end is the threaded end that moves and directly contacts the dent, while the passive end is that end designed to remain still, in the hands of the operator. This end could, and should, be made from some thick-wall tubing, or it will have to be drilled with a very long bit. I chose to make the passive end from tubing and an endcap, even though I have some pretty long aircraft bits.

In lieu of having aircraft-type drill bits, the longer member can be made from two pieces using a piece of thick-wall tubing and a solid endpiece. Spot welding or silversoldering will hold them together. The tubing must have an inside dimension of at least $5/16$-inch, (0.312-inch) to allow the threaded rod to traverse up and down when the moving endpiece slides up on the non-moving piece.

If you use the tubing method of building the passive end, you should put a solid piece on both ends of the tubing so that the moving endpiece has enough surface area on its slanted end to support its sliding motion.

For that reason, this design would be difficult to construct for a .410 shotgun.

The drawing shows the method using solid end pieces and tubing to keep the cost and machining down. The end pieces can be more easily heat-treated and then silversoldered to the tubing than a one-piece member can be heat-treated. For this reason, I would highly recommend that the dent remover be made with solid ends on tubing to save money and tool wear.

The end caps can be made with a lathe by normal methods. The drawing should be sufficient to guide anyone familiar with lathe operations, so I won't go further into the individual part construction. The end caps should be hardened and then silversoldered onto the tubing. The long threaded shaft can either be made from drill rod or any good pre-threaded rod stock. The end of the rod away from the operator can be threaded and then silversoldered to the moving end, and flats cut or filed into the operator's end. These flats will be used to help the operator keep the active end of the rod under control.

The stop collar is used to help the gunsmith place the dent raiser directly under the dent. It can either be bought from a local bearing company or made with very little effort. The collar can be made with a thumbscrew instead of a regular slot or hex socket screw, since it shouldn't experience any appreciable lateral thrust.

Any of the pieces, whether they be for the mechanical "bike handlebar" dent remover or mandrels, should be highly polished after being smoothed with sandpaper while spinning on the lathe. If you don't have access to a buffing wheel, the polishing can be done shoeshine style with strips of sandpaper followed by a cloth strip with rouge.

After the dent has been removed, the interior of the barrel polished and all of the abrasive residue removed from the gun, the entire firearm should be oiled.

Bead Sight Basics

It may seem like a simple matter indeed to unscrew an old shotgun sight bead and screw in another. Not so! Here's why...and how to do it right.

IF A SHOTGUN bead sight is improperly installed, with some of the threaded shank protruding into the bore, the results upon firing can he almost as bad as if the barrel were tightly stuffed with cleaning patches. Chances are the thin walls of barrel are going to split upon firing.

The installation of a shotgun sight bead is certainly within the reach of almost any shotgun owner provided he or she has access to a few simple tools and follows certain proven procedures.

Removing the Old Sight

Few existing shotgun bead sights will present any problem when being removed; most unscrew easily. However, if you should run across a stubborn thread, don't hesitate to use a good penetrating oil like WD-40, SS-P Super Penetrate, and the like. Apply the lubricant as per instructions on the container, wait about 15 minutes, and then try removing the sight with conventional pliers. If you want to save the sight you are removing, use pads in the plier jaws to prevent damage.

Should you accidently wrench off the bead from the threaded shank, or if the head is already off when you start the project—eliminating any gripping surface—the old threaded shank will have to be drilled out and a new thread tapped.

Most shotgun sight beads come in two sizes: 3x56 and 6x48—using #45 and #31 drills respectively. The tap sizes will be the same as the screw threads. Bead sight diameters range from 0.067-inch to 0.175-inch.

When drilling, use short drills as the longer ones tend to wander. Also use a drill jig if one is available. One of the best is available from B-Square Co., P.O. Box 11281, Ft. Worth, Texas 76110. B-Square's barrel sight drill jig is a precision V-block type drill guide with two #31 bushings located 0.5625-inch apart. The tool may also be used for both front and rear rifle sights. The jig is easy to use and will center one or both holes on any round barrel up to 1 inch in diameter. No center punching or measuring is required, and a #31 drill and 6x48 tap are included with the jig.

Once the hole is drilled, tap the hole with hand taps of three or four flutes—preferably with the use of a tap guide. Use a special tapping compound such as Tap Magic rather than conventional cutting oil.

With the sight hole drilled, tapped, and cleaned, be sure to select the proper size shank thread. If too large, you'll have a jammed sight; if too small, the sight will wobble and will eventually work out or else protrude down into the bore to cause problems as discussed previously.

Installing the Sight Bead

Start the new sight thread by hand or with a special shotgun sight installer available from Brownells, Inc. Run the threads to full depth and then scribe a line on the shank threads where they are flush with the inside of the barrel (bore).

Remove the sight and cut the shank off at the scribed line. This is best accomplished with a hand grinder and narrow emery wheel; the emery wheel will make a fast, smooth cut.

Reinstall the sight into the threaded hole. Then smooth up the remaining shank with a small file or polishing bob until the shank is exactly flush with the contour of the shotgun bore.

The operation should not take over 30 minutes and the job is safe if you make certain that none of the threaded shank protrudes down into the bore.

Benchworking Winchester Model 70 Rifles

Today's Model 70s don't qualify for "classic" status, but they're out in such number that you're bound to work on one some day. Here are some gunsmithing tips.

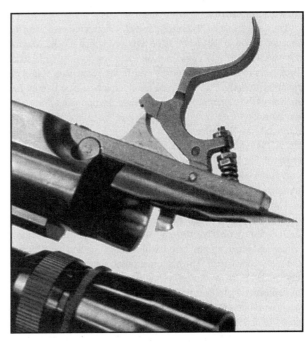

The Model 70 trigger is basic but strong. Three nuts on the threaded pin at the back control spring tension and overtravel.

By Dennis A. Wood

OVER THE LAST 100 years, Winchester has been shaken up, spun around and tossed in the air more times than any one company should be able to handle. But through it all—from ownership changes to bankruptcies—the company has steadily turned out firearms.

That the company stayed in business under sometimes difficult circumstances is a credit to guns like the Model 70 bolt-action rifle. This model outlasted many managements and has become almost legendary among hunting enthusiasts. I can recall reading the late Jack O'Connor's accounts of sheep hunting with his 270 caliber Model 70 when I was a young cub in the early 1960s.

You may recall the furor many sportsmen raised over the transition in 1964 to the "New Model 70." I could really never under-

stand the fuss because, in most respects, the new model's strength actually surpasses the old. For instance, the coned breech and the flat-faced bolt on the pre-'64 did not support and surround the cartridge head like the New Model does. The cut-out in the receiver's right side rail for the full-length extractor actually weakened the action. And unless you are going after critters that may want to eat you, the big Mauser-style extractor and controlled-round feeding is not all that necessary. However, USRAC has felt the pressure from consumers and is reintroducing that aspect in its new Super Grade. The nomenclature these days is "claw-controlled feeding."

These are but two examples of improvements Winchester made to its bolt actions after 1964, but there are other things you ought to know. Here they are.

Getting Started

Complete takedown is a prerequisite to thoroughly cleaning and blueing the Model 70. Before you start work, open the bolt and make sure the chamber is empty and the barrel clear. Then drop the floorplate to make sure there is nothing in the magazine.

In most respects, disassembly procedures are pretty much the same for the pre-'64, the New Model, and the Super Grade. Before removing the bolt on models with a two-position safety, place the safety in the safe or back position. If the rifle is equipped with a three-position safety, the intermediate position blocks the striker but still allows removal of the bolt. Because this style blocks the striker, it is considered by some to be the safest type on the market. While drawing the bolt rearward, depress the bolt stop/release at the left rear at the back of the receiver. Set the bolt assembly aside for attention later.

The three $^1/_4$-inch, 32-threads-per-inch action screws securing the barreled action to the stock can be removed with a #340-5 Magna-Tip screwdriver bit. These bits and handles are available from Brownells in sets or individually and fit the screw slots found on firearms properly. Pushing up on the floorplate-release button, just in front of the trigger guard bow, will drop the floorplate along with the cartridge follower and its spring. Once the front action screw is removed, the floorplate and its hinge can be removed from the stock. Taking out the fore and aft screws permits the trigger guard's removal. On Model 70s in the common calibers, the trigger guard bow is made of black painted aluminum, while steel is used on big bumpers like the 375 H&H and the 458 Winchester Magnum.

The aluminum bow can be replaced by the steel one if you are so inclined. USRAC's part number for the steel trigger guard is 28017. You will have to remove the floorplate-release button, spring and retaining pin from the aluminum one and install it into the steel replacement. The part order number for the whole assembly is 28117. Brownells sells an all-steel trigger guard bow made by Williams Manufacturing that drops right in the stock of those post-'64 models to replace the painted aluminum guard. These will cost $40 or $50.

Once the trigger guard is off, the magazine box can be taken out. Set it aside and separate the barreled action from the stock. Check the crown at the muzzle for any nicks or irregularities that will affect accuracy. If the stock is made of wood, check the inletting to make sure there is a good coat of sealing finish. Also inspect the barrel channel for glazed spots that may be putting undue pressure on the barrel. Such pressure points play havoc with accuracy and should be scraped away and the channel finished with a good wood sealant.

To gain access to the trigger assembly, place the barrel in a vise with padded jaws with the bottom of the receiver facing upward. The Model 70's trigger system is obviously quite simple but it is good and strong.

With a $^3/_{32}$-inch punch, drift the single trigger pin out of the receiver's left side, as it sits in your vise, to the right. While drifting the trigger pin, stop when the punch reaches the inside wall of the recess in which the trigger fits. This pin also secures the bolt stop/release and its spring. Leave the punch in place and pull the pin out while holding down the bolt stop/release with your thumb.

Once the trigger pin is all the way out, the bolt stop/release can be removed. Pull the punch out the way it went in, then remove the trigger and the spring that maintains pressure on the sear. Using a $^3/_{16}$-inch punch, drift the sear pin out. This pin has a larger diameter on the left side of the receiver as it sits in the vise and can only go one way. The sear and sear spring should be the last items removed.

The bolt assembly is the New Model 70's most complex part, containing a total of tewnty parts, but takedown is relatively easy. Hopefully, the safety remained at the midway condition or on safe. If for some reason the safety has found its way forward, it must be returned to the midway point or the bolt can't be disassembled. Clamp the cocking piece in a vise with smooth hard jaws, push forward on the breechbolt sleeve until there is about $^3/_8$-inch of the cocking piece protruding at the back of the bolt sleeve, then set the safety to the middle position. Now you can take the bolt apart.

Press down on the breechbolt sleeve lock and rotate the bolt sleeve counter-clockwise until the bolt sleeve comes out of the bolt body. The safety now needs to be placed in the forward position, which will relieve some slight tension on the striker spring. Removing the striker spring requires dexterity and some caution because the firing-pin washer can wind up in parts unknown if you don't stay focused. Place the back end of the cocking piece down on a non-slip surface like a piece of carpet or foam padding. I also wrap a sheet of paper towel around the spring to keep my fingers from slipping. Pull down on the spring and as you hold it, remove the "C" washer from its groove in the firing pin. Slowly relax the spring tension and catch the washer that was positioned between the "C" washer and spring. Now relax the spring completely and remove it. Hopefully, everything came off in good order and you're not crawling around on hands and knees looking for that little washer.

Back out the firing-pin stop screw with a #120-3 Magna-Tip bit. The firing pin and cocking piece will slide forward and out of the bolt sleeve. The firing pin and cocking piece are permanently pinned together into a solitary unit. If the firing pin breaks, the component will have to be specially fitted. It is important that you send the serial number of that particular firearm along with your order for a new one. This part must be fitted by a gunsmith and is not sold to consumers.

Mating this firing pin/cocking piece unit to the individual rifle is a try-and-fit proposition. There are no shortcuts. If the cutout on the side of the cocking piece does not line up properly with the safety, the firearm is not safe. You may need to remove a little metal, reassemble and try the safety until the fit is perfect. The shoulder that the wing safety rests against must have the rear angle maintained. Smoothing it up is no problem as long as the angle is maintained.

To remove the safety, the roll pin that secures it is drifted through toward the center hole in the bolt sleeve. Swing the safety to the rear, lifting it up and out. The safety plunger and spring is under tension and will come out quickly. Moisture has a tendency to collect in these small holes that capture small springs and plungers, so clean them with a good water-displacing oil. A dab of your favorite gun grease will keep these little cavities free of rust after reassembly.

WINCHESTER MODEL 70 AND 70 FEATHERWEIGHT BOLT-ACTION RIFLE

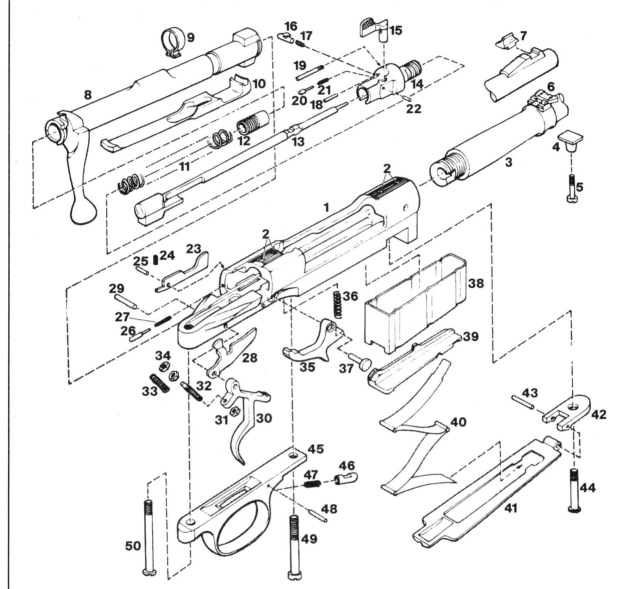

KEY

1 Receiver
2 Receiver Plug Screws
3 Barrel
4 Forearm Stud
5 Forearm Stud Screw
6 Rear Sight Assembly
7 Front Sight
8 Breechbolt
9 Extractor Ring
10 Extractor
11 Firing Pin Spring
12 Firing Pin Sleeve
13 Firing Pin
14 Breechbolt Sleeve

15 Safety Lock
16 Breechbolt Sleeve Lock
17 Breechbolt Sleeve Lock
 Spring
18 Breechbolt Sleeve Lock Pin
19 Firing Pin Stop Screw
20 Safety Lock Plunger
21 Safety Lock Plunger Spring
22 Safety Lock Stop Pin
23 Ejector
24 Ejector Spring
25 Ejector Pin
26 Bolt Stop Plunger
27 Bolt Stop Plunger Spring
28 Bolt Stop

29 Trigger Pin
30 Trigger
31 Trigger Stop Screw Nut
32 Trigger Stop Screw
33 Trigger Spring
34 Trigger Spring Adjusting
 Nuts
35 Sear
36 Sear Spring
37 Sear Pin
38 Magazine
39 Magazine Follower
40 Magazine Spring
41 Magazine Cover
42 Magazine Cover Hinge Plate

43 Magazine Cover Hinge Pin
44 Magazine Cover Hinge Plate
 Screw
45 Guard Bow
46 Magazine Cover Catch
47 Magazine Cover Catch
 Spring
48 Magazine Cover Catch Pin
49 Front Guard Bow Screw
50 Rear Guard Bow Screw

Parts Not Shown
 Buttplate
 Buttplate Screws
 Buttstock

Check the wing safety for burrs or irregularities on the stem that rests against the cocking piece. If you choose to polish the stem for smoother operation, avoid removing an excessive amount of material because the stem must have enough surface to bear fully on the cocking piece.

To reassemble, insert the safety plunger spring and plunger, then the safety itself. The roll pin holding these parts in place can be inserted only in the direction from which you drifted it out. Check to see that it does not protrude into the center hole for the cocking piece. Insert the firing-pin assembly into the bolt sleeve, replace the firing-pin stop screw until it bottoms, then back it off $1/8$-turn. A dab—don't overdo it—of thread sealer will keep the screw from backing out under recoil. With the wing safety forward, slide the striker spring onto the firing pin. As you did before, place the rear of the cocking piece and back of the bolt sleeve down on a padded surface and, while pulling down on the spring, slide the firing-pin washer on and install the "C" washer into the groove in the firing pin. It is important that the recess cut into the "C" washer be up or toward the front end of the firing pin. Relax the striker spring and this step is complete. To get the safety back into the intermediate position, repeat the steps described earlier.

Working The Bolt

We can now turn our attention to the bolt body, which contains the ejector and the extractor. You will find the ejector pin on the top of the left locking lug, in a hole that angles slightly down and toward the center of the bolt. Using a $1/16$-inch punch, drive the ejector pin down and out. The ejector and ejector spring come out quickly, so place your thumb over the face of the bolt body to contain them. Slide the two parts out the front, check their hole for accumulated crud, then clean it with water-displacing oil. Pipe cleaners get into these little areas easily.

The extractor fits into an undercut slot in the right locking lug of the bolt body. A hole in the extractor face will accommodate a $1/16$-inch punch. Once the punch is inserted, you can feel the tension on the extractor spring by pushing on it slightly. To remove the extractor, push down on the plunger while sliding the extractor itself toward the firing-pin hole. Here again, watch for the extractor plunger and spring to pop out. Once the extractor has been removed, look for and smooth out any burrs that will interfere with smooth operation. A good hard Arkansas stone works well. Clean the hole and apply a dab of good gun grease.

Check the bolt face for irregularities and make sure the firing pin hole is nice and round without burrs. At the back of the bolt, just behind and below the bolt handle, there is a notch in which the cocking piece rests while in the forward condition. If you find burrs, some judicious work with a hard Arkansas stone might be in order.

The ejector and extractor reassemble in reverse order of the way they were disassembled. Insert the ejector spring and then the ejector, making sure the cutout in the ejector lines up with the retaining-pin hole. Tap the pin into place and, using a $1/16$-inch punch, set the pin to just below the left locking lug's surface. Check to see that the pin does not protrude at the bottom. To install the extractor, insert the extractor spring, then the extractor plunger. With a small screwdriver, push down on the plunger while sliding the extractor into place until the plunger slips into its hole in the extractor.

Insert the bolt-sleeve assembly into the bolt body. Depress the bolt sleeve, and turn the bolt sleeve assembly clockwise until the threads engage. Turn the bolt sleeve until the bolt-sleeve lock fits into its notch at the rear of the bolt. The sear and sear spring can now be installed. The pin for these two items allows one-way insertion only. Once this step is complete, the trigger and bolt-stop can be installed.

As I said, the Model 70 trigger system is quite simple. Three nuts on the threaded pin at the back control trigger-spring tension and overtravel. The nuts are thin, measuring only about 0.070-inch in thickness. To work with these, I had two $1/4$-inch wrenches ground down to about 0.065-inch thick, but automotive ignition wrenches, if they're handy, will work just as well. I never adjust Model 70 triggers below $3^1/2$ pounds.

Working the Savage Model 110

Savage has sold tens of thousands of Model 110 rifles over the years to hunters seeking an inexpensive rifle. Here are some things that might need fixing.

By Frank Fry

THE SAVAGE MODEL 110 has been with us in one form or another since 1958 and, although it is not as visible nor as widely advertised as models from other manufacturers, it is seen often enough to warrant the gunsmith's attention.

The Model 110 has been produced in many variations and calibers, including magnums and models with detachable magazines. The current Model 110 is available with either wood or synthetic stocks and has a concealed box magazine.

As we begin work on the Savage 110, those cautions we hear so often must be repeated. First, make sure the chamber and magazine are empty before handling or starting work. Safety glasses are also recommended. (Wearing safety glasses should become automatic.) In addition, the professional gunsmith will use screwdrivers that have shaped tips that fit screw slots correctly. This will help to prevent burring screw slots or galling the sides of screw holes. Vises should have

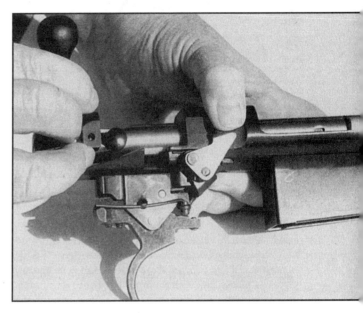

To remove the Savage's bolt, press down on the cocking indicator while pulling the trigger.

smooth, protective jaws to prevent marring the work. A clean bench mat to protect the work from the bench top also helps prevent marring of wood or metal parts. Finally, placing parts in containers as they are removed will help keep small parts from becoming lost.

Disassembly

Disassembly of the Model 110—as far as is practical for preventive maintenance, cleaning and oiling—is not difficult. Before starting, check the chamber again to assure it is empty.

Safety Operation. Note that the safety has three positions: all the way forward for fire, all the way to the rear for safe (which also locks the bolt handle from being raised), and a mid-position which keeps the trigger blocked and on "Safe." In practice, to load or unload, the safety is placed in the forward "Fire" position to raise the bolt handle, then the safety is pulled back to "Safe." Now the rifle can be loaded or unloaded with the trigger blocked. With the bolt handle raised, and the safety in the full rear or "Safe" position, the safety will automatically set in the middle location when the bolt is operated.

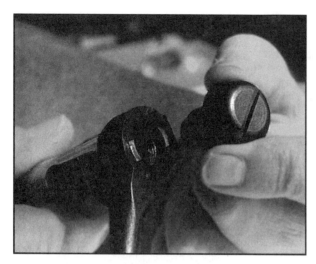

Removing the bolt-assembly screw allows you to get at all the insides for additional cleaning.

Bolt Removal. With the safety off and the bolt forward, pull the trigger and press down the cocking indicator (the lever just in front of the bolt handle). The bolt can now be slipped out of the receiver.

Action Removal. As with most bolt-action rifles, the Model 110 stock is fastened to the action with two stock or action screws. In this instance, Phillips-head screws are found in the front of the trigger guard and about 4 inches ahead of the guard in the forearm. After these screws have been removed, the barreled action can be lifted away from the stock. The plastic follower with attached spring will either stay in the stock or fall out, as it is not contained in the action or stock. The rifle is now field stripped.

Bolt Detail Disassembly

Far too often a gunsmith, either from ignorance or laziness, will not completely disassemble the bolt to remove solidified oils that may have built up inside.

To detail strip the bolt, the cocking-piece pin must be rotated to rest at the bottom of the cocking cam to relieve pressure from the bolt-assembly screw. As the firing-pin spring is quite strong, a vise to hold the bolt will make this job easier. The slot in the screw is curved so a piece of .080-inch flat stock will need to be carefully fitted to the slot to prevent damage to the tight screw. Now the slotted bolt-assembly screw can be removed.

After the screw has been removed, the bolt handle is lifted off the back of the bolt. Next, the rear baffle assembly can be pulled off the back of the bolt. The baffle-pressure ball, spring, and plunger remain in the baffle. Now pull the cocking-piece sleeve to the rear and the cocking piece pin can be pulled out of the bolt. The firing-pin assembly and cocking-piece sleeve will slide out the rear of the bolt.

To complete the disassembly of the bolt body, press out the bolt-head retaining pin. With the front baffle and friction washer now loose on the bolt-head stem, the bolt head slides out of the front of the bolt. A thorough cleaning of the bolt is easily accomplished at this point.

Further disassembly of the firing-pin assembly is strongly discouraged, as these parts are factory adjusted. The firing-pin spring is held under strong compression, and reassembly may be difficult. If, for some unforeseen reason, the firing-pin assembly does need further disassembly, the cocking piece can be unscrewed from the rear of the firing pin, thus releasing the cocking piece and cocking-piece sleeve-lock washer from the firing pin. If not contained, the cocking piece and sleeve lock will spring free from the strong firing-pin spring and can become lost.

If the sleeve lock or cocking piece does become lost, the entire rifle will have to be returned to the factory for replacement, because these are restricted parts. Another caution—and reason for leaving the firing-pin assembly together—is that firing-pin protrusion (the distance the firing-pin tip extends beyond the bolt face in the fired condition) is a critical factory-set dimension. If the cocking piece and firing-pin spring are removed, extreme care must be used to see that the firing-pin stop nut is not moved from the original factory-adjusted position.

To reassemble the firing-pin assembly, slide the spring over the firing pin and pull the spring down until the cocking-sleeve lock

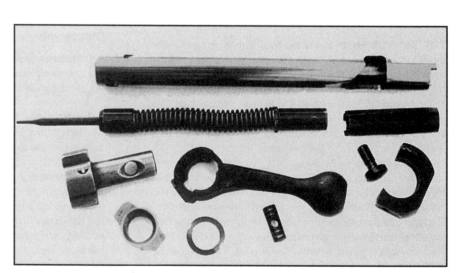

These are the major components of the Savage's bolt.

washer can be placed over the firing pin. The tongue in the washer fits on the milled flat of the pin. Now screw on the cocking piece. Line up the cocking-piece pin hole with the slot in the sleeve. Once again, caution is urged, as the firing pin is strong and damage can occur to its slender tip; any bend will degrade the function and reliability of ignition. (Note: Some firing-pin protection may be gained by inserting the firing-pin front into the rear of the bolt head while pushing down on the spring.)

To reassemble the remainder of the bolt, place the front baffle over the bolt front body. (The bolt guide on the front baffle must be on the bottom of the extractor side of the bolt head.) The friction washer is placed behind the baffle, and the unit slides into the front of the bolt body. Rotate the bolt head until it seats into the bolt body. Insert the bolt-head retaining pin with the center hole parallel to the bolt. Check the retaining-pin hole for alignment by inserting the firing pin into the bolt. The firing pin must slide through the hole and extend beyond the bolt face.

Now insert the cocking-piece sleeve over the cocking piece until the forward end of the slot is lined up with the hole in the cocking piece. Insert the cocking-piece pin. Finally, slide the rear baffle onto the bolt (flat side forward) with the friction ball located in the slot on the side of the bolt. The bolt handle drops over the rear of the bolt, extending to the same side as the large head on the cocking-sleeve pin.

Trigger Work

The Savage Model 110 uses a unique trigger system. There are no aftermarket replacement triggers produced for this model. All trigger adjustments need to be done slowly and carefully, as the trigger parts, screws, pins, and springs cannot be ordered from the factory. Damage to the screws or springs will require returning the entire gun to Savage. Aftermarket setscrews or pins that fit and function may be found, but may cause liability problems due to trigger malfunctions.

The trigger assembly comes from the factory with four screw adjustments. The screw all the way to the rear on the trigger adjusts the safety. If there is motion to the trigger while the safety is on, this screw can be turned in to remove the play. It must not be adjusted so tightly as to prevent the safety from moving into the safe position.

The second screw adjusts trigger overtravel. When pulled, the trigger must clear the sear by a sufficient amount to prevent any contact or drag of the sear at the break. Any more than minimum clearance gives a poor feel to let-off.

The forward screw controls sear engagement. Any adjustment to this screw requires that the safety be inspected to see that it goes on and is adjusted until trigger motion in the safe position is removed.

The remaining screw is found on the right side of the trigger housing and is euphemistically called the "trigger-pull adjusting screw." Screwing it in increases pressure on the trigger spring and increases the pull. Loosening it is supposed to decrease the pull. With the trigger-adjustment screw in its lightest position and the sear engagement in the shallowest adjustment, the pull will be light but erratic. It is possible that a slight stoning with a hard stone at the face of the sear where it contacts the trigger notch may smooth it up and help eliminate the erratic pull. As these rifles are primarily

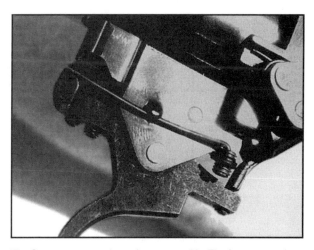

The Savage uses a unique trigger assembly. The four screws, from back to front, control safety adjustment, overtravel, engagement, and trigger pull.

designed for hunting, a light, target-type pull may not be advisable. The 112 Single Shot, which came as close to a competitive rifle as any member of the 110 series, used this trigger system, but suffered the same trigger drawbacks.

When dealing with triggers, remember that it's always better to make any adjustments toward heavier pulls rather than lighter—be safe and conservative.

Malfunctions

Reading the manual from the latest version of the Model 110 (those with Serial numbers above E963107) shows that Savage, like many manufacturers, reflects the current trend—fear of litigation and perhaps a distrust in the ability of gunsmiths in general. Out of some 58 separate parts listed in the instruction manual, half are restricted to either factory or "authorized" gunsmith installation.

Among those the factory will release are parts such as stock screws, sights, blank screws, magazine parts, and stocks. This leaves only a few internal parts available from the factory that most gun owners will have difficulty in replacing and will require the services of a gunsmith.

Those malfunctions that the factory will still allow us to work on are limited, and covered along with some additional factory/warranty gunsmith-only problems. (Factory or warranty gunsmith prohibitions apply to the latest versions.)

Ejection. The ejector is spring loaded and pinned into the bolt head in the same manner as the Remington 700-series rifles. As this ejector is quite thin, any bend in it will increase the possibility of binding and resultant ejection problems. Dirt is also another factor which causes sticky or erratic ejection. To change or clean the ejector, ejector spring, and hole, drive the ejector-retaining pin out from the top of the right-hand locking lug to the bottom. Be sure to trap the ejector and spring, as they will pop out when the punch is removed. Check the ejector hole for burrs or dirt.

When installing a new ejector, replace the ejector spring as well. Springs can collapse or lose their springiness in time; it's easy to

The extractor parts of the Savage rifle include the spring, ball, and the extractor itself. Always replace the spring when changing extractors.

install a new one at this point. Be sure to line up the ejector-pin slot with the bolt before installing the retaining pin.

Extraction. Failure to extract or leaving a case in the chamber can be caused by three major problems. One is dirt in the chamber, and that is cured by cleaning. If grit has galled the chamber, a light polishing with 320-grit cloth may help to smooth the surface. Don't change the dimensions—just remove roughness. Be sure to clean the chamber and bore to remove the polishing grit.

The second cause is found with the extractor itself. In this instance, the extractor will need to be removed and inspected. Dirt buildup can cause extraction difficulties, and if this is the cause, a good cleaning will eliminate the problem. Any chipping along the edge of the extractor can cause the extractor to slip over the case-extractor cut. If inspection shows the extractor is broken or chipped, replace it. The extractor spring should also be replaced for the reason given above.

The final cause is excessive headspace. This should be suspected if the extractor is clean and no chips or breakage are found (see section on headspace). The extractor is removed by pushing the face of the extractor into the bolt, and pushing the extractor hook to the outside of the locking lug. The extractor-pressure ball (a 0.125-inch-diameter steel ball) and spring will be released as the extractor slides out. Be sure to trap the ball and spring.

To insert the extractor, install the spring in the extractor-spring hole and push the pressure ball against the spring. Slide the extractor into its slot and over the ball to complete the installation. This is easier said than done, however, because the ball has a way of escaping, and you can waste a lot of time looking for it. Reassembling the extractor inside a plastic bag will trap any errant parts.

Feeding. Double feeding of shells from the magazine is caused by distorted magazine lips. Someone may have pried the box from the side and bent it in an attempt to remove the box. The cure is to replace the magazine box. To remove the magazine box, slide it as far to the front as possible, then use a wide screwdriver blade to pry the rear retaining lip forward until it clears the receiver. The box

can then be eased out of the receiver.

To reassemble the new box to the receiver, slide the front tongue of the box into the cut in the front of the magazine-box recess. Place the blade of a wide screwdriver at the junction of box and rear tab. With a sharp bump, drive the box forward and down to seat the magazine-box tab in its retaining slot. There is a cam on the rear of the action magazine cutout that will assist in reassembly.

The failure to pick up shells from the magazine will probably be the result of either a weak magazine spring, dirt, or galling, any of which can prevent the nylon magazine follower from moving smoothly. During routine cleaning, check the magazine follower for smoothness, and clean up any abraded spots.

The symptom of a weak spring is intermittent feeding, especially if the bolt is worked rapidly. A weak spring will not push the round into position rapidly enough for pickup. A broken spring will be obvious when the stock is removed. In both cases, spring replacement is indicated.

If the magazine spring has become detached from the follower because of an enlarged screw-attachment hole, the follower may tip down in front, burying bullet points in the magazine box. A new follower should be installed.

If the cocking pin fails to remain locked above the cocking cam, one cause is a worn notch above the cocking cam. The depression that holds the cocking pin can be recut to reshape the notch, or the bolt body can be replaced.

Factory Repairs

The following problems on a Model 110 above serial number E963107 will require repair by a Savage warranty gunsmith or by the factory. Parts for older models may be obtained from one of several companies specializing in "obsolete" items. When ordering parts, be sure to mention the serial number, model variant (110E, 110DL, etc.), caliber, part name, and part number.

If the gun fails to fire due to a broken firing pin or a weak firing-pin spring, these parts will need to be replaced. Match the factory firing-pin protrusion when replacing pins. Failure to cock due to broken cocking sleeves or cocking pins also requires that the broken parts be replaced.

Excessive Headspace. The symptoms of excessive headspace can include hard extraction, protruding primers, and incipient case separations, and may be caused by overloads. An overly oily chamber will also cause the case to appear as though headspace problems were present, and will eventually contribute to real headspace problems. If excessive headspace is suspected, a check with a No-Go gauge of the correct caliber will easily verify the suspicion.

If the No-Go gauge does close, replacing or setting the barrel back and rechambering are remedies that will cure the problem. If the No-Go gauge will not close, clean the barrel for possible over-oiling of bore and chamber. The use of an improper neck-sizing die on reloaded ammo can also give false headspace readings. If this is the cause, instruct the owner in proper reloading techniques.